NEPTUNE

NEPTUNE

THE ALLIED INVASION
OF EUROPE AND
THE D-DAY LANDINGS

CRAIG L. SYMONDS

OXFORD
UNIVERSITY PRESS

OXFORD

UNIVERSITY PRESS

Oxford University Press is a department of the
University of Oxford. It furthers the University's objective
of excellence in research, scholarship, and education
by publishing worldwide.

Oxford   New York

Auckland   Cape Town   Dar es Salaam   Hong Kong   Karachi
Kuala Lumpur   Madrid   Melbourne   Mexico City   Nairobi
New Delhi   Shanghai   Taipei   Toronto

With offices in

Argentina   Austria   Brazil   Chile   Czech Republic   France   Greece
Guatemala   Hungary   Italy   Japan   Poland   Portugal   Singapore
South Korea   Switzerland   Thailand   Turkey   Ukraine   Vietnam

Oxford is a registered trade mark of Oxford University Press
in the UK and certain other countries.

Published in the United States of America by
Oxford University Press
198 Madison Avenue, New York, NY 10016

© Craig L. Symonds 2014

Library of Congress Cataloging-in-Publication Data
Symonds, Craig L.
Neptune : the Allied invasion of Europe and the
D-Day landings / Craig L. Symonds.
pages   cm
Includes bibliographical references and index.
ISBN 978-0-19-998611-8 (hardback : acid-free paper)
1. Operation Neptune.   2. World War, 1939–1945—
Campaigns—France—Normandy.
3. World War, 1939–1945—Naval operations.
4. Military planning—History—20th century.   I. Title.
D756.5.N6S96   2014
940.54'21421—dc23
2013036647

1 3 5 7 9 8 6 4 2
Printed in the United States of America
on acid-free paper

For three great teachers:

Jeff Symonds, Susan Witt, and Carol Margaret Mason

CONTENTS

MAPS, CHARTS, AND TABLES

Neptune is a joint British–United States Operation, the object of which is to secure a lodgment on the Continent from which further offensive operations can be developed. It is part of a large strategic plan designed to bring about total defeat of Germany by means of heavy and concentrated assaults upon German-occupied Europe from the United Kingdom, the Mediterranean, and Russia.

—Top-secret Neptune operation order no. BB-44, May 20, 1944

For MANY, and for Americans in particular, the mention of D-Day conjures up an image of Omaha Beach, very likely that moment when the bow ramp of a landing craft drops into the surf and young soldiers, some of them teenagers, charge out to meet their fate. Whether because of Hollywood depictions or the haunting and harrowing photos taken by Robert Capa that day, it is a moment that has become etched in our national memory. And so it should. It reminds us of the terrible cost of war and of the sacrifices of those who bear it.

But it is a moment with a long backstory, one that has been told only in fragments and which is too often overlooked. Before the first landing craft nudged up onto the sand, before the first soldier stepped out onto the beach to face that merciless machine gun fire, a great deal had to happen. Men burdened with the responsibility of strategic decision making had to order it; others challenged to make it possible had to plan it; still others had to design and build the ships that carried the men and their equipment first from America to England and then, after months of training, across the Channel to occupied France. The Allied invasion of the Normandy beaches on June 6, 1944, bore the designation Operation Overlord, but everything that came before it, including the surge across the Channel and the landing itself, was part of Operation Neptune, and D-Day could not have taken place without it.

Neptune, the Roman god of the sea, is traditionally depicted as a bare-chested, muscular, white-bearded deity, often wielding a trident and driving a chariot pulled by seahorses. At the Quadrant Conference at Quebec in May 1943, where the Combined Chiefs of Staff of Britain and the United States confirmed the long-delayed decision to invade German-occupied France one year hence, it seemed an appropriate designation to apply to the massive amphibious operation that had just been approved. "Massive" is not an overstatement. Operation Neptune was the largest seaborne assault in human history, involving over six thousand vessels and more than a million men. This book is a study of how the British and Americans managed to overcome divergent strategic views, Russian impatience, German U-boats, insufficient shipping, training disasters, and a thousand other obstacles to bring the Allied armies to Normandy and keep them there.

Many of those at the Quebec conference who solemnly affirmed the decision to invade the European continent in the spring of 1944 wondered at the time if it represented anything more than wishful thinking, for the shipping needed to conduct such an invasion simply did not exist. The Americans, confident that their unrivaled industrial capability could meet any challenge, were far more sanguine than the British, who could barely conceive of an armada of six thousand ships. After all, ships were needed to maintain the lifeline of supplies from the United States to both Britain and Russia; more ships were needed to transport a million or more American soldiers across the ocean, and then to supply them with mail and cigarettes; still more were needed to ferry the jeeps, trucks, tanks, bombs, bullets, fuel, and all the other tools of war from the United States to England. And to guard these vessels from the predations of enemy U-boats, escort ships—destroyers, corvettes, and auxiliary aircraft carriers—were needed as well.

For the invasion itself, still more ships of a quite specialized type were needed to transport the invaders and their equipment across the Channel to the landing beaches, and then to evacuate the wounded and the prisoners back to Britain. And all of this had to be accomplished while still more ships—thousands of them—carried out a naval war against Japan halfway around the world. These ubiquitous demands put severe pressure on the decision makers. During World War II, a dearth of shipping was the key logistical constraint in Allied decision-making, and because of it, the most important Anglo-American strategic decisions of the war were less a product of what they *wanted* to do than of what they *could* do.

All the great milestone events of military history have a strategic element, a logistical element, and an operational element. Strategic planning for Neptune began even before the United States entered the war, with the formation and development of the Anglo-American partnership. From the moment the British Expeditionary Force evacuated the beaches of Dunkirk in late May and early June 1940, British planners—and soon enough American planners—began to consider how, when, and where the Western Allies could reenter the European continent in force. The urgency of such planning varied dramatically between 1941 and 1944, and almost as dramatically between the ostensible partners, with the British far less eager than the impetuous Americans, or after June 1941 the hard-pressed Russians, to sanction a swift return to the Continent. These issues became topics of sometimes sharp exchanges between the English-speaking allies. There were also disagreements, misunderstandings, and rivalries between and among the various services within each country, including disputes about the relative importance of an expanded Pacific War or an all-out commitment to strategic bombing. In the end, a consensus, if not quite unity, was achieved, and Europe was liberated, though it was, as Wellington said of Waterloo, a near-run thing.

A necessary second step involved the development of the wherewithal needed to secure the common goal. That included the men, of course, and between 1942 and 1944, millions of Americans were torn from their Iowa farms and Brooklyn tenements and transformed into soldiers and sailors.

It included women, too, who served not only in uniform but also in the factories and shipyards that produced the tools of war: the planes, tanks, trucks, and especially the ships needed to put a million men ashore on a hostile beach and sustain them there. There is an old saw among practitioners of the military art that "amateurs talk strategy; professionals talk logistics." In the spirit of that aphorism, this book illuminates the essential role of Allied, and particularly American, war production with a special emphasis on the construction of ships of every kind at hundreds of American shipyards. Astonishing as their productivity was during the war years, Americans learned that there were limits after all on what could be done. There was only so much steel, only so many workers, and only so much time.

The third element of the story is the operational one: the training, the embarkation, the landing, and the eventual mastery of the beaches, accomplished not only by the soldiers who won the battle and eventually the war but also by the men who swept the mines, carried the soldiers to the beach, cleared the beach obstacles, provided critical naval gunfire support, and of course kept the soldiers supplied with food and ammunition. A tendency to look back on historical events as inevitable encourages a belief that the outcome of the invasion was a foregone conclusion, that the Allied armada on D-Day was so enormous, and the planning so meticulous, that despite the horrors of Omaha Beach, success was a near certainty. It was not. The Allied armada was indeed large, but so, too, was the armada that left Spain in 1588 to conquer England. In studying Neptune-Overlord it is helpful, perhaps even essential, to confront the story as if the ending were unknown, as it certainly was for those who lived it.

In order to tell all of these stories, this book begins with the American entry into the war on December 7, 1941, and chronicles the strategic disputes, the logistical bottlenecks, and the all-too-human experiences of the soldiers and sailors themselves: the erstwhile civilians who found themselves herded aboard ships, sent across the Atlantic, trained in a variety of exotic specialties, and then thrown into a hurricane of violence. The goal is to follow the central thread of this Olympian event from the first tentative conversations by British and American officers in Washington in the winter of 1941 to the storming of the Normandy beaches in the summer of 1944.

In the belief that people are the driving force of history, this narrative highlights the particular contributions of key individuals whose actions and decisions determined the course of events. Some of them, such as Franklin Roosevelt and Winston Churchill, are obvious. Others who were household names at the time are too often overlooked or underappreciated today: George Marshall, Alan Brooke, Ernest King, Frederick Morgan, Bertram Ramsay, Harry Hopkins, and Louis Mountbatten, to name a few. Still others have become nearly anonymous some seventy years on: the junior officers, coxswains, gunners, demolition specialists, men of the Construction Battalion (CB, hence the name Seabees), and the ordinary sailors of the Navy and Coast Guard. The perspective here is that of the Anglo-American Allies, with a respectful nod to the Canadians, and because of that, the roles of the Russians, French, Italians, and even Germans are chronicled only insofar as they influenced Anglo-American decision making and operations.

One last note: in May 1995, on the fiftieth anniversary of V-E Day in Europe, I was taking time away from my position at the U.S. Naval Academy to spend a year teaching in the Department of Strategic Studies at Britannia Royal Naval College, the British naval academy. As part of the curriculum there, I participated in what civilian colleges call a field trip, but which military organizations call a staff ride, to the Normandy beaches. Along with two score of my students—British midshipmen on the cusp of their commissions—and Evan Davies, my colleague in the Strategic Studies Department, we crossed the Channel to Normandy, peeked into the still-extant German pillboxes and gun emplacements, and climbed the bluff from the beach to the American cemetery. There, arrayed across a broad stretch of impossibly green grass, was a virtual sea of white marble crosses—9,387 of them, I later learned—with occasional Stars of David in their midst. My students sensed the emotional impact of that vista, and one of them whispered, "We know you need a moment, sir. We'll be right over there." I did indeed need a moment. It is in long-delayed acknowledgment of the debt that all of us owe to the men entombed in that cemetery, and to tens of thousands of others, British, Canadian, and American, that I offer this story of their arrival on that historic and iconic beach.

NEPTUNE

CHAPTER 1

GERMANY FIRST

T HE PHONE RANG AT 1:47 IN THE AFTERNOON, Washington time,
just after President Franklin D. Roosevelt had finished his lunch of
soup and sandwiches in the Oval Study on the second floor of the White
House. A lifelong collector of stamps from around the world, Roosevelt
had a standing agreement with the State Department to send him the
stamps from each day's overseas mail, and he was just opening the most
recent batch when the phone rang. Harry Hopkins, the former director of
the Works Progress Administration who lived in the White House as Roosevelt's close personal advisor, was there, too, but it was Roosevelt who
reached across the desk to pick up the phone. The White House operator
told him that Secretary of the Navy Frank Knox was on the line insisting
that he talk with the president. "Put him on," Roosevelt said.

Knox wasted no time on formalities. "Mr. President, it looks like the
Japanese have attacked Pearl Harbor."

Roosevelt slammed the palm of his left hand down on the desk top with
a loud bang. "No!" he shouted.[1]

For Roosevelt, the surprise was less that the Japanese had attacked than *where* they had attacked. After all, the State Department's interminable negotiations with Japanese diplomats had ground to a stalemate in recent weeks, and he knew that significant elements of the Imperial Japanese Navy had recently left their ports in Japan's home islands and had gone to sea, heading south. That had been sufficiently alarming that Roosevelt had authorized official "war warnings" to all U.S. Pacific commands eleven days earlier. He would not have been surprised to learn that Japan had struck at French Indochina, British Malaya, or the Dutch East Indies—even, perhaps, the American-held Philippines. But, Navy man that he was, he was stunned, and initially incredulous, that the Japanese had managed to steam a major striking force more than two thousand miles across the Pacific undetected to target the American base at Pearl Harbor.

Soon enough, however, shock and incredulity gave way to anger and determination. His advisors, urgently summoned to the Oval Office that afternoon, found him uncharacteristically quiet and grim-faced. There was no apparent panic or confusion; indeed, several of his visitors commented on the president's outward calm. In a way, perhaps, the news was a relief from the ambiguity and uncertainty of the past several months. At least now he would no longer have to walk a precarious tightrope conducting stylized conversations with faultlessly polite but apparently untrustworthy Japanese diplomats. Nor would he have to parse the language of his public statements to avoid inflaming America's powerful and suspicious isolationist lobby, which strenuously opposed his open support for Britain in its war with Hitler's Germany. With the Japanese attack, all that was swept away. War would bring its own set of difficulties, sacrifice, and pain, but at least the die had been cast.[2]

Or so it seemed. Pearl Harbor meant war with Japan without question, but legally as well as geographically the United States remained apart from the war in Europe, and that was a problem, or at least a conundrum. One of the reasons Roosevelt had tried so hard to avoid a break with Japan was his conviction that Hitler's Germany was a far more serious threat—to the United States, to the West, and to mankind generally. Hitler's megalomaniacal ideology was the main reason, but in addition to that, Germany was a far more dangerous foe whose economy ($412 billion) was more than twice that of Japan's ($196 billion).* As Roosevelt saw it, Japan's ambitions in the Far East were worrying, but they could be dealt with later; Hitler was the immediate and existential problem. The German Wehrmacht had already subjugated more than a dozen European countries and was even then deep inside the Soviet Union. Great Britain clung to survival largely on the strength of the tenuous transatlantic supply line from America.[3]

It was to protect that supply line that some months before, Roosevelt had authorized new and more elastic guidelines for U.S. naval forces in the Atlantic. American destroyers now protected convoys bound for Britain as far as Iceland, and they cooperated with the British even beyond that. In September, a German U-boat skipper, frustrated by the interference of American destroyers with his target, had fired a torpedo at the USS *Greer*, and a few weeks later, on October 17, a German torpedo actually struck the USS *Kearny*, resulting in the loss of eleven U.S. sailors with another twenty-two wounded. To be sure, the *Kearny* was hardly an innocent bystander since she had been engaged in depth-charging the sub at the time, but the confrontation resulted in the first loss of American lives in the undeclared naval war. Less than two weeks later, a German torpedo sank the USS *Reuben James*, sending it to the bottom with a loss of 115 American sailors out of a crew of 160. These incidents might have marked the onset of a full-scale war, but instead both sides had backed away: Hitler because he had his hands full in Russia, and Roosevelt because he was uncertain that the American public would support a belligerent response. When questioned about it at one of his regular news conferences, the president replied, strictly off the record, "We don't want a declared war with Germany because we are acting in defense—self-defense....And to break off diplomatic relations, why, that won't do any good." Then he changed the subject.[4]

From the beginning, Roosevelt had crafted his foreign policy with a clear and calculating eye on what the Constitution would allow and what American public opinion would tolerate. He had tested the limits of both in trying

---

* The gross domestic product of the United States in 1941 was $1,094 billion, which was more than the GDP of Germany and Japan combined.

to forestall a British collapse, first by agreeing in September 1940 to give the hard-pressed Royal Navy fifty older American destroyers in exchange for long-term leases on British naval bases in the Caribbean and Newfoundland, and then, three months after that, by proposing and supporting passage of the Lend-Lease program. Those congressmen, newspaper editors, and clergymen who made up the vociferous and politically powerful isolationist movement in America were horrified by such policies, and they were absolutely apoplectic about the president's naval war against German U-boats. They charged that Roosevelt was deliberately trying to provoke a war with Germany for the sake of Britain, or if not open war, an excuse to expand the convoy program. They were not entirely wrong. Secretary of the Interior Harold Ickes confided to his diary in April, "We are longing for an incident that would give us a justification for setting up a system of convoying ships to England." Others, including Treasury Secretary Henry Morgenthau, thought the president was too diffident, and complained to *his* diary that instead of leading public opinion, the president was waiting for public opinion to catch up with him so that he could follow it. Had he been able to read their diary entries, Roosevelt might have thought that he had calibrated his policy about right.[5]

Now war had come, though it was a war against Japan, not Germany. To be sure, Japan was formally associated with Germany in the so-called Tripartite Pact, which also included Italy, but that agreement obligated the participants to support one another only when one of them was the *victim* of an attack, not when it inaugurated a war of choice, as Japan had done. Hitler was delighted that his American tormentors had been grievously wounded by the Japanese strike, but he was under no obligation to join the conflict it inaugurated. On the other hand, he might do it anyway. Thanks to the American code breakers, Roosevelt knew of a secret message from the German Foreign Office promising Japan that if she "became engaged in a war against the United States, Germany would of course join in the war immediately." Such promises from Hitler's government had meant little in the past, of course, though it was at least possible that this time he would fulfill his pledge and declare war on the United States.[6]

Roosevelt might have preempted him and asked Congress for a declaration of war against *both* Japan and Germany, and several of those who showed up in the White House that night for the emergency cabinet meeting suggested that he should do exactly that. Uncertain that Congress or the country would support him if he did so, Roosevelt preferred to wait and see what action Hitler would take. That afternoon, when Winston Churchill called from his country estate at Chequers to confirm the news reports and offer his condolences for the American losses at Pearl Harbor, Roosevelt assured him, "We are all in the same boat now." But that was not yet strictly true.[7]

IT WOULD BE EXTRAORDINARILY AWKWARD for the United States, and particularly for Roosevelt's policy, if Hitler did *not* declare war, for during the preceding two years, the United States had dramatically reoriented its war planning from a focus on Japan and the Pacific to the possibility, even the likelihood, of a two-front war against both Germany and Japan. The key component in the new plan—indeed, its vital element—was that in such a war, it would be necessary to defeat Germany first. This assessment marked a virtual revolution in American strategic planning; until then, U.S. Navy planners had focused their attention almost exclusively on what was called War Plan Orange.

Plan Orange was one of a series of so-called color plans whose origins reached back to the beginning of the century. They were contingency plans for possible conflicts against a whole variety of potential foes, some of them more likely than others. Besides Orange, which was the plan for war against Japan, there were plans for Germany (Black), England (Red), and Mexico (Green), plus many others. But it was Plan Orange that dominated the war-gaming exercises at the U.S. Naval War College in Newport, Rhode Island. There, on the giant checkerboard floor of Pringle Hall, officer-students maneuvered wooden models of battleships around to refight the World War I Battle of Jutland, and to imagine a similar confrontation against the Imperial Japanese Navy. Initially, at least, Plan Orange itself was relatively simple, if not simplistic. It posited an effort by Japan to seize the Philippines, which would trigger the mobilization of the American Pacific battle fleet in Hawaiian waters followed by a campaign across the Central Pacific that would culminate in a Jutland-like showdown with the Japanese somewhere in the Philippine Sea. While the plan grew in sophistication as it underwent periodic review and adjustment, the central elements of it remained at the heart of U.S. Navy planning, and it informed both budget requests and the annual fleet exercises held each spring to test the fleet's readiness.[8]

American planners began to reassess their assumptions as early as 1937. It was not because Japan seemed any less ambitious or dangerous; that very year, in fact, the Japanese invaded China to begin what they labeled "the China incident," but which was in fact a full-scale war of conquest. Rather, it was because the complexity of the international environment suggested the wisdom of broadening America's security outlook. To do that, Roosevelt sent Navy Captain Royal E. Ingersoll, head of the Navy's War Plans Division, to London to conduct private exploratory talks with the British about how the two nations might coordinate their forces in the Pacific and elsewhere in the event of war. It was the first foot in the door of a transatlantic relationship that would develop dramatically over the next four years. Two years later, in 1939, the key assumptions of Plan Orange were openly challenged when a U.S. Army–Navy Joint Planning Committee noted that a successful defense of the Caribbean and the Panama Canal against Germany would require "offensive measures in the Atlantic," and as a result, the U.S. Navy should adopt "a defensive attitude in the Eastern Pacific." That fall, the U.S. Army–Navy Joint Board scripted a whole new array of plans that retained the color coding for potential foes but grouped them in such a way as to envision possible wars against two or more "colors" at the same time. Inevitably, perhaps, these were dubbed "rainbow" plans. Despite these straws in the wind, most U.S. Navy leaders resisted a reorientation of defense policy away from the Pacific. To the admirals, Japan remained the primary and most probable enemy, and the ghost of Plan Orange continued to influence both their thinking and their training.[9]

That began to change after Hitler invaded Poland in September 1939, and especially after German forces sliced through Belgium and the Netherlands in the spring of 1940, drove the British from the beaches at Dunkirk, and compelled the French to sue for peace. On June 22, 1940, the very day that French generals signed an armistice that acknowledged their defeat, Roosevelt met with the Army chief of staff, George C. Marshall, and the chief of naval operations, Harold R. Stark, to discuss how the French collapse might affect American security interests.

Both Marshall and Stark were destined to play key roles in the war to come. Marshall was a specialist in planning and training who had served on the staff of John "Black Jack" Pershing during the First World War and had helped orchestrate the Meuse-Argonne offensive. Promoted to the rank of brigadier general in 1936, he pinned on the four stars of a full general when Roosevelt chose him for chief of staff, a post he assumed, significantly, on September 1, 1939, the very day Germany invaded Poland. For all his administrative gifts and keen intelligence, Marshall's greatest asset was his temperament. Quiet, dignified, and patient, he seldom raised his voice and never lost his temper. He was a superb judge of other men and kept a small notebook in which he listed the names of those officers who, in some future crisis, should be tapped for command responsibility.

Harold Raynsford Stark had taken up his duties as the eighth chief of naval operations a month earlier, on August 1, 1939. A 1903 graduate of the Naval Academy, he bore an unusual nickname. As a plebe (freshman) at the academy in 1899, he had been asked by an upperclassman if he was related to the American Revolutionary War general John Stark. The young plebe, no doubt standing at exaggerated attention, as befitted his status, confessed that he had never heard of General John Stark. At that, the upperclassman, with more forcefulness than accuracy, informed the young plebe that at the Revolutionary War's Battle of Bennington in Vermont, John Stark had proclaimed, "We will win today or Betty Stark will be a widow!" It was a piece of American patriotic lore that the upperclassman thought every plebe should know, especially one named Stark. So he instructed the hapless plebe that from that moment on he was to shout out that phrase whenever he encountered a senior midshipman. It was not long before Stark became universally known as "Betty" at the academy, and Betty Stark he remained for the rest

of his life. Even as chief of naval operations, Stark signed his memos—
including those to the president—simply as "Betty."*

Both Marshall and Stark advised Roosevelt that if the Germans got control of the French navy, it would tip the balance of naval power in the Atlantic. In such a case, they suggested, the American fleet at Pearl Harbor, which
Roosevelt had sent there to deter Japanese aggression in Asia, should be
transferred to the Atlantic. Roosevelt agreed in principle, but he chose to
wait until the status of the French navy was clarified. Some clarification
came eleven days later when the Royal Navy took the matter in hand and
executed a preemptive strike against the French fleet at Mers-el-Kebir in
Algiers, sinking a French battleship and heavily damaging six other ships,
killing more than twelve hundred Frenchmen in the process. Consequently,
though Roosevelt did send a battleship division as well as its two newest
battleships to the Atlantic in June 1941, nine American battleships remained
in the Pacific, including eight at Pearl Harbor, where they still were five
months later, on December 7.[10]

The German triumph in France led some American planners to conclude
that Europe, including Britain, was lost, and that the most practical thing the
United States could do now was reduce or even end its material support of
the British and hoard its arms for self-defense. Characteristically, Roosevelt
listened and nodded to those who offered such advice, but he attached so
many conditions as to make it effectively impossible. He viewed the survival of Britain as an essential component of American security. Instead of
cutting back on American support, he decided to send a "special observer"
to England to provide an independent source of war news. The initiative for
that came from the British ambassador, Philip Kerr, known by his title, Lord
Lothian. Lothian recalled to Roosevelt's mind the critical role that Rear
Admiral William S. Sims had played in the opening months of American
participation in World War I, when he had collaborated with the British to

---

* One irony of this tale is that John Stark's wife was actually named Molly, and what he
is supposed to have said at the Battle of Bennington is "We'll beat them before night or
Molly Stark's a widow." If the upperclassman had known his historical mythology a
little better, the future chief of naval operations might have gone through life as
"Molly" Stark.

produce a coordinated Atlantic strategy. Of course, Sims had gone to London only after an American declaration of war. Still, Roosevelt thought it was a good idea, and he nominated Rear Admiral Robert L. Ghormley for the post. Though technically Ghormley's mission was merely to discuss the standardization of arms, his presence in wartime London strengthened the link between the English-speaking countries, which may have been exactly what Lothian had in mind all along.[11]

That summer, Britain braced for a German invasion, though instead, in the first week of September, Germany began a sustained aerial bombing campaign of British ports and cities—the Blitz. As if impressed by that, on September 27, 1940, Japan formally joined the Tripartite Pact with Germany and Italy. Now a future American war against all three of the Axis powers seemed not only possible but likely—perhaps even inevitable. Instead of refocusing American attention on the Pacific, however, Japan's decision contributed to the growing emphasis on the Atlantic. In June, Marshall suggested that these circumstances "forced" the United States into "reframing our naval policy" to a "purely defensive" posture in the Pacific and making the "main effort on the Atlantic side." It was uncertain, however, that the Navy could be convinced of that, and it was at this moment that Stark played a vital role.[12]

On November 12, at the height of the German Blitz against London and two months after Japan joined the Tripartite Pact, Stark took it upon himself to send Secretary of the Navy Frank Knox a lengthy memorandum in which he embraced the emerging reorientation in American strategic thinking. In case of war, Stark wrote, "the reduction of Japanese offensive power" could be achieved "chiefly through economic blockade," while the United States devoted the bulk of its efforts to "a land offensive against the [European] Axis powers." That would require "a major naval and military effort in the Atlantic," during which time "we would...be able to do little more in the Pacific than remain on a strict defensive." He acknowledged that such a policy would allow Japan to consolidate its early conquests. Nevertheless, Stark believed the greater danger was that Germany would complete its mastery of Europe, including the conquest of Britain. If that happened, any future campaign to defeat Hitler would become significantly more difficult. It would mean that a subsequent invasion of Europe would have to be mounted from ports on the American Eastern Seaboard; instead of a twenty-mile-wide channel, an invasion fleet would have to span the width of the Atlantic Ocean.[13]

After laying out his argument, Stark presented four strategic alternatives, which he labeled A, B, C, and D. The last of them was his preferred option. Called "Plan Dog" in Navy lingo, it asserted that if the United States should find itself at war with both Germany and Japan, it would remain strictly on the defensive in the Pacific and devote its "full national offensive strength" to the defeat of Nazi Germany. "Should we be forced into a war with Japan," Stark wrote, "we should...avoid operations in the Far East or the mid-Pacific that will prevent the Navy from promptly moving to the Atlantic forces fully adequate to safeguard our interests and policies in the event of British collapse." Though others had been making similar arguments since June, Stark's advocacy was crucial, for it put the Army and the Navy on the same side of the strategic debate. Moreover, Stark went further than Marshall had by proposing that because of the likelihood of a future war against Germany, the United States should at once initiate a series of staff conversations for joint planning between British and American senior officers.[14]

Knox embraced both the argument and the conclusions of Stark's historic memo, and he commended it to the president. Roosevelt was characteristically noncommittal. He agreed wholeheartedly that Germany was the principal enemy. He was loath, however, to endorse any particular plan, for it was a central component of his administrative style to keep all his options open. He was also concerned about Stark's suggestion to open formal staff talks with the British, for he worried about the impact that might have on domestic American politics. Though he had just been reelected to an unprecedented third term (that very week, in fact), he knew that formal staff talks with an active belligerent would be an overt violation of American neutrality. If news of it leaked to the public, there would be a roar of outrage, and not merely from the isolationists. Consequently, while he approved the talks, he made sure that they would be purely professional, without any input from or participation by political leaders, and that nothing decided in them would be binding on the government.

THE ENSUING AMERICAN-BRITISH CONVERSATIONS, known historically as the ABC conference, took place in Washington from late January to early March 1941. Nonbinding they may have been, but the fact that they took place at all formalized the emerging Anglo-American partnership.

Roosevelt stayed out of it. Initially, he thought about asking Undersecretary of State Sumner Welles, a man whose advice he trusted, to attend the meetings and act as his eyes and ears, but on further thought he decided that only serving officers should participate. Sensitive to that, the Army–Navy Joint Planning Board stipulated, "In order to avoid commitment by the president, neither he nor any of his Cabinet should officially receive the British officers." Even Stark, whose idea the conference had been, took part only to the extent that he and Marshall offered a brief formal welcome to the team of British officers. Then they got out of the way.[15]

Stark and Marshall did, however, compile a list of the goals for the conferees, the central one of which was "to determine the best methods by which the armed forces of the United States and the British Commonwealth can defeat Germany and the powers allied with her, should the United States desire to resort to war." When they routed that memo past the president, Roosevelt picked up his pen, crossed out the word "desire," and replaced it with "be compelled." It was not his only change. The Marshall-Stark planning document offered six guidelines for the delegates, the first of which was "the defeat of Germany and her allies." Roosevelt was completely on board with that, but he paused while reading the next guideline: that the United States would exert "its principal military effort in the Atlantic or in the Mediterranean region." That reference to the Mediterranean bothered him. He did not want the United States to focus its main effort on the protection of British imperial interests from Gibraltar to Suez. Again he picked up his pen and inserted the word "navally" in front of "in the Mediterranean." "Navally" wasn't even a word, but at least it placed a theoretical limit on the role the United States might play there.[16]

All of the officers attending the conference wore civilian clothes. Not only was this in line with peacetime protocol in Washington, but it also helped disguise the fact that American and British officers were involved in war planning. Though technically it was a meeting between equals, the British were clearly the suitors. Everyone in the room knew how close Britain was to starvation and defeat in that cruel winter of 1940–41. The British desperately needed American materiel support, certainly far more than the Americans needed to chain themselves to a besieged and battered ally, one that many feared would not last out the year. On the other hand, the British representatives came to the meetings with clear and concrete objectives, whereas the Americans were there simply to mull over possible ways to implement newly revised contingency war plans.

Through two months of "conversations," the fourteen delegates came to appreciate that their views were largely congruent. The first important accomplishment was a mutual pledge to "collaborate continually in the formation and execution of strategical policies and plans." That alone constituted a significant success for the British, for it ensured an ongoing partnership and tied the United States more closely to Britain's fate. In addition, the British were ecstatic to learn that the Americans were willing to make the Atlantic and Europe the primary battlefield. "Since Germany is the predominant member of the Axis Powers," their report read, "the Atlantic and European area is considered to be the decisive theater." This was no more than Marshall and Stark had already concluded, but the news was a welcome revelation to the British. Notable as well was the fact that the final report, when it was completed in March, was sprinkled with phrases such as "When the United States enters the war..." and "When the United States becomes involved...," as if such a thing were a foregone conclusion. It gave the British hope—hope that soon became expectation.[17]

With all of the delegates committed to the defeat of Nazi Germany as the prime objective, the next question was how to achieve that goal. The report laid out a comprehensive strategy that listed seven "offensive policies" that would be applied to Germany. It was much too generalized to be called a "plan," but it did illustrate an overall strategic vision. Those seven policies included a blockade of the continent, the bombing of Germany from the air, the conduct of raids on the periphery of Hitler's empire, and support for the occupied nations. Only near the end did the report mention a military buildup "for an eventual offensive against Germany" itself.[18]

It is immediately evident that this program outlined a passive and peripheral strategy—the kind of indirect approach that the British had used against Napoleon's empire a century and a half earlier. Of course, anything more ambitious than that would have required military assets far beyond anything the British possessed in early 1941, and the Americans, who were not yet in the war, were in no position to push for anything more direct. Nevertheless, two aspects of this strategic blueprint deserve special scrutiny. One was the third goal on the list, which was "The early elimination of Italy as an active partner in the Axis." That seemed to contradict the guiding principle that Germany was the "preeminent" foe. If a conflict with Japan could be deferred until later, why didn't that same assumption apply to Italy? Very likely the reason was that in early 1941, the delegates perceived Italy as a weaker opponent whose defeat was within the theoretical reach of their limited assets, while the defeat of Germany was not. Nevertheless, the identification of Italy as a preliminary step on the road to Germany was thus implanted early in Allied strategic thinking and planning.[19]

The other noteworthy element in this list of "offensive policies" was the objective of capturing "positions from which to launch the eventual offensive" against Germany. This implied that the Allies did not *already* possess such positions—that, in other words, the "eventual" offensive against Germany would be launched not from the British Isles but from some other, as yet unidentified and currently uncaptured position. When connected with the goal of the "early" defeat of Italy, these two objectives foreshadowed the subsequent Allied campaign into North Africa and the Mediterranean. It is not clear whether the wording of either of these strategic goals signaled a deliberate attempt by the British to avoid a commitment to a direct assault on Germany from bases in England or whether they simply represented early and unfocused thinking constrained by limited resources. What is clear is that despite Roosevelt's insertion of the made-up word "navally" into the initial guidelines, the British were already thinking of attacking what Churchill would later label Europe's "soft underbelly."[20]

There was some evidence that the delegates were paying attention to the inevitable command problems that were likely to arise when four services from two nations sought to execute a coordinated military campaign. The Americans, historically wary of placing U.S. soldiers under foreign command, made sure to include a cautionary note: "As a general rule, the forces of each of the Associated Powers should operate under their own commander." And if a theater strategic commander somehow did end up controlling the forces of another nation, he was not to disperse national units but keep them unified so that, as much as possible, they could remain under the command of their own officers.[21]

One important outgrowth of the ABC conversations was the agreement to establish formal and permanent military missions in each capital. Each country agreed to send a senior admiral and a senior general to the capital of the other. Roosevelt had already sent Ghormley to London as an observer, but such representatives would now do much more than merely observe, for the new heads of mission were to engage in "collaboration in the formulation of Military Policies and plans" with their host nation, as well as "represent their own individual Military services." It was not quite a formal alliance, and the United States was still technically neutral, but the ligaments of unity were growing and strengthening.[22]

The lengthy report (twelve single-spaced typed pages plus another fifty-four pages of annexes), dated March 27, 1941, made the usual rounds in both capitals. In Washington, Secretary of the Navy Knox initialed his approval on May 23, and Secretary of War Henry Stimson gave his okay on June 2. But underneath those was a third notation, also handwritten: "Not Approved by President." It was not that Roosevelt disagreed with the report's conclusions or recommendations. After all, he had already indicated his strong support of a Germany-first strategy in case of war, and he believed that having a contingency plan on the shelf was all to the good. He was unwilling, however, to have his hands tied, or to be formally associated with a document that came perilously close to collaborating with a belligerent power. To this point at least, the Anglo-American partnership, such as it was, was limited to staff-level conversations and kept secret from the general public.[23]

EVEN AS BRITISH AND AMERICAN OFFICERS discussed possible future cooperation against Hitler's Germany, the U.S. Navy was already at war with his U-boats in the Atlantic. Only six days after the ABC conference ended, Roosevelt discussed new and more extensive responsibilities for the Navy in the U-boat war. He contemplated bringing more warships from the Pacific to the Atlantic, and ordered Stark to prepare an expanded and more aggressive convoy program. The new instruction, which Roosevelt endowed with the Orwellian name of "Hemispheric Defense Plan No. 1," authorized U.S. Navy warships to attack without warning any German U-boat operating in the western half of the Atlantic Ocean. Before it could be implemented, however, Japan signed a neutrality pact with the Soviet Union. That removed one more restraint on the Japanese, and convinced Roosevelt to retain in the Pacific the warships he had considered moving to the Atlantic. Instead, therefore, Roosevelt approved "Hemispheric Defense Plan No. 2," which authorized U.S. Navy warships merely to report the location of U-boats to convoys and to their escorts. Nevertheless, it was one more tentative step toward open warfare between the U.S. surface navy and German undersea hunters.[24]

Then on June 10 came news that a German U-boat (U-69) had sunk a United States merchant steamer, the *Robin Moor*. There had been no casualties, for the German U-boat commander had stopped the *Robin Moor*, demanded to see its papers, and then, deciding that it was carrying contraband goods (some target rifles and ammunition), ordered the passengers and crew to evacuate into lifeboats before sinking the ship. The incident had occurred weeks earlier, but news of it had been delayed until the lifeboats were found and the passengers rescued. Though it lacked the drama and the carnage of the *Lusitania* sinking back in 1915, it was an undeniable casus belli if Roosevelt wanted to make an issue of it. He might have issued an ultimatum, as Wilson had done back when Roosevelt had been his assistant secretary of the Navy. Instead, Roosevelt merely delivered a tough message to Congress that fell well short of an ultimatum. Hitler mostly ignored it. As it happened, he was preoccupied by other issues: two days later his armies plunged into the Soviet Union.[25]

With hindsight, it is evident that Hitler's decision to attack the Soviet Union while the British remained defiant on their island was the turning point of the Second World War. It meant a two-front war for Germany, and it roused the slumbering Russian bear, which eventually developed into a ferocious military giant. Hitler believed that the defeat of Russia would be only moderately more challenging than the defeat of France had been, and to ensure it, he applied overwhelming force. More than a hundred divisions crossed the Soviet frontier on that first day. The Germans achieved complete surprise and were soon deep inside the Soviet Union.

Roosevelt now had to decide whether Russia, like Britain, should be eligible to receive Lend-Lease matériel and equipment. It was one thing to provide war matériel to America's British "cousins," it was quite another to send arms and military equipment to Stalin and Communist Russia. In the end, pragmatism trumped ideology, and soon convoys of American ships were crossing the Atlantic bound not only for British ports but also on the long and arduous haul around the North Cape of Norway to Soviet ports on the White Sea. That strained American sealift capability further and also complicated the U.S. Navy's undeclared war against German U-boats.

Indeed, by midsummer the situation in the Atlantic was becoming critical. Frank Knox insisted that it was folly to dispatch valuable war supplies, which had been built by American workers and paid for with American money, via American ships, only to see those ships sunk en route to Britain. Stark agreed, arguing that unless the U.S. Navy became more active in convoy protection, the effort to supply Britain would become "hopeless." But how far could Roosevelt extend American naval protection over those convoys before it became a hostile act? He had already pushed the boundaries of neutrality beyond any generally accepted meaning of the term, and he was aware that there was a line that, if crossed, would constitute active belligerency. He worried far less about the legal niceties of such a line than he did about the reaction of American voters. Though he was a trained lawyer, his instincts were entirely political. Consequently, he acted incrementally, expanding America's commitment to convoy protection bit by bit, as if probing the limits of what the country would tolerate.

In mid-July, as Roosevelt and Hopkins sat in the White House, the president tore a map of the Atlantic Ocean out of the pages of *National Geographic*. Spreading it out on a table, he took a pencil and drew a north-south line on it from a point two hundred miles east of Iceland down to the

Azores, roughly approximating the twenty-sixth parallel. He suggested to Hopkins that the U.S. Navy should assume full responsibility for policing the area west of that line, thereby allowing the thinly stretched Royal Navy to focus its attention on the war zones closer to Europe. It was not only another step toward active American belligerency in the Atlantic but another tie linking the British and American navies.[26]

By now, the American Atlantic Fleet, under the leadership of Admiral Ernest J. King, was operating under full wartime conditions. Even before the *Greer* incident in September or the *Kearny* and *Reuben James* torpedoings in October, American warships in the Atlantic came to general quarters with sufficient regularity that it became almost routine. At night the ships ran blacked out, and day or night they steered zigzag courses to throw off any hostile submarine that might be lining up for a shot. It was both reasonable caution in an active war zone and valuable training for war if and when it came.

FROM TIME TO TIME, Roosevelt managed to escape from Washington and spend several days or even weeks at sea, sailing or fishing. He was good at both, and he genuinely enjoyed them. Ashore, even the most routine activities were difficult and occasionally humiliating, especially when it involved his having to be carried from one place to another. At sea, however, he could maneuver a sailboat with a simple command and a hand on the tiller; he could land the biggest of fish from his fighting chair using his powerful arms and shoulders, developed from years of compensating for his ruined legs. Immune to seasickness, he may also have derived satisfaction from the fact that while others struggled, often unsuccessfully, to maintain their dignity as the boat swooped and plunged through the waves, he always remained master of himself. Because some of his advisors could not match this aplomb in the midst of an active sea, they often dreaded invitations to accompany him.[27]

Roosevelt's offshore vacations were frequent enough that the press took little notice of it when in August 1941 the White House announced that the president was leaving on another fishing trip. On August 3 he boarded the presidential yacht *Potomac* at New London, Connecticut, and headed out to sea. After dark, however, the *Potomac* rendezvoused with U.S. Navy warships off Martha's Vineyard, and the president and his entourage transferred to the heavy cruiser *Augusta*, which then turned toward Canadian waters. The next day, as the presidential party steamed northward, reporters on chartered boats off Martha's Vineyard watched through binoculars as a man wearing an old sweater, sporting pince-nez glasses, and with a cigarette holder clamped firmly in his teeth sat at the stern of the *Potomac* with a fishing pole in his hands. The reporters sent daily bulletins ashore announcing that the president was enjoying his vacation. Even the Secret Service was fooled.[28]

The elaborate charade was designed to mislead both the Germans and the opposition press, for Roosevelt was on his way to meet the British prime minister in Placentia Bay, on the south coast of Newfoundland near Argentia. The meeting was Roosevelt's idea. It was a measure of how much the Anglo-American relationship had evolved since the ABC staff talks back in March. Whereas on that occasion he had remained aloof, he was now willing, even eager, to meet personally with Churchill, who more than anyone else personified Britain's resistance to Hitler's war machine. In addition, Roosevelt was the kind of face-to-face politician who was confident in his ability to affect events by the force of his personality. He wanted to take the measure of Churchill, to ensure that this "former naval person" understood American policy, and he also looked forward to hearing Churchill provide one of his already famous analytical disquisitions on the course of the war to date.

On August 9, the *Augusta* and the rest of the American squadron, which included a battleship and no fewer than seventeen destroyers, was anchored in Placentia Bay in a dense fog. Around noon, an enormous gray shape materialized out of the mist as the newest *King George V–class* Royal Navy battleship *Prince of Wales* cruised slowly into the anchorage. Displacing 44,000 tons and bristling with ten 14-inch guns, the *Prince of Wales* was the newest and largest of the Royal Navy's warships, and she still bore the scars of her recent successful fight with German battleship *Bismarck*. The fact that Churchill had chosen her to carry him to the rendezvous with Roosevelt was a measure of just how crucial he believed this meeting was.[29]

Roosevelt sent his naval aide, Captain John R. Beardall, over to invite Churchill and his staff to dine on board the *Augusta* that night. It was not to be a formal state dinner, the president told Beardall, just an informal gathering where he and the prime minister could talk comfortably. Churchill accepted, of course, and the evening was a great success. The two heads of government got on splendidly, and Churchill did not disappoint those who had anticipated a detailed and vivid *tour d'horizon* of the war.

The next morning, Roosevelt returned the visit by attending church services on board the *Prince of Wales*. Symbolically, at least, this was the high point of the conference. The officers and men of the two naval services sat together on the broad deck of the *Prince of Wales* and sang familiar hymns in a common language. It was Roosevelt himself who urged the inclusion of the Navy hymn "Eternal Father" with its reference to "those in peril on the sea." Afterward, Roosevelt toured the big new battleship, which was fated to be sunk only four months later in the South China Sea by Japanese bombers. Both men reveled in the tour, with Churchill acting the role of guide, showing off the crown jewel of the Royal Navy—*his* Royal Navy—while Roosevelt, an apt and eager student of all things naval, did not have to feign interest. A witness recalled that both the president and prime minister had "a fine time."[30]

The formal meetings themselves were mostly anticlimactic. Churchill urged Roosevelt to issue a hard-line ultimatum to the Japanese. He had his own purposes in doing so, of course, but Roosevelt demurred. Far from seeking a "back door to war," Roosevelt wanted to keep the Japanese at arm's length until Hitler could be dealt with. He told Churchill that rather than back the Japanese into a corner, he wanted to give them a "face saving out." In the end, Roosevelt sent Japan a somewhat ambiguous note proclaiming only that "further steps in pursuance...of military domination" would compel the United States to safeguard its "legitimate rights and interests."[31]

During the lengthy Atlantic crossing to Newfoundland, Churchill had prepared a position paper on how the war should be run if and when the United States got into it. His paper envisioned a war characterized by blockade, bombing, subversion, and propaganda. By isolating Germany from the outside, bombing it continually from the air, and constantly appealing to the citizens of the occupied countries to rise up, Churchill implied that Hitler's empire could be so weakened that it would collapse of its own dead weight. The document paid lip service to "landing forces on the continent," but only after Germany was on its last legs. Churchill hoped, even expected, that blockade, bombing, and subversion would "destroy the foundation upon which the [German] war machine rests—the economy which feeds it, the morale which sustains it, the supplies which nourish it…and the hopes of victory which inspire it." Churchill sent copies of this document to Marshall, Stark, and Major General Henry H. "Hap" Arnold, chief of the U.S. Army Air Corps.[32]

At the meeting of the senior officers the next day, the Americans exhibited a palpable coolness to Churchill's vision. To his suggestion that heavy bombers be given the highest production priority, Stark objected that this seemed inappropriate given that shipping was in such peril. Both Stark and Marshall found it odd that there was little mention of aid to the Soviet Union. Did the British not expect the Russians to hold out? The Americans worried, too, that Churchill's proposals contained only a vague reference to a possible land campaign on the continent, and then only when Germany was tottering and near defeat. It may have been Marshall who wrote this sentence in the American response: "Wars cannot be finally won without the use of land armies."[33]

Despite these apparent fissures in the Anglo-American war planning, the real significance of the meeting at Argentia was the personal connection made between the heads of government, and the only real news to emerge from it was the announcement of the Atlantic Charter. After the moving church service on Sunday, August 10, Roosevelt had suggested to Churchill, "We could draw up a joint declaration laying down certain broad principles which should guide our policies along the same road." That night, Churchill dictated the first draft of such a declaration, citing eight principles that would guide a postwar settlement, including "the right of all peoples to choose the form of government under which they will live." While offering few specifics, it outlined a vision for a peaceful and prosperous post-war world.[34]

The conference at Argentia marked a new milestone in the emerging Anglo-American partnership. From the first appointment of uniformed observers to England in 1937 to the secret staff talks in January through March 1941 and now the convivial exchanges on board *Augusta* and *Prince of Wales*, the United States had become as committed as a neutral nation could be to a strategic blueprint—however vague—for the defeat of Germany. It would begin with securing the Atlantic supply line, then ramp up into a massive bombing campaign while the Anglo-American partners assembled the men and matériel necessary for an eventual attack on Germany itself. When and where that invasion would take place were issues that were unaddressed.

Then on December 7, 1941, Japan attacked the United States.

WITHIN MINUTES of Frank Knox's phone call on that historic day, White House operators were summoning cabinet members for an emergency meeting. Stark called the president to confirm the attack, adding that the reports so far indicated that it had been a severe one, with substantial American losses in both ships and men. Roosevelt dictated a news release for the public. At three o'clock he met with the men of what would soon come to be known as his war cabinet: Marshall, Betty Stark, and the two service secretaries, Stimson and Knox, plus in this case Secretary of State Cordell Hull. As a rule, Roosevelt tended to work around Hull, who was never a member of the White House inner circle. His presence now was mostly a product of the fact that only moments before, Hull had met the Japanese negotiators in his office to receive their formal reply to the latest American peace proposal. Before they arrived, Roosevelt had called him with the news of Pearl Harbor. The president told Hull to receive the Japanese reply without comment, then coolly "bow them out." Hull, however, had been unable to remain mute. After reading the Japanese note with the two Japanese delegates standing in front of his desk, Hull looked up and said, "I have never seen a document that was more crowded with infamous falsehoods and distortions—infamous falsehoods and distortions on a scale so huge that I never imagined until today that any Government on this planet was capable of uttering them."[35]

For Roosevelt and his advisors, it was now no longer a question of contingency war planning. The contingency had arrived. Roosevelt instructed Stark to fight back, and the order to "execute unrestricted submarine and air warfare against Japan" went out to the fleet that first day. Longer-range plans, however, were now muddied. So much of the strategic planning of the past two years had focused on Germany and on cooperation with Britain to achieve Hitler's defeat. All of the men who now sat in Roosevelt's Oval Study had been part of that planning, and all of them still believed that Hitler was the more dangerous foe. They also believed it was more than likely that the United States would be at war with Germany soon enough. For now, however, more detailed planning would have to await events.[36]

Later that evening, after a meeting with his cabinet and another with the leaders of Congress, Roosevelt called his personal secretary, Grace Tully, into the Oval Study. "Sit down, Grace," he said. "I'm going before Congress tomorrow. I'd like to dictate my message. It will be short." He spoke slowly and deliberately, voicing the punctuation marks: "Yesterday comma December seventh comma…" When he finished, he told Tully to type it up double-spaced so that he could edit it. She was back in only a few minutes, and Roosevelt bent over the text with a pencil in his hand. He read the first sentence: "Yesterday, December 7, 1941, a date which will live in world history…" As serious a student as he was of world history, he felt the sentence lacked the impact he sought. He crossed out those words and above them wrote the single word "infamy."[37]

CHAPTER 2

ARCADIA

WINSTON CHURCHILL GOT THE NEWS later that night. He was spending the weekend at chequers, the estate in Buckinghamshire, north of London, that had served as the country home of British prime ministers since 1917. As it happened, he had just finished having dinner with two Americans: John G. "Gil" Winant, the U.S. ambassador, and Averell Harriman, whom Roosevelt had sent to England to coordinate Lend Lease shipments.* After dinner, Churchill switched on a small portable radio (a gift from Harry Hopkins) to hear the latest war news. The three men listened to reports about events in Russia and Libya. Then, near

---

* Though it is not clear that Churchill was aware of it, both Winant and Harriman were taking rather severe advantage of his hospitality. The married Winant was embarking on an amorous affair with Churchill's twenty-seven-year-old daughter Sarah, while the equally married fifty-year-old Harriman was sleeping with the prime minister's twenty-one-year-old daughter-in-law, Pamela, who was married to Churchill's only son, Randolph, serving in Egypt. Thirty years later, with much water having passed under the bridge, Averell, by then nearly eighty, and the fifty-one-year-old Pamela were married.

the end of the broadcast, there was an obscure reference to a Japanese air raid on American shipping in Pearl Harbor—or was it Pearl River? The fleeting reference and the fact that the story had not led the news was confusing. What exactly had happened? When Churchill's valet, Frank Sawyers, came in to clear the table, Churchill asked him about it, and Sawyers confirmed it. "The Japanese have attacked the Americans," he said. Churchill came out of his chair, pacing about the room and declaring that he would call the Foreign Office that very minute to arrange for a declaration of war against Japan. It was Winant who suggested that perhaps he should first call Washington. And so Churchill went to his study and placed a call to the White House. After a few minutes Roosevelt came on the line. "Mr. President, what's this about Japan?" Churchill asked. "It's quite true," Roosevelt told him. "They have attacked us at Pearl Harbor. We are all in the same boat now."[1]

Churchill's immediate and instinctive reaction was elation. Leaping at once to the conclusion that this would bring America fully into the war, he believed it meant nothing less than victory—not at once, of course, but eventually, and without question. For more than a year Britain had struggled virtually alone against Hitler's war machine, suffering privation due to the U-boat blockade, enduring almost daily bombing attacks, and anticipating imminent invasion. During those months, Churchill had personified British defiance and determination, alternately shaking his fist at the Nazis and mocking their pretensions while simultaneously calling for sacrifice ("blood, toil, tears, and sweat") from the British population. He had promised ultimate victory, but those promises had been more a measure of his resolve than genuine expectation. For all his bulldog defiance, he had been compelled to act the supplicant to the wealthy and powerful Americans, accepting the concessions, however demeaning, that Roosevelt demanded in exchange for American support in order to allay the suspicions of American isolationists and convince them that the United States was not giving anything away. When in June 1941 Hitler's armored divisions had smashed their way into Soviet Russia, England was no longer alone, and Churchill had begun to hope. Now, with the United States in the war, hope changed to certainty. He was convinced that with Russian manpower, American wealth, and British grit, "Hitler's fate was sealed." His mood soared. "England would live; Britain would live; the Commonwealth of Nations and the Empire would live." The evening was still young by Churchill's standards, and after seeing his guests off, he got to work at once, calling members of the cabinet and arranging for a special session of the House of Commons the next day. As usual for him, it was a late night. At last, in the early morning hours of December 8, he headed for bed. As he wrote later: "Satiated with emotion and sensation, I went to bed and slept the sleep of the saved and thankful."[2]

When he woke the next morning, his euphoria remained, though it was leavened now with his ubiquitous political calculation. He was convinced that Hitler would declare war on the United States and thus bring the Americans fully into the global conflict, but he worried that despite the tentative agreements of the ABC conference and the confirmation of those agreements at Argentia, the particular character of the Japanese attack might force Roosevelt to direct American wrath against Japan and relegate the war in Europe to a secondary theater. Churchill did not think that Roosevelt would willfully betray his commitment. He knew, however, that Roosevelt was an elected leader of a democratic society and necessarily sensitive to the mood and temper of his citizens. He thought there was "a serious danger that the United States might pursue the war against Japan in the Pacific and leave us to fight Germany."[3]

Equally worrisome was the possibility that the Americans might slow or even halt the river of goods and supplies that came from the United States via Lend-Lease (or, as the British called it, Lease-Lend). Britain had become dependent on this supply line, and an interruption of it would threaten Britain's survival as much as a triumph by the U-boats would. On this issue, Churchill's concern was not unfounded. One of the many knee-jerk reactions in the United States to the news of Pearl Harbor was a War Department order to stop all Lend-Lease shipments at once. In New York, thirty ships already loaded with war matériel for British armies in the Middle East received orders to postpone their departure. Alarmed, Churchill asked his friend Max Aitken, the British newspaper baron better known as Lord Beaverbrook, to call Harry Hopkins in Washington and see if he could straighten things out. Hopkins told Beaverbrook not to worry, that this was just a temporary misunderstanding. Hopkins was sure that once the United States began to mobilize for the war, "we will undoubtedly greatly increase our amounts." Still, the event reminded Churchill how precarious that supply line was, and how crucial it was to ensure its continuation. These considerations convinced him to make a personal visit to Washington as soon as possible.[4]

Churchill met with his war cabinet to get formal approval, then wrote to ask George VI for permission to leave the country in time of war. He made the reason clear: "We have … to be careful that our share of munitions and other aid which we are receiving from the United States does not suffer more than is, I fear, inevitable." With the king's approval in hand, Churchill sent a telegram to Roosevelt that same day inviting himself to Washington for a review of "the whole war plan in the light of reality and new facts."[5]

Roosevelt was not initially enthusiastic. He may have wondered about the wisdom of conducting a high-level meeting with his British counterpart while America was still reeling from the initial Japanese onslaught. The U.S. Navy was trying to put together a relief force for the besieged garrison of tiny Wake Island in the mid-Pacific, and the Army was seeking reinforcements for the men of General Douglas MacArthur's command in the Philippines. Pearl Harbor had quieted the isolationists, but they would become noisy again if they suspected that the British were coming over to assume direction of the war. Whatever his real concerns, Roosevelt couched his reservations in terms of anxiety for Churchill's safety in crossing the still-dangerous Atlantic once again. Churchill waved off such considerations and refused to be dissuaded.

The very next day, Hitler declared war on the United States. In one of his long and rambling speeches to the Reichstag, he portrayed the entire war as a German response to plots and threats from all quarters. Poland, Britain, France, and Russia had all been poised to attack, he insisted, only to be thwarted by bold defensive action by brave German soldiers. As for Germany's relationship with the United States, he cast it in personal terms as a confrontation between himself, a stalwart and hardworking champion of the German *Volk*, and the privileged and effete Roosevelt. "Roosevelt comes from a rich family and belongs to the class whose path is smoothed in the Democracies," he told the Reichstag deputies. "I am only the child of a small, poor family and had to fight my way by work and industry." The rich and privileged Roosevelt had been a complete failure as president, Hitler insisted, and "the only salvation for him lay in diverting public attention from home to foreign policy." As a result, "he himself began from March 1939 onwards, to meddle in European affairs which were no concern at all of the President of the U.S.A." Germany had been patient, Hitler asserted, but she had borne it long enough. He did not ask for a declaration of war; he simply announced that Germany was now at war with the United States. The deputies cheered.[6]

The United States was in the war at last—"up to the neck and in to the death," as Churchill put it—and the contingency plans of more than two years could be put into effect. Back in March, the tentative Anglo-American partners had determined that Germany was the most proximate threat and the most dangerous enemy. Would that decision still hold in the wake of Japanese infamy? To find out, Churchill prepared to cross the ocean for the second time in four months.[7]

CHURCHILL LEFT ENGLAND on December 14, one week to the day after Pearl Harbor. He sailed on the battleship *Duke of York*, sister ship of the *Prince of Wales*, which had carried him to the Argentia conference four months earlier. Soon after that meeting off Newfoundland, Churchill had dispatched the *Prince of Wales*, along with the battlecruiser *Repulse*, to the Far East to bolster the defense of Malaya and Singapore. Then on December 10, the very day he telegraphed Roosevelt to invite himself to Washington, he learned that both of those ships had met their doom at the hands of a Japanese air attack. It was a severe blow. "In all the war," Churchill wrote later, "I never received a more direct shock." As elated as he had been to learn that Japan's assault had brought the United States into the war, he now confronted the reality that the Japanese offensive had been astonishingly successful. With the demise of the mighty *Prince of Wales*, Churchill appreciated that throughout the Indian and Pacific Oceans, "Japan was supreme, and we were everywhere weak and naked."[8]

The *Duke of York* was also a big ship, and Churchill took along a substantial coterie, including several men who would play key roles in the design and execution of Anglo-American war plans right up to the invasion of Normandy two and a half years later. Arguably the most important of them was Field Marshal Sir John Dill, who represented the British Army. Dill's presence was a bit awkward since Churchill had only recently replaced him as Chief of the Imperial General Staff (CIGS) with General Alan Brooke. Churchill had concluded that despite an exemplary war record, Dill was simply too hidebound and conventional to continue as head of the British Army. One reason for the move may have been Dill's objection to giving the Mediterranean a higher priority in British strategic planning than the Far East. Then, too, Dill often declined to take seriously many of Churchill's more off-the-wall suggestions about gimmick weapons and eccentric strategies. The prime minister initially planned to put Dill on the shelf as governor of India. After Pearl Harbor, however, he decided to take Dill with him on the trip to Washington, leaving Brooke behind in London to mind the shop. Churchill thought that if things worked out, Dill might remain in Washington to represent British interests there. It proved to be an inspired notion, for Dill had a calm and diplomatic presence that helped smooth over the occasional and inevitable bumps in the alliance partnership. He proved invaluable not only at the forthcoming conference but throughout the war until his death in 1944.[9]

Another member of the British delegation was Admiral of the Fleet Sir Dudley Pound, who represented the Royal Navy. Sixty-four years old and in poor health, Pound was visibly past his physical prime. He had an unsettling tendency to nod off at meetings, then abruptly sit up and make a well-argued point before slumping back into his chair and closing his eyes. Air Marshal Sir Charles Portal represented the Royal Air Force. Sixteen years younger than Pound, he was more active and outspoken in meetings. Portal's Oxford degree gave him a certain intellectual cachet, and Marshall thought him "the best of the lot," though it was sometimes hard to tell whether Portal's principal constituency was Great Britain or the Royal Air Force. Another key member of the British team was Lord Beaverbrook, the wealthy Canadian-born newspaperman whom Churchill had put in charge of the Ministry of Supply. A self-made man who had become the owner of both the *Daily Express* and the *Evening Standard*, the elfin-looking Beaverbrook was a dynamo of energy and organization who had dramatically increased British war production. His most important credential, however, was his personal friendship with the prime minister, and he played a similar role for Churchill that Hopkins did for Roosevelt.[10]*

Churchill and his senior staff used the eight-day crossing to produce a number of position papers on various aspects of war management. Churchill wrote three of them himself, one each on the Atlantic, the Pacific, and strategic options for 1943. They were broad philosophical essays rather than specific plans (Hopkins, who was also on board, had warned him against arriving with detailed plans already in hand, for fear of triggering American suspicions). Since the Americans were still scrambling in the aftermath of Pearl Harbor, they had not prepared any position papers at all, and as a result the British memos became the basis for subsequent discussion. Churchill's goals for the conference were threefold: to reconfirm American commitment to the Germany-first strategy, to ensure the continuation of Lend-Lease goods, and to obtain approval for an early Allied campaign into North Africa.[11]

He need not have worried about the first two objectives. By now, the Americans were as committed to a Germany-first strategy as the British were. Nor was there any problem with the continuation of Lend-Lease, which, as Hopkins had predicted, soon increased rather than diminished. What was to prove the central issue, not only of the upcoming discussions in Washington but of Anglo-American conferences throughout the war, was how the defeat of Germany could best be secured. Churchill would soon discover that the American commitment to the Germany-first program made them eager to get on with it. For his part, Churchill did not oppose an eventual invasion of German-occupied Europe; indeed, he

---

* Beaverbrook resigned as minister of supply in February, shortly after returning to England from the Arcadia conference. Ostensibly it was because of his poor health, but Beaverbrook also objected to Churchill's decision to allow the Admiralty to control shipbuilding priorities, and he feuded openly with Clement Attlee, Churchill's deputy prime minister.

placed such an operation at the center of his planning documents. As a young man, Churchill had been fond of declaring, "The only punch worth throwing was a knockout punch." But not now. Not this year. He thought that if the Allies secured command of the seas and gained air superiority over the continent, and if they could produce the vast amount of materials necessary, an invasion of Europe might be possible "during the summer of 1943." Even then, he wrote, the invasion would require "nourishing on a lavish scale," and such an enterprise was simply not possible in 1942.[12]

Meanwhile, Churchill did not dismiss the suggestion in the ABC report that an accelerated bombing campaign and economic privation in Europe might lead to significant unrest among Hitler's unwilling subjects. He never gave up on the idea that "an internal collapse is always possible." That was no sure thing, of course, and so it was necessary to prepare "for the liberation of captive countries of Western and Southern Europe by the landing at suitable points, successively or simultaneously, of British and American armies strong enough to enable the conquered populations to revolt."[13]

A central conundrum in this view was that if an invasion was not possible until 1943, what were the Allies to do in the meantime? The summer of 1943 was eighteen months away, and surely the Allies could not spend all that time merely accumulating the necessary wherewithal for the eventual thrust onto the continent. This was especially true in light of the facts that the Russians were dying by the hundreds of thousands on the Eastern Front and the American public, eager to avenge Pearl Harbor, wanted to send forces to the Pacific. Given those pressures, it was absolutely essential to do *something* in the Atlantic theater in 1942, and for Churchill that something was obvious: "A campaign must be fought in 1942 to gain possession of, or conquer, the whole of the North African shore." He argued that such a campaign would close the ring around Hitler's European empire, forestall an Axis move into Iberia (Spain and Portugal), and, by regaining use of the Mediterranean sea lanes, obviate the need to send Middle East convoys all the way around Africa. Finally, it would compel Vichy France to choose sides once and for all. With the United States now in the war, French antipathy for the British would be ameliorated; they might even be encouraged to rejoin the Allied cause. At the very least, an Allied presence in North

Africa would compel the Germans to occupy the rest of France, which would tie down more German divisions and thereby provide relief to the hard-pressed Russians. For all these reasons, Churchill argued, "the Northwest African theater is one most favorable for Anglo-American operations." But first he had to sell that idea to the Americans.[14]

The *Duke of York* eased into the commodious anchorage at Hampton Roads, Virginia, on December 22. The official itinerary called for Churchill and his party to journey from there to Washington by boat, but Churchill was in a hurry, and he arranged to have a plane fly him from Hampton to Washington's National Airport, where he was met by Roosevelt. The two men greeted each other as old friends. During the drive to the White House, Churchill found it a bit jarring that despite the onset of war, much of the city was brightly lit with Christmas illuminations. It had been three years since there had been any Christmas illuminations in London. Churchill moved into the White House, where he was assigned the Rose bedroom on the second floor, directly across the hall from Harry Hopkins.[15]

Over the next several days, Churchill became, in effect, a member of the family. Given his habit of staying up late and sleeping in, he missed every breakfast, but he had lunch with the president and Hopkins each day, and he was there every afternoon for cocktails at what Roosevelt puckishly called "the Children's Hour." After drinks, which Roosevelt mixed himself, Churchill personally pushed Roosevelt in his wheelchair over to the elevator to go down to dinner. He later insisted that he did so "as a mark of respect," likening it to Sir Walter Raleigh spreading his cloak for Queen Elizabeth, a somewhat labored analogy. Aware of Churchill's nocturnal habits, Roosevelt stayed up later than he liked after dinner so as not to miss out on the conversations with Churchill and Hopkins. Both the British and American senior officers worried about these private sessions between president and prime minister. The Americans feared that the wily Churchill would convince Roosevelt to act in support of British interests rather than those of the United States. They were aware of Roosevelt's rather haphazard administrative style and his habit of agreeing, at least initially, with whatever views were presented to him most recently. Meanwhile, the British heads of service feared that decisions would be made, and deals struck, that would force them into some untenable or unrealistic commitment.[16]

In addition to Dill, Pound, and Portal, Churchill had also brought along a full suite of junior officers and servants, for Churchill was notoriously high-maintenance, and on some days there seemed to be more British officers with their red tabs (indicating a staff position) striding purposefully down the White House corridors than there were Americans. One of the young officers in the White House later recalled catching glimpses of Churchill "always with a sheaf of dispatches in hand, shuttling back and forth between his bedroom, Harry Hopkins's tiny office, and the president's study." In addition to his bedroom, Churchill also took over the Madison Room next to the Oval Study, where his staff installed what the prime minister called his traveling "map room," featuring giant theater maps with colored pins showing the current location of Allied and enemy forces around the world. Roosevelt greatly admired it, and after the conference was over, he ordered that a map room of his own be set up in the basement of the White House.[17]

As far as the American public was concerned, the highlights of the visit were the joint lighting of the White House tree on Christmas Eve by Roosevelt and Churchill, their attendance at the Foundry Methodist Church on Christmas morning, and Churchill's formal address to a joint session of Congress on the day after Christmas. All three events were triumphs for Anglo-American unity. Churchill won over the members of Congress immediately with his opening quip: "I cannot help reflecting that if my father had been American and my mother British, instead of the other way round, I might have got here on my own." Showman that he was, he brought the congressmen roaring to their feet when, in reference to the Japanese attack on Pearl Harbor, he growled, "What kind of a people do they think we are? Is it possible that they do not realize we shall never cease to persevere against them until they have been taught a lesson which they and the world will never forget?"[18]

The real work of the conference, however, took place out of the public eye, when the British and American heads of the military services met to contrive a joint strategy.

THE CONFERENCE WAS CODE-NAMED ARCADIA, a word that conjures a bucolic retreat where peace and serenity are broken only by the gentle song of birds or the lilting notes of a shepherd's flute. The crusty and humorless

Ernest J. King, whom Roosevelt had appointed U.S. Navy commander in chief (COMINCH) only six days before, opined that the name was "singularly infelicitous."[19]

Churchill wasted no time in pressing his agenda. At dinner on the very day he arrived, he broached the subject of an Anglo-American joint intervention into French North Africa. Roosevelt was not averse to the idea. Political animal that he was, he understood instinctively that if American troops did not become engaged somewhere in the European theater fairly soon, there would be tremendous pressure for them to be employed in the Pacific. Then they would have to be supported and supplied, and soon the Pacific would become the dominant theater, thereby wrecking the agreed-upon grand strategy. Since assaulting occupied Europe itself was beyond the Allies' capability in 1942, perhaps North Africa offered an interim solution. Moreover, Roosevelt had had his eye on Africa even before Pearl Harbor. An avid student of world geography from his youth (inspired in part by his world-class stamp collection), he had already picked out Dakar, a French colony on the westernmost tip of Africa, as a potential problem for both the Atlantic trade routes and for South American security. He saw that an Allied occupation of French Africa would prevent the Germans from developing Dakar into an important base. Churchill was convinced that "the President was thinking very much along the same lines as I was about action in French Northwest Africa."[20]

Churchill renewed his campaign the next day at the first official session of the Arcadia conference. He delivered a broad overview of the war, emphasizing the importance of the bombing campaign against Germany, the favorable prospects for an early victory in Libya, the conundrum of Vichy France (especially the disposition of the rest of the French fleet), and how the United States might contribute. He suggested that American soldiers might be sent to Iceland and Ireland to relieve British soldiers there, who would then become available for combat missions. It irked Marshall that Churchill assumed that American GIs were not ready yet for actual combat, though he also knew that he was probably right. Finally, Churchill brought up the idea of an Allied incursion into French North Africa, whether the French invited them in or not.[21]

When it was Roosevelt's turn, he seconded Churchill's emphasis on an accelerated bombing campaign, and he agreed that American ground forces could go to Iceland and Ireland. But he downplayed the idea of an Allied intervention in North Africa in favor of securing and maintaining global lines of communication. Churchill was disappointed; the president had seemed so much warmer about a North African campaign the night before. Apparently someone had gotten to him.[22]

Someone had—probably several someones. The American service chiefs were far less enthusiastic about a campaign into North Africa than their president was. One problem was shipping: there simply wasn't enough of it. Mounting an invasion of North Africa from the American East Coast meant crossing and recrossing the Atlantic Ocean—a distance of thirty-eight hundred miles—at a time when the U-boats were still winning the Battle of the Atlantic. And there were so many other demands on scarce shipping, including MacArthur's beleaguered forces in the Philippines, that it was hard to see how the necessary ships could be found. Moreover, in North Africa, so much depended on the French. Were the Anglo-Americans invited in, that was one thing, but to wrest control from a defending army was quite another. Thus cautioned, Roosevelt soft-pedaled his support of a North African campaign in his opening remarks. He would wait to see what the admirals and generals came up with.

After these formal introductions, Churchill and Roosevelt left, and the service chiefs got down to business.* On the American side, that group included both Marshall and Stark, plus King and Henry H. "Hap" Arnold, head of the Army Air Corps, which had been rechristened the U.S. Army Air Forces in June. Despite his nickname, Arnold was a ferocious defender of his service and, like Portal, a champion of strategic bombing. The British

---

* Churchill headed first to Canada, where he made a memorable address to the Canadian parliament, mocking Hitler's claim that he would wring England's neck like a chicken. In his growling baritone, Churchill remarked: "Some chicken...some neck." Then on January 6 he flew to Florida, where he stayed for several days in the winter home of the American Lend-Lease administrator (and later secretary of state) Edward Stettinius. There he enjoyed a genuine vacation, one of only a very few during the war.

delegation consisted of Dill, Pound, and Portal. Each country also had a civilian production expert on hand: Hopkins for Roosevelt, and Beaverbrook for Churchill. There was a small kerfuffle when, at their first meeting in the new Federal Reserve Building on Constitution Avenue, it was discovered that the room assigned to them was too small. Soon enough, however, they found a suitable space and began work in earnest.[23]

The British were undoubtedly pleased when Stark began the meeting by asserting that the British Isles "must be protected at all cost," and by reaffirming America's commitment to the Germany-first strategy. Thus one of the principal goals that had brought the British across the Atlantic was achieved in the first minutes. Beyond that, however, the British officers were rather taken aback to discover that the Americans had no particular proposals to offer, or even a very clear notion of what to do next. Dill wrote his successor, Alan Brooke, back in London, that "the country has not—repeat not—the slightest conception of what the war means, and their armed forces are more unready for war than it is possible to imagine." For their part, the Americans were suspicious of the political motives behind the British proposals, fearing that they concealed some hidden agenda connected to their own imperial interests. That suspicion was reinforced when Marshall learned that Roosevelt had agreed to divert U.S. ships headed for the Philippines to beleaguered Singapore. Marshall went to see Secretary Stimson about it, and together they confronted Roosevelt, who in his offhand way dismissed the story as "nonsense."[24]

The conversation continued on Christmas Day, the timing suggesting a lot about the sense of urgency. As one member of the American delegation wrote to a friend, "We just grind away all day long. . . . Christmas meant no more to us here than religion does to a dog." Christmas was Dill's sixty-first birthday, though an effort to surprise him with a singing telegram fell flat when the security guards refused to let the Western Union man in the door. Before revisiting Churchill's North Africa scheme, the chiefs reviewed the dire situation in the Far East where the Japanese rampage was still at full flood. Marshall brought up the fact that the Japanese had an advantage because they had unity of command, whereas the Allies had to work through four governments and at least eight service chiefs. To overcome the Japanese in the Far East, he argued, the Allies would need "unified command" in the field.[25]

Marshall had been thinking about this for some time. An avid student of history, he knew that the absence of unified command had caused problems in America's past wars. At the Virginia Military Institute he had studied almost literally on top of a Civil War battlefield, and he was very much aware of how the absence of unified command between the Union Army and Navy had undercut the North's numerical and matériel superiority. Marshall had also encountered the perils of disunity during the First World War when he had served on Pershing's staff. Not until the very end of the war did the Allies overcome the suspicious nationalism of the associated armies to create a unified command on the Western Front. As a result of both his reading and his experience, Marshall had urged closer Army-Navy cooperation during the interwar years, establishing a joint command of the Caribbean in December just days before Pearl Harbor. Now he argued that having separate and independent commands for the U.S. Army, the U.S. Navy, the British Army, and the Royal Navy was a recipe for duplication, confusion, and disaster. It was essential, in his mind, to have one man in charge.[26]

It is difficult in hindsight to appreciate what a radical proposal this was. The very idea of putting American soldiers under British command, or British soldiers under American command, or soldiers of any service under naval command, was little short of heresy. Even Stark instinctively recoiled, though King offered some encouragement. Portal suggested that perhaps "the committee here in Washington" could act as a kind of unified commander. But Marshall rejected the idea of command by committee out of hand. "I am convinced," he wrote, "that there must be one man in command of the entire theater—air, ground, and ships. We cannot manage by cooperation." The British already believed that the Americans were untested novices and that it would take some time—perhaps years—for them to become competent managers of war. They now imagined the consequences if battle-hardened British soldiers were placed under the direction of inexperienced and overeager West Pointers. They could not say any of this, of course—they needed the Americans desperately and could not afford to insult them, so instead they voiced skepticism about the whole notion of unified command.[27]

Marshall realized that he had sprung this idea on the delegates without having done the necessary staff work about how it would operate. It was unlike him. After the meeting, he pulled aside his young deputy, the newly promoted Brigadier General Dwight Eisenhower (whom everyone called "Ike"), and asked him to prepare a formal proposal for presentation the next day. Marshall told him that it should be written in the form of a letter of instruction to whoever was chosen to direct Allied forces in the Far East. Eisenhower stayed up late that night to write it. It probably never occurred to him as he did so that he was establishing the precedent for unified command that would later make possible his appointment as Supreme Allied Commander. Eisenhower's goal was to alleviate the suspicions of the British, and he therefore went out of his way to emphasize what a theater commander could *not* do. He could not relieve an officer of another service, he could not change the tactical organization, he could not use the supplies of one country to support another, and he could not "assume direct command" of the forces of other nations, only direct their strategic movements.[28]

Meanwhile, Marshall did the necessary legwork. He pitched the idea of unified command to Stimson, who liked it, and he and the secretary of war went again to see the president. Roosevelt listened and expressed general agreement, as he often did, then told Marshall to talk to Knox, for it would be essential to ensure that the Navy was in agreement. Even more than Knox, Marshall had to get the admirals on board, for few of them would welcome the idea of serving under an Army officer. Marshall met with the Navy's senior admirals in Stark's office. They remained skeptical, and they were especially concerned that the Army Air Force would somehow gain control of naval aviation. It was King who broke the logjam. To him it was simple logic that "effective operations would be impossible if three services, representing four different countries, should operate on their own without some immediate superior in the area." Once King signaled his support, the others fell into line.[29]

The British service chiefs were cautiously supportive about the idea, and a few were openly enthusiastic. After Marshall made his proposal, he was somewhat astonished when Pound ("the old admiral," as Marshall called him in his reminiscences) came hustling out of the meeting to catch up with him and vigorously shake his hand. Then Dill came up and literally threw his arms around him. For all their enthusiasm, however, it was evident that they would follow Churchill's lead, and the "former naval person" was likely to be a hard sell. In a conversation with Roosevelt in the White House on the night of December 27, Churchill maintained that unity of command might be all very well in principle, and might even be appropriate in a continental war, such as that of 1914–18, where the soldiers of the Allied armies had fought side by side, but in a global war, where forces were scattered all over the world, it was simply not practical. Beaverbrook and Hopkins were both present, and Beaverbrook took it upon himself to pass a note to Hopkins: "You should work on Churchill. He is being advised. He is open minded [on this] and needs discussion." On the basis of that, Hopkins arranged for Marshall to meet with Churchill one-on-one. With Hopkins's prodding, Churchill invited Marshall to come and see him in his White House bedroom the next morning. Very likely Churchill was confident he could overwhelm the soft-spoken American general with the force of his personality. It was a meeting of the irresistible force and the immovable object.[30]

Marshall found Churchill propped up in his bed with state papers spread out all around him—his usual morning workspace. Marshall declined the invitation to sit and remained on his feet, striding back and forth to make his presentation. He was, quite literally, a moving target. Churchill, as usual, began with a monologue. Marshall remembered that "he got off quite a spiel." Churchill insisted that "a ship was a very special thing" and could not be put under an army commander. "What would the army officer know about handling a ship?" he asked. Marshall shot right back: "Well, what the devil does a naval officer know about handling a tank?" though that was not the point. When Churchill began to recite the centuries-long tradition of naval independence, Marshall interrupted him: "I was not interested in Drake and Frobisher," he recalled saying, "but in [creating] a united front against an enemy which was fighting furiously." Churchill was not used to being challenged so directly. After a while he got out of bed and went into the bathroom. Marshall waited patiently, and eventually Churchill emerged from his ablutions wearing only a towel. Somewhat grudgingly, he agreed to discuss the issue with "his people," and in the end he gave way. "It was evident," he wrote later, "that we must meet the American view."[31]

It helped considerably that Marshall let it fall that the man he had in mind for a unified command in the Far East was an Englishman, General Sir Archibald Wavell, who in due course was appointed supreme commander of what was called ABDA, an acronym for Australian, British, Dutch, and American forces. Wavell held his command for only forty-nine days. For all their unity, the Allies simply lacked the wherewithal to stand up to the Japanese onslaught in the Far East, especially in the air. The unexpected and astonishing fall of Singapore on February 15 marked the collapse of the experiment, and ABDA was dissolved a week later. But Marshall's efforts had not been in vain, for they established the precedent for a unified theater command, and in the long term the principal beneficiary of that would be the man who had drawn up the proposal, Brigadier General Dwight D. Eisenhower.*

THE QUESTION OF NORTHWEST AFRICA proved more difficult. Churchill had endowed his plan for an Allied landing there with the code name Gymnast, and an even more ambitious scheme of occupying all of French Northwest Africa was called Super-Gymnast. As the Arcadia delegates sought to juggle their scarce resources to match the almost uncountable demands of global war, however, it became increasingly evident that such plans were little more than a chimera. As always, the bottleneck was shipping: there was simply not enough of it to continue the convoys to Britain and Russia, keep the lines of communication open in the Pacific, *and* mount

---

* An exception to the principle of unified command was the agreement reached at Arcadia that the United States Navy "will remain responsible for the whole Pacific Ocean east of [the] Philippine Islands." Of course, the U.S. Navy then had to negotiate its command responsibility with an equally assertive authority in the person of General Douglas MacArthur, who was subsequently endowed with command of what was called the Southwest Pacific Area (SoWesPac), including Australia and the Philippines, while the U.S. Navy presided over the Pacific Ocean Areas (POA) under the overall command of Admiral Chester Nimitz.

an invasion of Africa. Marshall acknowledged that he could probably assemble three divisions, one of them a Marine division, for the proposed
movement to North Africa, but that would leave no ships left to do anything else in the Atlantic. Churchill was crestfallen and declared that he
would be "frightfully unhappy" if they had to scrap their plans on account
of insufficient shipping. He suggested that perhaps the Allies could use battleships to carry troops. Roosevelt was dubious about that, though he
promised to see what he could "dig up." Given the realities of the shipping
problem, it seemed evident that an invasion of North Africa, at least in the
near term, was simply unrealistic.[32]

In spite of that, Roosevelt and Churchill wanted to keep the prospect of
Gymnast open. At one of the last meetings of the conference, on January
12, Roosevelt asked how soon an invasion of North Africa could be
launched, assuming that the shipping could be found to support it.
Churchill declared that it could be done by March 3—less than two months
away. Marshall demurred. He noted that "the shortage was not in troop carriers [alone] but in cargo carriers." It was not enough merely to put soldiers
ashore, even if the ships could be found to do so. They also had to be maintained there. King agreed. At the very least, he insisted, any such operation
would have to wait until mid-April.[33]

Despite the obvious skepticism evident in these responses, the eternally
optimistic Roosevelt announced that planning should begin at once for
what he labeled "General Marshall's plan." "We will make Beaverbrook and
Hopkins find [the] ships and will work on Super-GYMNAST at the earliest
possible date." Thus did the Allies take their first hesitant steps toward
North Africa and the Mediterranean.[34]

THERE WAS ONE MORE important result that came out of the Arcadia conference, one with significant long-term consequences for the Allied partnership. It emerged from the implementation of the ABDA command
under General Wavell. According to Eisenhower's memo, Wavell was to receive his orders from "an appropriate joint body." The problem was
that there was no such body to develop strategic plans. To create one, Roosevelt suggested that a permanent committee be set up composed of three

American and three British senior officers, with occasional representation from the Dutch and others on an advisory basis—in other words, a body very much like the one that had come together for the Arcadia conference. It seemed logical, too, that this permanent body should meet in Washington, not only in recognition of the fact that the United States was likely to provide the bulk of the men and materials during the war, but also because Washington was geographically located between the two theaters of war. Meeting in Washington would be easy enough for the American service chiefs, but clearly the British heads of service could not be expected to remain permanently in a foreign capital while a war was being fought at home. Someone other than the service chiefs would have to represent the British. The solution to this was near at hand. As Churchill had foreseen, Dill could stay on in Washington to represent the British Army, and the Royal Navy and Air Force could be represented by the senior members of those services on the British Joint Staff Mission in Washington. Stark would go to London as commander in chief of U.S. Naval Forces Europe (CINC-NAVEU), and that would allow King to take over the duties of chief of naval operations as well as COMINCH. The new decision-making and supervisory body thus created would be known as the Combined Chiefs of Staff (CCS).[35]

For the rest of the war, though the heads of government made the important strategic decisions, the CCS implemented those decisions, made the plans, drafted the orders, and pretty much ran the war. That included a responsibility to prioritize, allocate, and distribute the tools of war, which in practical terms meant distributing the products of American industry. This, of course, was another of the principal issues that had brought Churchill and his advisors, including Beaverbrook, across the ocean to talk to the Americans, and they were ready as ever with a specific proposal on the matter. The British urged the creation of a Supply Board that would establish procurement priorities for the war effort; similarly, a Munitions Board and a Shipping Control Board would set priorities in those fields. The Americans were suspicious. They wondered why a board composed of 50 percent British representatives should decide how to distribute material that was 100 percent American-produced. In the end, they agreed to establish two

boards, one American and one British, to recommend priorities. The recommendations would go to the Combined Chiefs, and *that* body would
make the final decisions. This additional power—to determine where to
send the ships, tanks, and planes of American industry—gave the Combined Chiefs additional control over the direction of the war.[36]

The British and American publics were entirely unaware of these negotiations, and for them the most important consequence of the Arcadia conference was the formal announcement, on January 1, 1942, of the
Declaration of the United Nations. Roosevelt came up with the term
"United Nations" to replace "Allies" because the United States and the
Soviet Union were not in fact allied—they were merely on the same side.
The new declaration was largely a restatement of the goals spelled out in
the Atlantic Charter but extended now to embrace all of the nations that
were at war with the Axis. It confirmed the principle of "national self-
determination" and announced that the signatory nations believed that
"complete victory over their enemies is essential to defend life, liberty, independence and religious freedom, and to preserve human rights and justice in
their own lands as well as in other lands." For that reason they were "now
engaged in a common struggle against savage and brutal forces seeking to
subjugate the world." There was some back-and-forth with the Russians about
the inclusion of the phrase "religious freedom," but in the end the Russians
agreed to sign, as did the representatives of twenty-five other nations.[37]

BY NOW, CHURCHILL WAS EAGER to get back to London to resume his
hands-on management of the war. Roosevelt and Hopkins personally escorted him, Pound, and Portal to the train station and bid them goodbye—
Dill, of course, was staying on. A special train took Churchill and his party
to Norfolk, where they boarded a big four-engine Boeing 314 Clipper flying
boat for a flight to Bermuda, where they were to reboard the *Duke of York*
for the six-day voyage back to England. Churchill, however, was impressed
with the size and comfort of the big flying boat, and he asked the pilot,
Kelly Rogers, if the plane could make it from Bermuda all the way to England. Rogers said it could, and so in the end that was how Churchill made
his return. It had been less than fifteen years since the world had celebrated

Charles Lindbergh's solo flight across the Atlantic, and now heads of government were making the flight. From then on, leading figures in the Anglo-American alliance would visit one another by air, thus shrinking the geographical gulf between them.[38]

Churchill's trip had been a resounding success. Both the Germany-first strategy and the continuation of Lend-Lease support had been reconfirmed, the Declaration of the United Nations created an umbrella under which all the countries fighting against Germany could shelter, and a mechanism for global strategic management had been established in the Combined Chiefs of Staff. Churchill later mused that "future historians" would view the founding of the Combined Chiefs of Staff as "the most valuable and lasting result" of the Arcadia conference. He had been forced to acquiesce to a unified command for the Far East, but the Americans had agreed to send several divisions of soldiers to Iceland and Ireland to relieve British divisions for the war in the Middle East. Moreover, though the American high command had not embraced his Gymnast plan for an invasion of North Africa, the idea had found favor with the man who mattered most: the American president. To be sure, some differences had emerged as well. It was obvious that the Americans were convinced that sooner or later, and preferably sooner, a full-scale amphibious assault aimed at Germany's heart would be necessary. Churchill accepted that reality, but he continued to hope that by 1943 such an invasion might constitute only the final shove that brought a tottering Nazi regime crashing down.[39]

On the negative side, the Arcadia conversations had exposed the Allied weaknesses in matériel that made an early invasion of any kind problematic. Even Gymnast would prove difficult unless the Allies could somehow overcome the quandary of insufficient shipping—too few troopships, cargo ships, tankers, and especially landing craft. To overcome that lacuna would necessitate not only an unprecedented building program but also neutralization of the German U-boat menace in the Atlantic. Before the Allies could seriously plan an invasion of any hostile shore, they would first have to secure the Atlantic sea-lanes, gain air superiority over the prospective enemy beaches, and assemble a stockpile of munitions and supplies. These were mostly issues of mobilization and productivity, and in time the Americans would solve them. Churchill had believed from the first that the American industrial cornucopia would prove decisive. He had known, too, that the war against Hitler would be a long, bloody slog, but at least now he believed he could see the way forward.

CHAPTER 3

"WE'VE GOT TO GO TO EUROPE AND FIGHT"

G EORGE MARSHALL'S COURTLY MANNERS, Virginia accent, and deferential demeanor sometimes led others to underestimate the steel within him. Roosevelt saw it early. Back in the fall of 1938, with the war still looming, the president brought together a roomful of his military advisors to discuss how to prepare the country for the coming storm. He had previously obtained congressional approval for a major naval buildup, and now he sought to do the same kind of thing for the Army. Marshall was in the room, but as a mere brigadier general, he sat at the end of a sofa, off to one side. Roosevelt outlined an aggressive program that emphasized the production of military aircraft. He told the assembled officers that he wanted an air force of twenty thousand planes. He had concluded that he probably could get Congress to approve only about half that number, he said, but that was acceptable because his real motive was to develop the industrial facilities for airplane production so that a more rapid armament could take place later if needed. To accomplish this goal, he went on, it would be necessary to funnel most of the increase in the Army's appropriation for that year into aircraft production and leave other programs pretty much as they were. He went around the room to ensure that all were in agreement with this idea, and his eye fell on the sandy-haired brigadier general at the end of the sofa. "Don't you think so, George?" he asked.

Marshall was a stickler for form who bristled silently at being called "George," even by the president of the United States. He had listened with growing alarm to Roosevelt's lengthy disquisition, fearful that such a program would leave U.S. ground forces mired in a state of continued unreadiness. He had said nothing while the president spoke, but now he had been asked his opinion, so he gave it: "I'm sorry, Mr. President, but I don't agree with that at all."

Roosevelt was visibly startled, though he did not follow up on Marshall's comment at the time. When the group adjourned and the men filed out the door into the anteroom, several of them turned to Marshall to offer their condolences for what they were certain was the end of a promising career. Instead, five months later, Roosevelt appointed Marshall chief of staff of the Army, with four-star rank.[1]

Marshall's particular combination of deference and candor, so evident in his remark to Roosevelt, also worked well in dealing with his naval counterparts (Stark and King) and with the British—even, as was evident at Arcadia, with the redoubtable Churchill. Months later, the judgmental and not entirely admiring British General Alan Brooke confided to his diary that while he did not think Marshall much of a strategist, he acknowledged that he was very good at "providing the necessary links between the political and military worlds." In a global coalition war, that skill would prove invaluable and make Marshall, as much as anyone in uniform, the architect of Allied victory.[2]

During the first six months of 1942, however, Marshall found himself on the losing side of a difficult and often frustrating campaign to convince first his fellow service chiefs, then the Combined Chiefs, and finally Churchill and Roosevelt that an early cross-Channel invasion of occupied France was the best and surest way to victory. From January through July 1942, Marshall employed reason, argument, and on one occasion blackmail to convince the heads of the American and British governments to accept the need for, and the wisdom of, his strategic vision. It was a campaign that tested his diplomacy, his debating skills, and often his patience, and in the end it was one that he would lose.

———————

THE COMBINED CHIEFS OF STAFF created at the Arcadia conference met more than two hundred times during the war, a number that does not include the scores of private discussions and informal conversations that took place on a near daily basis. The first meeting, held in the U.S. Public Health Building on Constitution Avenue because no other site was available, occurred on January 23, only nine days after Churchill returned to England. Marshall, King, and Arnold attended regularly, with occasional support from Eisenhower, whom Marshall had appointed in February to head the Army's War Plans Division.* Dill was the principal British spokesman, and he was seconded by Admiral Sir Charles Little, who led the British Joint Staff in Washington until he returned to England later in the year and was replaced by Admiral Sir Andrew Cunningham. The Royal Air Force was represented by Air Marshal D. C. S. Evill, whose name occasioned some amused comment. Others circulated in and out. A more permanent change occurred in July when Admiral William D. Leahy returned from his difficult and delicate assignment as the U.S. ambassador to Vichy France and Roosevelt made him his chief of staff in which capacity he joined the CCS as its titular head.

Early on, a kind of unofficial protocol emerged in which the Americans convened separately in the morning or over lunch to ensure that they were more or less in agreement before they met with their British counterparts in the afternoon. There was no official authority for these meetings of the American service chiefs, and no name for the group they formed, though others soon began to refer to it as the Joint Chiefs of Staff (JCS), a name that has stuck. Later in the war, Roosevelt sanctioned both the organization and the name with an executive order, but in the beginning it emerged out of convenience and necessity, an important first step toward cooperation— if not quite integration—among the American armed services, which up to

———————

* The War Plans Division was renamed the Operations Division in March 1942, though Eisenhower remained its director.

then had operated as autonomous entities. The meetings of both the Joint Chiefs and the Combined Chiefs soon came to dominate the work calendars of the principals. King estimated that despite his dual role during the war as both chief of naval operations and commander in chief of the U.S. Fleet, he spent two-thirds of all his time on either JCS or CCS matters.[3]

The CCS was not, however, a decision-making body. Everything it did was subject to oversight and reversal by the heads of governments. Churchill, who, in addition to his role as prime minister also held the portfolio of Minister of Defence, continued to direct British strategy from his basement war room in Whitehall. To him, both the British Chiefs of Staff in London and the Combined Chiefs of Staff in Washington were merely advisory bodies, and his larger-than-life personality dominated British strategic decision making throughout the war. For his part, Roosevelt was much less of a bully to his service chiefs, but his instinctive preference for a loose and informal (some said chaotic) administrative style unbound by clear wire diagrams or strict protocol allowed him to give the Joint and Combined Chiefs the freedom to make plans and to recommend policies—as long as everyone understood that in the end the final decisions were always his. Even then, he was as likely as not to change his mind.

Marshall began his campaign to obtain a commitment to an early cross-Channel offensive at the very first meeting of the CCS. As he saw it, if the strategic blueprint was "Germany first," then it was best to get on with it. He was distressed by the dispersion of scarce Allied resources to secondary theaters around the world, and he urged a focus on the vital center: Nazi Germany. Eisenhower agreed with that, writing, "We've got to go to Europe and fight—and we've got to quit wasting resources all over the world—and still more—wasting time." To Marshall and Eisenhower, it was self-evident that the Allies could not continue to send their resources all over the globe in penny-packet reactions to various Axis threats.[4]

Alas, in the first months of the war, some dispersal of assets was to a certain extent unavoidable, for the peril was global. The chilling effectiveness of the German U-boat offensive in the Atlantic was visible from the American coastline in the reflected light of burning oil tankers; in Africa, British forces in Libya struggled to hold on to Egypt. Both India and Burma were under threat from Japanese armies, and Chiang Kai-shek was calling for help in China. A Japanese force was closing in on the British citadel of Singapore, and MacArthur's forces had been driven back into the Bataan peninsula in the Philippines. Further south, the continent of Australia, including its precarious communications link to Hawaii, was endangered, and of course the principal theater of the war—more important than all the others combined—was in Russia, where nine million men slew one another by the tens of thousands along a twelve-hundred-mile front. A Russian collapse would be catastrophic and make any subsequent invasion of Europe all but impossible. Shoring up each of these threatened and precarious theaters with finite resources was like trying to plug eleven leaks in a dam using only five fingers. For several weeks, therefore, the Allies struggled to send whatever reinforcements they could scrape together to as many threatened fronts as the severely limited shipping would allow.[5]

It was amid these perils that Marshall began his quixotic effort to halt, or at least to limit, the dispersion of Allied assets and focus on the decisive theater. He asked Eisenhower to put together a formal plan for a rapid buildup of Allied forces in Britain, to be followed by a cross-Channel invasion of occupied France on or about April 1, 1943. Eisenhower began his report by noting that an attack in northern France was "the shortest route to the heart of Germany," and that it was only in northern France that the Allies could establish clear air superiority over the invasion beaches from airfields in Britain. And, of course, the establishment of an Allied front in northern France would provide "the maximum possible support to Russia." His proposal sounded a note of urgency in asserting that the decision to act "must be made now," for any such assault necessarily required "a long period of intensive preparation." The Marshall-Eisenhower plan was consistent with the one Churchill had presented at Arcadia, which also called for an invasion of France in 1943. Nevertheless, before offering the proposal to the Combined Chiefs, the politically sensitive Marshall first sought presidential approval.[6]

Marshall met with the president in his Oval Study on March 25. Others present included King and Knox for the Navy, Arnold for the Army Air Forces, and both Secretary Stimson and the ubiquitous Harry Hopkins.

The meeting did not begin well. Churchill-like, Roosevelt began with a rambling discourse in which he reviewed many of the problem areas throughout the world from the Middle East to China, with particular emphasis on the Mediterranean. Only with some effort did Marshall get the president to focus on the issue he had come to discuss: an early assault on Europe. As Marshall explained it, his plan had three elements, each subsequently endowed with a code name. A build-up phase (Bolero) would begin at once and involve "the movement to the British Isles of U.S. air and ground forces comprising approximately one million men." The invasion phase (Roundup) would consist of an amphibious assault by those men on "beachheads between Le Havre and Boulogne" in northern France on or about April 1, 1943. A third element (Sledgehammer) was a contingency plan for a small-scale invasion of France in the fall of 1942 in case of a Russian collapse, or if German forces became so "completely absorbed on the Russian front" that it created an opportunity. Though public speaking was not Marshall's strong suit, Stimson thought he "made a very fine presentation."[7]

Roosevelt listened carefully but showed little enthusiasm. One problem, surely, was that Marshall's plan envisioned no direct action against Germany, or anyone else for that matter, for over a year. What were American forces—those one million men—to do in the meantime? Asking the Russians to wait a full year for any significant relief was unlikely to strengthen their confidence in Anglo-American support. Stalin was instinctively suspicious, even paranoid, about his partnership with the western Allies, and he was already convinced that Churchill was willing to fight the Germans to the last Russian. (Or, as Churchill might have put it, to fight the Nazis to the last Communist.) Learning that the Anglo-Americans were planning to stay out of the European continent for another twelve months while the Russian army bore the entire burden of the war might encourage Stalin to reconsider his options. In addition, Roosevelt worried about the patience of the American public. The country was still enraged by the Japanese attack on Pearl Harbor, and sending soldiers off to cool their heels in England for a year or more would surely increase public pressure to send at least some of them to the Pacific. The president believed it was "very important to morale to give this country a feeling that they are in the war..., to have American troops somewhere in active fighting across the Atlantic." He was deeply committed to the Germany-first concept, but he feared that unless U.S. soldiers got into action somewhere in Europe soon—preferably that summer—that strategy might become politically unsustainable.[8]

These factors led Roosevelt to ask Marshall about North Africa. Though he had previously written to Churchill that Gymnast was not possible, he had done so principally because of the scarcity of shipping. On the other hand, if enough ships could be found to carry a million men to England, surely there would be enough for an assault on North Africa.[9]

Marshall opposed it. If the Russians showed signs of a collapse, he countered, Sledgehammer could be implemented, but to embrace an invasion of North Africa would draw resources away from the vital front and inevitably postpone the crucial and decisive thrust into northern France. Marshall's plan already included the dispatch of an American division to New Zealand and the delivery of planes to China; further dispersions would so scatter U.S. assets that the necessary buildup in England would be compromised.

Hopkins agreed. Though he, too, appreciated the importance of early action, he supported the central elements of Marshall's plan. On the other hand, Hopkins also saw that no plan was likely to succeed without Churchill's backing. Instead of submitting this plan to the Combined Chiefs, therefore, he suggested that Marshall should carry it personally to England to gain the prime minister's support. Roosevelt liked that idea, in part because it would allow him to keep the question in play and see what developed. He declared that Marshall should immediately fly to London to see Churchill and that Hopkins should go with him.[10]

Roosevelt wrote Churchill to tell him that Marshall and Hopkins were on their way with "a plan which I hope Russia will greet with enthusiasm," and which could be labeled "the plan of the United Nations." He followed that up with another cable in which he declared that Marshall's plan "had my heart and *mind* in it." Despite these endorsements, there was an inherent and fundamental disconnect between the views of the president and his Army chief of staff. To Marshall the key was an invasion of occupied Europe, something that could not be undertaken until the spring of 1943;

to Roosevelt, the most important thing was to do something quickly to keep the Russians and the American public in the game. Here was the conundrum: they could fight elsewhere in 1942, or they could fight in Europe in 1943, but they could probably not do both. They must choose.[11]

Roosevelt did not like to choose. Incorrigible optimist that he was, he continued to talk and act as if it would be possible to do both. In any case, the buildup phase (Bolero) could begin at once no matter what contingencies arose in the meantime. Whether that buildup fed Sledgehammer or Roundup—or even Gymnast—would depend on a number of factors, including British acquiescence. As Hopkins put it in a note to the president, "This will have to be worked out very carefully between you and Marshall, in the first instance, and you and Churchill, in the second."[12]

IN ENGLAND, CHURCHILL AND THE BRITISH prepared to receive their guests with a mixture of anticipation and uncertainty. It had been evident from the beginning that the Americans and the British had divergent views on grand strategy, some of which had emerged at Arcadia. Several factors contributed to this. The first was the British experience on the continent during the First World War. While the United States had remained neutral from 1914 to 1917, entering the war with significant numbers of troops only in the last few months of the conflict, an entire generation of British men and boys had died on the battlefields of France and Flanders.* The narrow escape of the British Expeditionary Force from Dunkirk in 1940 only reminded them that the continent was a dangerous place.

In addition, the British were very much aware of two other factors that made a swift return to the continent altogether impractical. The first was that for all their eager enthusiasm, the Americans simply did not have the available manpower to execute the early invasion they championed. Though mobilization in America was proceeding rapidly, it would be many months before the United States could deliver more than a token assault force to

---

* It is instructive to compare British losses in World War I (886,939 deaths out of a population of 45.4 million, or about 2 percent) to American losses in the Civil War (about 700,000 deaths—on both sides—out of a population of 31.5 million, or about 2.2 percent).

Britain for a cross-Channel attack. Marshall's plan called for the United States to ship some 800,000 men to England by the spring of 1943. Even if this schedule could be met, however, there would be only 105,000 Americans in Britain by the fall of 1942. So while a 1943 invasion might be feasible, any operation before that would have to be conducted mostly, if not exclusively, by British soldiers. Marshall acknowledged that he was "greatly embarrassed by the fact that we could propose only 2½ divisions to participate in a cross-Channel operation" in 1942. Rather than Sledgehammer, a more appropriate name for the contingency plan the Americans were suggesting might have been Croquet Mallet, for the Allies simply did not have the wherewithal for a full-scale invasion of northern France in 1942.[13]

Then there was the unresolved shipping problem. The astonishing productivity of American shipyards could possibly make an invasion armada a reality by 1943, assuming, that is, that the Allies could win the Battle of the Atlantic against German U-boats. But in 1942 there was not enough shipping for a cross-Channel invasion even if the troops to conduct it could somehow be found. Ferrying two infantry divisions and two tank regiments across the English Channel (the absolute minimum even for a serious raid) would require more sealift capability and landing craft than would be available by the fall of 1942.[14]

In addition to these tangible shortages, there was another problem on a more subjective level, and that was the British assumption—which they were careful to keep hidden—that American forces in any number were simply not ready for a confrontation with the Wehrmacht. Indeed, the eagerness of the Americans for an early invasion of Europe would have been amusing if it were not so alarming. Despite a lack of manpower, shipping, and experience, the Americans were—from the British perspective, at least—ludicrously eager to pitch into the fray against the most proficient armed force on the planet. The British found themselves in a situation akin to a parent trying to explain to his six-year-old why he cannot drive the car: you don't know how, and your feet don't reach the pedals. They couldn't say any of that, of course, for they desperately needed the Americans—their manpower, and especially their financial and industrial strength—to fight the war at all. And so they listened earnestly and feigned

agreement while disguising their skepticism. In the long run, this disin-
genuous pose damaged the mutual trust within the Anglo-American
partnership, especially when the British subsequently sought to rein in
American enthusiasm. As one senior British officer wrote later, it would
have been far better had they said from the beginning, "We are not going
into this until it is a cast-iron certainty." Instead, they responded with the
equivalent of a parental "We'll see."[15]

Finally, the British outlook was affected by Churchill's concern for the
political ramifications of strategic decisions. There is nothing the least bit
dishonest or inappropriate about such concerns. Securing political objectives is the very purpose of war. British objectives and American political
objectives, however, were not fully congruent. Churchill's emphasis on the
Mediterranean was driven in part by his strategic goal of (as he put it)
"closing the ring" around Germany. But it was also a product of his determination to protect British imperial interests, a goal that was antithetical to the
Americans. Gibraltar, Malta, and Suez were stepping-stones through the
Mediterranean to India, the jewel of the British Empire. It is noteworthy that
in addition to the formal title "King and Defender of the Faith," George VI,
like his predecessors back to Victoria, also bore the title "Emperor of India."
As the king's prime minister, Churchill took that seriously, and keeping
India and the rest of the British Empire intact was for him a principal war
goal. Some of the sharpest exchanges between Churchill and Roosevelt
during the war concerned the future political status of India. It was in reaction to American criticism of British rule in India that Churchill announced
to the Commons later that year: "I have not become the King's First
Minister in order to preside over the liquidation of the British Empire."

Despite these various concerns, the British did not reject the idea of a
1942 cross-Channel invasion out of hand. Indeed, the British Chiefs of
Staff spent many days and weeks studying various alternative scenarios for
landings in either the Pas de Calais or the Cotentin peninsula. They worked
up several plans for quick coastal raids or the establishment of a permanent
bridgehead, and some British officers became keen advocates of an early
offensive. But in the end, the numbers just did not add up. Any landing in
1942, even a small-scale raid, would have such a tiny margin of error as to

be nearly suicidal, and was unlikely to be of any significant help to the Russians. By the time Marshall and Hopkins arrived in England, Churchill had concluded that a cross-Channel operation in 1942 was simply out of the question.[16]

Marshall and Hopkins arrived on April 8, and they met the next day with General Alan Brooke, Dill's successor as chief of the Imperial General Staff and Marshall's counterpart.* Sporting a David Niven–style pencil mustache, Brooke was a small, neat, birdlike man, which was appropriate since bird watching and bird photography were his life's passion. From the beginning, however, Marshall and Brooke talked past each other. In part this was because of the phenomenon, observed by many over the years and generally attributed to George Bernard Shaw, that Americans and Britons were one people divided by a common language. Brooke, an Ulsterman, not only spoke with the Gaelic accent of Northern Ireland but did so in a rapid-fire delivery that often left the Americans entirely perplexed. Moreover, Brooke also had a lower dental plate that occasionally got in the way of his machine-gun pronouncements. Since the Americans were unwilling to pester him with constant requests to repeat himself, much of what he said flew past them without ever finding purchase. For his part, Brooke understood Marshall's soft Virginia-accented speech well enough—it was the content of that speech that he thought absurd. Brooke liked Marshall personally ("a pleasant and easy man to get on with," he noted in his diary) but found his arguments so "fantastic" that he concluded Marshall was "no strategist." Brooke conceded that Marshall was "a good general at raising armies," but "his strategical ability does not impress me at all!!"—the two exclamation points underscoring his incredulity.[17]

Marshall's central argument was that the Allies must somehow halt the drip, drip, drip of the continuous drain of resources to secondary theaters and get serious about the necessary buildup for the eventual invasion of

---

* Brooke's name occasionally creates confusion for American readers. He was elevated to the peerage at the end of the war, and in selecting his title he conflated his two names to become Viscount Alanbrooke, which is how his name appears in the notes and bibliography of this book. During the war, however, he was Alan Brooke, and his friends called him "Brooksie."

Europe. As he had explained it to Roosevelt, "The most important consideration is the gathering of the largest force of ground troops possible in the British Isles at the earliest possible date."[18]

What Brooke heard, however, was an American general insisting that a cross-Channel operation should be seriously considered for that fall, and to him that was utterly ridiculous. Rather than respond the way Marshall had to Roosevelt four years earlier ("I don't agree with that at all"), Brooke instead implied a general acquiescence, if not quite full acceptance. Coached by Churchill, Brooke feared that if the Americans were denied their preferred strategy, they might abandon the Germany-first concept and turn to the Pacific. So he agreed "in principle," but remained vague about specifics. Curiously, and a bit ironically, this was precisely the managerial gambit that Roosevelt often used when confronted with problems that he preferred not to engage.[19]

For most of a week, Marshall and Hopkins met with Brooke, Pound, and Portal to discuss what Brooke called "Marshall's scheme for [the] invasion of Europe." Their daytime meetings were generally followed by elaborate late-night dinners, generally hosted by Churchill. Marshall often flagged when social activities lasted well into the morning hours, but Brooke took it all in stride. It was, after all, part of his job to keep up with the prime minister. Indeed, Brooke expressed astonishment when Marshall told him that it was not unusual for him not to see the president for months at a time. Brooke responded ruefully that he was lucky if he could escape the prime minister for six hours.[20]

During the week, Brooke softened a bit in his reaction to Marshall ("The more I see of him the more I like him," he wrote), though he continued to believe the American scheme was not only wrongheaded but foolish. Nevertheless, on April 14 the British formally accepted the American plan, which Brooke recorded in his diary as "offensive action in Europe in 1942 perhaps, and in 1943 for certain." That was a fair summary of what Marshall sought. But Brooke's private reaction, confided to his diary, was that "it was not possible to take Marshall's 'castles in the air' too seriously." If Brooke was less than fully forthcoming to Marshall, Marshall was similarly guilty. His real plan, after all, was to use the *prospect* of a 1942 invasion to keep men and supplies coming to England so that they would not be sent off to some peripheral theater and thereby make a 1943 invasion impossible. Moreover, despite British agreement, Marshall recognized the reluctant and conditional nature of their acquiescence. To a colleague back in the States he wrote, "Virtually everyone agrees with us in principle, but many if not most hold reservations regarding this or that."[21]

Officially, at least, it was agreement and consensus all the way. Churchill wrote to Roosevelt on April 17, "We wholeheartedly agree with your conception of concentration against the main enemy." His only qualification was that because of recent triumphs by the Japanese in the Indian Ocean, including the fall of Rangoon in Burma, "a proportion of our combined resources must, for the moment, be set aside to halt the Japanese advance." He noted that "the campaign of 1943 is straightforward, and we are starting joint plans and preparations at once." Significantly, however, he added one more note toward the end: "We may, however, feel compelled to act this year." When Churchill wrote that, it was not Sledgehammer he had in mind. The Americans had barely left for home when Churchill sat down with Brooke and told him frankly that it was "impossible to establish a front" in France with the small number of landing craft available in 1942. Brooke was relieved to hear that the prime minister was so "amenable to reason," until Churchill told him that what *he* had in mind for 1942 was an invasion of Norway![22]

Roosevelt replied to Churchill's April 17 cable as if everything were settled. "I am delighted with the agreement which was reached between you and your military advisors and Marshall and Hopkins," the president wrote. "They have reported to me of the unanimity of opinion relative to the proposal which they carried with them."[23]

THAT APPARENT UNANIMITY began to evaporate almost at once, and the calls for a division here, a squadron there, and convoy support somewhere else continued. Early in May, Eisenhower noted privately, "Bolero is supposed to have the approval of the Pres and Prime Minister. But the struggle to get everyone behind it, and to keep the highest authority from wrecking it by making additional commitments of air-ship-troops everywhere is never ending." Moreover, the program received a near-mortal blow that summer in consequence of the arrival in Washington of two foreign emissaries: one of them a handsome, urbane, charming English aristocrat, and the other a bespectacled, humorless, cold-eyed Russian realist.[24]

The realist arrived first. Vyacheslav Mikhailovich Molotov was Stalin's foreign minister and the man who had negotiated the 1939 pact with Germany's Joachim von Ribbentrop to divide Poland between them—the document that gave Hitler the green light to invade Poland and start the war. Now, with Russia fighting for her survival, Molotov had flown from Moscow to ask what the Western Allies were willing to do to ease the pressure on the Red Army. In London Molotov signed a twenty-year Mutual Assistance Agreement with the British, but Churchill had declined to give him any guarantees about a second front, and so Molotov flew on to Washington, where he arrived on May 29 to talk to Roosevelt. As Churchill had done, he stayed in the White House during his visit, and there was an awkward moment at the very start when a White House butler unpacking his luggage found a loaded pistol alongside a loaf of brown bread and a sausage. Upon inquiring what he should do about the weapon, he was told to leave it where it was and say nothing. The fact that Molotov had felt the need to bring his own sustenance and means of self-defense speaks volumes about his state of mind.

Molotov was a tidy, diminutive man whose round spectacles gave him an owlish, academic aspect, and his prim and dour demeanor clashed jarringly with that of the ebullient and gregarious Roosevelt. Moreover, their conversations were complicated by the fact that each of their statements had to be laboriously translated. There were often lengthy delays as the two interpreters discussed the nuances of each comment between themselves before offering a translation, and as a result, the talks proceeded haltingly. Roosevelt asked Marshall, King, and Hopkins to be present at the first full meeting on May 30 when he invited Molotov to "put the situation before them" and "treat the subject in such detail as suited his convenience." Molotov got right to the point. Hitler "was the master of all Europe," he said, and given his strength, he "might throw in such reinforcements in manpower and material that the Red Army might *not* be able to hold out." He suggested that Hitler would try "to deal the Soviet Union a mighty crushing blow" that summer. He therefore wanted to know: could the Western Allies "undertake such offensive action as would draw off 40 German divisions"?[25]

Roosevelt responded that the United States considered it an "obligation to help the Soviets," but its efforts were severely constrained by the limits of "ocean transport." Molotov waved off that concern by asserting that "the difficulties...would not be any less in 1943." "If you postpone your decision," he said, "you will eventually have to bear the brunt of the war" and "next year will unquestionably be tougher than this one." He cut to the chase: his government wished to know "in frank terms" what position the Western Allies took "on the question of a second front." He had asked Churchill the same question, but the prime minister had deferred to Roosevelt. So now he asked the American president directly: could the United States "undertake such offensive action"?

Roosevelt turned to Marshall. Were developments "clear enough so that we could say to Mr. Stalin that we were preparing a second front"?

Marshall answered with a single syllable: "Yes."

Roosevelt then turned back to Molotov and told him he could "inform Mr. Stalin that we expect the formation of a second front *this year*."

No doubt alarmed by the chasm of difference between "preparing" a second front, which he had affirmed, and actually establishing one "this year," Marshall quickly added the far more conditional observation that "we were making every effort to build up a situation in which the creation of a second front would be possible." It was as far as he could go without openly contradicting the president.[26]

The rest of Molotov's visit passed more prosaically. Roosevelt raised other issues, including Finland, which the Russians had invaded in 1939, and the postwar management of the liberated territories, though at least twice he reiterated the American determination to "set up a second front in 1942." Roosevelt asked Molotov if the Soviets would accept a cutback on their promised Lend-Lease shipments in order to free up more shipping for that second front. At that, Molotov bristled. Demonstrating his instinctive distrust, he asked what would happen if Russia agreed to the cutbacks and no second front materialized. Roosevelt sought to reassure him, but

Molotov remained suspicious, and the question was shelved. The Allies would simply try to overcome the shipping problem.[27]

Meanwhile, it was necessary to draft a public statement about what exactly the two men had agreed upon. The key sentence in the final document was neither elegant nor definitive: "In the course of the conversations full understanding was reached with regard to the urgent tasks of creating a Second Front in Europe in 1942." While the statement contained the words "Second Front" and "1942," it was immediately evident that acknowledging the urgency of a task was hardly the same thing as a pledge to accomplish it. Apparently it was now the Americans' turn to say, "We'll see." Molotov accepted it because he perceived that it was all he was likely to get. Churchill accepted it because he thought it "might make the Germans apprehensive," though not for a minute did he assume that it meant a Western Front in France in 1942. To make sure Molotov understood that, he prepared an aide-mémoire to give to the Russian foreign minister when he passed through London en route back to Moscow. In it, Churchill was careful to state that although the British and Americans were "making preparations for a landing on the Continent," they could "give no promise in the matter." There it rested . . . for now.[28]

Despite the absence of a pledge, the meeting between Roosevelt and Molotov was critical, for the American president found the specter of a Soviet collapse so horrifying that he was reconfirmed in his view that an offensive somewhere in the European theater in 1942 was essential. To Churchill he reported that they "faced real trouble on the Russian front and must make our plans to meet it." Even if a 1942 invasion of Europe failed to gain a permanent toehold for the Allies, it might draw the Luftwaffe into an air battle over the beaches that could erode German air assets and would at least demonstrate good faith.[29]

No sooner did Molotov leave Washington than another visitor arrived. The new guest was Admiral Lord Louis Mountbatten, and there could hardly have been a greater contrast with the departed Molotov. A great-grandson of Queen Victoria, and second cousin to King George himself, Mountbatten was tall, attractive, sophisticated, and gracious. Churchill (who, like all of Mountbatten's friends, called him "Dickie") had named him chief of combined operations with oversight over the production of amphibious shipping. In that capacity, Mountbatten was simultaneously a lieutenant general in the British Army, a vice admiral in the Royal Navy, and an air vice marshal in the Royal Air Force. Mountbatten was eager to take on the Germans, but his careful study of landing craft availability had convinced him that a cross-Channel operation in 1942 was out of the question. He told the British chiefs that it was dishonest to continue to plan an operation they knew to be impossible. Aware of his views, Churchill dispatched him to the United States to insert some realism into American thinking.[30]

As Churchill no doubt expected, Mountbatten made a wonderful impression on the Americans; both Marshall and King thought him first-rate. More significant, however, was the five-hour conversation he had with Roosevelt in the White House. The president's fear of a Russian collapse had been intensified by Molotov's visit, and he asked Mountbatten "whether we could not get a footing on the Continent some time this year." Not only did Mountbatten explain the landing craft problem, but he also reminded Roosevelt that the Germans already had twenty-five mobile divisions in France, so "no landing that we could carry out could draw off any troops" from the Eastern Front. Roosevelt found that alarming and suggested that perhaps a "sacrifice" landing would be necessary anyway in order to show good faith to the Russians. When Mountbatten returned to England and shared that notion with Churchill, the prime minister decided that he must cross the Atlantic once again in order to squelch it. "I feel it is my duty to come see you," he wrote Roosevelt on June 13, and soon afterward he was in the air again, flying west.[31]

IT TOOK TWENTY-EIGHT HOURS for Churchill's flying boat to cross the Atlantic, and then he boarded another, much smaller plane to fly up to Hyde Park, on the Hudson, where Roosevelt was spending the weekend. Brooke had accompanied Churchill, but he stayed in Washington to meet with Marshall and the CCS. After a bumpy landing at the small Hyde Park airstrip, Churchill found a smiling Roosevelt sitting behind the wheel of his specially modified Ford that allowed him to drive without using foot pedals. The president was in a good mood, in part because of splendid news from the Pacific of an American naval victory near Midway that had resulted in the sinking of four Japanese aircraft carriers. That eased concern that assets might have to be funneled away from Europe to prop up the Allied position there. The president insisted on giving the prime minister a tour of the estate, and Churchill subsequently admitted that he had "some thoughtful moments" as Roosevelt steered his vehicle along the bluffs above the Hudson River with freewheeling joie de vivre.[32]

Meanwhile, Brooke sat down in Marshall's Washington office with Dill, King, and Eisenhower. It was a typical hot and sticky summer day in the capital ("stinking hot," Stimson called it in his diary), the building had no air-conditioning, and the British were still in their winter uniforms. Nevertheless, they got down to work at once. Brooke began by noting that the justification for the Bolero buildup was still valid—on that, at least, there was "complete unanimity of opinion." The problem was that they needed a contingency plan in case the Russians failed to hold out against the German spring offensive. It was clear, he said, that "logistic factors" made a cross-Channel invasion into France impossible for 1942, so some alternative to Sledgehammer must be found, and the only practical one was Gymnast—the invasion of North Africa. Marshall suggested that before abandoning Sledgehammer, they should wait to see whether the Russians held out, and how the buildup in England was progressing. Perhaps they could postpone making a decision until September 15. Brooke disagreed. That would be too late "to modify existing plans," and would come too late to help the Russians anyway. The planning must begin now for Gymnast. Dill concurred.[33]

Marshall felt betrayed. Just two months earlier, the British had agreed "wholeheartedly" to a strategic blueprint that they now insisted was impossible. Ernest King was equally annoyed and far less restrained. King's daughter once quipped that her father was the most even-tempered man in the U.S. Navy—he was always in a rage. Whether that was literally true, it was true enough now. King announced angrily that he was "entirely opposed to any idea of carrying out Gymnast in 1942." He lectured the British that "great risks" had been taken by American servicemen in the Pacific who went without needed equipment and supplies so that deliveries could be made to England for the invasion of Germany. To abandon that invasion now would mean that those sacrifices had been made in vain. Marshall, too, fought back, though with less emotion. The key to defeating Germany, he insisted, was "overwhelming power," and the only place where that could be applied was in "North West Europe." The Americans got unexpected support from the Royal Navy when Admiral Sir Charles Little declared that it was reckless to open yet another front in Africa when "we were not able to maintain our existing sea communications."[34]

In the end, it hardly mattered. The decision that counted was being made that same day up in Hyde Park. Marshall and King always worried when Roosevelt and Churchill met alone together, and they were right to be concerned. After their adventurous automobile tour of the estate, Roosevelt, Churchill, and Hopkins sat down in Roosevelt's small study, where, as Churchill ruefully noted, the Americans "did not seem to mind the intense heat." Any attempted invasion of France in 1942, Churchill asserted, "was certain to lead to disaster," besides which it "would not help the Russians," which, after all, was the main point. It was inconceivable that they should do nothing, so it was necessary to consider what was within their reach. In this way he worked his way back to the plan he had proposed at Arcadia: an invasion of French Northwest Africa.[35]

Roosevelt was far more agreeable to the idea than his uniformed chiefs were. He had never fully abandoned the idea of invading French Africa, and had signaled as much in a meeting with his war cabinet only three days before. As always, Marshall had vigorously opposed it, and because of that, though Roosevelt was now inclined to accept Churchill's logic, he would not commit himself without talking again to Marshall and King. To do that, Roosevelt, Churchill, and Hopkins boarded a train for an overnight journey back to Washington. Arriving early the next morning, Churchill was blissfully relieved to reenter his air-conditioned guest room in the White House, and after refreshing himself, he joined Roosevelt in his study. He had been there only a few minutes when a courier brought in a pink flimsy—a copy of a cablegram—and handed it to Roosevelt. The president read it silently, then told the courier to "give it to Winston." The first words of the message turned the prime minister chalk white: "Tobruk has fallen."[36]

Other than the evacuation from Dunkirk and the fall of Singapore, few catastrophes of the war constituted a heavier blow to British arms. Tobruk was the citadel of British power in Libya. A thirty-three-thousand-man British Commonwealth army held that citadel against a German army barely half its size. Churchill had counted on Tobruk to be the anvil for the hammer blow he hoped to strike in North Africa. Now with the citadel taken and its entire defending army made prisoner of war, it seemed possible that the Germans might drive all the way into Egypt. As he contemplated the consequences of this disaster, Churchill had to sit down.[37]

Roosevelt was instantly and instinctively sympathetic. "What can we do to help?" he asked. Churchill replied that American tanks—some of the new Sherman tanks—might allow the British to hold Egypt. On the spot, Roosevelt ordered Marshall to reconfigure the shipping tables to send three hundred Sherman tanks and a hundred self-propelled 105 mm guns to Egypt immediately. Apparently the president was willing to go further. As others drifted out of the room, he asked Marshall to stay. What did he think of sending an American division to the Middle East to fight alongside the British? Marshall was horrified. Here was a perfect example of the kind of dispersion of resources that he believed would doom the Allied cause. Not trusting himself to speak, he excused himself and left the room.[38]

There was one more strategy session in Washington before Churchill left to return to London in order to deal with the crisis in North Africa. At that meeting, Brooke met the American president for the first time. He had planned to change into his best uniform beforehand, but Churchill insisted there was no time and brought him along as he was. Brooke was impressed by Roosevelt ("a most attractive Personality," he wrote in his diary) and apologized for his dowdy uniform. Roosevelt waved it off and told him to take off his jacket and be comfortable.[39]

Aware that this was his last chance, Churchill pushed hard for an abandonment of Sledgehammer and a commitment to Gymnast. This time, however, Roosevelt was less amenable. Bolstered by memos from both Hopkins and Stimson (who wrote Roosevelt that "it would be a mistake . . . to risk BOLERO for the sake of GYMNAST"), as well as Marshall's stalwart defense, he resisted the eloquent appeals of the prime minister. The final memorandum stipulated that "Operations in Western Europe" would "yield greater political and strategic gains than operations in any other theater." On the other hand, that same memorandum stated that if "despite all efforts, success is improbable, we must be ready with an alternative," and that "the best alternative is Operation GYMNAST."[40]

Marshall sensed that the tide was flowing against him. To demonstrate to Churchill and the British that the Americans were making great strides toward the creation of an army that might yet be able to do something in Europe in 1942, he took the whole British delegation by train down to Fort Jackson, South Carolina, to watch a scheduled army exercise. South Carolina reminded Churchill of "the plains of India in hot weather," but he was an eager observer as ten thousand men and hundreds of vehicles maneuvered purposefully across the pine barrens. He was especially impressed by the spectacle of six hundred paratroopers dropping from the sky, and he enjoyed trying out the new "walkie-talkie" handheld radio. It did not, however, change his mind about the wisdom of hurling such troops as these against the coast of France. When he asked his military assistant, Hastings "Pug" Ismay, what he thought of the American maneuvers, Ismay replied, "To put these troops against continental troops would be murder."[41]

ROOSEVELT HAD MADE IT CLEAR that he wanted something to happen that year. Whatever that something was, Marshall wanted it to be in Europe, but it was becoming increasingly evident, even to him, that Sledge-hammer was doubtful. On July 8, Churchill finally pulled the plug, sending Roosevelt a cable that did not mince words: "No responsible British general, admiral, or air marshal is prepared to recommend Sledgehammer as a practicable operation in 1942," he wrote. Unsurprisingly, he had an alternative in mind: "I am sure myself that Gymnast is by far the best chance for effective relief to the Russian front in 1942."[42]

That left Marshall with only one card to play. He shared with Stimson an idea for a "showdown" with the British, and to some extent with the president, too. "As the British won't go through with what they agreed to," he told the secretary of war, "we will turn our backs on them and take up the war with Japan." Stimson encouraged him, and when Marshall brought the idea up with the JCS, King naturally thought it a splendid idea. So Marshall prepared a memo for the president in which he advocated a complete reversal of American strategy: "If the United States is to engage in any other operation than forceful, unswerving adherence to BOLERO plans," he wrote, "we are definitely of the opinion that we should turn to the Pacific and strike decisively against Japan; in other words, assume a defensive attitude against Germany, except for air operations; and use all available means in the Pacific."[43]

Long after the war was over, Marshall admitted to his biographer, Forrest Pogue, that his proposal had been "a bluff" designed to get the British to back down. Roosevelt, however, was an old poker player and recognized it for what it was. He received Marshall's astonishing memo at Hyde Park, discussed it briefly with Hopkins, and then called Marshall's bluff by asking him to show his cards: that is, to produce a detailed plan that included a list of Pacific targets, a timetable for the landings, a logistics program to support them, and an explanation of how such a move would help the Russians. Marshall had to confess he had no such plan, and so on Monday, July 13, Roosevelt officially rejected the proposal, saying that it would be like "taking up your dishes and going away." At the same time, he reiterated to Marshall that he must find a way to get United States troops into combat in the European theater *that year*, and to accomplish that, he was sending Marshall back to London with King and Hopkins to reach a final agreement with the British. He signed the memo "Franklin D. Roosevelt, Commander-in-Chief," a not-so-subtle reminder of the chain of command.[44]

Marshall, King, and Hopkins landed at Scotland's Prestwick Airport on July 18. Churchill had sent a special train to bring them to Chequers, where he planned an elaborate dinner. Marshall and King, however, still resentful of what they perceived to be British faithlessness, instead boarded a train that took them to Euston Station in London and made their way to Claridge's Hotel. Churchill was furious at the snub, and Hopkins took it upon himself to play peacemaker, going out to Chequers to try to calm the irate prime minister. He may have done more than that. Circumstantial evidence suggests that he also shared with Churchill that Roosevelt had taken the Pacific option off the table. That, of course, greatly strengthened Churchill's hand in holding out for Gymnast.[45]

The showdown came on July 22. Ordered by Roosevelt to obtain an agreement for a 1942 operation, Marshall and King pushed hard for Sledgehammer, or at least a modified version of it. Churchill and the British were unmovable. Churchill had made a *permanent* lodgment a condition of any cross-Channel effort, and the wherewithal to establish and maintain such a foothold simply did not exist. As Hopkins listened to the back-and-forth, he saw that the two sides had reached an impasse, and he scrawled a note to Marshall: "I feel damn depressed."[46]

Marshall suggested a compromise in which serious preparations would begin at once for Gymnast but a decision to execute it would be postponed until September in order to assess circumstances at the time. The British were willing to accept that, but Hopkins was not. He feared that postponing the decision until September would mean no action at all in 1942. He cabled the president privately to suggest that Roosevelt should intervene. He should not only support Gymnast, Hopkins suggested, but also set a date for its execution, suggesting October 30, 1942, which was, not coincidentally, four days before the congressional elections. Accepting Hopkins's advice, Roosevelt ordered Marshall and King to abandon Sledgehammer and choose instead one of several alternatives: North Africa, Norway, Egypt, or Iran. Given those choices, there was really only one possible outcome, and Hopkins cabled the final decision to Roosevelt that night in a single word: "Africa." Roosevelt's reply was similarly terse: "Thank God."[47]

Churchill, of course, was delighted, writing Roosevelt that it was now "full steam ahead" for the new plan, which he rechristened Torch. He happily embraced the proposal that an American should be designated as the overall commander of the operation, and even accepted the unpleasant duty of going to Moscow to break the bad news to Stalin. Churchill continued to act and to speak as if this commitment to Torch would have little effect on Roundup in 1943. He certainly implied as much to Stalin, telling the Russian leader that in addition to Torch, the Allies planned to land forty-eight divisions in France in the spring. He may even have believed it. Two months later he claimed, perhaps disingenuously, that he was "astonished" that the execution of Torch was likely to affect a 1943 cross-Channel invasion. Roosevelt, too, optimist that he was, clung to the notion that the

Allies could eat their cake and have it, too. As he told one officer, "he could see no reason why the withdrawal of a few troops in 1942 would prevent BOLERO in 1943."[48]

Marshall knew better. He saw clearly that once the Western Allies became fully committed, the momentum of events and the logistical realities of attempting to assemble, mount, and execute a large-scale amphibious assault in Africa would make a spring invasion of France in 1943 impossible. Bowing to reality, however, he acknowledged that the pressures of the moment, both political and logistical, compelled the decision for Torch. Time was running out. It was past midsummer, and the Germans had begun a two-pronged drive, code-named Case Blue, aimed at the capture of both the Baku oil fields and Stalin's namesake city, Stalingrad. Something had to be done, and Torch was the only thing that seemed doable. On July 30, Roosevelt formally announced that "as Commander-in-Chief, [he] had made the decision." The invasion of North Africa was now to be America's "principal objective," and the distribution of ships, men, and matériel for that operation was to take precedence over all other options, including Bolero. Disappointed but dutiful, Marshall prepared to execute the new strategy.[49]

CHAPTER 4

THE MEDITERRANEAN TAR BABY

EVEN BEFORE ROOSEVELT STEPPED IN to make the final decision for Gymnast/Torch at the end of July, Marshall sent Eisenhower to England to assume the role of commanding general of U.S. forces in the European theater. Eisenhower replaced Major General James E. Chaney, who suffered from two flaws: he maintained leisurely eight-hour work days, even wearing civilian clothes to the office, yet (according to Eisenhower) he betrayed "an excessive concern for minor regulations and rules." Chaney returned to the States to take over training for the Army Air Forces, and Eisenhower assumed command in England on June 24. Because of that, Ike was present at Claridge's Hotel in July when Marshall, King, and Hopkins laid their plans for the showdown with the British over Sledgehammer vs. Gymnast. Indeed, it was Eisenhower who wrote the briefing paper that had argued, "GYMNAST is strategically unsound as an operation either to support ROUNDUP or to render prompt assistance to the Russians." He was initially depressed by the decision to go to North Africa, predicting that future historians would mark July 22 as "the blackest day in history." Soon enough, however, he accepted and even embraced it. That was just as well, for within days he was tapped to be its commanding officer.[1]

Fifty-two years old in 1942 and already bald, Eisenhower was a Texan by birth, though he had been reared in Abilene, Kansas, which he always considered his home. Having delayed his application to West Point for two years after high school in order to work, he was older than most of his classmates, and he was twenty-five when he graduated more or less in the middle of his class in 1915. It was a great disappointment to him that he did not get overseas during the First World War and instead spent most of the war training tank units near Gettysburg, Pennsylvania. In the interwar years, his career was marked by a series of increasingly important staff positions under influential commanders: first Fox Conner, whom he always considered his mentor, then John J. Pershing, and finally Douglas MacArthur. His relationship with MacArthur was especially challenging since MacArthur preferred yes-men around him, and Eisenhower had to learn how to be loyal while remaining his own man—a delicate balancing act that prepared him to deal with the likes of Roosevelt and Churchill. Indeed, the key to both Eisenhower's rise in the Army and his success during the war was his measured temperament. In a note for his diary, he wrote: "In a war such as this, where high command invariably involves a Pres., a Prime Minister, 6 chiefs of staff, and a horde of lesser 'planners,' there has got to be a lot of patience." Like Marshall, who became his newest mentor, Ike was thoughtful and conscientious, a deliberate decision maker who worked long hours, maintained careful records, and ensured that everyone was kept well informed. Throughout it all he remained determinedly cheerful, often flashing that famous grin, which one officer thought was "worth twenty divisions." The only visible evidence that he was roiling inside was the cigarette that was almost always to be found in his hand, for he smoked up to four packs of Camels a day.[2]

In the ten months prior to his appointment to command Torch, Eisenhower had experienced an almost dizzying series of promotions. He made brigadier general in October 1941, major general in March 1942, and lieutenant general in July. Of course, there were any number of swift promotions in the rapidly expanding American army of 1941–42, but none quite like his—a rise that was all the more noteworthy in light of the fact that he had never commanded a body of men larger than a battalion, and he had never seen combat at all. Now endowed with the command of the largest and most complex undertaking of the war—indeed of American history— he began to gather the reins of command into his hands. He soon found that making plans was the easy part; it was implementing them that was hard, for coordinating all the various moving parts of this complex multinational operation was daunting. In the end, the material, logistical, organizational, and political difficulties of Torch demonstrated just how problematic an attempt to invade Europe in 1942 would have been. On the other hand, the experience proved invaluable in preparing Eisenhower to exercise even greater responsibility eighteen months later as the commander of Neptune-Overlord.

Eisenhower's first challenge was embracing the role of an *Allied* commander, not an *American* commander who had British troops serving under him. Though he (like Marshall) had advocated unified command for Allied operations from the start, it became immediately evident that the British and Americans had strikingly different command cultures and organizational habits. The American penchant for getting right to the point ran up against the British tradition of ensuring that all the boxes were properly checked before moving on to the next thing. Planning was slowed by the British preference for open discussion of most decisions at "large staff conference and committee meetings." American officers found this frustrating, and a few made disparaging remarks about it. Eisenhower acted quickly to stop such comments. He lectured his subordinates in no uncertain terms about the need for full cooperation. "The winning of the war," he insisted, "depends markedly upon...mutual feelings of respect and confidence." Any friction with the British at any level, he wrote, plays *"completely into the hands of our enemies,"* and he underscored the phrase for emphasis. He had no tolerance for inter-Allied feuding. He didn't mind if officers called each other a "son of a bitch," he told an associate; soldiers would do that. But if anyone referred to a *"British* son of a bitch," he was promptly sent packing. Throughout the war, Eisenhower's determination to erase national distinctions within his command was a central element of his leadership.[3]

Another constraint was Eisenhower's lack of control over political issues. One of those was whether to use British or American troops in the invasion. That question grew out of the complicated and uncertain political status of North Africa. The putatively independent Vichy French government retained colonial oversight over Morocco and Algeria, so, officially at least, an American invasion of North Africa would constitute an unprovoked attack on a neutral country, one with which the United States maintained nominally friendly relations. On the other hand, most Frenchmen continued to consider Germany their real enemy, and the Allied hope was that many of them would welcome the Americans as liberators.

That was not likely to be the case if British troops were involved. Though England and France had been allied against Germany in both world wars, that partnership had suffered a blow in May 1940 during the German blitzkrieg, when British forces had retreated to the Channel coast at Dunkirk to save themselves, leaving the French to face the Germans alone. To be sure, by then the military situation had utterly collapsed and the only other British options were destruction or surrender. Nevertheless, the French felt betrayed by what they considered their abandonment. Far worse, however, was the Royal Navy attack six weeks later on the French fleet at Mers-el-Kebir, near Oran in Algeria. The British had justified that attack as necessary to keep French naval assets out of German hands, but justified or not, it had been a deliberate and unprovoked assault in which more than twelve hundred Frenchmen had been killed. To the French, it was little different, and arguably even more infamous, than what the Japanese had done to the Americans at Pearl Harbor. Roosevelt feared that French anger would translate into fierce resistance to any invasion that included British troops, and he therefore wanted the North African assault to be an all-American show. Naturally enough, Churchill and the British did not want to be left out of this first Anglo-American counteroffensive of the war.[4]

A second issue was where the troops would land. French North Africa stretched for a thousand miles from the Atlantic Ocean to the Tunisian desert. The British wanted to secure a foothold as far inside the Mediterranean as possible. That way, they could move quickly into Tunisia and trap the German Afrika Korps between the invasion force and the British

Eighth Army in Egypt. American planners, dubious about sending forces through the Strait of Gibraltar and into the cul-de-sac of the Mediterranean, wanted the landings to take place outside the Mediterranean, on the Atlantic coast of French Morocco. Roosevelt himself personally insisted that "one of our landings must be on the Atlantic." The British found such concerns incomprehensible. They had been passing through the Strait of Gibraltar with impunity for more than two hundred years, and to them it was as friendly and familiar as the English Channel. In the end, these issues were resolved by compromise. The Allies would make three landings: an all-American effort on the Atlantic coast near Casablanca, and two Anglo-American landings on the Mediterranean coast at Oran and Algiers. These negotiations, however, played havoc with the timetable. Eisenhower did not get the green light until the first week of September, and only then could he begin to assemble the various pieces—the troops, the ships, and the supplies—that would make up the invasion groups.[5]

In the meantime, on August 19, the British launched a raid against the French Channel coast at Dieppe, about halfway between the Pas de Calais and Normandy. As he had made clear at Arcadia, Churchill's long-term strategic vision included periodic assaults against the periphery of Nazi-occupied Europe to test German defenses, give hope to the resistance, and perhaps draw the Luftwaffe into a battle of attrition. He had made Mountbatten the commander of combined operations precisely to oversee such raids, and the British had already carried out successful forays against Le Havre and St. Nazaire. The attack on Dieppe, however, was a disaster from the start. German defenses proved more than adequate, inflicting an appalling 60 percent casualty rate on the five thousand Canadians and one thousand British commandos who took part. Even the air battle went the way of the Germans: the Luftwaffe lost only 46 planes, while the Allies lost 106. If the operation had any silver lining at all, it was in providing important lessons about amphibious operations, including the difficulty of getting heavy tanks ashore from landing ships. Of the fifty-eight big 40-ton "Churchill" tanks embarked for the raid, fewer than half got to the beach at all, and fewer than half of those got as far as the seawall. Though the British sought to put the best face on it and kept the extent of the disaster a secret, the

Dieppe raid fell short of being a full-blown catastrophe only because of the limited numbers involved. The lesson was not lost on Eisenhower, who wrote his naval aide Harry Butcher on September 2 that in planning Torch, "we are undertaking something of a quite desperate nature."[6]

TO MANAGE OPERATION TORCH, Eisenhower moved his headquarters from No. 20 Grosvenor Square in London's Mayfair district to the larger Norfolk House on St. James's Square, a block off Pall Mall. Once the home of the Dukes of Norfolk, the original building had been razed just before the war to accommodate a rather charmless red brick office building. There, Eisenhower and his team of staff officers kept long hours dealing with the infinite number of details associated with mounting an invasion of Africa, now only two months away. Haste bred anxiety in the barely controlled chaos that characterized the daily schedule at Norfolk House. Ike's deputy Mark Clark (who preferred to use his middle name, Wayne) found that keeping track of all the various aspects of the global operation was all but impossible. Goods and equipment that had been ordered and shipped somehow disappeared. The U-boats were responsible for some of that, of course, but much of it was administrative confusion. Whatever the cause, the shortfalls had to be made up somehow, and staff officers scrambled to find replacements or substitutes. Their frustration led to frayed tempers and sharp words. Through it all, whatever he might feel personally, Eisenhower remained outwardly calm and confident. When Clark came to him frantic about yet another seemingly insoluble crisis, Eisenhower's most characteristic comment was, "Now just keep your shirt on, Wayne."[7]

Eisenhower also had to keep Churchill happy. The prime minister liked to be in the middle of things, and he insisted that both Eisenhower and Clark attend weekly luncheons and occasional late-night meetings at 10 Downing Street. The P.M. also hosted the Americans for weekends at Chequers. Churchill considered these meetings a great success. To Eisenhower they were one more time-consuming distraction from the work he had to do. In spite of that, he was unfailingly courteous, always complimented Churchill on the Irish stew that was often served, and managed to convince the prime minister that he was as delighted by these conferences as his host.[8]

The biggest problem confronting the planners at Norfolk House was the old one of shipping. There were not enough troopships for the invasion force, not enough cargo ships to carry the supplies, not enough escorts for protection, and, most of all, not enough landing craft to get the men, their supplies, and their vehicles from the transports to the beach. As Clark put it, "There was a continual crisis over shipping space and frequent changes in plans had to be made to overcome what was always a shortage of vessels." The prewar emphasis on building combatants had severely restricted the construction of auxiliaries, and losses in the Battle of the Atlantic made the problem worse. In consequence, the invasion armadas for all three beaches were improvised flotillas of whatever the Allies could lay their hands on. Prewar cruise ships became troopships, cargo vessels metamorphosed into attack transports, and even ferryboats from the Glasgow-Belfast run were called into service. To use the American idiom, the invasion fleets were jury-rigged, or as the British would say, lash-ups.[9]

Another problem was air cover. The landing beaches in Algeria could be protected, at least in part, by planes operating from the recently enlarged single airstrip at British Gibraltar, but the American landings in Morocco would depend entirely on carrier-borne aircraft, and most of the full-sized American aircraft carriers were in the Pacific. Indeed, only three days after the American invasion flotilla left Norfolk for Africa on October 23, U.S. carriers in the Pacific fought the Battle of the Santa Cruz Islands, which cost the Americans the USS *Hornet* (CV-8). The only carrier in the Atlantic was the much smaller USS *Ranger* (CV-4). To supplement her, the Americans relied on four small carriers that had been converted from oilers, each of them capable of carrying thirty planes.* These ships did excellent service, though their hasty conversion demonstrated again the ersatz character of the invasion force.

---

* These were the *Sangemon* (CVE-26), which gave her name to the class; the *Suwanee* (CVE-27); the *Chenango* (CVE-28); and the *Santee* (CVE-29).

By far the most daunting obstacle for the invaders was the dearth of landing craft. Getting armed men, each of them carrying fifty or sixty pounds of weapons and equipment, from the troopships to the beaches, along with their supplies and especially their vehicles, was the most difficult aspect of any amphibious operation. The U.S. Marines had pioneered amphibious tactics during the 1930s and had conducted a number of practice landings during the annual fleet exercises at Culebra in Puerto Rico. But due to the parsimonious budgets of those years, they improvised "landing craft" from ships' boats. That would not suffice for the kind of large-scale amphibious assaults needed to effect Torch. For that, the Allies needed specially designed vessels that were small enough to be carried aboard the troopships during the ocean crossing, yet large enough to carry a score or more soldiers and their equipment several miles to the beach. They needed to be of sufficiently shallow draft to get close to the beach—or even onto the beach—but also commodious enough to carry the jeeps, trucks, and tanks needed to sustain a landing force in a battle ashore. Though the Navy Department had experimented with early designs for a "tank lighter" in the 1930s, the vessel that proved most useful in this role was something called the Higgins boat.[10]

IN THE 1930S, A TEAM OF DESIGNERS working for boatbuilding entrepreneur Andrew Jackson Higgins had developed what was initially called a "Eureka boat" for trappers and oil explorers in the shallow swamps of the Louisiana delta. The U.S. Marines became interested in the Eureka boat for military purposes, and in the fall of 1940 Higgins obtained a contract with the Navy to build 335 of them. The boats that made up this first generation of landing craft were flat-bottomed plywood vessels thirty-six feet long with a spoon-shaped bow that allowed them to push up onto a shallow beach. They were initially powered by a gasoline engine, though diesel engines eventually proved more practical. Higgins was a charismatic and tenacious businessman who was occasionally frustrated in his prewar dealings with the Navy bureaucracy. Furious when the Navy reneged on a handshake deal for 131 tank carriers in favor of an inferior in-house design, Higgins publicly characterized the Naval Academy as a place where officers learned "fancy dancing, football, fencing, boxing—things like that," but, he insisted, "there are no officers...who know a goddam thing about small boat design." Navy leaders, in turn, considered him "an arrogant know it all."[11]

Pearl Harbor swept away most of the bureaucratic impediments, but it did not change the Navy's low priority for landing-craft production. In January 1942 the construction of carriers, destroyers, and even battleships seemed more urgent than building landing craft, which were initially listed eighth in the Navy's shipbuilding precedence. Two months later they were lowered to tenth. Nevertheless, by the summer of 1942, the Navy had authorized construction of nearly two thousand of them. Many of those were still in the construction pipeline as the deadline for Torch approached, and most would eventually be sent to the Pacific. Consequently, there were only a few hundred landing craft available for the landings in North Africa.

What made the Higgins boats so valuable was their peculiar design. Because of their flat bottom, spoonbill bow, and shallow draft (only twenty-six inches forward), they could run right up onto the beach. In newer versions, the bow was squared off and hinged at the bottom so that it could be dropped onto the sand to allow the men to rush out onto the beach dry-shod. Each boat could carry thirty-six soldiers plus a Navy crew of three, and the addition of the bow ramp meant that they could also carry jeeps and trucks, though at thirty-six feet long and just over ten feet wide, they could carry only one truck or two jeeps at a time. To improve on that, Higgins designed and built a fifty-foot model that was made of steel and equipped with a stronger ramp so that it could carry a thirty-four-ton Sherman tank. Characteristically, the Navy endowed each of these vessels with a slightly different acronym: the initial Higgins boat was a Landing Craft Personnel (LCP), and the ramped version was an LCP(R), later redesignated as a Landing Craft, Vehicle and Personnel (LCVP). The bigger, steel Higgins boats for carrying tanks ashore were designated as Landing Craft Mechanized (LCM), often called a "Mike boat."[12]

Higgins even assumed responsibility for training the coxswains who would operate these ungainly craft. Upon completing the course, they received a certificate from the "Higgins Eureka Motor Boat Operators School of New Orleans, U.S.A." At the school, they learned the distinctive characteristics of these unique craft. For example, the natural instinct of a boat operator heading for a beach at full speed was to throttle back as he approached the shore. To do so, however, meant that the vessel might ground on an offshore sandbar while still some distance from the beach. The coxswains had to be trained to keep the throttle wide open as they approached the shore in order to run the boat over any sandbars and up onto the beach as far as possible. Even while the men or vehicles were being discharged, the engine was held at full throttle to hold the boat in place.[13]

Important as they were, the Higgins boats were not a complete solution to the problem of assaulting a defended beach. As the battle for France had demonstrated, World War II was a mechanized war where tanks were an important component—arguably the key component—in any ground campaign. And as the debacle at Dieppe had shown, getting tanks onto a beach from ships offshore was particularly challenging. There were a limited number of LCMs (Mike boats), and in any case shuttling back and forth to carry one or two tanks ashore at a time simply would not do. Some way had to be found to land many tanks—scores of them, even hundreds of them—all at once. Eventually this would be resolved by what was perhaps the most important vessel of the war: the Landing Ship, Tank (LST). In the fall of 1942, however, there was no such vessel in the U.S. Navy. And so, once again, the Allies had to improvise. The Americans addressed the issue by purchasing the *Seatrain New Jersey*, a commercial ship that had been built to carry a hundred fully loaded railroad cars between New York and Havana—in effect, a kind of early container ship. Purchased only days before the Torch invasion armada left Norfolk, she was rechristened USS *Lakehurst* (APM-1) and loaded with 250 Sherman tanks. That was certainly enough armor to make an impact on the battlefield; the problem was that the *Lakehurst*'s V-shaped hull meant that she drew more than twenty-three feet of water when fully loaded, and could not discharge her cargo over a beach. None of those 250 tanks could come ashore until the Allies seized a working seaport.[14]

The British addressed the problem differently. They had been thinking about the difficulty of unloading tanks across a defended beach much longer than the Americans—since Dunkirk, in fact—and they had tried it at Dieppe, though with less than resounding success. As a result, they had developed an early prototype of a tank landing ship. Like so much else, the impetus for this vessel came from the fertile mind of Winston Churchill. Early on, he advocated a ship that could carry sixty heavy tanks and steam right up onto the beach to unload them through massive bow doors that opened like a giant cupboard. Unable to build such vessels from the keel up due to the scarcity of both steel and building ways, the British converted a handful of existing flat-bottomed oil tankers originally designed to operate in the shallow waters of Venezuela's Lake Maracaibo. As with the American reliance on the *Seatrain New Jersey*, it was not a perfect solution. While these ships drew only four feet of water at the bow, they drew fifteen feet at the stern, and as a result, on any beach with a gradual incline, the ship's stern was likely to touch bottom while the bow was still some twenty or thirty feet from the shore. That required extending a very long and rather precarious bow ramp to the beach. By the time of Torch, the British had one large version of such a ship (called a "Winston"), and three smaller versions (called "Winettes").* The Winettes could carry up to twenty of the American-made Grant tanks, but their long bow ramps took thirteen minutes to deploy, which was not ideal when under fire.[†]

In addition to the transports and the landing ships, each of the invasion forces also required a warship escort, not only to ensure safe arrival at the beach but also to provide naval gunfire support against targets ashore. By agreement, the U.S. Navy would escort the American invasion force across the Atlantic from Norfolk to Morocco, and the Royal Navy would do the same for the invasion groups from Scotland to Algiers and Oran. The

---

* It is noteworthy that the Winston was designed to carry the Churchill tank, a circumstance that underscores both the impact that the prime minister had on virtually every aspect of British weaponry as well as on planning and strategy, and his unembarrassed willingness to accept these tributes as appropriate. Though the official designation for the Winettes was "LST(1)," they were substantially different from the American-built LSTs that were used at Normandy a year and a half later.

[†] There were two versions of the thirty-ton M3 tank. Those sent to Britain under Lend-Lease were dubbed the "General Grant"; those retained and used by the Americans were dubbed the "General Lee." Thus it could be said that the British deployed a "Yankee" tank while the Americans used a "rebel" tank. Both versions suffered from the fact that they carried a relatively small gun (37 mm) and were therefore no match for the German Mark IV tank, which had a 75 mm gun.

American warship contingent included the brand-new battleship USS *Massachusetts* (BB-59) plus the much older *New York* (BB-34) and *Texas* (BB-35) as well as seven cruisers and no fewer than thirty-eight destroyers. More destroyers would have been preferable, but in the late summer of 1942, destroyers were in demand everywhere: the Battle of the Atlantic against German U-boats was at full tide, and that very week in the Pacific, U.S. Navy destroyers engaged in a series of fierce surface engagements in the Solomon Islands. In this, as in all things, the Allies would make do with what there was. The British warships committed to Torch, dubbed "Force H" and "Force X," included the *Duke of York* (the battleship that had carried Churchill to the Arcadia conference), the *Nelson*, two battlecruisers (ships with armament similar to a battleship but more lightly armored), three cruisers, and seventeen destroyers, one of them Dutch. To assemble this force, the Royal Navy had to draw from the Home Fleet, reduce the Atlantic escorts, and temporarily suspend the convoys to Russia.[15]

Eisenhower's job was to bring all the elements together—the troopships, the transports, the aircraft carriers, the landing craft, and the warships, both British and American, plus the tanks, trucks, and jeeps, and the thousands of tons of supplies, plus more than a hundred thousand men—in a complex maritime quadrille. Keeping track of all the various pieces of this giant puzzle was all but overwhelming. Eisenhower bemoaned the fact that "there is no way in many instances of knowing exactly what we have here. Many supplies are still unclassified and are not yet unloaded at depots. Time for unloading, sorting, cataloging, and for subsequent boxing, crating, marking, and loading simply does not exist." Nevertheless, the unforgiving timetable dictated that the operation begin before the winter storms arrived, and so work continued around the clock.[16]

In early November, Eisenhower boarded a B-17 "Flying Fortress" and flew from England to Gibraltar where he set up headquarters in a small, dank chamber carved out of the rock itself.* He had set all the pieces in motion; now it was a matter of what he described as an "interminable, almost

---

* The pilot of Eisenhower's plane was Major Paul Tibbets, who three years later, as Colonel Tibbets, would fly the B-29 *Enola Gay* to Hiroshima carrying an atomic bomb.

unendurable wait" to see whether they fit together. The wait was especially nerve-racking because the ships en route to the invasion beaches all operated under radio silence. He may have been in command, but he had no idea what was happening, and he felt utterly helpless. "We cannot find out anything!" he scrawled in his diary in frustration.[17]

ON OCTOBER 23, 1942, A LONG COLUMN of ships that included twenty-eight transports packed with 33,843 American soldiers began filing slowly out of Hampton Roads, Virginia, and into Chesapeake Bay to begin a four-thousand-mile journey to the coast of Africa. That same day in Egypt, forces of the British Eighth Army attacked the German Afrika Corps at El Alamein. The British pounded the outnumbered Germans for ten days, eventually winning a signal victory—indeed, the first major British victory of the war against a German army. It was a promising omen.

While the British assailed the Germans at El Alamein, the American convoy steamed eastward across the Atlantic. Destroyers scouted ahead, with watch standers scouring the sea for the telltale "feather" of an enemy periscope. Navy patrol planes circled overhead; two silver blimps drifted lazily nearby. On board the task force flagship, the heavy cruiser USS *Augusta* (CA-31), were both Major General George Patton, who commanded the embarked troops, and Rear Admiral H. Kent Hewitt, who commanded the armada itself, officially designated Task Force 34. The contrast between the two men was jarring. Patton was impeccably attired, with every badge and button in place; Hewitt's uniform often looked like he had slept in it. Patton was a former Olympic athlete who presented himself with an assertive, almost challenging military bearing; Hewitt had a perceptible double chin and an easy relaxed manner. Patton was flamboyant, profane, and quick-triggered; Hewitt was understated, low-key, and deliberate. Despite his appearance, Hewitt was bright and competent and every bit a professional. Patton wasn't so sure. When, prior to sailing, Hewitt suggested that there were still a number of problems they had to work out, Patton threw a tantrum and accused Hewitt of being defeatist. Concerned by Patton's reaction, Hewitt went to King, who talked to Marshall, and Patton eventually climbed down enough to allow a working relationship, though he never quite accepted Hewitt as a true warrior, writing home to his wife that "poor old Kent" was "such an old lady."[18]

Three days out, the convoy from Norfolk rendezvoused with the warships of the covering force that had steamed south from Casco Bay in Maine, and soon afterward it joined up with the carrier force steaming up from Bermuda. The transports and cargo vessels formed up into nine columns with the ships following one another at thousand-yard intervals. Cruisers and destroyers scouted out to both sides; the oilers for refueling trailed behind. After them came USS *Ranger*, the four smaller carriers, and their escorts. Altogether, the formation covered some six hundred square miles of ocean.[19]

The troopships were tightly packed. Upon boarding, each soldier had been handed a canvas cot with a metal frame that he hung on the bulkhead, where there were slots for them in tiers of four. In many cases the men were not billeted with their company mates since in order to keep track of who had embarked, the men had filed aboard in alphabetical order rather than by unit. That meant that officers were unsure of where their men were, or even what ship they were on. Officers tried to track down the men of their command using the short-range talk-between-ships (TBS) radio, but the Navy soon put a stop to it because the airwaves were being so clogged with messages it sounded, in the words of one Navy officer, like "a Chinese laundry at New Years." Unsurprisingly, many of the GIs suffered horribly from seasickness. Crowded as the ships were, the men could not all be allowed on deck at one time, and most of them spent the two-week crossing below decks as the ships rolled in the Atlantic swells while the convoy executed a zigzag course to discourage submarine attacks. The conditions were hardly improved by the miasma of odors that resulted not only from thousands of unwashed soldiers living and sleeping together in a confined space but also—and especially—by the lingering stench of *mal de mer* that could never quite be eliminated.[20]

One day before the Americans left Norfolk, forty-six British cargo ships escorted by eighteen warships left the Firth of Clyde in Scotland bound for Oran on the north coast of Algeria. A day behind them came thirty-nine more transport ships carrying the men for the Eastern Assault Force bound

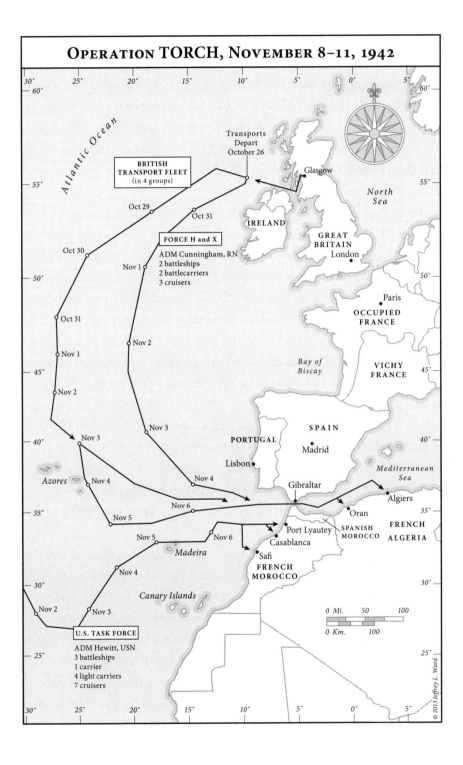

OPERATION TORCH, NOVEMBER 8–11, 1942

Atlantic Ocean

North Sea

Transports Depart October 26

Glasgow

BRITISH TRANSPORT FLEET (in 4 groups)

IRELAND

GREAT BRITAIN
London

Oct 29

Oct 31

FORCE H and X
ADM Cunningham, RN
2 battleships
2 battlecarriers
3 cruisers

Oct 30

Nov 1

Paris

OCCUPIED FRANCE

Oct 31

Nov 2

Bay of Biscay

VICHY FRANCE

Nov 1

Nov 2

Nov 3

SPAIN

PORTUGAL

Madrid

Nov 3

Nov 3

Azores

Nov 4

Nov 4

Lisbon

Mediterranean Sea

Gibraltar

Algiers

Nov 6

Nov 5

Oran

FRENCH ALGERIA

Nov 5

Nov 6

SPANISH MOROCCO

Madeira

Port Lyautey

Casablanca

Nov 4

Safi

FRENCH MOROCCO

Canary Islands

Nov 2

Nov 3

U.S. TASK FORCE

ADM Hewitt, USN
3 battleships
1 carrier
4 light carriers
7 cruisers

0 Mi.   50   100

0 Km.   100

© 2013 Jeffrey L. Ward

for Algiers. The British and American soldiers on board these ships had a somewhat shorter journey than those in Task Force 34, and some of the Americans found the experience rather novel, even enjoyable. They were especially pleased to be included in the British tradition of "splicing the main brace" each day, when a ration of rum was served out to all hands. They were less enchanted by the other British tradition of afternoon tea, and they were positively repelled by the food, which consisted almost exclusively of boiled mutton.[21]

Altogether, the Allies committed more than six hundred ships to Operation Torch. Keeping this massive movement secret was a major concern, not only to achieve surprise on the beach but to avoid German U-boats en route. Consequently, the convoys from both Norfolk and Britain took deceptive routes to give the impression that they might be bound elsewhere, such as the Azores or South Africa. Even after the convoys from England passed through the Strait of Gibraltar and into the Mediterranean, they continued eastward, as if headed for the besieged island of Malta, before they abruptly turned south for the African coast. The mission was kept secret from the French as well, and as a result, no one knew how the French would react when the Allied troops came ashore. Would the British and Americans be greeted as liberators or invaders? There had been some discussion about sharing plans with the French in the hope of working out an arrangement in advance, though to do so risked compromising the whole operation. In the end, the decision was made to keep everything secret until the last moment.

The Allies did make one effort to obtain French cooperation. On the night of October 23, the same day the American invasion convoy left Norfolk, Eisenhower's deputy commander, Mark Clark, arrived by prearrangement off the African coast near Algiers as a passenger on a British submarine. After some clandestine blinking of lights with a contact onshore, Clark climbed gingerly into a canvas kayak called a folbot and paddled to the beach with a handful of British commandos to meet a French major general named Charles Mast, who had indicated his readiness to use his influence to encourage French cooperation with an Allied invasion. It was a risky, perhaps even foolhardy undertaking since Clark was privy not only to all the plans for Torch but also to what was called the Ultra secret: that the Allies had broken the German signal codes. Were Clark to be captured and tortured, all that would be in jeopardy. Moreover, the mission was of questionable value since Clark was not authorized to tell Mast anything specific about the pending invasion, including the date, which made it impossible for Mast to arrange for any meaningful cooperation.

The episode meeting was dramatic enough. At one point, news that the police were en route forced Clark and the others to hide in the cellar while policemen searched the house where they were meeting. Later, Clark and the commandos raced down to the beach, where Clark removed his trousers in order to swim out to a swamped folbot. He came back ashore unsuccessful and spent the rest of the night trouserless, hiding among the trees.* In the end, Clark made it safely back to the waiting sub, though his clandestine mission resolved nothing, and when the Allied convoys approached the target beaches on the night of November 7, no one knew how the French would react. The Americans agreed beforehand that if they received hostile fire, they were to report, "Batter up!" and the order to return fire would be "Play ball!"[22]

In hindsight, it might have been worth risking the secrecy of the operation to bring the French more fully into Allied confidence, for instead of being greeted as friends, the Americans met fierce resistance. Some of this was because the French navy, frustrated by the fact that it had not had the opportunity to fire a shot during the 1940 campaign against the Germans, was eager to defend not only French territory but honor. In addition, when the shellfire erupted out of the predawn darkness on November 8, it was only natural for the French to respond in kind. At a few minutes past 6:00 a.m., Hewitt ordered, "Play ball!"[23]

Though there were no Germans in either Morocco or Algeria, the landings there constituted the first Anglo-American counterattack against Hitler's empire. Given that, it was absolutely essential that the Allies succeed. Failing

---

* This story soon made the rounds of those few who were aware of the mission. When Clark later met King George VI in Buckingham Palace, the king tweaked him by saying: "You're the one who took that fabulous trip. Didn't you, by the way, get stranded on the beach without your pants?"

in this first effort would badly damage Allied morale and confidence and send the planners back to the drawing board. Russia would feel abandoned, and the peoples of the occupied nations would lose whatever hope they had. It would delay indefinitely any invasion of Europe. Finally, the landings would test, really for the first time, the ability of the Allies to conduct a large-scale multinational amphibious operation against a defended shore. As Hewitt put it, "The TORCH Operation served as a severe material test." Much, then, was riding on what happened in the early morning hours of November 8, 1942.[24]

THE ALLIED LANDINGS OCCURRED on a front that was seven hundred miles wide—from the Moroccan city of Safi, a hundred miles south of Casablanca, to Algiers, on Africa's northern coast. At each site, the Allies landed on several different beaches with code names such as Red One and Blue Two. Because of the importance of securing undamaged port facilities before they could be sabotaged, the Allies also tried the unusual gambit of sending specially selected warships filled with British and American commandos charging directly into the harbors of several of the port cities.

At Oran, that assignment went to two British corvettes, *Hartland* and *Walney*, both of them former U.S. Coast Guard cutters. The planners hoped to achieve surprise, but when the ships entered the harbor, crewmen on board could hear sirens wailing ashore. Then the shore lights went out, the searchlights came on, and the batteries opened fire. The two corvettes pressed on and even managed to land a small shore party in some canoes. Soon enough, however, both ships were burning wrecks. Of the 393 commandos onboard, 189 were killed outright and another 157 wounded—a casualty rate of 88 percent.[25]

The results were not quite as horrific at Algiers, though only one of the two destroyers assigned to the mission managed to make it into the harbor. The initial idea here had been to wait until three hours after the landings to send in the two destroyers, in the hope that by then some kind of accommodation might have been worked out with the French. But the landings were late, and the British destroyers *Broke* and *Malcolm* encountered the same kind of heavy battery fire as the corvettes had at Oran. The *Malcolm* was hit several times and set afire, so it had to withdraw. The *Broke* got through on her third try, and even landed her embarked American commandos under Lieutenant Colonel Edwin T. Swenson. Swenson led his men inland, secured the facilities, and set up a defensive perimeter, while the *Broke* remained alongside the pier to provide support. Soon, however, the *Broke* came under such heavy and accurate fire from the shore batteries that her captain sounded the recall. By then, the shore party was also under heavy fire, and Swenson decided his men could not make it back to the ship. He opted to stay. The crippled *Broke* was towed out to sea and later sank. Swenson and his command held off a force of French colonial infantry from Senegal backed by Renault tanks for several hours before surrendering at 12:30.[26]

British and American forces coming ashore elsewhere met with widely divergent reactions. At Algiers, Allied commandos encountered furious resistance as they sought to secure French coastal guns, but at a landing beach twelve miles to the west, the Americans were greeted with cries of "Vive les américains!" In the suburbs of Algiers, there was house-to-house fighting before French and American officers negotiated a cease-fire. A final armistice was delayed by French concern that if they openly welcomed the Americans and the incursion proved to be only a raid, the Germans would return afterward and exact fearful revenge. Once it was clear that the Allies had come to stay, it became possible to work out a series of cease-fires that led eventually to an armistice that included the release of Swenson and his men.[27]

It was different in Morocco, where American readiness to conduct an amphibious landing faced a much sterner test. This was especially true at Fedala (now Mohammedia), five miles north of Casablanca, the site of the largest American assault. The British had wanted to bypass Morocco altogether, but Marshall and King, fearful of being cut off at Gibraltar, saw the control of Morocco as essential and convinced Roosevelt to insist upon landings there. Now the Americans would pay the price for that insistence. Almost from the start, the landings in Morocco, and especially at Fedala, revealed just how much work the Allies still needed to do before they could even consider a cross-Channel invasion.

The American transports dropped anchor off Fedala in the early morning hours of November 8. Within minutes they began hoisting out the Higgins boats, and soon the soldiers were climbing down into them on nets made of chains. It was dark, the ships were blacked out, and the sea was rough. The chains were slippery, and men reached out gingerly in the dark for the footholds. More than a few ended up in the water, and some were injured when the Higgins boats bobbing alongside collided with the hull of the transports. Even after the landing craft successfully cast off from their mother ships, many had to go around from ship to ship to find the particular units they had been designated to transport. As a result, the first wave was an hour and fifteen minutes late in heading for the beaches.[28]

Once the landing craft were finally on their way, the coxswains often took them to the wrong beaches, in part because it was still full dark, and in part because they did not have adequate maps. The only coastal reconnaissance the Allies had conducted was to peer at the target beaches through submarine periscopes, and the vague maps that resulted failed to give the coxswains a clear understanding of the terrain features. The results would have been comic had they not been so disastrous. For example, two landing boats from the transport *William P. Biddle* got so disoriented they not only missed their assigned beach but motored into Casablanca harbor, five miles away, and stopped a passing French patrol boat to ask directions. The French opened fire, sinking both of the landing craft and taking the survivors prisoner.[29]

On the beaches themselves, the landings were unopposed, but the surf was heavier than anticipated, and the big waves lifted up the plywood Higgins boats and slammed them down on the sand with a mighty thump, often doing damage to the hull as well as to the embarked soldiers. The boats all crowded together along the beach, and the big waves threw them into one another. Several broached, their sterns cast up onto the sand so that they lay parallel to the beach instead of perpendicular to it. Unable to back off, the inexperienced crews simply abandoned them. Afterward, Hewitt reported that Higgins boats were "definitely unsuited for landing through a surf higher than seven feet." The soldiers, too, had trouble with the high surf. When they scrambled out of the boats, many were knocked off their feet by the waves. Overloaded as they were with heavy gear, some were unable to regain their footing and drowned in water that was only three or four feet deep.[30]

There were other problems. The electric ramp-operating mechanisms on some of the boats failed, and the ramps had to be cranked down manually. This took more time and played havoc with the schedule. Worse, once the ramps were deployed, the backwash from the receding waves ran into the well of the boats and flooded some of them, making it difficult or impossible to get off the beach again. As a result, many of the scarce Higgins boats were so wrecked after the first landing they became inoperable. On one beach, only seven of twenty-five Higgins boats were able to extricate themselves and return to the transports for a second load, and of those seven, five more were wrecked during the next trip. On another beach, twenty-one of thirty-two boats were smashed up in the initial assault. The historian Samuel Eliot Morison estimates that "altogether between 137 and 160 out of 347 landing boats in the Center Attack Group, 40 to 46 percent of the total, were expended" on the beaches that morning. The steel LCMs carrying the Sherman tanks fared better in the heavy surf, but they encountered a different problem: many of the tanks rolled off the LCMs and immediately sank up to the middle of their treads in the soft sand and couldn't get off the beach.[31]

All in all, the American ship-to-shore movement at Fedala was anything but a model of efficiency. It was evident to all that had this landing been directed at a prepared enemy determined to resist, it would have been a disaster. Even as it was, it came near enough to failure. Hewitt noted that the landings suffered from "insufficient training, improper debarkation priorities, and inadequate means." Major General Lucian Truscott went further, declaring, "The combination of inexperienced landing craft crews, poor navigation, and desperate hurry resulting from the lateness of the hour, finally turned the debarkation into a hit-or-miss affair that would have spelled disaster against a well-armed enemy intent upon resistance."[32]

The Americans did eventually get most of their men and equipment ashore. By dusk of the first day, the surviving Higgins boats had delivered a total of 7,750 men to the beaches. More followed the next day, and more the day after that. By then Patton was leading an advance southward toward Casablanca. Efforts to convince the French that their best interest lay in welcoming the Americans bumped up against French concepts of duty and honor, and the Americans met heavy resistance. French cruisers and destroyers charged out of Casablanca harbor, steaming boldly into the midst of the invasion fleet. The brand-new *Richelieu*-class battleship *Jean Bart*, though unfinished and immobile in port, fired her big 15-inch guns at American ships offshore. Luckily, the USS *Massachusetts* landed a 16-inch shell on the only turret of the *Jean Bart* that could bear on the American fleet, jamming it and putting it temporarily out of action.

Casablanca surrendered on November 11 (fittingly, Armistice Day), but the delays in executing the landings and the battle for the city meant that the transports and cargo ships had to remain off the landing beaches longer than intended. That gave the German U-boats an opportunity to find them. As Hewitt noted, "the anchorage at Fedhala was not a completely secure one," and the American ships were sitting ducks. Spending four days in one spot proved to be one day too many. On the evening of November 11, U-173 fired a spread of torpedoes into the anchorage, hitting the transport *Joseph Hewes*, the tanker *Winooski*, and the destroyer *Hambleton*, all within a ten-minute period. The next day, torpedoes from U-130 struck three more troopships, all of which sank, though by then they had discharged their priceless cargo. Nevertheless, the losses demonstrated the inherent danger of lingering too long off an invasion beach.[33]

Elsewhere, the assault went more according to plan. At Safi, a hundred miles to the south, the attempt to seize a port by a *coup de main* actually worked. Two American destroyers, *Bernadou* and *Cole*, carrying 197 commandos, steamed boldly into the port. The French opened fire, but French defenses at Safi were less robust than at Algiers or Oran, and the American commandos stormed ashore and secured the port. That allowed the big tank carrier *Lakehurst* to follow them in and unload her cargo of Sherman tanks at the jetty. By November 12, the Americans had their foothold in Morocco.[34]

SECURING THE BEACHHEAD was only the first step. Within twenty-four hours of the initial landings, Eisenhower was urging Allied forces to "rush eastward without delay" in order to seize Tunisia before the Germans brought in reinforcements. At first he hoped to do this within a matter of days. After two weeks, he was hoping "to complete the occupation... by mid December." By the end of the year, he was looking for success "early in March." With almost comical understatement, the official historian of the campaign wrote in 1957: "Succeeding operations in the Mediterranean area proved more extensive than intended."[35]

The "rush eastward" was derailed by several factors. One was the need to consolidate the ports to ensure the continued movement of supplies; another was the need to build new airfields and repair existing ones in order to provide air cover for the advance; a third was that American forces and their equipment had to be moved from Morocco to Algeria, a movement exacerbated by the perpetual shipping problem. Ike noted that "from the day we started," the problem of inadequate shipping restricted his movements. Now, once again, "the old shipping problem rises up to smite us." Instead of sending the 250 Sherman tanks that had landed at Safi to Algeria by sea, they were hauled more than eight hundred miles overland on North Africa's rickety and unreliable single-track railroad. Nor did the weather cooperate. The postponement of the assault from October to November meant that the ensuing ground campaign took place during the rainy season, when swift movement—or any movement—was inhibited by muddy roads.[36]

Then, too, Eisenhower was sidetracked and frustrated by interminable negotiations with various French leaders. Concluding that the Americans had come to stay, the French agreed to join the anti-Axis alliance. But there was a bitter debate among several self-appointed candidates about who should emerge as the leader of the French contingent in that alliance. The Allies had counted on General Henri Giraud to rally the French to their side, but Giraud declared that he would play no role at all unless he was given supreme command of all Allied forces. As always, Eisenhower remained outwardly calm, though inside he was seething, and he unburdened himself to Marshall. "I find myself getting absolutely furious with these stupid Frogs," he wrote, bemoaning "the necessity of dealing with little, selfish, conceited worms that call themselves men." Eventually, Eisenhower made a deal with Admiral Jean-François Darlan granting the Frenchman authority over all of

North Africa in exchange for his cooperation. Eisenhower may have thought that one "Frog" was as good (or as bad) as another, but Darlan had been a prominent Nazi collaborator, and the British and American public response to the arrangement was outrage. Ike survived the criticism, and the awkwardness of working with a former collaborator ended when Darlan was assassinated by a French monarchist on Christmas Eve.[37]

Most of all, however, the Allied advance into Tunisia was slowed by the Germans, who rushed reinforcements into North Africa and established strong defensive positions before the British and Americans could exploit the surprise of their initial landings. As a result, what was supposed to be a quick dash turned into a lengthy slog. The low point was a surprise German counterattack at Kasserine Pass in February 1943. Directed by Field Marshal Erwin Rommel, who justified his reputation as "the Desert Fox" in this campaign, two German Panzer divisions smashed through American defenses and advanced for three days before withdrawing. The Americans lost some twenty-five hundred men and more than a hundred tanks. This debacle was a wake-up call for American arms, and for Eisenhower as well. It forced Ike to reassess his assumptions about the timetable, and to make several changes in command, including urging the promotion of George Patton. Some British soldiers, who had been fighting in North Africa since June 1940, saw Kasserine Pass as a kind of comeuppance for the brash Americans. A few punned on the popular George M. Cohan World War I song "Over There" by replacing the line "The Yanks are coming" with "The Yanks are running."[38]

Eventually Eisenhower and the Americans recovered, but it took six months—until May 1943—for the British and Americans to drive Axis forces from the continent. It was a significant victory: at a cost of seventy thousand casualties, more than half of them British, the Allies inflicted similar losses on the Germans and Italians, and also took more than a quarter of a million prisoners. Of course, even after this victory, the Allies were no nearer to Berlin than they had been in Scotland, and during that same period, the Russians had been continuously engaged in the ferocious Battle of Stalingrad, inflicting more than three-quarters of a million casualties on the Germans while suffering over a million casualties of their own. Despite the North African victory, the Russians might still ask, with some asperity, if the western Allies were holding up their end.

Notwithstanding Stalin's disparagement, Torch was very likely all that was possible for the Anglo-American forces in 1942. The many errors and disappointments of the campaign proved that Churchill and the British had been correct in their assertion that the Allies were not ready to leap across the Channel. By the end of the campaign, even the most sanguine American—Eisenhower included—had come to appreciate that if they had launched their plywood Higgins boats and modified Caribbean freighters filled with inexperienced soldiers and untested commanders against German-occupied France in the fall of 1942, the consequences would have been fully as disastrous as the British had predicted.

IN THE LATE NINETEENTH CENTURY, the American folklorist Joel Chandler Harris published a series of tales from the Old South derived from stories he had heard while living among the South's African-American community. In one of the best-known of those tales, B'rer Rabbit confounds his nemesis B'rer Fox by constructing a mannequin made of tar—a tar baby—and placing it by the road. When B'rer Fox becomes annoyed that the mute figure refuses to acknowledge his greeting, he strikes it with his fist, which sticks fast. Angered, he then strikes it with his other fist, and then with his feet, until he is entirely embedded in sticky tar and rendered helpless.

Though there was no trickster figure to lure the Allies into their Mediterranean adventure, in November 1942 the Allies had hurled their fist into North Africa and it had stuck. In the extended campaign for Tunisia, they employed their other fist. By the time the Allies secured the victory in May 1943, there were eight hundred thousand British and American soldiers in North Africa. As Marshall and Eisenhower had predicted, the lengthy campaign all but ensured that the invasion of Europe would be delayed for at least a year. Churchill had argued from the beginning that an invasion of the European continent in 1942 was simply beyond reach. Now, however, it seemed likely that Torch had made a cross-Channel invasion the following year equally impractical. Still, the landings in North Africa and the campaign for Tunisia did constitute an important, even vital apprenticeship for the Americans, whose learning curve, perilously steep in 1942, had flattened considerably by May 1943.

Some of those men wondered if, now that the long campaign was over, they might be going home for a bit of leave. They were soon disabused of that. Major General Charles Ryder, commander of the American 34th Infantry Division, set them straight: "We shall fight in Europe," he told them, "and we shall find that in comparison, the Tunisian campaign was but a maneuver with live ammunition."[39]

CHAPTER 5

CASABLANCA TO COSSAC

FROM THE OUTSET, the Allied invasion of French North Africa had been a product of Churchill's fixation on a peripheral strategy plus Roosevelt's determination to do *something* in 1942. Now the something had been done, and the principal decision makers confronted the question of what to do next. Back in September, Churchill and Roosevelt had assured Marshall that once North Africa was secured, the Allies would be in a position to execute Bolero-Roundup in the New Year. Marshall had suspected from the start that executing Torch would make a 1943 invasion unlikely, and the disappointments and delays of the ensuing campaign only reinforced that assumption. Though he continued to believe that a surge across the channel was the best and shortest path to victory, his new proposal was significantly less ambitious. Rather than execute Roundup, he wanted to land an Allied force on the Brest peninsula later that summer to secure a beachhead that could be exploited in the spring of 1944.

Two factors worked against him. The first was the momentum of events. By January 1943 the Allies had half a million men plus all their supporting equipment in North Africa, and that number would rise to eight hundred thousand by May. It would be far simpler to use that force locally, to cross the narrow waist of the Mediterranean to Sicily or Sardinia, than to move all of it, or most of it, back to England for an assault on Brest. The second factor, as always, was shipping. Losses in the Pacific during the fierce battles around Guadalcanal, losses to the U-boats in the Atlantic, and of course losses during Torch all affected both sealift and amphibious capability. Given that, the British argued that it made much more sense to continue operations in the Mediterranean than to try to move hundreds of thousands of men from there to England. The Catch-22 of this option was that another operation in the Mediterranean would deplete Allied shipping even more and delay a cross-Channel move yet again—perhaps indefinitely.[1]

Roosevelt kept an open mind. He took Marshall's earnest advocacy of a cross-Channel operation seriously, but he also wanted to talk to Churchill again, and he was especially eager to hear Stalin's views. He proposed another meeting. Churchill was more than willing. "As soon as we have knocked the Germans out of Tunisia," the prime minister wrote to Roosevelt two weeks after the Torch landings, "we should proceed with a military conference." Roosevelt suggested that they meet somewhere in Africa, in part because an African venue might allow Stalin to attend, and in part because he foresaw the political benefits that would accrue from being photographed reviewing American troops on a recent battlefield. Roosevelt initially thought "a secure place south of Algiers" might do, though in the end he accepted Marshall's suggestion to hold the meeting near Casablanca in French Morocco. Soon thereafter, during movie night at the White House, it suited the president's puckish sense of humor to screen the new Humphrey Bogart–Ingrid Bergman film *Casablanca*. Since the forthcoming trip was still a closely held secret, only he and a few others got the joke.[2]

Roosevelt enjoyed the fact that the trip would be both historic and more than a little adventurous. He would be the first American president to fly in an airplane or to visit Africa while in office, and the first commander in chief to leave the country in time of war. As always, the trip was kept utterly secret, and the clandestine atmosphere only added to the president's boyish enthusiasm. (Hopkins thought he "acted like a sixteen-year-old.") The presidential party stole surreptitiously out of Washington late at night on January 9 and headed south by train to Miami. There he and his entourage boarded a plane for Trinidad, where Admiral William Leahy, Roosevelt's chief of staff, who had been battling a stomach virus, declared himself too ill to continue. The rest of the party flew south again to Belem, on the Brazilian coast. There were some obligatory meetings with local leaders before the official party boarded a flying boat for an eighteen-and-a-half-hour overnight crossing of the Atlantic. The plane splashed down in the mouth of the Gambia River in western Africa, and from there it was back onto another plane that flew the presidential party over the Atlas Mountains to an airstrip only two miles from the hotel that had been secured for the conference.[3]

As it happened, Stalin did not attend. He declared that he would not leave the Soviet Union so long as there were German soldiers on Russian soil. Perhaps, too, he felt that his refusal underscored the fact that while the western allies traveled around attending conferences, he was actually fighting a war.

Partly because of travel fatigue, and partly because of the prime minister's nocturnal habits, most of the business sessions involving Churchill and Roosevelt took place in the late afternoon and evening. That allowed the Combined Chiefs to meet in the mornings to thrash out strategic alternatives before presenting their views to the heads of government in the afternoon. In effect, the generals and admirals proposed, and the political leaders disposed. The schedule also allowed time for some family reunions. Churchill arranged to have his son, Randolph, released temporarily from his post with the British Eighth Army in Egypt; both Elliot Roosevelt, who was with the U.S. Army, and Franklin junior, a lieutenant in the Navy, were present. Even Harry Hopkins's son Robert, whom he had not seen in years and who was now an Army Air Forces photographer, was there.

The Combined Chiefs got together for their first session on January 14. The British were well prepared as usual, and Brooke led off with an hour-long presentation that emphasized the great results to be expected by invading Sicily. Such a move, Brooke argued, would "compel the Germans to disperse their forces," and thereby give greater assistance to the Russians than an invasion of France would. Pound argued that continued Mediterranean operations were all but inevitable since the limitations of Allied shipping made any other option impossible. Portal then took up the cause by asserting that continued pressure in the Mediterranean, along with unrelenting strategic bombing, would bring Germany to her knees.[4]

These arguments were neither new nor surprising to the Americans, for they were not significantly different from what Churchill had proposed a year earlier at the Arcadia conference. Marshall and the Americans remained skeptical, convinced that "an operation from the United Kingdom" was essential to ultimate victory. If the arguments had not changed, the circumstances had. The Torch landings and the subsequent North African ground campaign had revealed serious shortcomings in both American training and available assets. It was perhaps to be expected that the judgmental George Patton would find fault with the combat readiness of U.S. soldiers, many of them only a few months out of civilian life, but even Marshall was shocked when, during an evening walk outside Casablanca, he encountered a unit of newly arrived American soldiers and found the men so sloppily dressed and undisciplined that they were, in his view, "not usable for any battle against the Germans." The British certainly agreed. Field Marshal Harold Alexander wrote to Brooke that the Americans "simply do not know their job as soldiers." That was not true of every American, of course, but it was clear that more training and more experience would improve the odds of future battlefield confrontations.[5]

As for the sealift problem, the Torch landings had used up almost exactly half of the Allies' available landing craft, and at Casablanca, Eisenhower reported that a subsequent move to Sicily would entail the loss of 50 to 75 percent of what was left. Landing craft, apparently, were like Kleenex: good for one use and then discarded. This was especially true for the small Higgins boats. The problem of underprepared American soldiers could be overcome with training and experience, but if the Allies expended most or all of their remaining landing craft in another Mediterranean operation, there would be few or none left for a cross-Channel invasion. Marshall was cold-bloodedly realistic in observing that "we could replace troops" lost in any Mediterranean campaign, but that "a heavy loss in shipping...might completely destroy any opportunity for successful operations against the enemy in the near future."[6]

In reply to these concerns, Brooke adopted the demeanor of a long-suffering schoolmaster forced to deal with a class of particularly slow-witted pupils. "All matters have to be carefully explained and reexplained [to the Americans] before they can be absorbed," he wrote in his diary that night. "They can't be pushed and hurried, and must be made gradually to assimilate our proposed policy." Brooke got support from Mountbatten, the director of combined operations, who suggested that instead of attempting to redeploy landing craft from the Mediterranean back to England, which would be a lengthy and tedious process, new landing craft should be brought over from America on the same transports that carried the U.S. troops. That way, the arriving GIs would have landing vessels available for amphibious training, and the landing craft already in the Mediterranean could remain there and be put to good use in local follow-on operations.[7]

Like Marshall, Brooke sought relief from the negotiations by taking walks, though in his case, they doubled as birding expeditions. (Brooke recorded excitedly in his diary that he spotted "sanderlings, ring plover, grey plover, and turnstones!") During the sessions, he sought to reassure Marshall that the buildup of American forces in England could continue even as operations unfolded in the Mediterranean. He envisioned the movement of twelve thousand American GIs a month to Britain throughout the spring and summer, so by August there would be nine to twelve divisions in southern England for a thrust across the Channel if a "crack" in the German defenses provided an opportunity. And Brooke assured Marshall that "we should definitely count on reentering the Continent in 1944 on a large scale." Of course, they had said much the same thing a year earlier about a 1943 invasion.[8]

This dispute was not merely about available resources or even strategy. At its heart it was the product of a fundamentally different understanding of the very purpose of a cross-Channel invasion. From the beginning, the British had envisioned any such assault as the final coup de grâce to be applied to an enemy utterly worn out by prolonged struggle and constant bombing; to them, no invasion should be attempted until Germany was visibly faltering and on the brink of collapse. The American view was quite different. To them, the invasion was not to ratify a victory already won; it was to seize that victory by brute force. To the British, it was to be a victory lap; to the Americans it was a death grapple. In the long history of the alliance, this gap in perceptions was never bridged.[9]

After three days, the two sides were no closer to an agreement than they had been at the start. Brooke pushed for Sicily, Marshall for Brest, and King for expanded operations in the Pacific, and at times the conversations became "very heated." It was Dill who broke the deadlock. As a British officer who lived in Washington and met every day with the JCS, he had a foot in each camp, and he knew just how much each side could give in order to reach an agreement. Moreover, Dill was one of the few besides Churchill who could stand up to Brooke. In a private meeting, Brooke told Dill that he would "not move an inch," and Dill shot back, "Oh yes, you will!" After some effort, he obtained Brooke's grudging agreement to several minor points. Then he went to see Marshall, and wrung similar concessions from him. As a result, when the Combined Chiefs met with Roosevelt on January 18, they were able to tell him that they had reached an agreement. The invasion of Sicily, code-named Husky, would go ahead, but the Allies would simultaneously continue the buildup of troops in England "for a thrust across the Channel in the event that the German strength in France decreases."[10]

Though technically a compromise, Marshall and the Americans had once again given way on the main point. King was pleased that the war against the U-boats would receive the highest priority, and he secured approval to proceed with a Pacific offensive in the fall; Marshall got approval for a buildup of Allied forces in England. Nonetheless, the British won the big prize: authorization for an expanded Mediterranean campaign, a campaign that, once under way, would very likely draw more and more assets into the fight. Once again, the Allies had agreed to punch the tar baby, and the Americans knew that they had been outmaneuvered. Following the final session, the American brigadier general Albert C. Wedemeyer, who had assumed Ike's old job as head of war planning, was resting in his room when Vivian Dykes, his British counterpart, stopped by for a drink. Wedemeyer and Dykes were old friends, having served together at Fort Myer in Virginia before the war. When Dykes sat down, Wedemeyer looked at him sharply and said, "Your people have no intention of ever crossing the channel." It was not so much an accusation as a statement, and Dykes did not deny it. Instead he sucked thoughtfully on his pipe and responded, "There is no accounting for Winston."[11]

For his part, "Winston" appreciated that the Americans might feel hard done by (to use the British phrase) at the outcome of the conference, and he sought to ease their disappointment by suggesting that perhaps it was time to name a commander for the cross-Channel attack. Though Brooke hoped that when the time came, he might be that eventual commander, others expected that it would probably be an American, most likely Marshall. Given that, Churchill proposed the appointment of a British chief of staff as a deputy commander. Marshall supported the idea. While Churchill's purpose may have been to offer the Americans a harmless consolation prize, Marshall saw that appointing a deputy commander or a chief of staff for the big invasion made such an invasion real in ways that mere assurances of future support did not. It also meant that the organizational and administrative work could begin at once, and that would speed the execution of the invasion when it finally did occur. And so, on January 22, the CCS agreed "that a British Chief of Staff, together with an independent U.S.-British staff should be appointed at once for the control, planning and training of cross-channel operations in 1943." Whatever Churchill's motives in suggesting it, it was the first tangible step toward the beaches of Normandy.[12]

Nine days later in Stalingrad, German field marshal Friedrich von Paulus surrendered 91,000 men including sixteen generals, all that was left of his army of 265,000, to the Russians. It was the greatest Allied victory of the war, and almost certainly Stalin reflected on the fact that while the British and the Americans talked, the Russians fought—and won—battles. To ensure that no one missed the point, on February 23, the anniversary of the founding of the Red Army, Stalin released an order of the day that contained this sentence: "In view of the absence of a second front in Europe, the Red Army alone bears the whole burden of the war."[13]

One more aspect of the Casablanca conference requires mention here, if only because it commanded so much attention from newspapers at the time and from historians since. After the final session of the conference on January 24, Roosevelt and Churchill met with reporters to showcase the grudging truce they had managed to engineer between Henri Giraud and Charles de Gaulle. Somewhat awkwardly, the two French rivals shook hands for the benefit of the cameras, and afterward Roosevelt announced, almost cavalierly, that the Allies had agreed to demand the "unconditional surrender" of the Axis powers.

Roosevelt later claimed that as he watched Giraud and de Gaulle shaking hands, it reminded him of Grant and Lee at Appomattox, and that recalled to his mind Grant's demand for unconditional surrender at Fort Donelson. The idea of announcing a policy of unconditional surrender, he asserted, just popped into his head. Like many of Roosevelt's stories, this was more fable than fact. He had discussed the policy with the Joint Chiefs at their planning session in the White House almost three weeks earlier, on January 7, and had confirmed it with Churchill at Casablanca. Moreover, it was not a flippant or thoughtless notion. Roosevelt knew that the Nazis had seized power in the 1930s in part by claiming that Germany had never been defeated on the battlefield in World War I but instead had been "stabbed in the back" by Jews, social liberals, and communists at home. He wanted to ensure that no such claim could be made this time. Moreover, making unconditional surrender an official policy would reassure Stalin that Britain and America would not make a separate deal with Germany behind his back, and perhaps it would also restrain Stalin from trying to make a deal of his own.[14]

Afterward, there was much conversation in the press and elsewhere about whether announcing a policy of unconditional surrender effectively backed the Axis into a corner and thereby made less likely an early end to the war. Some speculated that the announcement undercut efforts by dissidents in Germany who wanted to remove Hitler from power. Whatever the merits of such speculations, it is unlikely that Roosevelt's announcement changed either the course of the war or Stalin's views on a separate peace. In the meantime, there were more immediate and tangible issues at hand: there was still North Africa to be conquered, Sicily to be invaded, and a chief of staff to be appointed for the cross-Channel invasion of Europe.

IN MARCH 1943, while Eisenhower was reorganizing his forces in the wake of the humiliating American defeat at Kasserine Pass, a relatively obscure British major general named Frederick Morgan learned that he had been selected to coordinate "plans for cross-Channel operations this year and next year." No one—Morgan included—was quite sure how seriously to take the assignment. After all, one of the elements of British strategy was a massive disinformation campaign, subsequently codenamed Fortitude, a vast conspiracy involving bogus radio transmissions, nonexistent units, and even double agents, that was designed to keep the Germans confused and off balance. And, as his new orders made clear, one of Morgan's responsibilities was to conduct "an elaborate camouflage and deception scheme" to tie down German forces along the Channel coast. On the other hand, his orders also specified two other objectives: "a return to the Continent in the event of German disintegration" and the development of plans for "a full scale assault against the Continent in 1944 as early as possible." Of course, having three assignments somewhat muddied the waters and led Morgan to wonder what had priority: the misdirection campaign, the possible but entirely contingent emergency operation, or planning for an actual full-scale assault. Whatever the intentions of those who had written his orders, Morgan had no option but to take all three charges seriously.[15]

The eldest son of a middle-class businessman in Kent, Morgan had not attended Sandhurst—the Royal Military Academy, designed to turn "gentlemen cadets" into line officers, and the school where Churchill had won his commission as a young subaltern. Instead, Morgan had matriculated at Woolrich, the military school for artillery and engineering officers. Rather than focus on leadership and tactics, his curriculum had centered on trigonometry and engineering. His background and scientific training set him apart from the scions of the aristocracy who dominated the higher ranks of the British Army, and in class-conscious Britain, that mattered. At least he looked the part. Forty-nine years old in 1943, Morgan might have been conjured by central casting in Hollywood to play the role of a British officer. He was slim and pale with sandy hair— light brown with hints of red—a fine straight nose, a brush mustache just beginning to gray, and, like Eisenhower, was seldom to be seen without a cigarette held between the first two fingers of his left hand. He approached problems with seriousness of purpose, an organized mind, a professional commitment, and a wry sense of humor.[16]

With Eisenhower in Africa, Morgan took over the available space in Norfolk House and began to assemble a staff. The group had to have a name—an identity—and it was Morgan who came up with COSSAC, an acronym for "Chief of Staff, Supreme Allied Commander," though no one knew yet who that commander would be. Not only was it logical, but it served a secondary purpose of contributing to the disinformation campaign, since many individuals outside Norfolk House assumed that the unit must have something to do with the Russians, who, after all, were the ones who had Cossacks.

Morgan and his nascent COSSAC team took up their multiple and even contradictory assignments in April and May. As part of the disinformation campaign, they sought to encourage the German assumption that the Allies might assault either Norway or the Pas de Calais in France that summer. For Norway, they invented a new and entirely fictional force—the British Fourth Army—which was supposedly headquartered at Edinburgh, and they coordinated the release of hundreds of coded radio signals that implied both its existence and its purpose. It was subtly done and may have helped convince Hitler to keep a substantial force in Norway to defend it from this phantom army. For France, the COSSAC team managed a program of "controlled leakage" to convince the Germans that yet another fictional army—the British Sixth Army—was encamped around Luton, north of London, and preparing to attack Calais. It was only partially successful. To be sure, the disinformation campaign kept the Germans guessing, but in December 1943, Vice Admiral Friedrich Rieve of the Kriegsmarine speculated in his official war diary that "the Seine River estuary as well as the Cotentin Peninsula" constituted the most likely target for Allied "amphibious assaults on the greatest scale."[17]

In addition to these impostures, COSSAC also developed a plan to move quickly onto the continent in case of a German collapse. Though such a thing seemed remote in the spring of 1943, Britons remembered how swiftly the Germans had fallen apart in 1918, and Churchill in particular never quite abandoned the notion that another such collapse might occur at any moment. If it did, and if the western Allies were unready to reenter the Continent, Stalin's armies might march through Berlin and all the way to the Channel—a prospect nearly as appalling as leaving Hitler in charge. So Morgan's team assembled a plan for a kind of updated Sledgehammer that they dubbed Roundhammer—a conflation of Roundup and Sledgehammer.[18]

It was the third assignment—the creation and development of a plan for a full-scale invasion of continental Europe in the spring of 1944—that dominated the COSSAC agenda. It is unclear how seriously Churchill intended this charge to be. Neither he nor the Combined Chiefs gave Morgan any specific guidance; Morgan did not even have access to Eisenhower's 1942 plan for Roundup. For all practical purposes, he had to start from scratch with no preconditions or limitations. Professional that he was, he simply got on with it.

He began by identifying an appropriate landing beach for the assault and then calculating the number of divisions needed to secure it. For this he needed detailed maps, and the CCS had not supplied him with these, either. Morgan had to send his aide to scrounge around the London bookshops for Michelin travel maps. These were then cut up and taped together onto the wall at Norfolk House. The resulting montage, Morgan later claimed, triggered an epiphany. By spreading out the coastal maps from Spain to Holland, he saw that instead of being an island on the periphery of Europe, England was really at the enter of a giant arc of possible targets. Nevertheless, after much study, Morgan and his team narrowed their focus to two sites on the French north coast: the Pas de Calais, where the English Channel narrowed to only nineteen miles, and the coast of Normandy east of the Cotentin peninsula, an area known as Calvados and famous for its potent apple brandy.[19]

The advantage of the Pas de Calais was that the beachhead could be covered by land-based air from Allied bases in East Anglia, and the short distance between Dover and Calais meant a quick turnaround for scarce Allied landing craft. The downside was that these very factors made it the obvious target, and because of that, the Pas de Calais was the most heavily defended stretch of coastline in German-occupied France. As for Normandy, it had good beaches and nearby ports, but it was farther away, which meant that Allied planes would have a shorter time over the beaches and landing craft would have a longer turnaround, effectively doubling the number of vessels needed. Then, too, the terrain behind the beaches at Normandy was carved up by hedgerows in a landscape that was known locally as the *bocage* country. That would make a breakout from the landing beaches more difficult.

To choose between these alternatives, Morgan assigned teams of officers to make the best possible case for each site. They engaged in a kind of parliamentary debate as each team argued its case and defended it against verbal challenges. It was a useful way to bring out the strengths and weaknesses of each site, though it also bred a spirit of competition between the study groups as their passionate arguments transformed them into genuine advocates rather than merely briefers. In the end, Morgan concluded that despite the obvious geographical advantages of the Pas de Calais, Normandy offered the best chance to spring a surprise.[20]

The second issue Morgan had to deal with was how many Allied divisions would be needed. The coast of Normandy could accommodate only so many men at a time, and that necessarily limited the initial landing to only a few divisions. The more important question for the planners was the total number of divisions needed to complete the conquest of occupied France and drive on to Berlin. Back during the Arcadia conference, Churchill had suggested that such a campaign would require forty divisions (twenty British and twenty American); the Eisenhower-Marshall Roundup plan had called for forty-eight divisions (eighteen British and thirty American). In his plan, Morgan envisioned no fewer than one hundred divisions (fifteen British and eighty-five American). Assuming a division strength of fifteen thousand men, Morgan's plan called for the deployment of one and a half million men. It was stunningly ambitious. In the entire war from Pearl Harbor to V-J Day, the United States managed to create a total of only eighty-nine Army divisions, and Morgan's preliminary plan called for the deployment of eighty-five of them in a single operation. The monumental scale of his plan contributed to the perception by some, both inside and outside Norfolk House, that Morgan and his team were not serious.*

Indeed, that perception—that Morgan and his COSSAC team were part of the disinformation campaign rather than a legitimate planning group—contributed to Morgan's most intractable problem, which was that many in the British military bureaucracy did not take him or his command seriously. By now detailed planning was well under way for Husky, the invasion of Sicily, which was set for July. After that, who knew: maybe Sardinia, Greece, Italy, even the Dodecanese Islands had been mentioned. By contrast, Morgan's project seemed both distant and uncertain, another time-consuming exercise, perhaps even (as Morgan himself often assumed) a hoax. Such doubts bred what Morgan later called a "corrosive and potentially explosive" mood at Norfolk House. Despite that, there was no alternative except to work as hard as they could whatever the final result of their labors.[21]

EISENHOWER'S LONG-DELAYED VICTORY in Tunisia prompted yet another round of high-level talks about what to do after the presumed success of Husky. In mid-May, Churchill and the British chiefs of staff flew again to Washington for another conference, this one code-named Trident. It was Churchill who led off and by asking the key question: "TORCH was over, HUSKY was near, what should come next?" Of course Churchill never asked a question unless he already had the answer ready, and he quickly supplied it: "To get Italy out of the war by whatever means might be best."[22]

At every top-level conference so far, the British had come better prepared than the Americans, arriving with both elaborate arguments and detailed plans already in hand, and inevitably those plans had become the

---

* The United States fielded a total of 94 divisions during the war, including Marine Corps divisions in the Pacific. For purposes of comparison, Nazi Germany fielded 375 divisions, and the Soviet Union 491. Though German and Russian divisions were significantly smaller than a full-strength U.S. Army division, especially by 1944, the overall level of American mobilization was far less than that of either its British and Russian allies or its European foe.

basis for ensuing discussion. This time, however, the Americans were ready for them. For one thing, Marshall had managed to secure an agreement from Roosevelt that their principal objective during Trident would be "to pin down the British to a cross-Channel invasion of Europe at the earliest practicable date." In addition, Wedemeyer, still smarting from his defeat at Casablanca, had prepared a set of detailed plans of his own. And finally, the relationship between the western Allies had undergone a subtle but significant sea change in the four months since Casablanca. During the Arcadia conference in January 1942, and even during the Casablanca meeting a year later, Britain had significantly more men under arms and engaged with the enemy than the United States, despite a population less than one-third that of its bigger and richer ally. When Commonwealth units were included, the United States was very much the junior partner in terms of active combat troops. Not until the middle of 1944 did the number of U.S. soldiers in uniform begin to rival that of its British ally. Nevertheless, by May 1943, the balance was beginning to shift, and American productivity—always the Allies' trump card—was surging dramatically. In his opening remarks at Trident, Roosevelt made a point of noting that the industrial output of the United States surpassed that of Germany and Japan combined. He hardly needed to add that many of the products of that industrial cornucopia were being sent to England under Lend-Lease.[23]

Churchill knew he would need all of his eloquence to convince the Americans to continue the peripheral strategy he preferred. He opened by noting how much things had changed in a year. The last time he had been hosted in the White House, news had arrived of the fall of Tobruk; now all of Africa was in Allied hands. Sicily would fall soon, and the next step, clearly, was the invasion of Italy to take her out of the war altogether. If Churchill expected that Roosevelt would applaud such a goal, he was surely disappointed when the American president disputed Churchill's assertion that the fall of Italy would provide succor to the Russians. Indeed, Roosevelt suggested that an Allied occupation of Italy might have the opposite effect, releasing German troops from the Italian boot for service on the Eastern Front. Moreover, the president revealed an agenda of his own. "ROUNDUP and SLEDGEHAMMER have been talked about for two years," he said, "but as yet none of these operations had been accepted as a concrete plan to be carried out at a certain time." While he conceded that there was "no possibility" of a cross-Channel operation that year, he declared that such an operation "should be decided upon definitely as an operation for the spring of 1944." In a direct challenge to Churchill's strategic vision, Roosevelt asserted that "the most effective way of forcing Germany to fight was by carrying out a cross-Channel operation."[24]

If Churchill was taken aback, he did not show it. After all, Roosevelt had acknowledged that an invasion of Europe was not possible that year, and clearly something else would have to be done in the meantime with the twenty Allied divisions already in the Mediterranean. Whatever that something turned out to be, it would very likely create a momentum of its own, and after that, well…they would see. Though it seemed "imperative" to Churchill "to use our great armies to attack Italy," he was willing to let the Combined Chiefs "thrash it out." While they did, he joined Roosevelt and Harry Hopkins for an automobile trip to "Shangri-La," the presidential summer retreat in the Catoctin Hills of Maryland (now Camp David). Passing through the Maryland town of Frederick en route, Churchill, who was a serious student of the American Civil War, remarked that it was in Frederick where the elderly Barbara Frietchie had defiantly flown the national flag above her door when Lee's column of soldiers had marched through in 1862. That inspired Hopkins to recite the famous couplet from John Greenleaf Whittier's poem about her: "Shoot if you must this old gray head, but spare your country's flag she said." There was a brief pause, and then, to the amazement of all, Churchill recited all thirty stanzas of the poem from memory, an astonishing display of recall—though he later acknowledged that he might have missed a line or two.[25]

Meanwhile, back in Washington the CCS took up the familiar issues. There were no surprises left, for the arguments were by now entirely predictable. The Americans, with Roosevelt's chief of staff, Admiral William D. Leahy, in the chair, insisted upon a massive concentration of force in England for an attack across the Channel; the British, led by Alan Brooke, countered that no such attack was possible until at least the spring of 1944 and that something else must be done in the meantime. Brooke echoed

Churchill and emphasized the importance of "knocking Italy out of the war," but the Americans were having none of it. It was a measure of Marshall's growing impatience that he uncharacteristically snapped back that rather than "knocking Italy out of the war," perhaps they should direct their attention to "knocking Germany out of the war." He pointed out that "operations invariably created a vacuum in which it was essential to pour in more and more means." Torch was supposed to have required a total of 185,000 U.S. soldiers, but there were now more than 400,000 American GIs in North Africa. Meanwhile, of the 279,000 American soldiers who had been shipped to England, fewer than 20,000 ground troops remained there because "all available U.S. resources had been sent to North Africa." Both Torch and Husky had been approved "in order to do something this year while preparing for cross-Channel operations," yet no meaningful preparations had been made. Given that, Marshall announced that the program sketched out by the British was "not acceptable to the United States."[26]

The British argued that the realities of the shipping problem made any transfer of assets from North Africa to England virtually impossible. Indeed, the dearth of shipping continued to dominate any discussion of Allied plans. Fears that the Germans might cut the transatlantic supply lines had eased, thanks to stronger convoy escorts, accelerated shipbuilding in the States, and the tremendous advantage gained by having broken the code that the Germans used to vector U-boats toward Allied convoys. Nevertheless, there were continuous new demands on shipping in the Pacific, and in the Mediterranean, too, including the need to transport a million prisoners of war from North Africa at the rate of thirty thousand a month. Shipping was so scarce that the Allies felt compelled to decline a plea from seventy thousand Bulgarian Jews who sought rescue from the Axis, a decision that in hindsight would come to look especially callous. Eisenhower reported that he was "thirty ships short of what he needed" even to conduct Operation Husky. Where would the ships come from to reorient operations from the Mediterranean to England? The American answer was that they would simply build more. In fact, the Americans were now building new cargo ships—most of them Liberty ships—faster than the Germans could sink

ALLIED SHIPPING LOSSES VS. CONSTRUCTION OF NEW SHIPS, 1942–1944

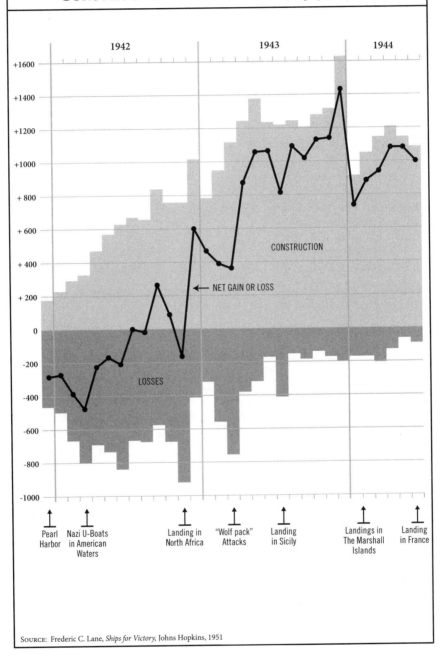

SOURCE: Frederic C. Lane, *Ships for Victory,* Johns Hopkins, 1951

them (see chart). The anticipated availability of all that new shipping, nearly all of it built in the United States, gave the Americans significant leverage in the strategic debate.[27]

Three days of wrangling changed few minds, and once again the conference ended with what was officially a compromise. Unlike previous compromises, however, in which the Allies had approved one or another peripheral attack and made a cross-Channel movement conditional upon circumstances, this time it was the other way around. The final agreement authorized a cross-Channel invasion of France with a firm target date of May 1, 1944, and it made the invasion of Italy, or any other Mediterranean operation, dependent on circumstances, leaving the decision to the judgment of the theater commander, Dwight Eisenhower. The agreement also acknowledged the importance of defeating "the U-boat menace" and granted King permission to conduct a campaign of "unremitting pressure against Japan," a foot in the door that triggered what would become the Central Pacific Drive.[28]

It was significant that the "Draft of Agreed Decisions" included specific details. The cross-Channel force would consist of twenty-nine divisions. This was a much smaller force than Morgan had proposed, and smaller than either the forty divisions Churchill had suggested eighteen months earlier or the forty-eight divisions Marshall had envisioned for Roundup. Moreover, due to the limited sealift capability, Morgan was instructed to plan for an *initial* assault force of only three divisions. These early estimates would be subsequently revisited and modified. Nevertheless, it was the first time the Allies had agreed to commit a precise number of troops to an invasion on a specific date. Most important of all from the American viewpoint, the agreement specified that forces would be transferred from the Mediterranean back to England to form the core of this invasion force. If all of the pieces could be assembled—the men, the ships, the supplies, and especially the landing craft—the Allies would begin the great invasion on May 1, 1944.[29]

Churchill was not ready to throw in the towel. He had come to Washington to secure an agreement for the invasion of Italy, and because that decision had been delegated to Eisenhower, he now resolved to go to Algiers and sell the idea to Ike. He invited Roosevelt to come along. The president demurred and suggested that Marshall should go instead. Three days later, Churchill and Marshall flew to Gibraltar, and then on to Algiers, where the British prime minister turned the full force of his personality on Eisenhower. Ike later acknowledged that "Churchill was at his eloquent best" during this visit. He was certainly persistent. Ike complained privately to his friend and naval aide, Harry Butcher, that it was physically exhausting to listen to Churchill relentlessly press his case over and over. Eisenhower was not averse to the idea of an Italian campaign. His concern was that it would inhibit future options. As Marshall had written him in a private letter, "an all out invasion of Italy inevitably presents very serious consequences in the way of shipping... which would put a stop to serious offensive operations elsewhere." Ike wrote back: "My views agree completely with yours." Even if an Allied invasion of Italy was fully successful, the need to keep the Italian nation fed and supplied with coal so that her people did not starve or freeze over the winter would further absorb scarce Allied shipping and thereby restrict European operations. In any case, Eisenhower reminded Churchill that their ability to do anything in the Mediterranean after Husky depended on how quickly and how efficiently Sicily could be taken. "If Sicily proved to be relatively easy," he told the prime minister, a subsequent move into Italy might be possible, but if the battle for Sicily proved long and difficult, any such invasion was unlikely. Churchill remained his confident and ebullient self, telling Eisenhower that he "looked forward to having Christmas dinner with Ike in Rome."[30]

In the end, Churchill got his way, mainly because the campaign in Sicily was remarkably successful. The initial landings on July 10 went so smoothly that Mountbatten, watching from offshore, thought "the whole show looked like a rehearsal." Only twelve days later, Patton's Seventh Army captured Palermo, on the Sicilian north coast, and two days after that, the Italian government effectively removed Mussolini from power with a vote of no confidence. Il Duce's replacement, Prime Minister Pietro Badoglio, sent out peace feelers to the Allies, and on September 3, the same day an armistice was ratified, British forces crossed the narrow Strait of Messina into Italy. A week later, Kent Hewitt's naval task force delivered Mark Clark's mostly American Fifth Army to the beaches near Salerno, south of Naples,

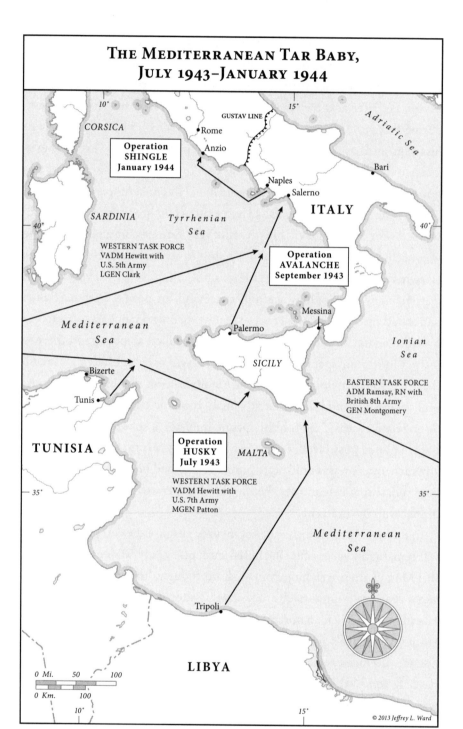

THE MEDITERRANEAN TAR BABY,
JULY 1943–JANUARY 1944

CORSICA

Rome

GUSTAV LINE

Adriatic Sea

Operation SHINGLE January 1944

Anzio

Naples

Salerno

Bari

ITALY

SARDINIA

Tyrrhenian Sea

WESTERN TASK FORCE
VADM Hewitt with
U.S. 5th Army
LGEN Clark

Operation AVALANCHE September 1943

Messina

Palermo

Mediterranean Sea

SICILY

Ionian Sea

Bizerte

Tunis

EASTERN TASK FORCE
ADM Ramsay, RN with
British 8th Army
GEN Montgomery

TUNISIA

Operation HUSKY July 1943

MALTA

WESTERN TASK FORCE
VADM Hewitt with
U.S. 7th Army
MGEN Patton

Mediterranean Sea

Tripoli

LIBYA

0 Mi.   50   100
0 Km.   100

© 2013 Jeffrey L. Ward

in what was code-named Operation Avalanche. Here the landings were touch-and-go, and at one point Clark actually considered a withdrawal, though in the end the Allies managed to hang on. Technically, at least, Italy had been "knocked out" of the war, thus fulfilling Churchill's ambition. Nevertheless, the German Tenth Army remained in Italy, and it dug in along what the Allies called the Gustav Line. The campaign soon bogged down into a lengthy slugfest. Once again the Mediterranean tar baby had absorbed the Allies' punch and held it fast. Fighting in Italy lasted until the end of the war.[31]

IT DID NOT, HOWEVER, DERAIL the decision made at Trident. While Morgan's revised instructions called for him to continue with the "deception scheme," they now emphasized that his principal focus should be on "mounting an operation with target date of May 1, 1944 to secure a lodgment on the Continent from which further operations can be carried out." There was still no designated operational commander. Churchill told reporters that preparations had not yet reached the point when "the executive commander has to be chosen," and so Morgan, as COSSAC, continued to plan a major amphibious operation without knowing who would execute it.[32]

Worse, Morgan found little support from the British military establishment. Institutional reluctance to invest heavily either materially or emotionally in a major cross-Channel operation was in part a legacy of Dunkirk as well as of dark memories of Passchendaele and the Somme. In addition, Britons at almost every level had difficulty absorbing the idea that so vast an operation was even possible. The Americans threw around absurd numbers: Roosevelt mandated the construction of twenty-four million tons of shipping, while Marshall claimed to be raising an army of sixteen million men. The British found it hard to get their heads around such numbers. As Morgan put it, it was almost impossible for British officers "to overcome entirely the effects of a lifetime of niggling, cheeseparing, parsimony, and making do" that had characterized their entire professional experience. And finally, Morgan encountered difficulty navigating the British political bureaucracy, that hodgepodge of offices and committees, some of them a legacy of pre-Victorian England, that constituted the middle echelon of the British government. (One Royal Navy veteran quipped that British officials moved "at the rate of frozen molasses traveling across sand paper.") The combination of the ambitious goal, the proximate deadline, tepid coopera-tion from the military bureaucracy, and skepticism from the top all fed frus-tration and even anger within the COSSAC group.[33]

It was Mountbatten who stepped in to apply the balm. In June, he invited the entire COSSAC team to his summer home, Largs, on the west coast of Scotland. When Morgan and the other officers arrived there on June 28, their general mood was somber, even defeatist. Morgan feared that some members of his team had decided the mission was hopeless. The retreat to the Scottish highlands, however, proved a tonic. Morgan himself felt the change that first evening when he walked the grounds of the estate with the tall, handsome, and buoyantly confident Mountbatten. The new mood was aided by a felicitous coincidence later that night when the conferees watched from Mountbatten's rooftop as a convoy of ships departed the Firth of Clyde carrying soldiers to the invasion of Sicily, now twelve days away. On the spur of the moment, a small signal lamp was set up on the roof and a message of "Godspeed" blinked out to the embarked soldiers. Whether it was the change in venue, Mountbatten's irresistible confidence, the fine June weather, or the vision of soldiers off to do their duty, a new sense of optimism infused the COSSAC planners. Within days, deadlocks were overcome and a plan finalized for a May landing on the Normandy beaches.[34]

Morgan's orders required him to provide a detailed operational plan to the CCS by the first of August. Two weeks before that deadline, he pre-sented a preliminary report to the British chiefs of staff. In it, Morgan asserted, first, that he believed the operation was feasible. To be sure, ship-ping would be a difficulty, and the number of landing craft would have to be increased dramatically, but these difficulties were surmountable. Second, he announced COSSAC's conclusion that the landings should take place on a three-division front on the Normandy beaches near Bayeux. A larger initial landing force would be desirable, but the limited number of landing craft was the controlling factor. In an effort to extend the optimism of the Largs retreat to the chiefs of staff, Morgan reminded them that it was essential for the government to embrace the plan fully, and to take "all possible steps" to support it. That meant that "action must start now and every possible effort made by all means in our power... to speed up our own preparations." There was, he told them, "not one moment to spare."[35]

According to Morgan, the reaction of the British chiefs of staff was "not demonstrably enthusiastic." Even allowing for traditional British reserve, their response was disappointing, and some members of the COSSAC team were angered that their hard work was so casually received. When Morgan asked if he could forward the plan to the American chiefs of staff, permission was denied. The British were about to leave for another conference in Quebec (code name Quadrant) and they wanted to keep the cards in their hands. This created a serious professional dilemma for Morgan. He was a British officer, but COSSAC was an Allied organ, set up to be "neither British nor American, but equally answerable to both... governments." He knew the Combined Chiefs would have to approve the plan before anything could be done, yet he was denied permission to share the plan with the Americans.[36]

Morgan resolved his dilemma by ensuring that an advance team of COSSAC members, some of them Americans and all of them familiar with the plan, sailed for the United States a few days ahead of the British delegation. Once there, they briefed not only their American counterparts but Roosevelt himself, both in Washington and again at Hyde Park. By then Churchill was also en route, this time on the *Queen Mary*. Lounging in his bunk with cigar in hand, he listened impassively as staff officers read aloud the details of the COSSAC plan to invade the beaches of Normandy eight months hence.[37]

At the Quebec conference, the British did not attempt to overturn the decision that had been made at Trident; instead they emphasized the importance of keeping the Germans distracted by conducting a vigorous and aggressive campaign in Italy. The Americans remained deeply suspicious that this was simply another manifestation of British obstructionism. That suspicion fed Marshall's opposition, which in turn provoked Brooke's impatience. "It is quite impossible to argue with him [Marshall]," Brooke wrote in his diary, "as he does not begin to understand a strategic problem." The undercurrent of inter-Allied hostility was best personified by the American chief of naval operations, Ernest King, who announced challengingly that he would not authorize "a single additional warship" to another Mediterranean adventure, and (according to the official minutes) employed some "very undiplomatic language" in the process. After so many contentious months, the British and Americans simply did not fully trust each other.[38]

A decisive element in resolving the dispute was the fact that the United States was by now clearly emerging as the senior partner. It was the United States that was producing the ships, the planes, the tanks, and, soon enough, the manpower that would be used in the proposed operation, and this gave the Americans incalculable leverage. It was also the key factor in deciding who would become Supreme Allied Commander. Ever since Eisenhower had been named to command Torch back in 1942, some Britons, Brooke included, had expected that a British officer would command the eventual cross-Channel operation. According to Brooke, Churchill had promised him the command at least three times. Such an appointment had seemed logical in 1942, perhaps even in early 1943, but by the late summer of that year, the growing preponderance of American strength undermined such an expectation. At Quebec, Churchill himself suggested to Roosevelt that an American should be named to command the cross-Channel invasion. Roosevelt was gratified, perhaps even relieved.

Churchill then broke the news to Brooke. Churchill wrote later that Brooke "bore the great disappointment with soldierly dignity," but in fact it was a terrible blow. Years later, Brooke wrote that as he listened to Churchill deliver the news, he felt "swamped by a dark cloud of despair." Almost as bad was the casual, matter-of-fact way Churchill did it. "Not for one moment did he realize what this meant to me," Brooke wrote. "He offered no sympathy, no regret."[39]

Other issues got a hearing at Quebec as well. The CCS discussed the Burma campaign, the role of China in the Pacific War, even Sumatra in the Dutch East Indies. Indeed, Churchill adopted Sumatra as his new hobbyhorse, arguing that the Allies should seize airfields there in order to bomb Singapore. Even Brooke recognized this as another peripheral diversion and sought to rein him in, with little success. Still nursing resentment of his cavalier treatment, Brooke recorded in his diary that Churchill "behaved like a spoilt child that wants a toy in a shop."[40]

There was an odd moment on August 19 when Mountbatten insisted on demonstrating the practicality of his somewhat bizarre idea to use giant, specially constituted slabs of ice as mobile aircraft platforms in the North Atlantic. He arranged to have two blocks of ice brought in to the dining room of the Château Frontenac, which was being used as a conference room. One of them was ordinary frozen water; the other was composed of 5 percent wood pulp, which yielded a frozen substance that Mountbatten called "Pycrete." To demonstrate its resilience, he challenged the members of the CCS to try to break it. Hap Arnold gave it a try, spitting on his hands and swinging a heavy meat cleaver, though with no visible effect. Then, drawing his pistol, Mountbatten announced that he would fire a bullet into each frozen block to show how different they were. That announcement led to a sudden scraping of chairs as admirals and generals scrambled to get out of the way. Mountbatten fired a bullet into the first block of ice, which shattered spectacularly. Then he took aim at the block of Pycrete. The bullet bounced off the hardened ice and ricocheted about the room, causing three- and four-star admirals and generals to dive for the floor. Brooke and General Sir Leslie Hollis actually collided, skull to skull, under the table. Outside the room, junior staffers wondered if the Americans and British had finally started shooting at each other.[41]

Compared to that, the final agreement was anticlimactic. Churchill and Roosevelt formally approved "the outline plan of General Morgan," and the CCS endowed it with a name: Operation Overlord. The naval aspect of the plan, including the sealift to England and the cross-Channel movement itself, was Operation Neptune. Like many others, Morgan was struck by the historical weight of the moment. As he put it later, "This campaign would absorb the bulk of the resources of United States and the British Empire. If they did not suffice, the future hardly bore thinking about."[42]

CHAPTER 6

BRITS AND YANKS

A T CASABLANCA, BROOKE HAD SUGGESTED that even during an active campaign in the Mediterranean, the United States could still maintain a buildup of troops in England at the rate of twelve thousand men per month. At that rate, he noted, there would be some 135,000 American soldiers—about nine divisions—in England by August 1943, in position for a swift cross-Channel assault in case of a German collapse. Of course, Germany did not collapse that summer, nor did the Americans manage to ship twelve thousand GIs a month to England. Instead, the number averaged only a fraction of Brooke's proposed goal—in March, for example, only twelve *hundred* GIs arrived. As a result, by mid-May, when the Trident conferees agreed to invade France a year hence, while there were more than a hundred thousand U.S. support personnel on or near the airfields in East Anglia, there were fewer than twenty thousand American combat troops in England—barely one division. Clearly, if the Allies were serious about a cross-Channel invasion in less than twelve months, the movement of American troops to England would have to increase dramatically.

And it did. Once Neptune-Overlord was approved at Trident and ratified at Quebec, the transatlantic trickle of American soldiers turned into a flood. In June, nearly fifty thousand GIs arrived at British ports, all but overwhelming the ability of the British to accommodate them. Another fifty thousand arrived in July, and nearly that many in August. Eighty thousand arrived in September. In October, the numbers topped a hundred thousand, and for each of the next seven months, an average of nearly 150,000 Americans arrived in Britain. (See Table 1, page 124.)

For nearly four hundred years, the movement of humanity between Europe and America had been overwhelmingly westward as immigrants took passage for the New World. Now that tide was reversed, and in particularly dramatic fashion, for the American "invasion" of Britain took place not over centuries or even decades but in a single calendar year. Not only did this phenomenon test the sealift capability of the Allies, but it greatly affected the soldiers themselves, most of whom had never been outside their home states, much less out of the country, and of course it dramatically affected the citizens of the United Kingdom who became their hosts. As one Briton recalled, "The American invasion rated second only to the bombs as the outstanding feature of wartime life."[1]

Most of those who took part in this mass migration were young men in their late teens and early twenties. They had volunteered, or been conscripted, and sent to training camps where, in a dizzying sequence, they were barbered, inoculated, and issued uniforms. They learned how to salute (and whom to salute), how to march, and how to shoot. Then, after a brief leave home, some, though not all, received more instruction at an advanced training center. Before a year had passed, they hoisted their olive-drab duffel bags, stenciled with their names and units, and boarded trains and buses that took them to one or another port of embarkation, New York being by far the largest. There they were mustered on a pier and marched up a gangplank onto a ship. Only a few had ever been on a ship before—or even seen one. They did not know where they were bound, and made guesses about their destination based on the type of clothing they had been issued. Though they were filled with the confidence (and the arrogance) of youth, few had ever fired a shot in anger, and for the most part they were utterly ignorant of what lay ahead.

Table 1   U.S. Troop Strength in Britain, June 1942–May 1944

Month	Number of Men Arriving Each Month	Total Present in England	Ground Forces Available	AAF, Support, and HQ Personnel
1942				
June	19,446	54,845	38,699	16,146
July	26,159	81,273	39,386	41,887
August	73,869	152,007	72,100	79,907
September	28,809	188,497	79,757	108,740
October	39,838	233,794	90,483	143,311
November	7,752	170,227	5,656	164,571
December	9,322	134,808	17,480	117,328
1943				
January	13,351	122,097	19,431	102,660
February	1,406	104,510	19,173	85,337
March	1,277	109,549	19,205	90,344
April	2,078	110,818	19,184	91,634
May	19,220	132,776	19,204	113,573
June	49,972	184,015	22,813	161,202
July	53,274	238,028	24,283	213,745
August	41,681	278,742	39,934	238,808
September	81,116	361,794	62,583	299,211
October	105,557	466,562	116,665	349,897
November	173,860*	784,631	197,677	686,954
December	133,716	773,753	265,325	508,428
1944				
January	166,405	937,308	343,972	593,366
February	136,684	1,084,057	442,474	641,583
March	124,412	1,199,077	488,379	710,698
April	216,699	1,422,276	599,428	822,848
May	108,463	1,526,965	620,504	906,461

* Includes troops returning to England from North Africa

The ocean voyage was memorable, indeed unforgettable, for virtually all of them, though in quite different ways. Shipping remained an enormous problem for the Allies, and in recognition of that Churchill offered the use of "the Queens"—Britain's large passenger steamers, including the *Queen Mary* and the *Queen Elizabeth*. These magnificent ships, one completed in 1936, the other in 1940, had been designed to carry two thousand passengers, cosseted by a crew of just under a thousand, in hotel-style luxury. Refitted for war use, they carried far more men in far less comfort. On early trips they carried six thousand men per crossing. That was soon increased to ten thousand, and then to fifteen thousand, which meant that the accommodations were Spartan indeed. To make room for everyone, the crew drained the swimming pools and used it as deck space. The soldiers slept in canvas bunks attached to metal frames that were stacked four deep along the bulkheads. Worse, they were "double-bunked," or what was sometimes called "hot bunking," which meant that a soldier got possession of a sleeping space for a twelve-hour period, then had to give it up to another man for the next twelve hours. The officers got cabins, though instead of the four people the cabins had been designed to accommodate, each now housed sixteen to twenty. Often half of them slept in the cabin while the others made do in the passageways rolled up in blankets; the next night they switched places. The heat and the stale air led some to carry their blanket up to the forward deck to sleep in the chill weather topside. Others slept on the mess tables. In spite of that, those assigned to one of the "Queens" counted themselves lucky, because the ships were fast—at twenty-five knots, they were too fast for a German U-boat to track them. That meant they could sail singly, without escort, and cross the Atlantic in five days.[2]

Most Americans came over in much slower troop transports that had to sail as part of a convoy, moving at the speed of the slowest ship—generally at ten knots or less. That not only made them more vulnerable to the U-boats but also meant spending three weeks or more at sea. A typical troop convoy consisted of between twenty and thirty transport ships organized into eight, nine, or ten columns of three or four ships each, constituting a formation that might be five or six miles wide. The ships followed one another at relatively close intervals—a thousand yards or less. Even at such close quarters, it was difficult to maintain station blacked out at night or in the North Atlantic fog, when it became almost impossible for an officer of the deck to see the ship directly in front of him. Foghorns sounding from several directions at once provided an imperfect guide to officers who sought to stay in formation while avoiding a collision. In such circumstances, ships would deploy what was called a "sea sled," a device towed astern that had a scoop on the bottom and a spout at the top. The high plume of water it generated provided a visual guide to the officer of the deck on the next ship in column.[3]

Troop convoys sailed with an especially heavy escort, often consisting of a U.S. Navy cruiser as the escort flagship, plus six to eight destroyers. By 1943, many troop convoys also included an escort aircraft carrier, a relatively new type of vessel that was particularly effective against the U-boat threat. Even so, the convoys executed a zigzag course, periodically changing their heading all at once, a maneuver that inevitably produced temporary confusion and disorder until the skippers managed to regain their assigned positions in the convoy pattern. By now, the Allies had secured the upper hand in the U-boat war, due in part to the construction of more than 260 new American escort destroyers, as well as the highly secret (Ultra) decrypts of German radio messages that allowed the code breakers to give convoys advance notice of where danger lurked. That made the crossings much safer, if not necessarily more comfortable. In the whole of the war, though the Germans sank nearly twenty-eight hundred Allied ships, not one troopship escorted by U.S. Navy ships was ever lost.*

The troopships were crewed by civilians in the merchant marine. Only the gun crews who manned the 3- or 5-inch gun for use against submarines and the 20 mm anti-aircraft guns were in the U.S. Navy. It was tough duty. The soldiers had to endure only one crossing, but the ships' crews remained on board for the round trip, and then repeated the journey again and again. Still, because the merchant sailors were paid more than either the soldiers or the Navy men, there was some inevitable grousing and petty rivalry. The Army ran the galley (kitchen) and the sick bay (hospital). For the soldiers, this was the worst of all possible worlds: despite being consigned to Neptune's element, they never enjoyed the rumored ambrosia of Navy chow and had to make do with Army rations.

Food was a particular concern for those who sailed on British ships such as the "Queens." Of course, the GIs complained about food as a matter of

---

* Late in 1944 a Belgian troopship, the *Leopoldville*, carrying American soldiers from England to Cherbourg and escorted by Royal Navy warships, was sunk by the Germans with the loss of 802 American soldiers.

habit, but on British ships they had more justification than usual. As a rule, they were served two meals a day in six sittings to accommodate the large numbers. Even then, they had to eat standing up, for there was not enough room for tables and chairs. Breakfast generally consisted of a bowl of sticky oatmeal, sometimes with prunes in it. When it wasn't oatmeal, they might be served kippered herring or kidney stew. Such fare would have met with groans even ashore, but it was particularly discouraging at sea. As one GI asked rhetorically: "Can you imagine anything worse than kippered herring for breakfast after a rough night at sea?" Dinner was often stewed mutton and cabbage. It was edible, but endlessly repetitive. As a result, most of the men who made the crossing lost weight, some as much as twenty to thirty pounds.[4]

Men also wasted away due to seasickness. The slow convoys were especially likely to induce *mal de mer*, for the slow speed made the troopships liable to heavy rolling, and the zigzag course only added to the sense of instability. Not everyone suffered from seasickness, and those who were immune sometimes made fun of those who suffered. But it was no joke. Men who could get out to the open deck lined the rails shoulder to shoulder and threw up into the rolling and pitching sea. Those below deck threw up into their helmets if they could get to them in time, or, as one recalled, "they would hang over the side of their bunks and throw up onto everybody's bunk below them." It was more than annoying; many suffered so horribly they prayed for death. And some found it. On virtually every crossing, men who could stand it no longer threw themselves over the side or shot themselves with their own rifles. This became common enough that when a soldier became badly ill, his carbine was taken away. At least one man died of internal hemorrhaging from dry heaving for five days.[5]

The only "entertainment" on board consisted of occasional lectures about what to expect when they arrived, supplemented by a few pamphlets. A movie, *Welcome to Britain*, narrated by Burgess Meredith, consisted of lessons in what *not* to do. It portrayed a loud, noisy, drunken American soldier insulting British food and British valor, making fun of Scottish kilts, and, when invited into a British family's home, eating up its entire rations for a month. A pamphlet carried a similar message. "Be friendly but don't intrude," it advised. "Don't make fun of British speech or accents." One rule that the GIs found particularly hard to follow was "Don't criticise the food, beer, or cigarettes." A relatively easy one was "Never criticise the King or Queen."[6]

The first Americans to arrive in the British Isles were those who had been sent to Ulster, the six counties of Northern Ireland, only weeks after Pearl Harbor. They stepped ashore in Belfast on January 26, 1942, to be welcomed by a crowd of dignitaries and a band from the Royal Ulster Rifles playing its version of "The Star Spangled Banner." The government of the Republic of Ireland, however, was far less enthralled. Irish president Eamon de Valera portrayed the arrival of the Americans in Ulster as an "invasion" and their occupation as a violation of national self-determination. There were few serious incidents, however, and by the end of 1943 there were more than sixty-five thousand American GIs in Northern Ireland. By mid-1944 their numbers had grown to nearly seventy-four thousand.[7]

A far larger number of Americans—more than a million of them— arrived in England in the aftermath of the decisions at Washington and Quebec in 1943, most of them disembarking at various ports on the west coast of Britain between Bristol and Liverpool. For many of these new arrivals, the first reaction was how impossibly green everything was, which began to make sense when they realized how frequently it rained. For others, the dominant impression was the physical evidence of the consequences of war. Those who arrived in Liverpool could count the hulks of sunken ships littering the harbor. When his transport docked at Avonmouth, near Bristol, one GI recalled seeing his "first look at bomb damage," all the more impressive because at least some of it was apparently quite recent. He and his fellow soldiers suddenly appreciated that death could come from the sky at any moment, and with that understanding, "fear ran through the ship like a shot." Other GIs had a quite different reaction. Having read about the Blitz and seen movie newsreels depicting the damage it wrought, they had concluded that there were probably not two bricks still standing on top of each other in all of Britain. Yet here were whole streets that were perfectly intact, with pedestrians and cyclists (though few automobile drivers) going about their business.[8]

Those Americans who traveled in one of the slow convoys—which was most of them—were happy enough to set foot on solid ground again, though some found it surprisingly difficult. As they moved down the gangplank and stepped onto the soil of Britain, they "rolled and staggered" as if drunk, unable to readjust to walking on a platform that didn't pitch and roll. After disembarking and being jostled into formation, they were marched off to the local train station. Many were astonished by the miniature (to American eyes) trains whose passenger coaches were divided into small closed compartments that ran down one side of the car. Some asked where the club car was, and were disappointed to be told that there was none. The GIs never knew where they were during their travel within England because all the identifying signs in the train stations had been removed to confuse the Germans in case of an invasion. Some GIs took the trains all the way south to the Channel coast, into Plymouth or Portsmouth, where the bomb damage was more extensive. On one train filled with newly arrived Americans, there had been a lot of joking and laughing during the trip south until the train slowed down to enter a city. The GIs then saw "row after row, street after street of gutted two-story houses," and the entire train suddenly became completely silent.[9]

Other trains discharged their human cargo at anonymous campsites well away from the coast. Those who arrived in the summer of 1943 often found themselves assigned to vacated British barracks: two-story brick Victorian-era cavalry barracks with one toilet per floor. One set of barracks even dated back to the Napoleonic era. After these were filled, GIs were more likely to be sent to newly constructed campsites on the Salisbury Plain in south-central England, best known to Americans as the site of Stonehenge. After the men piled out of the trucks, they were handed sandwiches and coffee and sent off to stow their gear. "We were given one horse blanket and a folding cot," one veteran recalled, "and pointed to the sleeping quarters."[10]

The man charged with supervising the logistical arrangements for this influx was Major General John Clifford Hodges Lee, who ran the Services of Supply (SOS) command. Lee was a humorless, self-centered, and uncompromising martinet who wore his Old Testament religiosity on his sleeve. Eisenhower called him a "modern Cromwell"; Patton, with less restraint, called him "a pompous little son-of-a-bitch." Lee was also a fawning admirer of the British aristocracy and enjoyed socializing with titled peers and traveling in high style with a private train and a fleet of cars. Before the war was over, Eisenhower would feel compelled to caution him about his extravagance lest it "give the impression of [a] disregard for public expenditures." He was known by his initials as J. C. H. Lee, and many on his staff and others who worked for him whispered among themselves that the initials actually stood for "Jesus Christ Himself."[11]

But he got things done. Lee and his staff crafted the orders that led to the construction of campsites, warehouses, airfields, and supply depots that made the American occupation of southern England possible. American equipment and supplies soon began filling up some twenty million square feet of warehouse space and then overflowed into another forty-three million square feet of open storage. The preparation of these facilities exposed one of several cultural differences between the two English-speaking societies. British work crews first ensured that all the paperwork was properly completed, that every level of the command had signed off on the work order, then prepared blueprints and carefully surveyed the ground before setting to work. The Americans, by contrast, stormed onto a site and immediately set the dirt flying. Witnessing these different approaches, Morgan later offered this example of a typical American response to being assigned a construction job: "Yes sir ... 100 percent. You bet. As for your 'skedule,' it's a cinch ... This is right up our alley. Why, this little outfit of mine, when we were 'way back in Texas' ... " and so on.[12]

In preparing quarters for the arriving GIs, both British and American work teams relied principally on what were known as Nissen huts: semi-cylindrical corrugated steel barns that were the British equivalent of Quonset huts, but much smaller. Thirty-six feet long (about the length of a Higgins boat), they housed eighteen to twenty GIs in Spartan discomfort, with no plumbing or electricity and only an iron stove at one end to provide heat. A camp designed to hold a thousand men required 123 such buildings, half of them barracks, plus office space, a guardhouse, garages, kitchen, and storage buildings. It took forty acres to accommodate such a camp, and simple arithmetic reveals that to house a million men occupied 40,000 acres of farmland or grazing land in a country where food was already scarce. Locals were astonished by the speed in which farmland was transformed into fully functioning camps. "One evening there had been empty fields," a farmer recalled, "the next morning there were mushroom towns of bell-tents, lorry parks, jeep lines, and field kitchens."[13]

Even so, the camps could not be built fast enough to house the tens of thousands of Americans who arrived weekly, and soon enough the new arrivals were being billeted in local hotels. The hotel owners received compensation from the British government, though they were not asked to give their permission. One widow who owned a small tourist hotel in the seaside town of Torquay—a hotel much like Fawlty Towers, depicted in the popular late 1970s British television series—found this out in most dramatic fashion. She had been informed by the authorities that her property was being commandeered by the Americans. It was nonetheless a shock on the night of January 29, 1944, when trucks pulled up to her door and soldiers began clomping into the building in their "heavy army boots" and headed upstairs. All that night, and for some days afterward, the woman and her daughter huddled fearfully in their ground-floor apartment listening to the foot traffic on the other side of the door and hearing the strange accents of her alien occupiers. Eventually, however, she met some of her "guests" and gradually got to know them. Soon enough she began inviting them downstairs to listen to the radio in the evenings. When they finally left months later, there were hugs and tears all around.[14]

In a few cases, Americans were billeted in private homes. The authorities resisted such an intrusive option. After all, the Quartering Act of 1774, which had obligated Bostonians to house British soldiers in their inns and homes, had helped spark a revolution. Now that the shoe was on the other foot, some wondered if the British would tolerate an imposed obligation to take American GIs into their homes. Controversial as it was, there seemed to be no other solution. Some half a million men needed to be housed in the seven counties of the so-called West Country, from Land's End in Cornwall to Portsmouth in Hampshire, and nearly a hundred thousand of them were billeted in private homes. At first it proved awkward. As a platoon of American soldiers marched down the street of a village, the officer in charge

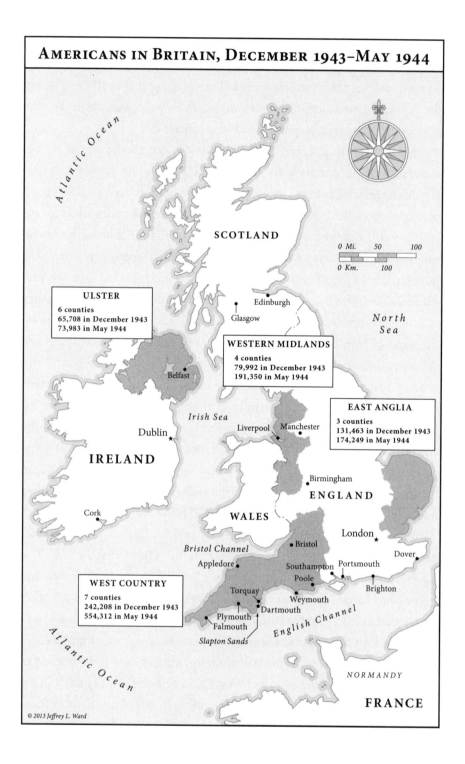

AMERICANS IN BRITAIN, DECEMBER 1943–MAY 1944

Atlantic Ocean

SCOTLAND

0 Mi.   50   100
0 Km.   100

ULSTER
6 counties
65,708 in December 1943
73,983 in May 1944

Edinburgh
Glasgow

North Sea

WESTERN MIDLANDS
4 counties
79,992 in December 1943
191,350 in May 1944

Belfast

Irish Sea

EAST ANGLIA
3 counties
131,463 in December 1943
174,249 in May 1944

Dublin ★

Liverpool   Manchester

IRELAND

Birmingham

ENGLAND

Cork

WALES

London ★

Dover

Bristol Channel

• Bristol

Appledore •

Southampton   Portsmouth
Poole

Brighton

WEST COUNTRY
7 counties
242,208 in December 1943
554,312 in May 1944

Torquay
Weymouth
Dartmouth

Plymouth •
Falmouth

English Channel

Slapton Sands

Atlantic Ocean

NORMANDY

FRANCE

© 2013 Jeffrey L. Ward

would order a halt. Consulting his clipboard to confirm the street number, he would then announce: "Two men are going to live here. Okay, Jones and Smith, go up, knock on the door, and introduce yourselves. That's where you're going to live." Then the column marched on. Jones and Smith had no option but to walk up to the door and knock. Awkward as those first moments were, for the most part the program was quite successful. The soldiers themselves considered it "a great treat," and the homeowners received a small stipend, critical to many families in a society that had never managed to climb fully out of the Depression before the war struck. By and large the British welcomed the Americans, and some remained in contact with them for the rest of their lives.[15]

For their part, the GIs recognized that they were not in Kansas anymore. One big difference was simply the scale of things. The huts were more crowded, the roads much narrower, the shops smaller, and the space allotted for almost any activity severely restricted. Britain was not only a small country, it was, to American eyes, a tiny country with miniature-scale everything, from trains to food portions. The natives were just as impressed with the much larger scale of almost everything American, from their big trucks to their big American teeth. One Hampshire resident watching the arrival of the Americans from her window recorded her astonishment at "the size of everything." And it was not only the size but the quantity. She stood "positively spellbound by the unending procession of American military equipment" as it rolled past her home. In a society where scarcity had been the hallmark of daily life for most of a generation, such abundance was positively world-shattering.[16]

Feeding and supplying an army of a million men was an enormous logistics problem, and given the limits of Allied shipping, it made sense to supply the American occupiers with locally produced food whenever possible. The British were willing enough, even in some cases eager, to take on this responsibility, seeing it as a way to pay back the United States for all the support it had provided through Lend-Lease. They even referred to it as "reverse Lend-Lease." The difficulty was that the American troops recoiled at the kind of fare that was available in Britain in 1943. This was not entirely unexpected. Roosevelt himself had decreed the year before that "American

soldiers could not live on British rations." From the start, the GIs were allocated more meat (12 ounces per day) than British soldiers (8 ounces per
day), and far more than the ration for British civilians (4 ounces per day).
On the other hand, most of that meat was mutton, or sometimes pork. For
many Americans, "meat" was synonymous with "beef," and beef was in very
short supply in England, where most of the cattle were dairy cows. American sailors fared little better. In September 1943, Stark had decreed that
U.S. naval personnel should call on the Royal Navy for "general stores, services, fresh provisions, and fresh vegetables, bread, cakes, and pastries." Un-
fortunately, the Royal Navy was no better off than the troops ashore, and
sailors on U.S. ships got mostly powdered eggs, powdered milk, and powdered potatoes. Their principal meat was Spam, "with some bologna thrown
in now and then." For soldiers and sailors alike, vegetables were also a
problem. They were plentiful enough, but the GIs objected to both the type
and the quality. The most readily available vegetable was Brussels sprouts,
which Americans almost universally despised.* Even the bread, instead of
being made of enriched wheat flour, was made of barley and oats.[17]

If food was a source of complaint, the Americans in Britain seemed never
to be short of what the British called "sweets": candy and gum. From the
beginning, Marshall had recognized that a civilian conscript army had to
have access to certain benefits, including Hershey bars, chewing gum, and
Coca-Cola, as well as American-made cigarettes, regular mail service, and a
well-stocked post exchange, or PX. Despite the shipping problem, each
American division was allocated thirty-two thousand tons of supplies,
which gave the U.S. Army a higher "tail-to-teeth" ratio (tons of supply per
front-line soldier) than any other military service in the world. Almost at
once, these American luxuries became a kind of ersatz currency in the developing relationship between American occupiers and British residents.
Chewing gum had been all but unknown in Britain until the arrival of the

---

* The scarcity of vegetables extended to the upper ranks. When a member of Ike's staff had a
chance to include a private package on an airplane coming from the States, he begged an
American supply officer to ship him a crate of fresh vegetables. When it arrived, the entire
staff gathered around to see what wonderful comestibles it contained, though when the lid
was pried off, it revealed an entire crate of fresh Brussels sprouts.

Americans, but the GIs seemed to be constantly working on a wad of gum with their big white American teeth. British children, especially the boys, found that they were nearly always successful when they approached a GI to ask: "Any gum, chum?" Soon it was a common sight to see British schoolboys happily chomping away on their sticks of American gum.[18]

Quite beyond the question of housing and food, the interaction of the Americans with their British hosts involved a number of more complex issues. British law had long established the precedent that soldiers of any nationality were "subject to all the duties and liabilities of an ordinary citizen" when in the British Isles. That meant they had to abide by the same laws, and were subject to the same penalties, as everyone else. Under U.S. law, however, American soldiers who committed a crime, regardless of where that crime occurred, were subject only to U.S. military law and only to U.S. military courts. It was an indication of British willingness to do almost anything to accommodate the Americans that Parliament quickly passed a special act exempting American soldiers from prosecution for any crimes they might commit in England. Interestingly, the law did not apply to the Canadians, French, Poles, Norwegians, or any other nationality that also had soldiers in England—only to Americans.[19]

That kind of special treatment bred resentment among some Britons, especially those in uniform. Eisenhower recognized that the British soldiers had grounds for resenting the favored treatment that American soldiers received. "Our scale of pay is much higher," he noted, "our ration is more elaborate; the amount devoted by the [American] Red Cross and the Government for recreation and amusement is greater." In addition, British soldiers felt that the carefree Americans simply did not take things seriously enough. Even when on watch, British officers noted that American soldiers "leaned on their rifles, chewed gum, and smoked cigarettes, and generally adopted a most unsoldierly-like attitude." Off duty, they swaggered into the pubs, talked loudly about how they had come over to pull British chestnuts out of the fire, then plunked down ostentatiously large bills while ordering their pints. A poll taken by a British newspaper revealed that the Americans were less well regarded in England than the Czechs, Dutch, Russians, French, or even the Italians, who until late 1943 were their erstwhile enemies. British soldiers resented the Americans' new, clean liberty uniforms that included a necktie, which made them all look like officers. And they resented the medals they wore, including the European Theater of Operations (ETO) medal, issued to every soldier who arrived. As the British put it, the Americans got medals for "just showing up." Would these men really be able to stand up to the Germans when the time came? One British officer suggested, though only within his own circle, that perhaps the best thing to do was to assign British officers to command American soldiers, in much the same way they commanded colonial troops from India or South Africa, so that they could put a little starch into them.[20]

One particularly sensitive point was the relationship between American GIs and British women. Because Britain had been at war since 1939, with British soldiers fighting on battlefields from Burma to Egypt (and now in Sicily and Italy), the military-age male population of Britain was little in evidence in 1943. British women were too fully occupied to sit around waiting for them. Nearly half a million British women were in the armed services themselves, and virtually all the rest worked, for there was no unemployment in wartime Britain. Indeed, a wartime British law required that any man who worked less than sixty hours a week and any woman who worked less than fifty-five hours a week also had to serve at least one night a week on fire watch. Of course, all this was new since the war began, and it had bred a dramatic change in the social dynamic. Before the war, respectable women did not go out unescorted, especially in the evening, but due to the dearth of possible escorts those rules no longer applied. Given the new social fluidity, the arrival of a million free-spending, joke-cracking Americans was all but explosive. Brenda Devereux, who was a teenager in the Channel port city of Bournemouth, recalled that when the Americans hit town, "they swaggered, they boasted, and they threw their money about," unlike British men, who found such behavior vulgar and tawdry. Brenda was "captivated." "How we loved it," she gushed. British men, especially British soldiers, blamed the erosion of the old standards on the GIs who, in the famous phrase of the day, were "overpaid, oversexed, and over here." But many Americans felt that equal responsibility belonged to British women, who, liberated from the straitjacketed life of the prewar years, often welcomed the advances of the GIs with enthusiasm. As one GI put it, "The English girls were a lot friendlier than English men."[21]

In an effort to control the burgeoning social revolution, the British government created an agency to provide social outlets for the occupiers. They authorized clubs and other centers for social interaction. However, the fare was sparse, the music bland, and the mood sedate. Americans much preferred the clubs set up and run by the American Red Cross, where the beer was cold, the cigarettes were American-made, and the radios were tuned to the jive sounds of the American Armed Forces Network instead of the drear and pedantic BBC. The British resented the obvious American preference for replicating a piece of the USA in Britain rather than integrating into British culture. Anthony Eden, the British foreign secretary, complained about it to John Dill. "We had hoped," he wrote in August 1943, "that the presence of large numbers of American troops...would have done much to develop mutual understanding." Instead, he reported, "American military authorities in England tend to discourage fraternization as a waste of time." Similarly, the director of the BBC, Godfrey Adams, betrayed his pique when he remarked that "the American Army authorities are anxious to have everything over here of their own—their own equipment, of course; their own food, their own sports kit to play their own games, and so forth. In a word, pretty well all they require from this country is a piece of land to camp on until the 'second front' opens."[22]

One slice of American culture that migrated across the Atlantic with the soldiers was the tradition of racial separation and discrimination. As David Reynolds writes in his excellent history of the American "occupation" of Britain, the experience "proved something of a sociological laboratory for black GIs." The U.S. Army of World War II was still segregated, though black soldiers made up 10 percent of the whole, serving mainly as drivers, as cooks, and on laundry detail, the kind of work that is done mostly by contract laborers in the twenty-first century. When Major General James E. Chaney had been in command, he strongly recommended that no black soldiers be sent to England at all. Roosevelt overruled him, declaring that 10 percent of the Army should be composed of black soldiers, and that this proportion should be reflected in all command theaters.* After Eisenhower replaced Chaney in England, he sought to reduce racial tensions by issuing an order that "the spreading of derogatory statements concerning the character of any group of United States troops, either white or colored, must be considered as conduct prejudicial to good order and military discipline." Nevertheless, black American soldiers in England were billeted separately, ate separately, and were generally restricted to their own area unless they were making a delivery or assigned to a work project. White Americans, both officers and enlisted, accepted this as perfectly normal.[23]

The British, however, had no legacy of domestic slavery and no tradition of race separation; at the time, there were fewer than eight thousand black residents in all of England. Consequently, while Americans of any color were novel and therefore innately interesting, black Americans were especially intriguing. Moreover, while white Americans often displayed a brash confidence, blacks were polite, deferential, even courtly. In many venues, the black soldiers were more popular with the British than the white soldiers were. "Everybody here adores the negro troops," a woman in Wiltshire wrote, "but nobody likes the white Americans. They swagger about as if they were the only people fighting the war, they all get so drunk…, while the negroes are very polite." A story that was popular at the time, and which was still being told in Devon a half century later, involved the reaction of one local when asked what he thought of the American soldiers. "They're right fine blokes," he said, "but I don't much care for the white buggers they brought with 'em."[24]

For many Americans, especially from the South, the very idea that white women of any nationality would "walk out" with black men was not only disorienting but intolerable. Often the very presence of black soldiers in a pub led to fights, as white American soldiers sought to defend the cultural traditions they had been born to. On rare occasions the fights were serious

---

* The U.S. Navy also had a lengthy tradition of racial segregation and a policy of restricting black recruits to service positions, in particular as "mess boys"—essentially servants for officers. In 1942, Roosevelt had insisted that the Navy begin to open more specialties to blacks, including those of gunner, signalman, yeoman, and quartermaster.

enough that men were killed. The British were horrified by this and some-times came to the aid of black soldiers who were under attack from a crowd of angry white Americans. In the end, however, the British were compelled to adjust. Their perceived need for American military partnership proved the trump card, and the British accepted, without embracing, the racial code imposed on them by the Americans. Pubs were designated as either black or white, or in some cases blacks and whites were allowed access only on alternate days.[25]

THE PRINCIPAL ACTIVITY of the American troops in England was training—especially training for amphibious assault. Except for those veterans of the North African campaign who were transferred back to Britain in November 1943, most of the GIs were raw recruits in their teens and early twenties, and their officers hoped to complete their combat training in England. Morgan ordered that "advanced amphibious training... be initiated without delay." In such training, not only did Brits and Yanks have to learn to work together, but so did Army and Navy units, which was no sure thing. Moreover, it was essential "to familiarize troops and naval units with conditions peculiar to [the] English Channel." The goal was to conduct combined training exercises "under conditions similar to those which prevail in the Channel."[26]

To effect this training, the Americans made a number of requests to the British Government for large tracts of land for military exercises. In addition to the forty thousand acres used to house the Americans, and well over twice that amount devoted to American air bases in East Anglia, the United States in September 1943 requested an additional 191,000 acres in southern England for armored training. The British minister of agriculture protested that this would devastate the country's food and dairy production at a time when Britain could barely feed its people, much less its voracious guests. Nevertheless, though the size of the tract was reduced to 141,000 acres (220 square miles), the British agreed to this, too, assigning much of the Salisbury Plain and the Channel coast west of the Dart River to the American Army.[27]

Generous as that was, it seemed severely restricted by American standards. For comparative purposes, when George Patton set up a desert training area in America in the months before Operation Torch, he had appropriated a site in California that was over ten *million* acres (sixteen thousand square miles). In England, that would have constituted one-third of the entire country. The necessarily restricted area set aside for training in Britain meant that much of that training consisted of small arms practice and road marches, with only limited opportunity to maneuver in units larger than a battalion. One American soldier estimated that he had marched some three thousand miles while in England, but during all that time, he had very little training in combat exercises. Navy signalman Paul Fauks recalled that "there wasn't a lot of training," and when there was, it consisted of going into a field, pitching a tent, digging a hole, and sending out practice messages in code. Such exercises soon "became repetitive and very boring." It didn't help that even in southern England the nights were cold and damp in what one officer called "the moisture-laden, bone-chilling Devon countryside."[28]

If the training was boring and repetitive and the weather often cold, at least the surroundings were picturesque. Aside from Cornwall, the County of Devon is the westernmost piece of England, stretching from Dartmouth, Paignton, and Torquay on the Channel coast fifty miles north to the Bristol Channel. A barren and rocky moor (Dartmoor) occupied the middle of it, but it was along the coasts that the Americans established their bases for amphibious exercises: Appledore, on the north coast near Barnstaple, and Slapton Sands, on the English Channel just west of Dartmouth. To many Americans, South Devon in particular looked exactly like what they imagined England to be: small cottages dotting low rolling hills that were checkerboarded with vivid green pastures separated by hedgerows. In a typical reaction, one GI noted upon arrival, "The land…is lovely, divided by hedgerows, green and beautiful." Those hedgerows looked benign enough, though in fact they were thick rock walls from which a heavy growth had sprouted over several centuries. Indeed, one reason for choosing South Devon as a training site in the first place was that the hedgerows there were superficially similar to those in the *bocage* country in Normandy where the Americans would have to fight after they had seized the beaches.[29]

Devon was also desirable because of its relative isolation. Large-scale amphibious training could proceed there without attracting too much attention. South Devon was therefore endowed with the new title of "The American Army Battle School," and to ensure that the training was realistic, with full use of live fire, the three thousand or so residents were told that they would have to move out, abandoning their farms and villages, their churches and their pubs—indeed, empty the countryside altogether—in order to make way for the Americans. This came as a complete shock to the Devonians. It was one thing to turn farmland over to the Americans for their campsites and their armored training; it was quite another to tell Englishmen who had lived there all their lives to get out. Some of the families in South Devon had been there for as long as anyone could remember; in a few of the villages, the Norman churches dated back to the twelfth century. It is one more measure of the British willingness to bend over backward to accommodate the Americans that the Churchill government approved this eviction. With very short notice, the residents of South Devon packed up and left, hoping that the Americans would do no more damage to their homes and farms than was necessary. GIs who arrived at one Norman church in a now-abandoned village found this note tacked to the door:

> This church has stood for several hundred years. Around it has grown a community which has lived in these houses and tilled these fields ever since there was a church. This church, this churchyard in which their loved ones lie at rest, these homes, these fields are as dear to those who have left them as are the homes and graves which you, our Allies, have left behind you. They hope to return one day, as you hope to return to yours, to find them waiting to welcome them home.[30]

While the isolation of South Devon was an advantage in many ways, it was also a logistical nightmare. Between those green but solid hedgerows, the country lanes, most of them unpaved, were barely wide enough for a single vehicle or horse cart. Occasional turnouts allowed one vehicle to pass another. Should two vehicles meet face-to-face, one or the other of them had to back down to the nearest turnout so they could squeeze past each other. In prewar days, drivers might pause there to discuss the weather or local events before proceeding. Once the hundreds of thousands of Americans began arriving, however, the country lanes became the source of much cursing and gear grinding by the drivers of the oversize two-and-a-half-ton American trucks (the famous "deuce and a half") that plied the roads in an almost unending stream from the summer of 1943 until the invasion began the following year. The Americans built 17 miles of new roads, widened 230 miles more, and built five new bridges, but in spite of that, between July 1943 and March 1944 there were some twenty-four thousand reported traffic collisions on these country lanes, a full quarter of them at speeds of less than five miles per hour, which suggests they were incurred as vehicles sought—unsuccessfully—to maneuver past each other while their drivers colored the air with scatological imprecations.[31]

FROM THE BEGINNING, the Anglo-American partnership had traveled a bumpy road. Despite subsequent talk about the "special relationship," and the much-publicized friendship between Churchill and Roosevelt, the tension between the two English-speaking allies never fully disappeared. First at the conference table, then in North Africa and Sicily, and finally in England, the cultural collision of Brits and Yanks threatened but never quite broke the partnership. Mostly this was due to mutual need. The British needed American men, American money, and American equipment, and they were willing to surrender convenience, pride, and even a little bit of sovereignty to get them. The Americans needed the British, too. Most of all, perhaps, they needed Britain itself—the base from which the invasion would be launched, though they also needed British experience even if they too often undervalued it.

If the cultural and institutional differences were evident in the Allies' divergent approaches to grand strategy, they were also evident in the day-to-day operations of the military forces. As Morgan put it, "It seems that the word 'command' has two different meanings in our two services." In the United States Army and Navy, it was common practice for senior officers to outline an objective along with a rough timetable, and then delegate the details of its execution to their subordinates. The British found that approach slipshod at best, and very likely dangerous. In their view, it was essential to ensure that there was complete agreement and understanding of virtually every facet of an operation up and down the chain of command. This was especially true of any operation in which Winston Churchill had a stake. Indeed, it was Churchill himself who offered what was perhaps the most overt expression of this view. "In practice," he wrote, "it is found not sufficient for a Government to give a General a directive to beat the enemy and wait to see what happens." To him it was clear that "a definite measure of guidance and control is required from the Staffs and from High Government authorities." By which, of course, he meant himself.[32]

Another significant difference, not unrelated to the first, was that while the Americans were always in a hurry, the British tended to adopt a more careful, analytical approach to most issues, an approach that struck the Americans as old-fogeyism. The British were aware that the Americans thought them cold and reluctant. One very senior British officer wrote his wife, "No doubt after years of war we look more closely at things before we say what we will or will not do, whereas the Yanks are new at this game and have the enthusiasm of beginners." He also recognized an important reality: "They are as good for us as we are for them."[33]

To the British, evidence of this "enthusiasm of beginners" was manifest in the American tendency to throw around nearly unimaginable numbers and seemingly impossible deadlines. The very idea of assembling two million men and five thousand ships in a relatively short period of time struck the British as not only naive but evidence of hubris. In this, at least, both sides were right. The Americans *were* naive, and their boastful confidence certainly bordered on hubris; they undoubtedly benefited from a strong dose of British realism, especially in 1942. Yet the British also underestimated the American ability to produce previously unthinkable numbers of ships, planes, and tanks. Morgan saw all of this in his dealings with both sides. When the Americans proposed a particular operation, Morgan wrote, a common British response was something like this:

My dear boy, is all this really necessary? Well, if it really is, couldn't we do it just as well with half the bother? At any rate we can't get anywhere near the numbers you want....And as for time, I don't see how it could possibly be done in less than at least a week longer than you seem prepared to give us....We'll have a crack at it, only don't expect much of a show.[34]

All too often, Americans found this tongue-in-cheek stereotype uncomfortably accurate. Bred to the notion that swift action and undeviating focus on the objective was the way to get things done, Americans found the British agonizingly indirect. When American Navy Captain James E. Arnold received orders as the naval officer in charge (NOIC) for one of the landing operations, he sought out his British counterpart to discuss how they could cooperate. He showed up at British headquarters and introduced himself: "I'm Captain Arnold, U.S. Navy, and I'm looking for NOIC, British forces. I wanted to discuss—" At that point he was interrupted: "Aye, sit down and have a spot of tea." Such exchanges were not necessarily typical, but they were common enough to suggest that the cultural and professional gulf between the two nations affected planning and training for Neptune-Overlord.[35]

The origin of this Anglo-American gulf was not merely cultural—it was also experience-based. The vastly different roles that each country had played during the First World War colored all the exchanges between Brits and Yanks in the Second. In August 1943, Secretary of War Stimson wrote to Roosevelt, "The shadows of Passchendaele and Dunkerque still hang too heavily over the imagination of these [British] leaders. Though they have rendered lip service to the [cross-Channel] operation, their hearts are not in it." That much was evident. As late as November 25, 1943, barely five months before the date set for the invasion of Europe, the British chief of staff argued, "We must not...regard OVERLORD on a fixed date as the pivot of our whole strategy on which all else turns." The British, Stimson said, believed in "pinprick warfare" and were convinced that "Germany can be beaten by a series of attritions in northern Italy, in the eastern Mediterranean, in Greece, in the Balkans, in Rumania and other satellite countries and that the only fighting which needs to be done will be done by Russia."[36]

He was not entirely wrong. And yet, in spite of the dissimilar experiences that informed their divergent approaches to war, and in spite of the cultural gulf between the gum-chewing, wisecracking Yanks and the temperamentally restrained, tea-drinking Brits, by the end of 1943 they were bound together by mutual need, and poised on the brink of history. It now seemed likely that the manpower resources for the invasion could be assembled in time to meet the agreed-upon deadline of May 1, 1944. To be sure, most of those men were inexperienced, many were insufficiently trained, and others were still en route, but they were well armed, well fed, and certainly eager enough. Two questions, however, remained unanswered: Could the Allies assemble the sealift capability needed to get them across the Channel and onto the Normandy beaches? And who would command the operation?

CHAPTER 7

"SOME GOD-DAMMED THINGS CALLED LSTS"

S HIPPING. from the very day of Pearl Harbor and even before, Allied strategic planning had been severely circumscribed by the scarcity of available shipping. As Brooke noted in January 1943, "The shortage of shipping was a stranglehold on all offensive operations." It was not that the Allies had failed to see this coming. As early as 1936, the United States had begun subsidizing the construction of fifty new merchant ships a year under the Merchant Marine Act. Three years later, the government doubled the number of subsidized ships to one hundred, and doubled it again the next year. In January 1941, nearly a full year before Pearl Harbor, Roosevelt had declared an "unlimited national emergency" and used that to justify an even bigger shipbuilding program. Nevertheless, once the war began, the need to supply both Britain and Russia while simultaneously fighting a war in the Pacific revealed just how desperately short of shipping the Allies were. And it got worse. During 1942, German U-boats sank more than a thousand Allied ships in the North Atlantic. For a time it seemed possible that this U-boat onslaught might eliminate Allied sealift capability altogether.[1]

Defending the Atlantic convoys required hundreds of new destroyers, especially the new, smaller, destroyer escorts (DEs), plus dozens of small auxiliary aircraft carriers (CVEs). As Secretary of the Navy Frank Knox wrote in February 1943, it would be impossible to conduct any operations in Europe at all "unless escort vessels can be provided much more rapidly." It seemed clear to him that building new escorts was the nation's highest industrial priority. King agreed. Arguing that "one ship saved was worth two ships sunk," he, too, wanted to put escort ship construction at the top of the nation's priority list.[2]

On the other hand, it was equally critical to build more cargo ships. At the very least, the Allies had to replace the hundreds of ships already sunk by the Germans, and others being lost almost daily. The deputy administrator of the War Shipping Administration, Lewis W. Douglas, protested that making escorts the highest priority would jeopardize the program for building cargo ships and weaken the ability of the Allies to maintain the transatlantic convoys. After all, escorts would be useless if there was nothing for them to escort. Knox disagreed. "It does us little good," he wrote, "to produce one hundred cargo ships a month if we do not produce enough escort vessels during that month to enable us to protect them when they go to sea." In a kind of chicken-and-egg dilemma, the Allies had to decide whether it was more critical to build escorts to protect the convoys, or replace the cargo ships they were supposed to protect.[3]

And now there was a third imperative. All of the agreements solemnly accepted by the Combined Chiefs of Staff and the heads of government about invading occupied France on May 1, 1944, would be meaningless if the Allies could not produce the thousands of landing ships and landing craft needed to carry the invasion force to the beaches. Landing craft had constituted a bottleneck for the Torch landings, and again for the invasion of Sicily and Italy. The invasion of France would require far more. Without literally thousands of new landing craft, any talk of a cross-Channel operation was simply fatuous.[4]

There is an inextricable connection between strategic planning and logistical realities, and ship construction is especially determinative. Even more than in the production of tanks, trucks, or planes, shipbuilding requires a particularly long gestation period that begins with the accumulation of raw materials and leads through steel mills, fabrication shops, machine shops, and assembly plants before eventually arriving in the building ways. It is a complex puzzle involving tens of thousands of interconnected parts. As a result, decisions made about construction priorities in 1943 decisively affected what was operationally possible in 1944. The American industrial colossus was impressive, but it was not infinite. If Neptune-Overlord was to become a reality—if those hundreds of thousands of soldiers crowding into southern England were to be lifted across the Channel and deposited onto the beaches of Normandy—the Allies had to produce the thousands of landing craft needed to carry them there.

Back in 1942, Roosevelt had created the War Production Board (WPB). In theory, at least, part of its job was to establish priority categories for all sorts of products, not just ships but also machine tools, cranes, valves, forgings, engine parts, and the hundreds of other industrial tools of war. The WPB set up a system in which the highest priority items received a rating of A-1. Inevitably, however, one or another command or interest group came forward to explain why a particular product needed to be elevated above the others, and soon there was an AA-1 category, and not long after that an AAA-1 category. By mid-1943 such ratings had become all but meaningless because so many items had been assigned the highest priority. At that point, the WPB created a new standard: an urgency rating. After confirmation of the decision for Neptune-Overlord in August 1943, only one American shipbuilding program carried an urgency rating: landing craft. The decision came late in the game, however, and the friction of war proved particularly powerful in slowing the production of desperately needed landing craft. In the end, the Allies simply ran out of time.[5]

———————

THE TERM "LANDING CRAFT" encompasses forty-six different types of vessels,* ranging from oceangoing transport and cargo ships that displaced

* In general, any vessel over two hundred tons was called a "ship," and those under two hundred tons were called "craft," though this was not universally true. Both the LCI (landing craft, infantry) and LCT (landing craft, tank) displaced more than two hundred tons but were nevertheless labeled as craft.

ten thousand tons or more down to the thirty-six-foot Higgins boats that carried the soldiers to the beach.[6] The alphabet soup of acronyms for all these vessels can be confusing, even to experts, and for that reason, it is useful to lump them into three broad categories:

1. The most numerous, indeed nearly ubiquitous, type of landing craft was the small, flat-bottomed personnel carriers developed by Andrew Jackson Higgins at his shipyard in Louisiana (see Chapter 4). Popularly known as Higgins boats, they were initially designated as Landing Craft, Personnel (LCP) by the Navy. These displaced only six tons each and were carried aboard larger ships, suspended on davits that could lower them into the sea alongside the mother ship. Soldiers would then climb down chain or rope nets into the holds, which had no seats or benches, making some feel like they were inside a railroad boxcar with no roof. Each boat had a Navy crew of three whose job was to ferry their human cargo several miles to the beach. By the time of the Trident conference in May 1943, the United States had produced nearly four thousand of these craft. (See Table 2, page 161.) Many had gone to the Pacific, others had been employed in the Torch landing in North Africa, and still others were sent to the Mediterranean for the invasions of Sicily and Italy.

By May 1943, however, the LCP was no longer being manufactured, for it had been replaced by a slightly larger and more resilient variant that displaced eight tons and carried both soldiers and vehicles, including jeeps and light trucks, though not tanks. These were also produced by the Higgins Company and still called Higgins boats, though the Navy's designation for them was Landing Craft, Vehicle and Personnel (LCVP). Like the earlier LCPs, they were carried aboard larger ships, and suspended on davits. They were an improvement over their slightly smaller predecessors in several ways. First, the draft forward was only twelve inches, which allowed them to land on beaches that had a very gradual slope (as at Normandy). They were also faster (12 mph) and had a longer range (one hundred miles) than the LCP, and they carried two .30 caliber machine guns aft. The first of them was built in November 1942, slightly too late for Torch, but over the next eighteen months American shipyards turned out an astonishing twelve thousand of them, making them the most numerous of any vessel built during the war. They were the workhorses of the amphibious war, carrying soldiers and Marines to beaches from Sicily to Saipan.[7]

Another vessel in this general category was the somewhat larger Landing Craft, Mechanized (LCM), sometimes called a Mike boat since "Mike" was the phonetic code for the letter *M*. The 1944 Navy training manual called the LCM "a big and chunky older brother to the LCVP." Of all-steel construction, each Mike boat displaced thirty tons and could carry a single Sherman tank, which is why they were sometimes called "tank lighters." They had twin diesel engines, which made them quite maneuverable, though that also meant they required a particularly skilled coxswain. With a range of 130 miles, they could cross the Channel on their own, though they, too, had to be brought across the Atlantic as deck cargo on larger vessels, often several at once. By the time of the landings in Normandy, the United States had produced more than eight thousand of these small tank carriers.[8]

2. A second category of landing craft consisted of larger vessels that were capable of crossing the English Channel on their own to deliver tanks and infantry onto the assault beach. The larger of them was the Landing Craft, Infantry, or LCI, which the sailors affectionately called "Elsies." The most common type was the LCI(L)—the second *L* standing for "large"—which were just over 158 feet long and displaced 230 tons. They could carry up to two hundred men each, though they were relatively fragile with little armor, and since they lacked bow doors, they could not carry vehicles of any kind. To disembark their human cargo, they pushed as far up onto the beach as they could and deployed twin ramps on either side of the bow.

The other vessel in this general category was the Landing Craft, Tank (LCT), which could carry four or five tanks or heavy trucks in its open cargo bay. In the course of the war, both Britain and the United States produced several versions of the LCT. By 1943, the United States was building the Mark VI, which at 119 feet was considerably shorter than an LCI but both sturdier and better armored, displacing 286 tons. The key feature of this type of landing craft was that upon beaching, it could open its bow doors, deploy a ramp onto the sand, and allow the trucks or tanks in its open well deck to drive out under their own power.

RELATIVE SIZES OF ALLIED LANDING CRAFT

USS Texas (BB-35)

USS Herndon (DD-638)

LST

LCI (L)

LCT (USN version)

LCM (Mike boat or tank lighter)

LCVP (Higgins boat)

Rhino Ferry

While both the LCI and the LCT could cross the English Channel on their own, neither had been designed for a transatlantic voyage. Many of the LCIs did it anyway, but most of the LCTs came to England as deck cargo. In some cases they arrived in sections and were welded together in British shipyards, though the general practice was for them to be carried piggyback on the deck of a larger ship. When the paired ships arrived in England, the host ship would transfer water in her ballast tanks to create a deliberate list to one side, and the 286-ton LCT would slide sideways down greased wooden beams to land alongside with a spectacular splash.[9]

3. The third type of amphibious vessel was both the largest and by far the most important. It was also the ship that became the industrial and logistical bottleneck for the Allies, not only for the Normandy invasion, but worldwide. This was the Landing Ship, Tank (LST). Described by one authority as "a large, empty, self-propelled box," it was an oceangoing ship that displaced 1,625 tons when empty and could carry twenty Sherman tanks, thirty heavy trucks, or twenty-one hundred tons of cargo in its cavernous hold, plus as many as forty light trucks or jeeps lashed to its upper deck. It also had bunk space for up to 350 soldiers. Because of its flat bottom, which gave it a draft of only a foot and a half forward when empty and four to seven feet when fully loaded, it could steam right up onto a beach despite its great size and discharge its cargo through massive bow doors. The British had pioneered this kind of large-capacity tank carrier with the "Winstons" and "Winettes" used at Dieppe, and because of that the American-built LSTs were sometimes referred to as the LST-2. Very quickly, however, the American version eclipsed its British prototype and was soon universally known simply as the LST.[10]

A case can be made that LSTs were the most important ships of the Second World War, yet few loved or admired them. To begin with, they were very poor sailors. With their blunt bow (to accommodate the big doors) and flat bottom (to ensure shallow draft), they were, as one sailor put it, "shaped like a bathtub," and they wallowed badly even in calm seas. In any kind of mild chop they would smack down heavily on each successive wave with a teeth-rattling thump. As one veteran recalled: "Some ships go over the waves; some of them go through the waves; some go under the waves; but an LST just clubs them to death." In an active sea, the LSTs also tended to "shimmy and vibrate," and the torque exerted on the lengthy hull as it slipped precariously down a quartering wave was so powerful that observers on the bridge could see the hull actually twist. If the ship was loaded with a full cargo of jeeps and light trucks on its weather deck, the vehicles would rise and fall rhythmically as if driving in unison over a hilly countryside. On rare occasions, the movement of the ship's hull became so violent it could rip open the welds that held the ship together, opening a seam, as one sailor put it, like a run in a woman's stocking.[11]

Given these sailing characteristics, seasickness was endemic, and the LSTs were uncomfortable in other ways, too. To conserve space for the barn-like hold, the crew's quarters were squeezed into a small space aft under the fantail and consisted of hinged bunks stacked three high. The ship's head was directly behind these bunks, and one veteran recalled that the LSTs "stank of diesel oil, backed-up toilets, and vomit." The LSTs did not even have names. Instead, like the smaller LCIs and LCTs, the ungainly and unloved LSTs were distinguished only by their hull number, such as LST-235 or LST-393.* It was almost as if the Navy bureaucracy was ashamed of these ugly ducklings and sought to deny them the distinction of a christening. Finally, the LSTs were slow, seldom able to exceed ten knots, and crewmembers joked that "LST" actually stood for "Large Slow Target." For all that, they were absolutely essential to any large-scale amphibious operation, and vital for success at Normandy.[12]

Before the war was over, the United States would build more than a thousand LSTs, but by May 1943, when the conferees at Trident approved the plan for an invasion of Europe one year hence, only 241 of them had been completed. Moreover, all but a handful of them were in the Pacific or the Mediterranean. The COSSAC plan for the cross-Channel invasion called for a concentration of 230 LSTs in southern England by early 1944 in

---

* Both of the sample LST hull numbers cited here are for ships that participated in the Normandy invasion and which are preserved today as historic artifacts. LST-235, at Evansville, Indiana, is the only LST in the world that is still operational; LST-393 is not operational but is open to visitors as a museum in Muskegon, Michigan.

order to execute Neptune-Overlord on May 1. Instead, a variety of factors conspired to hinder both their production and concentration, and very soon it became evident that a shortage of LSTs was the Achilles' heel of the entire Allied invasion effort. Indeed, the history of the LST construction program offers singular insight into both the friction of war and the confluence of strategy and logistics.

BORROWING HEAVILY ON BRITISH PLANS, naval architect John Niedermair, who ran the Preliminary Design Branch at the U.S. Navy's Bureau of Ships (BuShips), drew up the blueprints for an American LST early in 1942, and the first keel was laid in June of that year. One curious but valuable aspect of Niedermair's design was that the LSTs were equipped with ballast tanks which, when filled, would prevent them from bobbing like a cork when unladen, but which could be pumped out when carrying a full load so that the draft remained relatively stable.

Though LSTs were full-sized, oceangoing ships with a length of 327 feet 9 inches and a 50-foot beam, the majority of American LSTs were built inland, mostly along the Ohio River, at cities from Pittsburgh, Pennsylvania, to Evansville, Indiana. They were constructed on building ways parallel to the river and were launched sideways, an event that generated an impressive wave that slapped up onto the opposite riverbank. The first LST hit the water in Pittsburgh in October 1942, only weeks before the Torch landings. Manned by a skeleton crew and placed in the charge of a river pilot, it made its way fifteen hundred miles down the Ohio and Mississippi Rivers on a nine-day journey to New Orleans. The Navy men on board followed the civilians around to learn how the ship worked. Many remembered that journey as "a great adventure," since for most of them it was the first time they had been under way on board a ship. The LSTs were formally commissioned in the town of Algiers, Louisiana, across the river from New Orleans. There, the boat davits were installed and they were equipped with Higgins boats— initially two or three to a side. Then, proudly bearing a commissioning pennant, they steamed out the mouth of the great river and into the Gulf of Mexico. Some lingered for a week or two near Panama City for a series of beaching exercises; others rounded Key West and headed up the Atlantic coast to the Navy's Amphibious Training Base at Little Creek, Virginia, where the Commander Amphibious Forces supplied new officers and the rest of the crew.[13]

For the most part, the crews on the LSTs were as fresh and untested as the ships themselves. The complement for an LST was nine officers and 110 sailors, a larger number than on a comparably sized cargo ship because of the need to man the guns when at general quarters. Save for the commanding officer, usually a Navy lieutenant in his twenties, most of the officers were ninety-day wonders who had come straight from civilian life and endured thirteen weeks of midshipman training at one of several designated colleges before being sent directly to a ship. As one graduate of the program recalled, "we learned close order drill, plane identification and signal flag recognition. That was about it." As for the crew, a handful of petty officers brought critical experience; most of the rest were teenagers straight from boot camp. One officer recalled that on his ship, "the ages of our crew ranged from 17 to 22. Not one of them had ever seen the ocean."[14]

Manning the smaller LCIs and LCTs was even more problematic. They often boasted only a single commissioned officer, and like the department heads on the LSTs, they were often complete novices. When Ensign Philip Goulding reported on board the LCI(L) 506, the commanding officer, a lieutenant, junior grade, asked him: "Goulding, do you know anything?"

"No, sir," Goulding replied earnestly. "I just got out of midshipman's school. I don't know anything at all."

To Goulding's astonishment, the lieutenant slapped his hand down on the wardroom table and exclaimed: "Thank God for that. Nobody on this ship knows anything and I was afraid those idiots were going to send me someone to spoil it. Siddown and have a cup of coffee."[15]

The training in Chesapeake Bay seldom lasted more than a few weeks. The officers and crew on the big LSTs learned how to run the engines, operate the bow doors, and maneuver the ship while under way. They worked on emergency procedures, tactical maneuvering, precision anchoring, mooring alongside, and underway refueling. As on all Navy ships, officers sought to keep the crew physically fit, though this occasionally proved problematic, and even humorous. While the large open deck of an LST provided lots of room for calisthenics, the constant rolling of the ship made it something of an adventure. As the sailors lined up and began doing jumping jacks, the rolling ship moved beneath them so that after each jump, they landed a few inches away from where they had started. As the ship slowly rolled to starboard, the files of jumping men "moved slowly across the deck to the port rail, and then, as the ship righted itself, they bounded slowly back to starboard." Watching this from the bridge, one officer wondered if "in a prolonged roll, the crew would dance right over the side."[16]

Combat training consisted of learning how to shoot the 3-inch gun on the stern and the 20 mm anti-aircraft guns, or later the 40 mm Bofors gun. Often there was only one day to practice firing those guns, aiming at a target sleeve towed at the end of a long tether by a Navy airplane whose pilot was almost certainly very nervous. Beaching exercises were especially nerve-racking. It was frightening to steam directly toward the shore. It was so counterintuitive that during the first attempt, men on board instinctively grabbed on to whatever they could, anticipating a jarring collision, if not worse. Then, too, if the LST grounded on the beach at anything other than a fairly precise 90-degree angle, it was likely to slew off to one side, an effect called broaching, which meant it would end up sideways on the beach and probably require a tow to get off again.[17]

Once an LST successfully pushed itself up onto a beach, its massive bow doors opened like a cupboard, a twenty-three-foot bow ramp was lowered, and the tanks, trucks, and jeeps inside its hold drove off onto the sand under their own power. Huge fans ventilated the cargo hold so that the exhaust from all those gasoline engines firing up at once did not asphyxiate the crew. After the hold was emptied, the vehicles on the upper deck could be unloaded. In early models of the LST, an elevator on the foredeck lowered them one by one down to the cargo hold. That proved time-consuming, however, and beginning with LST-491, laid down in July 1943, a ramp replaced the elevator so that the vehicles on the weather deck could simply drive down the ramp and out the bow doors.[18]

After unloading, the LSTs needed to retract from the beach. To do that, each was equipped with a special anchor at the stern that was attached to a steel cable wound around a massive winch. As the LST steamed in toward the beach, crew members dropped the anchor well offshore and paid out the cable as necessary. It was important to pick the right moment to execute that maneuver, for if the crew dropped the anchor too soon, the cable would run right off the spool and disappear into the sea. After disgorging its cargo, a gasoline-powered motor engaged the winch, the anchor dug into the bottom, and the LST hauled itself off the beach stern first, assisted by its own engines. The sequence of orders was: "Up ramp. Close bow doors. Haul around on the stern anchor. All engines back one third."[19]

It was helpful if the LSTs landed on a rising tide at or near the high-tide mark. If they attempted to discharge their cargo at low tide, the last vehicles to drive off might be swamped by the rising tide; if they unloaded during a falling tide, by the time the last vehicle debarked, the ship could find itself thoroughly aground, high and dry like a beached whale, a circumstance known as "drying out." When that happened, there was no choice but to wait for the next high tide to retract.

THE FIRST LSTS WERE PART of a large construction program authorized early in 1942 for Operation Roundup. In March of that year, Secretary of War Stimson urged Roosevelt to "lean with all your strength on the ruthless rearrangement of shipping allotments" to ensure a sufficiency of landing craft for the invasion, and the next month Roosevelt declared that landing craft should have priority over "any other program." The Navy dutifully informed its contractors that "landing craft would take precedence over all other programs in the A-1 category," then still the highest priority rating. In May 1942, contracts were let to build three hundred new LSTs, and on July 1, they were officially elevated to the top of the priority list.[20]

The moment did not last. The July 22 decision to invade North Africa made Roundup unlikely for 1943, and both Leahy and King argued that landing craft construction should be scaled back in favor of building escorts for the convoys. The British protested mildly, suggesting that the new LSTs could be sent to England anyway in case "an opportunity for operations on the Continent in 1943 might arise." King thought that was a terrible idea, and said so in his usual emphatic way. He argued that it made no sense to build LSTs to be warehoused in Britain for an unlikely contingency. German bombers might blow them out of the water before they could be of use to anyone. He proposed that any LSTs that were already under construction should be completed, but they should then "be allocated to that theater where they were most needed," by which he meant the Pacific. Meanwhile, the contracts for all LSTs not yet laid down should be cancelled to allow for the construction of more destroyers and escort carriers for convoy protection. The CCS agreed, and on September 16, 1942, the War Production Board cancelled the contracts for one hundred of the new LSTs, as well as forty-eight LCI(L)s. Whereas in the spring of 1942, eighteen American shipyards had been engaged in the construction of LSTs, by September 1943, only eight were so employed. Though landing craft in general remained in the AA-1 category, their place in the priority list slid to twelfth, behind minesweepers. By the end of 1942, the United States had produced a total of only twenty-three LSTs.[21]

The decision made sense at the time. The prospects for Roundup were doubtful at best, and the Allies were desperately short of escorts. The British First Sea Lord reported that the Royal Navy was two hundred escort vessels short of simply being able to maintain current operations, and Frank Knox told Roosevelt that the U.S. Navy was 981 escorts short of a full complement. The new emphasis on building escorts in 1942 did much to ease this shortage and helped turn the tide in the Battle of the Atlantic in 1943. Indeed, the "crossover point" at which Allied ship construction began to exceed losses to U-boats occurred in November 1942, during the North African campaign. (See Chart, page 113.)

Still, the decision to restrict LST construction in the late summer of 1942 did affect the Allies' ability to meet the requirements set down by COSSAC for the invasion of France in 1944. The Allies tried to rejuvenate the LST program after the Trident conference in May 1943, and to effect that, four of the shipyards that had been retooled for destroyers were ordered to shift back again to accommodate LSTs. But it was much easier to order it than to do it. Retooling a shipyard was not simply a matter of throwing a switch. Parts already fabricated for one kind of vessel had to be set aside and the whole program restarted from the beginning of the logistical pipeline. As a result, some yards did not get fully back on line producing LSTs until March 1944.[22]

Another factor that affected the LST shortage, one that was far more perplexing, was the evident lack of any particular urgency on the part of the principal decision makers—even after the Trident and Quebec conferences. Instead of responding to the May 1 deadline for D-Day with enthusiasm and alacrity, the U.S. military bureaucracy exhibited a curious kind of malaise, at least insofar as LST construction was concerned. The Joint Chiefs did formally recommend a 25 percent increase in landing craft production. That instruction, however, did not specify that LSTs were a particular priority. As a result, though the production of the small Higgins boats (LCVPs) jumped from 567 in June to over 1,000 in July, there was no similar acceleration in LST construction—indeed, during those same months, LST production actually fell from twenty-seven to twenty-four per month. When Morgan expressed concern that the shortfall in landing craft could upset the Allied timetable, Donald Nelson, head of the War Production Board, assured him that all was well. "Don't you believe a word of it," Nelson told Morgan. "By early 1944 we shall have so much of the darned stuff that we shall be hard put to find a use for it all." The reality was much different. New orders for LSTs were not placed until December 9, less than five months from the date scheduled for D-Day. Only then could the various subcontractors begin to retool their shops to manufacture the more than thirty thousand different components that made up an LST.[23]

A third factor that affected productivity was the competition for raw materials. If shipbuilding was a major bottleneck in Allied strategic planning, steel plate was a major bottleneck in shipbuilding. Between 1940 and 1943, American steel mills increased production from four million tons a year to thirteen million tons, an increase of over 300 percent. In that same period, however, shipyard consumption of steel plate increased from half a million tons to seven and a half million tons, an increase of 1,500 percent. Indeed, by 1943, shipbuilding consumed more than half of all the steel plate rolled in the United States, and the principal consumer of that steel plate was the United States Maritime Commission, which produced the other U.S. ship with a legitimate claim to being called the most important vessel of the Second World War—the Liberty ship. For much of the war, Liberty ships carried the munitions and supplies that kept Britain and Russia in the war and sustained Allied trade and Allied operations worldwide. Before the war was over, American shipyards would turn out more than twenty-seven hundred of them.[24]

At 14,500 tons each, Liberty ships were more than three times larger than LSTs, and they were voracious consumers of steel plate. Back in February 1942, Roosevelt had challenged retired Rear Admiral Emory Scott Land, who ran the Maritime Commission, to build eight million tons of shipping that year, and ten million tons more in 1943. These were audacious numbers; in 1941, even with the spur provided by the government's subsidy program, the American shipbuilding industry had produced a total of only 1.1 million tons of shipping. Now FDR wanted eighteen times that. It is not clear where he got the numbers; he may have simply plucked them out of the air to impress Land with the importance of building as many ships as he could as fast as possible. At the time, both Land and his deputy, Rear Admiral Howard Vickery, believed achieving such a goal was unlikely. Nevertheless, with a Herculean effort, by 1943 Land and Vickery seemed to be on their way to accomplishing it. At that point, Roosevelt raised the bar, setting a new objective of twenty-four million tons. His attitude seemed to be: *If you achieved the goal I set, I must not have set it high enough.* Such astonishing levels of productivity, however, absorbed unprecedented amounts of raw materials, especially steel plate, and that affected the renewed effort to build LSTs. As the 1944 War Production Board report put it, "Competition among various agencies of the Armed Services for available material was keen." That competition also involved machine tools, electric motors, welding rods, generators, reduction gears, bearings, pumps, and hundreds of other vital components. Despite America's role as the "Great Arsenal of Democracy" (Roosevelt's term), it was a zero-sum game after all: one more Liberty ship might well mean one, two, or even three, fewer LSTs. The competition for resources between landing craft and other construction projects demonstrated that American industrial capacity was not infinite.[25]

Table 2   U.S. Landing Ship and Landing Craft Production, January 1942–May 1944

Month	LST	LCI(L)	LCT	Mike Boats (LCM)*	Higgins (LCP)**	boats LCVP	Total
January 1942	0	0	0	18	116	0	134
February 1942	0	0	0	10	0	0	10
March 1942	0	0	0	0	117	0	117
April 1942	0	0	0	1	174	0	175
May 1942	0	0	0	27	248	0	275
June 1942	0	0	1	35	344	0	380
July 1942	0	0	1	118	480	0	599
August 1942	0	0	45	307	600	0	952
September 1942	0	1	156	131	477	0	765
October 1942	1	25	152	203	394	0	775
November 1942	18	59	101	244	466	75	963
December 1942	43	68	11	168	345	140	775
January 1943	46	70	3	114	37	205	475
February 1943	61	47	0	156	44	319	627
March 1943	28	22	0	406	18	655	1,129
April 1943	17	10	0	143	57	405	632
May 1943	27	3	0	236	0	416	682
June 1943	27	9	1	146	0	567	750
July 1943	24	16	0	244	0	1,073	1,357
August 1943	22	22	10	401	0	812	1,267
September 1943	23	23	32	502	0	943	1,523
October 1943	16	25	44	585	50	836	1,556
November 1943	20	28	46	563	50	921	1,628
December 1943	25	30	38	523	50	875	1,541
January 1944	28	35	65	578	50	833	1,589
February 1944	18	34	84	641	50	932	1,759
March 1944	28	54	81	594	50	811	1,618
April 1944	50	69	100	470	50	744	1,483
May 1944	82	78	83	487	50	792	1,572

* Includes both Mark III and Mark VI.
** Includes both LCP(L) and LCP(R).

The LST construction program also had to compete for manpower. With millions of Americans in the Army, the labor pool for shipbuilding consisted mainly of three groups: those who had been rated 4-F by their draft boards, older workers, and women. Just as millions of young men were turned into soldiers in a matter of weeks in Army boot camps, so, too, were inexperienced and unskilled workers turned almost instantly into shipbuilders. Teenager Clendel Williams was rated 4-F by his draft board because he was underweight (six feet one inch and 118 pounds), so he sought a job at the Evansville, Indiana, shipyard. "The interviewer only glanced at my application," he wrote later. "There was no physical, nor an eye examination. One person took my picture and another one fingerprinted me. Within a few minutes I was handed a badge with my picture and number 4214 on it." After attending welding school "for a few weeks," he was certified as a "three position welder" and set to work building LSTs. Women also joined the workforce in unprecedented numbers. Though this aspect of what was, in effect, a social revolution was most evident in the aviation industry, women also went to work in the nation's shipyards as drafters, drivers, and welders. Indeed, the shipbuilding industry had its own version of "Rosie the Riveter" in "Wendy the Welder." By the end of the war, a full third of the ninety thousand workers at the Richmond, California, shipyard were women.[26]

In most of the shipyards, the workers employed the task system. Teams specialized in a particular function—cutting sheet metal, fabrication, electrical, piping, or carpentry—and they completed all the work of that type on one ship before moving on to the next ship on the next building way. They labored in three shifts around the clock, earning fifty cents an hour, which, after deducting $1.40 for "old age benefits" (the new Social Security program), yielded $18.60 for a forty-hour week, though sixty-hour weeks were common. Workers who left at the end of the day shift at 4:00 p.m. jostled past hundreds of others coming in for the swing shift. At dusk, giant floodlights on towering stanchions lit up the shipyards, and the work continued without a pause. At midnight, workers from the swing shift gave way to those working the night shift, and so it went around the clock, seven days a week. The welding machines were in use twenty-four hours a day, handed off from one shift to another. Yet due to the finite number of building ways, the production of LSTs continued to lag behind anticipated need.[27]

One effort to deal with the labor shortage was Andrew Jackson Higgins's idea to hire large numbers of underemployed black workers to build Liberty ships. By local tradition, blacks were not admitted to skilled-labor jobs in the South, including shipbuilding, because white workers simply refused to work alongside them. As a result, thousands of able-bodied blacks remained idle even as the demand for labor grew. Higgins's idea was to build two separate shipways, one employing all white workers and the other relying on only black workers. Segregated they might be, but at least black workers would find lucrative employment that was otherwise unavailable. Higgins planned to challenge the workers on each building way to demonstrate their skill and work ethic by outproducing the other group— an approach that might have led either to healthy competition or a race riot. In any case, it never happened, for in making the switch from Liberty ships and LSTs to escorts in 1942, the contracts Higgins had been promised were among those that were cancelled.[28]

FOR THE NORMANDY LANDINGS, the COSSAC plan called for 250 LCI(L) personnel carriers, 900 LCTs, 480 Mike boats, more than 1,000 Higgins boats, and 230 LSTs. The construction of all of these except LSTs proceeded apace. Smaller landing craft, such as the Higgins boats, did not require building ways and could be contracted out to independent boatyards and metal fabricating firms, some of them hundreds of miles from deep water. In the last six months of 1943, even as the construction of LSTs lagged, more than five thousand Higgins boats were delivered to the fleet.

One event that did affect the production schedule of these smaller boats, as well as the LSTs, occurred almost exactly halfway around the world on November 20, 1943. On that date, five thousand U.S. Marines assaulted the tiny island of Betio in Tarawa Atoll, the first step in what would become known as the Central Pacific Drive, a campaign that would lead from Kwajalein to Saipan, Iwo Jima, and Okinawa. At Tarawa, however, the Higgins boats got hung up on the offshore coral reefs despite their shallow draft. That compelled many of the Marines to wade more than a quarter mile to the beach, suffering horrible casualties in the process. As a result, the Marines requested a dramatic increase in the number of tracked amphibious vessels (LVTs or "amphtracks") that could crawl over such reefs. The November schedule had initially called for 2,055 of these, but as a result of the lessons learned at Tarawa, the December schedule included more than 4,000 of them, virtually doubling the requirement. It was one more obligation crowded onto an already congested construction schedule.[29]

Finally, assembling a sufficient number of LSTs for Neptune-Overlord was not simply a matter of production; it was also a question of distribution. Besides those sent to the Pacific, there were 104 LSTs still in the Mediterranean in late 1943. Since Allied soldiers were already ashore on the Italian boot, the need for landing craft in that theater had diminished significantly, and Morgan's plan called for fifty-six of those LSTs to return to England in January 1944 to prepare for the cross-Channel operation. As the campaign in Italy dragged on, however, Churchill conceived of an end run around the German defensive line in Italy by conducting an amphibious landing at Anzio. Though Eisenhower was less enthusiastic about this maneuver than most of his subordinates, he agreed that it was desirable in order to avoid "a series of slow and costly frontal attacks." Of course, to conduct that operation meant keeping a number of landing craft, and especially the essential LSTs, in the Mediterranean. "I do not wish to interfere with the preparations for OVERLORD," Eisenhower wrote to the Combined Chiefs, "but I have felt it my duty to lay before you my requirements."[30]

Churchill argued that the departure of the LSTs for England could be delayed several months without any serious consequences because the ships and crews in question were already veterans of multiple operations and would not need additional training after they arrived in the United Kingdom. Of course, that argument overlooked the fact that while the ships' crews might be experienced, the troops they would carry were not, so it would be helpful, arguably even essential, to have the LSTs in England for training several months before they set out across the Channel. Nevertheless, on October 29, orders went out to suspend "all shipments of landing craft to U.K. from Mediterranean area." In the end, the fifty-six LSTs participated in the landings at Anzio (dubbed Operation Shingle) on

January 22, 1944. (See map, page 116.) It was another fist hurled into the Mediterranean tar baby, for the troops at Anzio became trapped in a coastal cul-de-sac and the campaign bogged down again. Churchill acknowledged his disappointment in a particularly vivid sentence: "I had hoped that we were hurling a wild cat on to the shore, but all we got was a stranded whale." Stranded or not, the forces in the Anzio bridgehead had to be supplied, and much of their supplies had to be carried on LSTs, a fact that kept those ships, like the men they supplied, imprisoned in the Mediterranean.[31]

Scrambling to close the gap between the shrinking availability and the increasing need, the Combined Chiefs took steps to ensure that none of the LSTs were being "wasted" conducting ancillary missions. Because they had a commodious hold and the ability to discharge cargo anywhere without a pier, jetty, or heavy-lift cranes, theater commanders found LSTs useful for all sorts of logistic work. A few of them, especially in the Pacific, even used them as "afloat storage" for ammunition and supplies. Aware of this, King ordered all commanders to "rigidly restrict use of landing craft to first am-phibious assault operations," adding an unusual note: "This is mandatory." Similarly, Churchill wrote to Brooke to ask about LSTs being "absorbed in purely supply work to the prevention of their amphibious duties." The prime minister was annoyed that "such valuable forces [were] being so completely wasted."[32]

Meanwhile, back in the United States, despite an "urgency" priority and twenty-four-hour-a-day work schedules, the production of new LSTs remained modest, even disappointing. Roosevelt authorized the new director of war mobilization, James (Jimmy) Byrnes, to make landing craft the single highest construction priority, over Army trucks, Navy ships, and even Russian assistance. By the end of 1943, the United States had built a total of 398 LSTs, but over half of them were in the Pacific and more than a hundred were still in the Mediterranean. That left fewer than a hundred for an operation that Morgan estimated would require 230. By the spring of 1944, the situation was becoming serious. Secretary of the Navy Knox tried to put the best face on it he could in a letter to Betty Stark in London. He asserted that "we are right up to schedule—in fact, ahead of schedule—for landing craft of all types *except LSTs*, and we might be short five or six of these on the date required. We have cut out entirely the building of Destroyer Escorts, and are concentrating those yards on landing craft production."[33]

Was it too late? To be sure, LSTs were at last making their way across the Atlantic, albeit slowly, and many of them also carried a fully loaded LCT strapped to the deck as cargo. To the men on board, this was a decidedly mixed blessing. It allowed the executive officer on the LST to integrate the crew of the LCT into the watch bill for the crossing, which meant that watch standers did not have to serve "watch-and-watch"—four hours on and four hours off, around the clock. On the other hand, the added weight topside made the LSTs even more liable to heavy rolling than usual. It was hard to say whether the extra help on watch compensated for the rough ride. As one put it, "You have never ridden a ship until you have ridden an LST in the North Atlantic in the month of February." Another sailor described the experience with particular vividness: "One minute the ship was carried to the crest of a wave, at which time one could look down into the valley of water below, and the next minute the ship would sink down to the bottom of the trough and then one would look at a wall of water, towering almost vertically above the ship on all sides." It was difficult—even dangerous—just to sit on the toilet since the swift rise and fall of the hull often sent the occupant crashing into the overhead and then plunging down back onto the toilet seat.[34]

Despite Knox's attempt to reassure Stark, it was soon evident that the Allies would be short several dozen LSTs on the projected date for D-Day, and that many of the LSTs that did arrive would be in no condition for a major effort for weeks if not months afterward. That meant either going ahead with inadequate shipping or postponing the invasion. Churchill may not have been entirely disappointed by the prospect of a delay, for he had already suggested a postponement until June; nonetheless, he found it absurd, as he wrote to Marshall, that "the destinies of two great empires . . . seemed to be tied up in some god-dammed things called LSTs."[35]

ONE ISSUE THAT WAS FINALLY RESOLVED that winter was the appointment of a commanding general. At Quebec in August, Morgan had been granted a third star and endowed with de facto command of the

cross-Channel attack "pending the appointment of the Supreme Commander." As D-Day neared, Morgan's temporary status became increasingly
awkward, and the need to make a permanent appointment more urgent.
When he had conceded to Roosevelt the authority to make that appointment, Churchill had assumed that Roosevelt would name George C.
Marshall to the post, and at the time, that was exactly what the president
planned to do. FDR believed that Marshall had more than paid his dues
with the JCS and CCS and that he deserved an opportunity to become, as
the president put it, "the Pershing of the Second World War" by commanding the great invasion. Even Morgan urged Roosevelt to name Marshall to
command, and to do it soon, telling him during an October visit to America
that even though the invasion was still six months away, some matters had
to be put in motion immediately in order to ensure readiness on D-Day.
Roosevelt listened but did not commit himself.[36]

Nevertheless, the assumption on both sides of the Atlantic was that Marshall would soon be named to command the cross-Channel invasion and
that Eisenhower would return from the Mediterranean to assume the job of
chief of staff so that a British officer could take command in the Mediterranean. Marshall even began to put his household effects into storage in
preparation for an imminent move to Europe. Secretary of War Stimson did
no more than reflect the general consensus when he wrote to Roosevelt
that making Marshall the supreme commander was obvious. Making an
analogy with the Civil War, Stimson noted that while "Mr. Lincoln had to
fumble through a process of trial and error with dreadful losses until he was
able to discover the right choice," no such casting about was needed on this
occasion. "General Marshall already has a towering eminence of reputation
as a tried soldier and as a broad-minded and skillful administrator."[37]

But that was exactly the problem. Marshall was such a "skilful administrator" that it was not clear that Eisenhower or anyone else could replace
him. Who would run the war while Marshall was running the invasion? The
fact that Eisenhower had been Marshall's acolyte and would now become
his theoretical superior as chief of staff added another layer of awkwardness. Though Roosevelt had all but promised Marshall the command (as
Churchill had done to Brooke before snatching it back), as September

turned to October, and October to November, the president made no formal announcement about it.

One reason for his hesitation was the pushback he was getting from the other members of the Joint Chiefs. Both Ernie King and Hap Arnold insisted that Marshall could not be spared from his current job. Secretly they may have believed that no one else could manage the mercurial president and give him not only the kind of direct and honest advice he expected and deserved but also the subtle guidance and direction that, in their opinion, he needed. They also suggested that appointing Marshall to command Overlord would be a demotion from being chief of staff. As Arnold wrote General Thomas T. Handy, the assistant chief of staff for operations, sending Marshall to Europe to command Overlord would make him "just another Theater Commander." Roosevelt might have resisted these objections from the JCS, but soon Marshall's pending appointment became a political issue as well. Rumors that Marshall would be relieved from his post and sent to Europe found their way into the press. Republican newspapers, ever suspicious of nefarious plotting by the New Dealers, portrayed it as a scheme to get the forthright and honest Marshall out of the way.[38]

Marshall himself maintained a professional silence about the whole issue, but he did have concerns about how wide the supreme commander's authority would reach. He believed that whoever commanded Overlord should also have strategic control of Mediterranean operations. An advocate of unified command since Arcadia, Marshall was convinced that it was essential that one man "should exercise command over the Allied force commanders in the Mediterranean, in northwest Europe, and of the strategic air forces." That was anathema to Churchill, not only because it would put the entire European war in the hands of an American but also because the prime minister continued to harbor hopes of extending Mediterranean operations into the Balkans and the Greek Islands, something that was unthinkable if an American was in charge. As far as the British were concerned, Overlord would be an independent and completely separate command, and a British officer would have his own independent command in the Mediterranean. Such a narrowing of the authority of the supreme commander made it somewhat less "supreme," and was one more factor for Roosevelt to consider.[39]

Roosevelt had still not made a decision, or at least had not yet announced one, when he left to attend yet another conference with Churchill—and, for the first time, with Stalin—at Tehran in November 1943. En route to that meeting, Roosevelt and Churchill stopped in Cairo, where they met with the Chinese leader Chiang Kai-shek. There, Roosevelt first broached with Marshall the possibility that he might not be selected to command Overlord after all. The president hated personal confrontation and therefore sent his alter ego, Harry Hopkins, to sound out the general on the question. Marshall told Hopkins that he would "wholeheartedly" accept any decision the president made. Thus assured, Roosevelt himself talked to Marshall the next day. Roosevelt wanted to know how Marshall felt about the possibility of staying on in Washington as chief of staff. Marshall again professed that he would be happy with any job the president assigned to him, and asserted that "the issue was too great for any personal feelings to be considered." At the end of their conversation, Roosevelt signaled his likely intent by telling Marshall, "I feel I could not sleep at night with you out of the country."[40]

At Tehran, a number of the old issues were revisited. Churchill could not help reprising some of his now-familiar, even tedious arguments about continuing Mediterranean operations at the expense of delaying Overlord by a month or two, but he elicited little support. Stalin made it clear that such an option would provide no significant relief to the embattled Red Army. Russian armies, he noted, were facing 210 German divisions on the Eastern Front, plus 50 more divisions made up of Hungarians, Finns, and Romanians, for a total of 260 enemy divisions—perhaps two million men. He hardly needed to add that this was ten times the number of Germans the western Allies faced in Italy, and fifty times the force that the Anglo-Americans planned to put ashore in Normandy, though the numbers were skewed by the fact that British and American divisions were nearly twice as large as the actual (as opposed to the theoretical) size of German divisions.[41]

The issue of landing craft came up as well. Marshall acknowledged that "the question of adequate landing craft," especially "those capable of carrying 40 tanks" [sic], was "the chief problem" in planning the cross-Channel attack, though he assured the Russians that "the schedule of production had been stepped up" and he was confident that Overlord could take place on time as planned.[42]

It was Stalin who raised the issue of who would command it. When Roosevelt told him that the decision had not yet been made, the Russian premier stated that while he did not expect to have a voice in the decision, *someone* should be named, he should be named soon, and he should have complete authority. Though he did not say so, the implication was that unless and until the Anglo-Americans named a commander, it was hard to take their promises of an imminent invasion seriously.[43]

That may have encouraged Roosevelt finally to get off the fence. He had hesitated until now partly because it was his administrative style to delay. In addition, however, despite a somewhat selfish desire to keep Marshall in Washington, he did not want to deprive him of his place in history. Student of history that he was, the president knew that generals who operated behind the scenes seldom won the kind of public credit that fell to successful operational commanders. He resolved his dilemma by convincing himself that this war was different, that future historians would not—could not—overlook Marshall's manifest contributions even without an active field command. That meant that Marshall could stay in Washington, where he was essential, and still earn his place in the history books.[44]

Having made the decision, Roosevelt did not wait long to act on it. Returning from the Tehran Conference, the president summoned Eisenhower to meet him in Cairo prior to a quick trip to Sicily to hand out some medals. As soon as the two men settled into the back of the president's car at the airport, Roosevelt turned to Eisenhower and said, "Well, Ike, you are going to command OVERLORD."[45]

CHAPTER 8

SHAEF AND ANCXF

ISENHOWER LEFT NORTH AFRICA on the last day of the year to fly back to the United States. Between quick trips to visit his son, a cadet at West Point, and his mother in Kansas, he spent a quiet few days with his wife at the Greenbrier resort in West Virginia, which was being used as a convalescent hospital by the Army. After that, Ike traveled to Washington to discuss his new command with Marshall. He had planned to return to Africa afterward to say goodbye to the "happy family" he had worked with for more than a year, but Marshall encouraged him to fly instead directly to England. On January 15, he flew to the Azores, and then on to Prestwick Airport, near Glasgow, where he boarded a train for London, arriving there on January 17. With that, COSSAC ceased to exist and was replaced by a new acronym: SHAEF, which stood for Supreme Headquarters, Allied Expeditionary Force.[1]

By then, a number of the men that would make up the command team for Neptune-Overlord were already in place, and Eisenhower had promised Marshall that he would "disturb the present setup as little as possible." There was, however, the problem of what to do with Morgan, now a lieutenant general, who had presided over the Overlord planning for the last six months, and who knew the issues and circumstances better than anyone. Morgan had known from the start that he would eventually step aside for a more exalted boss, but he had assumed that he would remain as deputy commander, or perhaps chief of staff. Instead, Eisenhower selected a British air marshal, Sir Arthur Tedder, as his deputy commander. Eisenhower was convinced that the coordination of air and ground forces during the invasion would be critical, and he had worked closely and companionably with the handsome, pipe-smoking Tedder in the Mediterranean. Eisenhower also brought his own chief of staff from North Africa, the gruff and irreverent but highly efficient Major General Walter Bedell Smith, whom Ike (and others) called "Beetle." Eisenhower tried to let Morgan down easy, complimenting him on "the fine work" that he and the COSSAC team had done, and assuring him that Brooke had "an important job awaiting you." That turned out not to be the case, however, and Morgan stayed on as a deputy to Smith, helping to manage the staff work with two other three-stars: Sir Humphrey Gale and James Robb. To his credit, he bore neither Eisenhower nor Brooke any ill will and continued to labor with cheerful enthusiasm, though with tongue in cheek he told an associate that he knew the reason he had been retained on the staff: "If something goes wrong they want me right here to put the blame on."[2]

The rest of the SHAEF command team remained largely intact. Because the overall commander of Neptune-Overlord was an American, the three men who would exercise direct command of the ground, air, and sea aspects of the invasion were all British. Churchill himself had picked the commander of the ground forces. Though Eisenhower would have preferred Sir Harold Alexander, the prime minister instead chose Field Marshal Bernard Law Montgomery to head what was labeled the 21st Army Group, made up of American, British, and Canadian forces. Fifty-six years old in 1944 (three years older than Eisenhower), Montgomery had become famous in Britain after his victory at El Alamein in 1942, which had won him a knighthood. Though his actual performance in that campaign was more competent than brilliant, his status as national hero apparently went to his head, for he exuded an ego-driven self-confidence that many, including Tedder, found embarrassing, even offensive. George Patton (who found fault with many) thought him "a little fellow of average ability [who] thinks himself a Napoleon—he is not." Even Eisenhower, who got along with almost everyone, found Montgomery a strain to work with and confessed to Brooke that he did not know how to handle him. In some respects, Montgomery was the Douglas MacArthur of the European war—a man with evident military talents who was victimized by his own unbridled ego, his haughty demeanor, and a tendency to preen. He was also somewhat dismissive of Americans, believing that they exhibited more boisterous enthusiasm than good sense, and he thought they had made a "dog's breakfast" of the campaign in Italy. He was therefore glad to put Italy behind him and fly to London to prepare the decisive stroke of the war.[3]

Command of the air assets for Overlord went to Air Marshal Sir Trafford Leigh-Mallory, a former fighter pilot whose friends called him "L-M." Leigh-Mallory would soon be overshadowed by Ike's deputy, the bomber pilot Tedder, but it was just as well that SHAEF had so much Air Force brass in the high command, for almost at once squabbling erupted over how to utilize air assets during the invasion. The Combined Chiefs of Staff in Washington suggested that the organization of tactical air forces for Overlord should rest in its hands. Eisenhower resisted that, arguing successfully that control of the air forces over the invasion beach must reside with the invasion commander—that is, himself. The next battle was with the champions of strategic bombing. Both British Air Marshal Sir Arthur Harris, known as "Bomber Harris," and American Lieutenant General Andrew "Tooey" Spaatz, were convinced that Germany could be bombed into submission if the air attacks were relentless. They were therefore reluctant to withdraw their bombers from that mission to support the invasion. Eisenhower won that fight, too. Even then, Spaatz and others argued that the bombers should conduct an "oil strategy" by targeting wells and refineries, rather than the "transportation strategy" against railroads and bridges that Ike wanted in order to isolate the invasion beaches. And finally, there was a dispute about which air forces would support which invasion beach. Some thought that American planes should cover American beaches while

British planes covered British beaches. Eisenhower rejected that out of hand, insisting, as he had from the start, on an integrated effort. In the end, Eisenhower won all these disputes, relying heavily on Tedder and Leigh-Mallory to do so.[4]

Of course, at root Neptune-Overlord was an amphibious operation, and the designation of an overall naval commander was critical. The officer assigned the job of Allied Naval Commander, Expeditionary Force, which yielded the rather cumbersome acronym ANCXF, was Admiral Sir Bertram Home Ramsay—"Bertie" to his friends. Ramsay, who turned sixty-one on January 20, was the oldest of the SHAEF commanders and physically unprepossessing: of average stature with a plain round face and thinning, though surprisingly dark, hair. The son and brother of British Army generals, he had joined the Royal Navy in 1898 at the age of fifteen, undergoing initial training aboard HMS *Britannia*, an old three-deck ship-of-the-line, not unlike those of the Napoleonic era, that served as Britain's Naval Academy until 1905.

Like Eisenhower, Ramsay had spent much of his career as a staff officer, working for very senior officers. He had been flag lieutenant to the commanding officers of both the Atlantic and Mediterranean fleets, and flag commander to Admiral Sir John Jellicoe during a round-the-world cruise on the battlecruiser HMS *New Zealand*. He had a strong work ethic and high personal standards that he tended to apply to others as well as to himself, writing in his diary, "My faults are that I can't sit still and see things done in an antiquated and un-progressive way." This "shortness of manner," as one put it, occasionally got him into trouble. Indeed, it very nearly ended his career in the 1930s when, as a rear admiral, he resigned as chief of staff to Admiral Sir Roger Backhouse after only four months on the job because he felt that Backhouse was insisting on doing all the staff work himself. Their parting was amicable and Backhouse bore him no ill will, but his voluntary abdication of such a high-profile position cast a shadow on his career, and for the next four years he was without an assignment, a status made official in October 1938 when his name was moved to the retired list. Ramsay rather enjoyed the hiatus, marrying an heiress half his age and settling down to the comfortable life of a gentleman landowner.[5]

Curiously, it was Backhouse, when he became First Sea Lord, who rescued Ramsay from Coventry by appointing him flag officer in charge at
Dover during the Munich crisis in the fall of 1938. Ramsay still held that
position two years later when the Germans smashed through Allied
defenses in the lowlands and the British Expeditionary Force retreated to
the beaches near Dunkirk. As the man on the spot, it was Ramsay who cho-
reographed the evacuation of more than 338,000 men from the Dunkirk
beaches, including nearly 140,000 French, Polish, and Belgian soldiers. It
was all but a miracle, and it proved the making of him. In 1942, Ramsay was
promoted to full admiral and appointed Commander, Expeditionary
Forces with responsibility for the "general direction of all naval forces engaged in large-scale landing operations." In that capacity he played key roles
in both the Torch and Husky operations in the Mediterranean.[6]

Ramsay received his appointment to command the naval forces for Neptune in October 1943, a full six weeks before Eisenhower got the job as
supreme commander, and he was already ensconced at Norfolk House
when Eisenhower arrived there in January 1944. He got along well with
Eisenhower, whom he considered "a sensible chap," and with his British
colleagues as well. He was one of very few who could call Montgomery
"Monty" and get away with it, and he thought Tedder both "intelligent and
sympathetic."[7]

In fact, all of the British service commanders for Neptune-Overlord got
along well, making up "a most cheerful party," in Montgomery's words.
Ramsay actually lived with Montgomery, since both men took rooms at St.
Paul's School, which had been turned over to the armed forces for the duration. That allowed them to swap ideas and build a sense of interservice
teamwork. Of course Montgomery always considered himself the captain
of the team. Ramsay occasionally took it upon himself to remind Monty
that he was not, in fact, the boss. On January 12 when Montgomery scheduled a meeting at St. Paul's prior to Eisenhower's arrival, the conference
room was set up with a U-shaped table and place cards put out to denote
the various participants. The placards for Ramsay and Leigh-Mallory read
"Naval C-in-C," and "Air C-in-C," while others read "U.S. Army," "U.S. Air
Force," and so on. But the place card for Montgomery at the head of the

NEPTUNE-OVERLORD COMMAND STRUCTURE

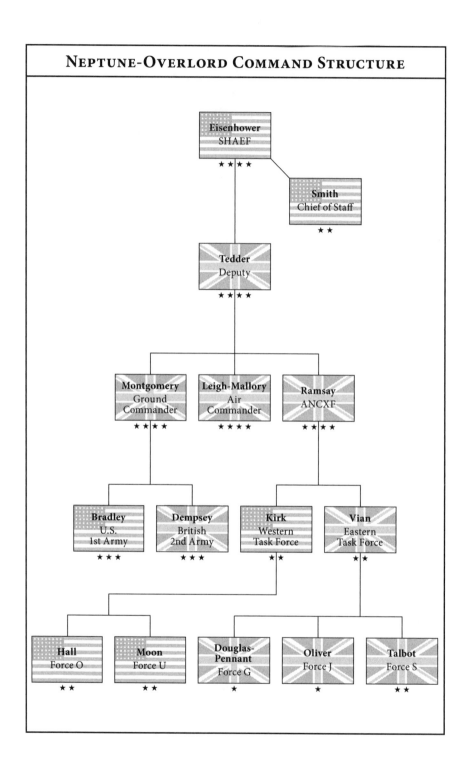

table read simply: "C-in-C." Arriving a bit early, Ramsay looked over these arrangements, turned to Leigh-Mallory, and remarked, "I say, L-M. What is this? There are three ruddy Cs-in-C in this set up." Before Montgomery arrived, they rearranged the placards and the chairs so that the three of them sat side by side at the head of the table. Montgomery said nothing about it at the time, though when Ramsay confronted him about it later, he insisted that the table arrangements had not been his doing, and he apologized for any perceived slight.[8]

ALMOST FROM THE START, there was general agreement among the "Cs-in-C" that the plan Morgan had crafted for Overlord simply would not do. Morgan had based all his plans on an initial assault force of three reinforced divisions, not because he believed three divisions were sufficient but because the Combined Chiefs had told him there would be only enough sealift for three divisions, and Morgan had planned accordingly. Now that the invasion was more than a vague ambition, it struck almost everyone that a three-division assault force was entirely too weak. After all, the Allies had employed seven divisions for the landings on Sicily. Even before he knew he was going to be appointed to command Overlord, Eisenhower had concluded that the invasion of France "was being made on too narrow a front and with insufficient land forces." Before he left for the United States on New Year's Eve, he sent for Montgomery, who was preparing to fly to London, and told him to do what he could to "increase the troop lift in OVERLORD."[9]

By the time Eisenhower arrived in London in mid-January, his trio of commanders had all agreed that the initial invasion force had to be increased from three divisions to five. Since this also necessitated adding two new landing beaches, it effectively doubled the length of the invasion front, which would now extend from the Cotentin Peninsula on the west to the Orne River on the east, a distance of nearly fifty miles. Five reinforced divisions would attack in the initial assault, with two more to follow that same afternoon. In his memoirs, Montgomery claimed credit for insisting on this increased commitment, though, in fact, the initiative had come from Eisenhower. Montgomery's principal contribution was to encourage an additional three-division paratroop drop—a "vertical envelopment," in military terminology—behind the beaches, two on the Cotentin Peninsula, behind the westernmost beach, and another near Caen, at the eastern end of the Bay of the Seine. That brought the initial assault on D-Day to a total of ten Allied divisions. The problem, of course, was sealift. All of Morgan's calculations for the naval requirements had been based on a three-division assault, and the number of landing ships, landing craft, escort vessels, and gunfire support ships detailed in the COSSAC plan were wholly inadequate for a five-division assault.

There was, however, a relatively easy solution at hand. The overall Neptune-Overlord plan confirmed at Quebec had included a diversionary Allied landing in southern France. At Tehran, this diversion received enthusiastic support from Stalin, who believed it would force the Germans to face threats from two directions at once and allow the Normandy "hammer" to slam down on the southern "anvil." As a result, the initial diversion was expanded into a two-division assault and code-named Anvil. The Americans had proposed the diversion in the first place as a way to rein in Churchill's ambitions for other, more tangential Mediterranean adventures, but then Stalin's support made it an integral part of the strategic plan. The difficulty was that while Anvil confronted the Germans with a potential two-front campaign in France, it also compelled the Allies to conduct two simultaneous landings, and that meant more landing craft and more support ships, including the essential LSTs. Once the SHAEF team determined on the necessity of a five-division initial assault in Normandy, it was evident that one way to resolve the problem of insufficient landing craft for Neptune was to cancel Anvil and transfer the necessary naval assets from the Mediterranean to England. All of Eisenhower's British service commanders, including his own chief of staff, Beetle Smith, found this a compelling, even obvious, solution.[10]

Eisenhower was loath to do it. In part, his opposition was a product of his own analysis. He believed that Anvil would greatly aid Overlord by forcing the Germans to disperse their military assets, and he was aware of how valuable it would be to have several seaports in southern France to funnel supplies into the country once the ground campaign took off. He was also sensitive to the political implications. Stalin had made it clear that he considered Overlord and Anvil to be a single inseparable operation. The cancellation of either might well have negative repercussions for the alliance. In addition to that, however, Eisenhower defended Anvil because he knew that Marshall supported it, and he was reluctant to oppose his mentor. Consequently, in his first report as SHAEF to the Combined Chiefs, rather than advocate the cancellation of Anvil, Eisenhower instead queried them about getting additional sealift in order to do both operations.

Ramsay was disappointed. He viewed Eisenhower's desire to conduct both Neptune and Anvil as an unwillingness to come to grips with reality. Though Ramsay had previously written his wife that Eisenhower was "a sensible chap," he now confided to his diary that, "Ike is waffling and seeking to have his cake and eat it [too]." In Ramsay's view, there was simply no alternative to canceling Anvil and moving the needed sealift vessels from the Mediterranean to England. Instead of risking both operations by dividing up the limited shipping for two assaults, it was far better to ensure success for one of them, and that one, obviously, was Neptune. To Ramsay, the solution was self-evident and unavoidable: "Anvil must be cancelled."[11]

This newest Anglo-American disagreement reflected the difference between British and American views of the relationship between logistics and strategy. To the British it was simply self-evident that operational planning had to adjust to the realities of logistical limits. Their view was that if there weren't enough ships for two landings, one landing had to go. The Americans, accustomed to greater matériel abundance, took the view that if there weren't enough ships for two landings, the obvious solution was to get more ships.

To do exactly that, Eisenhower sent a lengthy telegram to the Combined Chiefs in Washington detailing the sealift requirements for a five-division assault on Normandy. Specifically, he wanted 271 more landing craft, including forty-seven more of the scarce LSTs. Nor was that all, for in order to escort those landing ships and landing craft safely across the Channel, and to support the landings, Ike also wanted thirty-six more destroyers, five additional cruisers, and one or two battleships. Adding up all of the naval assets needed for the expanded cross-Channel operation, the new plan called for more than twelve hundred warships, four thousand landing craft, and fifteen hundred other vessels—nearly seven thousand vessels in all if one included the small Higgins boats and British LCAs. Eisenhower acknowledged that it might be difficult to obtain all those resources quickly, and expressed his willingness to postpone the attack for a month if necessary. "Rather...than risk failure with reduced forces on the earlier date," he wrote, "I would accept postponement of a month if I were assured of obtaining the strength required." Eisenhower concluded his lengthy cable by asking for "an immediate decision."[12]

He didn't get one. The arrival of his memo in Washington triggered another lengthy debate within the CCS, one that pitted not only Overlord against Anvil, but also Europe against the Pacific. That very month, U.S. naval forces seized targets in the Marshall Islands at Kwajalein, Majuro, and Eniwetok, operations that also required large numbers of landing craft. King was suspicious that the CCS were looking toward the Pacific as a kind of resource pool for Overlord, and he reminded the CCS that the original Neptune plan had called for the British to provide the naval support for the invasion of Europe. Rather than a prompt yes or no, therefore, Eisenhower received a rather curious reply that came not from the Combined Chiefs but from the American Joint Chiefs. It was neither an approval nor a rejection, but a list of questions that implied skepticism about Eisenhower's calculations. In particular, the JCS wanted to know "the basis you used in arriving at the additional resources required." How many landing craft did he have? What was their capacity? What was the justification for more warships? In effect, the JCS wanted Eisenhower to do the math and to show his work. The Supreme Allied Commander might have taken offense at the challenging tone of that reply—Montgomery and Ramsay certainly did. True to his character, however, Eisenhower patiently responded to all of the questions, though he reiterated that he needed an answer soon, for it was impossible to make any meaningful plans until he knew whether he was to have the needed sealift. "All plans and training considerations hang on the answer," he wrote.[13]

In Eisenhower's detailed item-by-item response, he listed the number of ships he had, along with their function and their capacity, and allowed the numbers to speak for themselves. Taking the number of serviceable LSTs already in England (173) and adding twenty-five more per month (the production numbers given him by the JCS) would give him 248 LSTs on D-Day. Because several of them had to be used as command ships and fighter-director ships, he would be left with almost exactly the 230 that Morgan had calculated would be necessary for a three-division assault, but clearly considerably short of what was needed for a five-division assault. "We have gone into this matter carefully," Eisenhower wrote, "and as far as we know every serviceable landing craft that is worth having is allocated to OVERLORD." And it wasn't enough.[14]

In receipt of Eisenhower's detailed cable, the JCS agreed to postpone D-Day from May 1 to May 31 in order to build up Allied sealift. They also agreed to preserve the Anvil landings. To make that possible, however, Ike would have to make do with forty-eight fewer LSTs and fifty-one fewer LCI(L)s than he had requested. Some of the shortfall could be made up by adding more transports and American attack cargo ships (AKAs), but it reduced the margin of safety to near zero. Eisenhower was betting on American productivity, writing Marshall that "one extra month of landing craft production, including LSTs, should help a lot." Ramsay thought otherwise. In his opinion, the decision to continue with Anvil was "outrageous." Even with an extra month to build more ships, he was convinced that the necessary sealift for Neptune "cannot be obtained without some of [the] Anvil lift."[15]

All of Eisenhower's hopes for Anvil were predicated on a swift and successful conclusion to the campaign in Italy so that ships from the Mediterranean could be used for both Neptune and Anvil. But as January turned to February, the Allied forces around Anzio remained virtually imprisoned in their precarious beachhead, sustained there by the very landing ships that Eisenhower wanted and needed. On February 5 the British Chiefs of Staff insisted that the stalemate in Italy made Anvil "neither possible nor desirable," and urged that any landing craft in the Mediterranean not needed to sustain the Anzio beachhead should be moved at once to England for Overlord. Less than a year before, the British had pushed hard for expanded Mediterranean operations and the Americans had insisted on the primacy of a cross-Channel attack. Now it was the other way around.[16]

Eisenhower continued to defend the Anvil operation, though privately he began to lose heart. "It looks like ANVIL is doomed," he wrote in a memorandum for his diary. "I hate this." Though it was the stalled campaign in Italy that intensified the crisis, the real culprit, in his view, was the war in the Pacific. That war was "absorbing far too much of our limited resources in landing craft," he wrote. Despite the initial strategic decision to fight Germany first—an agreement to which all parties had subscribed—"we are fighting two wars at once—which is wrong."[17]

For months, the several constituencies squabbled over the scarce landing craft, and especially the LSTs. Alan Brooke, who was in the middle of it, wrote in his diary that distributing LSTs was like "one of those awful jigsaw problems when it becomes very difficult to fit in all the right pieces." In fact, it was more like a slide puzzle: vessels shifted from one theater to another necessarily left a vacuum somewhere else. Eisenhower proposed bringing twenty LSTs and twenty-one LCI(L)s from the Mediterranean in exchange for AKAs equipped with boat davits for amphibious operations. The JCS offered a different solution: sending twenty-six LSTs in the Mediterranean to Britain for Overlord in exchange for twenty-six new LSTs from America originally scheduled for the Pacific. Sir Henry "Jumbo" Wilson, who was the Allied commander in Italy, wondered why the new LSTs from America couldn't go directly to Britain so he could keep the twenty-six he had. The answer was that the new LSTs wouldn't be ready until late May or early June, which was obviously too late for Overlord. But as far as Wilson was concerned, that was too late for him, too, for it would leave him without any LSTs for nearly three months. Brooke and the British Chiefs of Staff insisted that an attempt to execute Anvil would strip Wilson of his operational reserve and jeopardize the entire campaign in Italy. The Americans were not especially alarmed by such a prospect, since they were perfectly willing to close down the Italian campaign in exchange for opening a new front in southern France. But instead of seeing that as a rational choice, the British, and especially Brooke, saw it as evidence of American obtuseness. On Valentine's Day, Eisenhower wrote to Marshall that "the LST appears to be the one great question in the landing craft problem to which no really satisfactory answer now seems apparent."[18]

Throughout this period, the waters were muddied further by Churchill, whose behavior was even more eccentric than usual. The prime minister had suffered a physical collapse after the Tehran conference, and he spent a full month in Marrakech gathering the strength simply to fly back to Britain. Even after his return in mid-January, his behavior was erratic. He seemed to have trouble tracking a line of argument, and he became obsessed by tangential issues such as his old notion of conducting a landing on Sumatra. Brooke was nearly apoplectic in trying to keep him focused on the issues at hand. "I just cannot get him to face the true facts!" Brooke wrote in frustration. "It is a ghastly situation."[19]

Meanwhile, as February turned to March, there was still no resolution concerning Anvil. Ramsay found "the continual delay ... [v]ery unsatisfactory," and wrote in his diary, "This battle of the Chiefs of Staff is wearing everyone down." Tempers grew short. After yet one more cable from America in which the Joint Chiefs confirmed their support for Anvil, Brooke all but threw up his hands. "Marshall is quite hopeless," he wrote in his diary. "I have seldom seen a poorer strategist! He cannot see beyond the end of his nose." In Brooke's view, Ike was no better. "Eisenhower has got absolutely no strategical outlook and is really totally unfit for the post he holds," Brooke wrote, though he had to admit, "He makes up [for it], however, by the way he works for good cooperation between allies."[20]

By March, Eisenhower was wavering. Much as he wanted to support Marshall, he saw that clinging to Anvil not only was logistically dubious but was damaging the alliance. Moreover, he just could not make the numbers add up. If he counted every LST currently on hand and raised the "serviceability" ratio from 85 percent to an unrealistic 95 percent, then added all the ships currently in the construction pipeline, he would still be fifteen LSTs short on D-Day. In addition, there was the inevitable attrition consequent to all of the hazards of simply going to sea in wartime. By March, several LSTs had been sunk by the U-boats or damaged in training exercises; one of them (LST-228) broke her anchor chain in Horta, the chief port of the Azores, and crashed into the rocks. Such losses, unfortunate at any time, were especially worrisome given the circumstances. On March 20, Eisenhower gave up. He reluctantly confessed to Marshall that it was simply not possible to conduct Neptune-Overlord without drawing upon "the landing craft hitherto hypothecated for a possible ANVIL." To drive the point home in a particularly vivid way, he told Marshall that without the vessels from the Mediterranean, there would be enough sealift at Normandy for only "the first three tides." After that, "we will have no repeat no LSTs reaching the beaches after the morning of D plus 1 until the morning of D plus 4." Though smaller landing craft would be available, the Allied landing force would be effectively stranded on the Normandy beaches for three days without any LSTs available for either major reinforcement or, if necessary, evacuation. The addition of the twenty-six LSTs and forty LCI(L)s from the Mediterranean would give Eisenhower and Ramsay "some margin of safety as well as flexibility in the assault."[21]

In the end, the solution for Anvil was the same as for Overlord: it was postponed. Overlord had already been delayed for a month in order to allow time to build more landing craft. Now Anvil was delayed until midsummer so that all or most of the Mediterranean sealift capability could be used for Overlord, then redeployed back to the Mediterranean afterward for a future Anvil. Of course that meant there would be no simultaneous double pincer, but there seemed to be no other solution.

Brooke was relieved ("At last!" he wrote in his diary), though he was hardly forgiving. He remained angry at the Americans, and particularly at Marshall, for trying to manipulate the crisis. From his point of view, the American offer of twenty-six new LSTs for the Mediterranean had been an effort "to blackmail us into agreeing with them." After Anvil was postponed, the Americans withdrew the offer and sent the LSTs, as originally planned, to the Pacific. "History will never forgive them," Brooke wrote, "for bargaining equipment against strategy." Brooke's bitterness may have been exacerbated by his continuing row with Churchill, for his assessment of Marshall was hugely unfair. Marshall's support for Anvil had been genuine, and it was with real regret that he abandoned it, accepting at last the fact that sometimes logistics do trump strategy. Ramsay's reaction to the news that Anvil was put off was restrained but heartfelt: "Thank Goodness."[22]

The issue was settled at last, but it was now April 19, 1944, three months and two days after Eisenhower had arrived in London to assume the responsibilities of Supreme Commander. Even with the four weeks he had gained by the postponement of the Normandy landings, D-Day was only six weeks away.

OF COURSE THE ALLIES had not been completely idle during those three months. More than four hundred thousand additional American GIs had disembarked at English ports since January—two hundred thousand of them in April alone. More ships, too, had arrived, some of them LSTs with LCTs riding piggyback on their hulls, and all of them stuffed with supplies of every kind, from beans to bullets. With them came more than twenty-two thousand U.S. Navy officers and men, most of whom were billeted ashore, eight thousand of them at Plymouth, three thousand at Falmouth, and two thousand at Dartmouth. Training, and especially joint training, was accelerated. While Eisenhower worried over grand strategy and the viability of Anvil, his trio of commanders—Montgomery, Leigh-Mallory, and Ramsay—supervised programs designed to prepare their forces for the great invasion, though their dissimilar styles made for dramatically different approaches.

As the commander of an Army group, Montgomery supervised two armies: the American First Army under command of the homely but well-liked General Omar Bradley, and the British Second Army (which included the Canadian Third Division) under the tall and gaunt General Miles Dempsey. The various elements of their commands were spread out in more than a hundred camps all over England, and Montgomery spent most of his time traveling about the country visiting them, sometimes two or three a day. He did so using a special train (which he called the "Rapier") on which the abstemious Montgomery allowed no drinking or smoking.* At each stop, the local commander held a parade so that the troops could pass in review. Montgomery was convinced it was essential for him to see the troops, and even more important for them to see him. He once told

---

* Montgomery's intolerance of smoking led to some awkward moments when he and Eisenhower worked together. At one early meeting, Ike lit up a Camel, and Monty looked up and asked accusingly: "Who's smoking?" Eisenhower stubbed out the cigarette, and for the sake of Allied harmony he never did it again, but he quietly resented it.

George VI that his beret alone was worth three divisions because when soldiers saw it across a battlefield, they would cry, "There's Monty!" and become unbeatable. After almost every one of these formal parades, Montgomery made an effort to interact personally with the soldiers. Often he called for the men to "stand easy," then wandered among them, shaking hands and making chitchat. At some of the larger events, he would signal that they should break ranks and crowd up to the reviewing stand for an informal talk. If there wasn't a reviewing stand, he might climb on top of a jeep and wave the soldiers to gather round. His actions were based on a conviction that "stout hearts" (his words) were at least as important as technical training. Paraphrasing Napoleon, he asserted that, "It is 'the man' that counts, and not only the machine." What he meant was that winning battles was due as much to individual courage as to technical or mechanical superiority, but few who heard him were left in any doubt about who "the man" was. Significantly, Montgomery spent much of February sitting for a formal oil portrait.[23]

After visiting virtually every Army base on the island, Montgomery began giving speeches at factories and work centers. He told his listeners that "we were all one great army," and that "we must all rally to the task and finish off the war." He was well received everywhere he went, which contributed to his already healthy self-regard, but it was unclear to some whether he was preparing for a military operation or running for public office. In his postwar memoirs, he noted, "The people seemed to think I had some magic prescription for victory and that I had been sent to lead them to better things." Almost certainly he thought so, too. Both Churchill and Eisenhower worried that Montgomery was not focusing on the pressing need for realistic training, and Ramsay was particularly frustrated by his lengthy absences. "His knowledge of the technique of the operation is very small," Ramsay wrote in his diary. He worried that rather than make command decisions himself, Montgomery left almost everything to his staff. "He does *no* work at all," Ramsay wrote in disgust.[24]

For his part, Ramsay established his headquarters at Southwick House, a few miles inland from Portsmouth. A large, impressive manor house with a colonnaded front, it had been turned over to the Royal Navy as a School of

Navigation to replace the one that had been bombed out in Portsmouth, and as such, it bore the name HMS *Dryad*, though it certainly never went to sea. Once an elegant private estate, the grounds were marred now by hundreds of the ubiquitous Nissen huts. A giant map of the English Channel was installed on one wall of the main house showing all the ports in southern England where Allied troops were congregated, as well as the target beaches in Normandy. Tiny wooden ship icons could be moved about on the map to show the location, both current and intended, of Allied vessels.

One of Ramsay's first decisions after moving into Southwick House was to request the appointment of Admiral Sir Philip Vian as his deputy commander. It was a natural selection for a number of reasons, including the fact that Ramsay and Vian were close friends. Ramsay had spent the New Year's holiday at Vian's house in Hampshire, where they had played golf despite the weather and spent the evenings playing card games with Vian's children.[25] In addition to their personal friendship, Vian was a natural choice because, like Montgomery, he was something of a national hero in Britain. Early in the war, he had pursued a German supply ship, the *Altmark*, into then-neutral Norwegian waters in order to rescue three hundred British merchant seamen being held on board as prisoners, an act for which he was awarded the Distinguished Service Order (DSO). Two years later in the Mediterranean, Vian won a knighthood after a series of desperate actions in defense of convoys fighting their way from Egypt to the besieged island of Malta, south of Sicily.*

Vian had also commanded what was labeled "Force V" during the Husky landings in Sicily and the Avalanche landings near Salerno, in which role he had worked closely with Ramsay. After that, Churchill decided to name him to succeed Louis Mountbatten as head of amphibious forces. When Vian reported to the Admiralty in 1943, however, he learned that Ramsay had requested him as his deputy for the cross-Channel invasion, and that

---

* Fans of naval literature who are familiar with C. S. Forester's classic novel *The Ship* may be aware that it is based on the Second Battle of Sirte, fought on March 22, 1942, in which Vian fought off several attacks from a superior Italian surface force and German air forces.

put Vian in an awkward position. To him, being second in command of Neptune was a far more desirable billet than being the administrative head of amphibious operations. He was therefore concerned when Churchill invited him to dinner, unsure of what he would say if the prime minister offered him Mountbatten's job. As usual at Chequers, dinner was quite late, and the guests didn't sit down to eat until nearly 11:00 p.m. The party broke up at 2:30 in the morning without any job offer being extended, and Vian thought he was off the hook. Apparently the dinner had been an audition, however, because Churchill sent for him at eight the next morning, receiving him in his bed, and made the expected offer. Vian swallowed hard and told the prime minister that he would prefer the job with Ramsay, "which was operational and a fighting one." Churchill did not press the issue. He may have been pleased that a veteran Royal Navy officer preferred a fighting command to administration, and perhaps wished that he could have one, too.[26]

Vian's responsibilities under Ramsay were redefined after the cross-Channel operation was expanded from three divisions to five, for that meant there would be five landing beaches as well, too many for a single naval task force to cover. Ramsay's command was divided in half: a Western Task Force responsible for the two American beaches (initially code-named Oboe and Uncle), and an Eastern Task Force for the two British beaches (Sword and Gold) and the Canadian beach (Juno). In that new arrangement, it seemed only logical that Vian should assume command of the Eastern (British) Task Force, and he jumped at the opportunity. Instead of being second in command of the whole operation, he would be first in command of half of it.[27]

The new assignment seemed a natural for Vian, a fighting admiral with an enviable war record. Curiously, however, administering the various elements of a disparate command did not come naturally to him. Impetuous as he was in fending off Italian battleships, he seemed ill at ease administering a force that consisted of hundreds of LCMs, LCTs, LCI(L)s, and LSTs, as well as minesweepers, destroyers, and cruisers. He often referred issues that he might have handled himself up the chain to Ramsay's office, and soon enough Ramsay's staff began to grouse about it. After a long meeting with Vian on March 3, Ramsay wrote in his diary that his Eastern Task Force commander "strikes me as being a little helpless." "In fact," he wrote, "I feel that I am organizing his part of the show as well as my own."[28]

That was certainly not the case with the officer assigned to command the Western (American) Task Force, Rear Admiral Alan G. Kirk. As with Vian, Ramsay also enjoyed a friendly relationship with Kirk, one that had begun two years before when Kirk had been the American naval attaché during Ramsay's command tenure at Dover. They, too, had been regular golf partners, and knew each other as "Alan" and "Bertie." Like Vian, Kirk had played an active role in the landings in Sicily, after which, at the request of Admiral King, he had flown out to the Pacific to discuss amphibious operations with members of Chester Nimitz's staff. In the fall of 1943, however, he was back in England and assigned to Ramsay's staff. Upon his return, Kirk called Ramsay up and invited him to have lunch. Ramsay's cool refusal suggested to Kirk that he had made a gaffe. Since their golfing days, Ramsay had gained two more stars and was now vastly Kirk's superior. To make amends, Kirk hurried over to Ramsay's headquarters to report to him formally and officially.[29]

Just as Vian had assumed that he would be Ramsay's deputy, Kirk's initial assumption was that he would be Ramsay's chief of staff. But with Ramsay's command now split, Kirk was the logical person to take over the Western (American) Task Force. For Kirk, this was great news, for, like Vian, he much preferred a fighting billet to administrative duties. Some weeks before, he had reported to the British First Sea Lord, Admiral Andrew Cunningham, whom he had known for years, and Cunningham had teased him by saying that as Ramsay's chief of staff, he was likely to miss out on most of the action. During the invasion, Cunningham told him, "you'll be with Admiral Ramsay in a big bomb shelter down the south coast of England."

"Oh no," Kirk replied. "I don't expect to be there at all. I expect to be on my flagship off the coast of Normandy."

His riposte was as much bravado and bantering as genuine expectation, but as it happened, he was correct. His appointment to command the Western Task Force meant that he would be an active, indeed central, player in the invasion.[30]

Unlike Vian, Kirk settled into the management of his diverse and far-flung naval command with ease and authority—perhaps with a bit too much authority, in Ramsay's opinion. As disappointed as Ramsay was with Vian's hesitancy to grasp the reins of command, he soon became alarmed at Kirk's tendency to overstep his bounds. Mostly this was a product of the very different leadership protocols in the Royal Navy and the United States Navy. As Kirk put it, "Our system of command was to tell the fellow what you wanted him to do and why you wanted him to do it," and then to leave it up to the on-scene commander to "decide for himself *how* he's going to do it." Ramsay, however, did not want his subordinates running off willy-nilly to do their own thing, especially during the decisive campaign of the war. Kirk noted disapprovingly that "all the planning was done in Norfolk House by Admiral Ramsay and his staff in the minutest detail." Written orders arrived from London in thick packets, and if any change needed to be made, it all had to be referred back up the chain of command to be reconsidered. If the change was approved, another thick folder of orders was sure to follow.* Kirk and his staff instinctively rebelled at these circumstances, and occasionally they complained about it. When they did, Ramsay was unmoved. Kirk noted that whenever his staff suggested that "we could do it better this way or that way," the result was a "tough little comment" from headquarters putting them in their place.[31]

Despite this tension, Ramsay sought to pay lip service, at least, to the idea of a fully integrated naval command. From the very start, one of Eisenhower's guiding principles had been the complete integration of Anglo-American forces. It was in deference to that command guidance that Ramsay wrote to Kirk early in their relationship: "The operations we are planning together call for a degree of cooperation between our Navies which had hitherto never even been contemplated." The idea, Ramsay

* When Ramsay issued the official Neptune operational order on April 10, it was eleven hundred pages long and nearly four inches thick. All orders connected with Neptune and Overlord were stamped "BIGOT" in large red letters, which was the equivalent of "Top Secret." It derived from the fact that back in 1942, the secret orders for the Torch invasion had been stamped "To Gibraltar" or simply "To Gib." "BIGOT" was "To Gib" spelled backward. Those privy to top-secret information were said to be "bigoted."

wrote, was to create the kind of partnership in which it would possible to conclude that "there existed not two Navies but one nation." In that spirit, each of Ramsay's task force commanders was in charge of all the ships, of whatever nationality (including French, Dutch, and Norwegian), within their respective area.[32]

All this left Admiral Harold Stark somewhat out in the cold. The former U.S. chief of naval operations knew that he had been packed off to England in the first place to make room for Ernie King to assume a dual role as both CNO and COMINCH, and also because the incubus of Pearl Harbor still hung about him like an aura. Then, too, Roosevelt may have decided that Stark was simply not tough enough to be wartime CNO. Officially, at least, Stark was Commander in Chief, U.S. Naval Forces, Europe, and recently he had been endowed with another title: Commander, Twelfth Fleet. Those titles meant little, however, since Ramsay and his task force commanders absorbed literally every ship and landing craft they could get their hands on. As a result, the Twelfth Fleet existed mainly as an abstraction, and it became Stark's main job to ensure that Ramsay had the tools and the manpower he needed to be successful. In that mission, Stark got invaluable support from Navy Captain (later Rear Admiral) Howard A. Flanigan, a 1910 Naval Academy graduate and World War I veteran who had been recalled to active service after the United States entered the war. He proved an imaginative and resourceful administrator, who demonstrated an uncanny ability to fulfill (if perhaps illicitly) even the most exotic matériel requests.[33]

QUITE APART FROM THESE COMPLICATIONS OF COMMAND, the issue that continued to dominate Allied planning was whether there would be enough ships available to execute the crossing at all. The problem of insufficient sealift had been partially resolved with the decisions to postpone the Normandy landing until June—it was now officially scheduled for June 5—and to postpone Anvil until the late summer. It also helped that April and May were the most robust months yet for LST construction: American shipyards turned out fifty of them in April, and an astonishing eighty-two in May. Still unresolved, however, was the shortage of warships to escort the landing vessels across the Channel and provide gunfire support for the landing. As early as January 21, Ramsay had provided Eisenhower with specifics about the naval implications of a five-division assault, and Ike had included those estimates in his request to the JCS. Though the Joint Chiefs had agreed to postpone the assault and to accelerate LST production, they had not responded to the request for more combatant ships.[34]

A factor complicating Eisenhower's request was that King and the U.S. Navy were in the midst of choreographing a major offensive in the Pacific that was scheduled to take place only a few days after the D-Day landings. A massive American strike force of seven aircraft carriers, eight light carriers, and seven fast battleships, plus scores of cruisers and destroyers as well as transports and landing ships—more than seven hundred ships altogether—was scheduled to strike Saipan in the Marianas on June 15. The Allies' ability to launch two major seaborne offensives on opposite sides of the globe less than two weeks apart was testimony to the remarkable productivity of American industry, but it was also evidence that the Germany-first strategy had been all but abandoned.

One reason King and the Americans felt they could undertake the Saipan offensive was that according to the original agreement set down at Quebec and confirmed at Cairo, the escort and combat vessels for Neptune would be provided primarily by the Royal Navy "with some augmentation from the United States." Alas, with the expansion from three to five divisions on five different beaches, and the creation of separate British and American task forces, the warship requirements for Neptune now exceeded the Royal Navy's resources. The First Sea Lord, Admiral Cunningham, was able to add only the cruiser *Sheffield*, which had a bent propeller shaft, and the battleship *Nelson*, which was scheduled to go into the yards at Philadelphia in May for modernization. In March, Ramsay sat down with his staff to work out the numbers. After studying the escort and bombardment schedules, he concluded that he needed a minimum of one additional battleship, seven more cruisers, and fourteen destroyers. That raised his total warship requirement to six battleships, twenty-five cruisers, and no fewer than fifty-six destroyers. He acknowledged that this was "a huge force," and that "the R.N. can't possibly meet this bill." Regardless of earlier agreements, he knew the additional ships would have to come from the United States Navy, which in his view was "meet, right and proper."[35]

Eisenhower backed him up. Indeed, if anything he raised the ante. "If the decision is made to send U.S. naval vessels," he wrote to Marshall, "three or four battleships" would be better than "a corresponding number of cruisers." Ike found the thought of those big 14-inch shells smashing into German pillboxes and artillery positions "very comforting." Eisenhower's request triggered a visit from King's deputy chief of staff, Rear Admiral Charles M. Cooke Jr., called "Savvy" Cooke since his Naval Academy days in tribute to his academic brilliance. Cooke met first with Kirk and his subordinates, including Rear Admiral John Lesslie Hall Jr., who at this point served as Kirk's deputy and was in charge of training. Kirk had a reputation for straight talk, but it was Hall who was blunt to the point of insubordination. He told Cooke he did not understand "how in the world" King could deny adequate gunfire support to so important an operation as Neptune. It was "ridiculous," Hall asserted, to send squadron after squadron of destroyers across the Atlantic on convoy duty and not keep even one of them in British waters for "the most important landing in the history of the United States." Cooke was taken aback, and told Hall, "You have no right to talk that way." Hall was not intimidated. "Who in God's world has a better right to talk that way than I have?" he asked truculently. In the end, Hall suffered no consequences for his outburst, and King eventually ordered three older battleships, two more cruisers, and twenty more destroyers from the U.S. Navy to join the Neptune force, bringing the total number of U.S. destroyers to thirty-four.[36]

At the same time, however, King also sent Rear Admiral Bernhard Bieri to England with orders to join Ramsay's staff. Apparently King's view was that if Ramsay was going to have some U.S. Navy ships, he was also going to have a U.S. Navy man on his staff. Ramsay bristled at that, since he assumed, correctly, that he alone had the authority to appoint the members of his staff. Even Eisenhower thought it presumptive, if not in fact offensive. Beetle Smith told Bieri that if Ramsay wanted to send him home, he was within his rights. Instead, Ramsay accepted Bieri, though he also made sure that he understood he worked for ANCXF and not for King. Ramsay put Bieri to work on a committee doing postwar planning.[37]

There were other shortages besides shipping. On April 17, Stark sent King a long cable arguing that "despite every effort to spread all available personnel in Ukay [U.K.] just as far as they will go," he was concerned about "important deficits" that threatened the viability of the cross-Channel movement. Among the deficiencies: there were not enough officers for the LCTs, not enough medical personnel to treat the expected casualties, too few intelligence officers and communications personnel, and not enough tugs. Most of these problems were relatively minor and fixable, but they could not be ignored.[38]

While Ramsay, Stark, and King sparred over available warships and shortfalls in other areas, the training never stopped, especially amphibious training. A hundred years before, the French military theorist Antoine-Henri Jomini had declared that amphibious operations were "among the most difficult in war," an adage that had become a mantra in the military academies and war colleges of Western nations. Certainly the Allies had seen ample evidence of Jomini's cautionary dictum, from Dieppe to Torch to Tarawa. With so much riding on the outcome of this particular amphibious operation, it was essential that the soldiers of Montgomery's 21st Army Group and the sailors of Ramsay's naval command develop a clear and practiced protocol in the few weeks left before they crossed the Channel. Training—training that was as realistic as it was possible to make it—was the next hurdle.

CHAPTER 9

DUCK, FOX, BEAVER, TIGER

D URING 1943, most of the training received by those million and a half soldiers spread out in a hundred or more camps all across southern England had consisted primarily of lengthy route marches. Due mainly to the shortage of landing ships and landing craft, few of them had ever participated in an amphibious landing or even been on board an amphibious ship. One Army officer at the American training base at Appledore on Devon's north coast did the best he could with what he had. He had logs laid out on the practice beach in the shape of a Higgins boat and ordered his men to huddle together inside the rectangular outline. Then, on his signal, they ran out the landward end to take positions farther up the beach. While perhaps better than nothing at all, it was hardly an effective substitute for an actual landing.

Equally important was the training needed by the Navy and Coast Guard officers and men on the thousands of vessels that would carry these soldiers to the beaches. Those LSTs transferred from the Mediterranean after Anvil was postponed did have experienced crews, but on their arrival in England, those ships were augmented by hundreds of new recruits, most of them right out of boot camp. And the only seagoing experience of the men on the newest LSTs arriving from America was their journey across the Atlantic. They were, as one officer put it, "green as corn."[1]

As for the smaller LCTs, as Betty Stark had pointed out to King, they had only one commissioned officer each, most of them young ensigns with just a few months' service. Indeed, they did not even have the experience of having crossed the Atlantic under way, since their ships had been carried as deck cargo on the larger LSTs. Given that, it seemed desirable to Stark to add a second officer to each vessel. It was not clear how adding one more brand-new and inexperienced ensign to each LCT would significantly improve its efficiency, but it seemed a good idea at the time. To fill that perceived need, the officer training program back in the States was cut short. College graduates who had been enrolled in the Navy's V-7 officer training program for only a few weeks suddenly got orders to pack their sea bags and report to New York for embarkation.[2]

Arriving in Glasgow, they took trains south to one or another Channel port. Ninety-two of them were dispatched to Dartmouth, where they encountered the rather awesome spectacle of nearly a hundred LCTs lined up hull to hull across the Dart River. The ninety-two new arrivals became instant executive officers, virtually all of them serving under a captain who was in many cases only a few months their senior. It was rumored among the new execs that one of the LCT skippers, an ensign named Clifford Underwood, was actually thirty years old and married![3]

The British, too, worried about having enough junior officers to command the hundreds of smaller amphibious ships. To address that need, they opened a special naval cadet school at Lochaiort in Scotland where the officer candidates focused almost entirely on amphibious issues. They did not even get training in deep-sea navigation. Some veteran Royal Navy officers muttered that the graduates should not have commissions at all if they could not handle a ship on the high seas, though in the end most acknowledged that it was, as one put it, "a matter of necessity rather than choice.[4]

British and American LCTs were grouped into flotillas of a dozen vessels each, and the flotilla commanders were young, too, most of them lieutenants in their mid- to late twenties. Their first task was to ensure that the LCTs were operationally ready. In addition to such cosmetic things as providing a fresh coat of paint, they had to ensure that engines and the guns actually worked. Once the vessels were certified as functional, the flotilla commanders began taking them out into the Channel, where the new skippers (and their even newer execs) learned how to respond to flag and light signals so they could maintain their positions in a formation and turn simultaneously from a column ahead into a line abreast. They maneuvered first in groups of eight to twelve, then twenty to thirty, and finally more than a hundred. They learned how to land their craft on a beach and successfully retract. And they conducted endless man-overboard drills, fire drills, and first-aid drills.[5]

Beginning early in 1944, British and American landing craft began to conduct small-scale rehearsals of amphibious landings with their army counterparts. In Channel ports from Fowey in Cornwall to Salcombe in Devon and Poole in Dorset, American LCT skippers worked closely with the elements of the 1st and 29th U.S. Infantry divisions that made up part of Major General Leonard Gerow's V Corps and the 4th division that was part of J. Lawton Collins's VII Corps. Farther east, up the England Channel, Royal Navy LCTs conducted exercises from the Solent to the Thames estuary with units of Dempsey's British Second Army, which included the Canadian Third Division.

For the Americans, the center of much of this activity was the Amphibious Training School at Slapton Sands, only a few miles west of Dartmouth. In at least one respect, Slapton Sands was a misnomer, for there was no sand there at all. Like the American target beaches across the Channel (now renamed Omaha and Utah), the beach at Slapton was composed of shingle: billions of small wave-polished black and gray pebbles. The site had other physical characteristics that were similar to Omaha Beach and especially Utah Beach. Not only did the rolling countryside of South Devon resemble the *bocage* country of Normandy, but behind the beach at Slapton Sands was a brackish marshy inlet called Slapton Ley. Since there was a similar body of marshland behind Utah Beach, the landings at Slapton would allow the would-be invaders to rehearse bridging this obstacle.[6]

Beginning in the midwinter chill of January 1944, the practice landings at Slapton Sands and elsewhere continued through February and March and into April as the days gradually lengthened and the Channel waters became slightly less frigid. Most of the smaller exercises did not involve the big LSTs, and the smaller LCTs did much of the work. A crew member on LCT-276 recalled the exercises fondly: "We sailed into Devon and Cornwall County seaside cities and towns where [the soldiers] were stationed. Both of the counties were renowned for their beauty, fine hotels, and quaint pubs. In between the practices, there was enough time to be able to enjoy them." Ninety miles to the north on the Bristol Channel, the official "Boat Operational Schedule" for the Appledore Training Center showed similar activity, and still more exercises took place even farther north in the Firth of Clyde in Scotland, though uncertain weather and chilly seas often wreaked havoc with the schedule. In all of these exercises, the soldiers and sailors learned the protocols of each other's service, and soon enough the practice sessions became routine, or as routine as inherently dangerous amphibious landings could be. "We loaded and unloaded various troops and equipment time after time," one sailor recalled. "We were never sure if each practice might be the real thing."[7]

The Allied planners who organized these training sessions gradually raised the stakes. The exercises became larger and more realistic until they began to approximate the feel of a live-fire assault. The planners sowed mines in the waters leading to the beach so that the minesweepers could sweep them up, and they designated targets onshore as enemy bunkers or gun emplacements so that the destroyers could practice taking them out with naval gunfire. One gunner recalled being assigned the window on the upper left side of a specific house as his target. In many of the exercises, the first troops ashore belonged to the Special Engineer Brigades, whose job it would be to disarm or destroy the mines. The infantry came next, splashing ashore through the frigid Channel surf and charging inland to set up a defensive perimeter. LCTs and the smaller Mike boats brought ashore the trucks, tanks, and jeeps needed to exploit the landing. With live ammunition passing over their heads from the destroyers offshore, and mines exploding both offshore and on the beach, it looked and felt a lot like real war.

Dangerous as it was, Allied officers were convinced that occasional casualties were the price of readiness, and that it would save lives in the end.[8]

ALTHOUGH THE LSTS had been specifically designed to run up onto the sand and discharge their cargoes directly onto the beach, that was not advisable or even possible during the initial assault phase, when enemy artillery dominated the landing site. German guns ashore might smash up so many of the scarce LSTs that it would become impossible for the Allies to sustain the flow of essential reinforcements and equipment. Only after the big guns were captured or suppressed would it be safe to bring the LSTs ashore. Until then, smaller vessels such as the LCTs would have to shuttle the men and equipment from the LSTs to the beach.

That was no simple matter. Since the LSTs remained stationary, the young skippers of the LCTs had to maneuver into position. The anchored LST would have its bow doors open and its ramp partially deployed, hovering ten or a dozen feet above the sea, and the LCT skipper had to maneuver underneath that heavy ramp while his own vessel was heaving and rolling with the Channel swells. Once the LCT was positioned perpendicularly across the bow of the LST, the ramp was lowered until it rested on the thwart of the smaller vessel. With the ramp in place and secured, vehicles could then be driven under their own power from the tank deck of the LST across what was now a narrow metal bridge into the exposed deck of the LCT. The weight of each truck or tank not only caused the LCT to settle lower in the water, it also acted to push it away from the LST and put a tremendous strain on the lines holding the ships together.[9]

Sometimes LCTs took on loads further offshore from the even larger Attack Transports (APA), and this, too, was no picnic. The big transports had three mooring zones alongside where an LCT could tie up, and as the LCT approached, a coordinator on the transport assigned it a specific zone. To maneuver into place, the LCT skipper used a speaking tube to give helm orders to the quartermaster in the chart house one level below him while simultaneously giving orders to the engine room. Mooring at the bow or the stern of an APA was difficult enough, but mooring amidships was a nightmare, especially if there were already other LCTs moored ahead and astern. Often, an LCT commander would try to "crab" his vessel into the narrow space by coming alongside fairly fast (to ensure that the rudders would take hold), then backing down on all three screws at once while holding the helm hard over, hoping to slide into place. If he misjudged the moment, it could result in a collision, sometimes with significant damage. Another approach was to make what the LCT skippers called a "Chinese landing," which meant coming alongside stern first and backing into the space. It was much like parallel-parking a car—if the car was 120 feet long, weighed 286 tons, and had no brakes.[10]

Even when the LCT was safely moored alongside, the danger was not past. Since the LCT was coming to collect a cargo, it was empty and "tossed up and down like a cork," as one skipper put it. The mooring lines had to be loose enough to accommodate this movement but tight enough to keep the LCT alongside. Fenders were thrown over the side to minimize damage as the two vessels thumped violently together. Then the real work began: cranes on the big transport ship would lower the jeeps, trucks, and other cargo over the side of the transport down into the empty LCT. With the LCT rising and plunging, choosing the right moment to unshackle a two-and-a-half-ton truck was a touchy and even dangerous task. Eventually the cargo shift would be complete, and the LCT could unmoor and head for the beach.[11]

An alternative to using LCTs to do this was to employ what was called a "rhino ferry," which was essentially a self-propelled raft made up of giant pontoons constructed out of sheet metal. A rhino ferry could hardly be called a vessel, for it had no hold, no cabin, and no working parts at all other than two outboard motors that allowed it to move independently at about two or three knots. They were manned by men of the Construction Battalion, called CBs or Seabees. Despite their minimalist design, the rhino ferries proved so effective in rehearsals that on D-Day many of the LSTs towed a rhino ferry behind them during the Channel crossing.[12]

The worker bees of the landing exercises were the little Higgins boats (American) and LCAs (British). They were used not only to carry troops and light vehicles (mostly jeeps) to the shore but also for a wide variety of mundane tasks: carrying messages from ship to ship during periods of radio silence, ferrying officers between ship and shore, conducting rescue work, picking up supplies, and making mail runs. They were essentially the jeeps of the naval war.

Though the German air Blitz of English cities had ended, occasional bombing raids punctuated the Allied training schedule and added another level of wartime realism. Often the German planes came over at night, and the gunners on the hundreds of Allied ships opened fire, sending thousands of rounds of red tracer fire into the dark sky. On mornings after such raids, many of the ships in the harbor found their decks littered with shell fragments, most of it spent ordnance that had fallen back to earth. During these raids, the Germans frequently dropped mines in the harbor, which kept Allied minesweepers busy. Minesweeping was a noisy activity, as explosions took place all across the harbor. The concussions were so great that men on ships half a mile away could feel them in their feet. Even so, the sweepers occasionally missed one or two. Watching from the deck of his LST one day, Donald W. Nutley observed a Higgins boat making a mail run across Plymouth Harbor when it hit a mine and exploded. The coxswain was hurled off the boat like so much wreckage. Nutley watched as the man flew "high into the air, end over end, and landed flat out on the deck of an LCT with a loud thud." Naturally, he assumed the man had been killed. Then, "all of a sudden, he got up, staggered around like a drunk," and walked away.[13]

THE COMMAND TEAM in charge of training included not only Ramsay, Vian, and Kirk but also two U.S. Navy rear admirals, John Wilkes and John "Jimmy" Lesslie Hall Jr. Wilkes's job was largely administrative, since he was responsible for the landing craft themselves as well as the practice facilities and the enormous supply depot at Exeter. In this capacity, he bore the delightful acronym of COMLANDCRAB. While Wilkes supervised the craft themselves, Hall's job was to schedule and organize the exercises, which he did from an office in the British Naval Academy at Dartmouth. Hall's job soon underwent a dramatic change, however. The expansion of the initial landing force to five divisions not only led to the division of Ramsay's command into Eastern and Western Task Forces under Vian and Kirk, it also caused those task forces to be subdivided into task groups, one for each beach. Three of them were under Vian's supervision: Force S for Sword Beach, Force J for Juno Beach, and Force G for Gold Beach. The other two, under Kirk's command, were Force U for Utah Beach and Force O for Omaha Beach. And each of them got a separate commander.

The men selected to command the two American task groups were very different from each other. Jimmy Hall gave up his training command to take over Force O, which would carry Leonard Gerow's V Corps to Omaha Beach. Like most career officers, Hall was happy to trade an administrative post for an active afloat command. His singular characteristic, both as a personality and as an officer, was a hearty self-confidence. On his Naval Academy yearbook page, Hall's classmates described him as "a big, blonde, good-natured Virginian" with a "deep bass voice" who was "a friend to everyone." Like Eisenhower, he was older than most of his classmates because prior to attending the Naval Academy, he had spent three years at William and Mary College, where his father was an English professor famous in academic circles for his translation of *Beowulf*. A standout athlete at William and Mary, Hall had starred in football, basketball, and baseball. This was before the NCAA had rules limiting the eligibility of athletes, and Hall played all three of those sports for four more years at Navy, later recalling, "My last year at the Academy, I played every second of the Army football game, every second of every basketball game, and every inning of every baseball game."* Upon his graduation in 1913, he was awarded the sword presented to the academy's best all-around athlete. His size, his age, and his athletic prowess all contributed to an ebullient self-confidence.[14]

Though Hall spent most of his naval career as a battleship-destroyer man, he had as much or more experience in amphibious operations as anyone in the theater. He had been Hewitt's chief of staff during the Torch landings and had organized the U.S. Amphibious Force for the invasions of

---

* When Hall suited up for the baseball game against Army in 1913, the left fielder on the opposing team was Omar Bradley. (Army won the game 2–1.) Because of that shared history, the two-star admiral felt no qualms calling the three-star general "Brad" when they met thirty years later to plan the rehearsals for D-Day. The 1914 Army baseball team, on which Bradley also played, subsequently became famous for the fact that every member of the starting nine became a general.

both Sicily and Italy. When he arrived in England, he impressed Ramsay as "a fine type of seaman, bluff and obstinate, & a fine leader." That bluff obstinacy occasionally got him into trouble, such as when he told Savvy Cooke that "it was ridiculous" for King and the JCS to refuse to supply the cross-Channel force with the warships that were needed. He occasionally saw fit to lecture Army generals as well. After assuming his new job as Force O commander and studying the numbers carefully, he went personally to Montgomery's headquarters to explain to him that the shipping crisis might well mean a reduction in the size of the initial cross-Channel lift. When he got there, Montgomery was absent, off on yet another speaking trip, so Hall explained the situation to Monty's chief of staff, Brigadier General Francis "Freddy" Guingand. Guingand heard him out and then replied, "General Montgomery would not accept a reduction of that nature." Hall made it clear that he wasn't there to get Montgomery's approval, and that it was not a matter of what Montgomery would "accept." It was a matter of what was possible. "General, apparently you misunderstand the job I've been assigned," Hall told Guingand. "I'm down here to tell you how you would do it if you had to accept." It is probably just as well that Montgomery was not there.[15]

The other American naval command was Force U, for Utah Beach. That job might have gone to Wilkes, and in fact, Kirk wrote to King to "strongly recommend" Wilkes for the post because of his experience in Sicily and his "general familiarity with the plan." King had other ideas. Wilkes remained ashore as the administrator of landing craft, and the command of Force U went instead to Rear Admiral Don P. Moon, who had served as King's operational plans officer and had been slotted to command a naval task force for Anvil. Now that Anvil was postponed, King sent Moon to England to command Force U. Ramsay expressed satisfaction with Moon when he arrived in March, noting in his diary that Moon was "a fine type of U.S. officer. Efficient & alert. He should do well." Moon, however, was very different from Hall. If bluff self-confidence was Hall's principal characteristic, Moon's was a ferocious work ethic, the product of a fierce determination "to always do one's best." Even as a midshipman, what Moon's classmates remembered most about him was his "infinite capacity for hard work." Instead of the easy dominance that had characterized Hall's participation in sports, Moon earned a spot on the academy fencing team only by "dogged persistence," which allowed him to become "a very tolerable *sabreur*." Less flatteringly, Moon's classmates also described him as "persistent and conservative, without the curse of imagination, or disturbing outburst of animal spirits." In the language of the academy, he was a grind.[16]

Moon's work ethic was an inherent characteristic, but it was very likely exacerbated by both experience and circumstance. Back in July 1942, Moon had commanded the escort for convoy PQ-17, bound for Russia around the North Cape. It had progressed as far as the Barents Sea, north of Norway, when the British Admiralty, having misread a code intercept, concluded that a large German surface force was in the area and ordered the convoy to scatter. That was a dreadful mistake, for it made the ships easy pickings for the U-boats and aircraft, and in the end, twenty-three of the thirty-seven merchant ships in the convoy were lost. It was hardly Moon's fault, but the memory of it may have contributed to his determination to ensure that he did not overlook any detail. Then, too, his subsequent assignment in Washington, working directly for the demanding and punctilious Ernest King, could make anyone detail oriented.

Another factor contributing to Moon's regimen of hard work was his late appointment to the command of Force U. Having initially been sent to the Mediterranean, he arrived in England only in March. Whereas both Kirk and Hall had six months or more in the theater, Moon had less than three months to prepare for the invasion. Among other things, that meant that he never had a chance to compile a compatible staff, which contributed to his tendency to try to do too much himself. Thus as a result of character, experience, and circumstance, Moon became obsessed with work in the spring of 1944. He worked until well past midnight nearly every day, then was up and back at it again at four the next morning. Hall told him that "he was trying to do too much himself" and that "he would have to delegate more authority," but Moon continued to burn the candle at both ends.[17]

Even the Army officers who worked with Moon noted his obsessive attention to detail. Collins, the commander of the VII Corps, became concerned about Moon's tendency "to do too much himself instead of giving responsibilities to his staff." He tried to get Moon interested in a walk or a game of tennis, but Moon always begged off, pleading that he was too busy. Collins's repeated invitations, however, may have been the impetus for Moon's order one day that everyone on the staff should go out and play a baseball game, though he himself did not play.[18]

Both Hall and Moon accelerated the training exercises for their commands. In addition to the innumerable small exercises, there were also several major rehearsals, most of them endowed with the name of some water-loving and presumably amphibious creature. Hall's Force O participated in three large-scale rehearsals in January code-named Duck I, II, and III. They were followed by Exercise Fox, and then a series of smaller operations called Muskrat, Otter, and Mink. Gerow, the V Corps commander, was not happy with the early exercises. He thought the embarkation had taken too long, the supplies had been late in coming ashore, the troops had carried too much gear, and the men seemed confused about what to do. He wondered aloud whether in an actual landing any of them would have gotten off the beach alive.[19]

Hoping for a better show, Ramsay, Kirk, and Gerow all boarded Hall's command ship, USS *Ancon*, on March 10 to observe Exercise Fox. It was a "nice sunny morning," and all went according to plan. The two cruisers and eight destroyers shelled the beach at Slapton Sands, further blasting the already ruined Royal Sands Hotel, which had been designated as the enemy headquarters. Then hundreds of landing craft carried the men and equipment of the 1st Infantry Division ashore. The rhino ferries were particularly effective in transferring tanks and trucks from the LSTs to the beach. There was still some confusion in Army-Navy communications, but the only serious difficulty was that a few of the tanks had trouble crossing the pebbly beach and bogged down. Despite that, Ramsay was pleased. Even before the exercise, he had confided to his diary that he had begun to "view the future with more confidence as regards the purely naval aspects." Significantly, perhaps, no one expressed an opinion about how the exercise might have turned out if it had not been a "nice sunny morning."[20]

Ramsay was also pleased with the outcome of Exercise Beaver two weeks later, in which Moon's Force U, in its first full-scale exercise, carried elements of Collins's VII Corps from Plymouth, Dartmouth, and Brixham to

Slapton Sands. The beach assault took place on time and according to plan. The Special Engineer Brigades cleared paths through the obstacles with their bulldozers, tractors, and motorized road graders; the assault units secured the beachhead and made a rapid advance inland; and the Navy managed to keep the troops supplied, bringing some eighteen hundred tons of supplies and ammunition ashore by nightfall.[21]

WHILE THE PRACTICE LANDINGS CONTINUED, others sought creative and innovative ways to enhance Allied chances in the great invasion. The most ambitious of these was a proposal to construct one or more artificial harbors off the landing beaches. The origins of this project dated back to the summer of 1943 when the COSSAC planners were discussing the seizure of Cherbourg. They had drawn up a schedule to get the first wave of Allied forces ashore, but it was evident that without the use of Cherbourg's port facilities, it would be difficult to expand the initial foothold. What if Cherbourg did not fall in accordance with the Allied schedule? In the midst of that discussion, British Commodore John Hughes-Hallet said, apparently in jest, "Well, all I can say is, if we can't capture a port we must take one with us." There was general laughter around the table, until someone said: Well, why not?[22]

The initial idea was to sink some old ships off the landing beaches to serve as a breakwater in case of unsettled weather. From the beginning, this was both a British idea and a British program. At the Quebec conference, advocates of the scheme set up a demonstration in a hotel bathroom. Admirals and generals crowded into the loo to watch as Mountbatten's science advisor, Professor J. D. Bernal, placed some small paper boats in one end of a partially filled bathtub. An officer then swirled the water around in the other end with a back brush. That caused the paper boats to bounce around, and they soon swamped and sank. After replacing them with new paper boats, Bernal then placed a barrier in the tub. (In one version of the story it was a life vest, in another a loofah.) Again the officer vigorously swirled up the water, but this time the barrier absorbed the wavelets, and the paper boats were undisturbed. It was hardly a scientific experiment, but it carried the day, and the plan to erect an artificial breakwater off the landing beaches became part of the Neptune-Overlord plan that was adopted at Quebec.[23]

Over the ensuing months, however, this relatively modest proposal took on a life of its own and morphed into a far more ambitious program. Spurred on by Churchill, who was ever an enthusiast of innovative approaches to war, it grew to include one or more artificial harbors with special off-loading piers and causeways into the beach. Eisenhower had already suggested that because tanks might bog down in the shingle of the invasion beaches, it would be desirable to construct a causeway from the low-tide mark to the top of the beach. Now British planners went beyond that to propose the construction of causeways from pier heads well offshore all the way into the beach itself.[24]

The overall project was given the name Mulberry. The breakwater was called a "gooseberry," which was to be made up of derelict vessels dubbed "corncobs." Like some lab experiment gone horribly awry, the program eventually grew out of all proportion to the original idea. The 149 Phoenix caissons needed to construct artificial harbors alone consumed more than half a million cubic yards of concrete, thirty thousand tons of iron reinforcement bars, fifteen million feet of steel tubing, and fifty miles of steel wire.[25]

These enormous demands drew upon already scarce matériel and labor resources and occupied shipways and building yards needed to maintain and repair the landing craft and warships. Even if all the pieces of the Mulberry program could be assembled in time—which was by no means certain—there were not enough tugs to move them all into place. Instead of cooling enthusiasm for the project, however, these discoveries triggered a frenzied effort to find more resources. Stark warned King that unless many more tugs could be made available, the project could not be completed in time to meet the perceived need.[26]

In the cultural legacy of the eventual Allied victory, the artificial harbors off the Normandy beaches have come to symbolize the ultimate triumph of Anglo-American ingenuity and resourcefulness. Yet many of the operational commanders both at the time and afterward were markedly restrained in their enthusiasm. After inspecting a site where the gigantic Phoenix caissons were being fabricated, Ramsay decided they were "even more formidable & abortion like than I anticipated." He thought it would be "the devil" to tow them into place, and wondered if they would make much of a difference in the end. Right up to D-Day itself, he referred openly to "those damned Mulberries." Even Hughes-Hallet, whose offhand remark had set it all in motion, came to see the Mulberry project as an example of "wasteful and ridiculous excess."[27]

Besides the artificial harbors, another Allied initiative was dubbed Pluto, which stood for "pipeline under the ocean" and was designed to meet the Allied army's voracious appetite for fuel. The jeeps, trucks, and tanks carried to the beach by the thousands of landing craft would require enormous amounts of gasoline and diesel fuel to keep going during the land campaign. Carrying that fuel across the Channel in a virtually infinite number of jerrycans (initial estimates were for 26.3 million of them) seemed both daunting and a bit absurd, but until Cherbourg was taken, there was no port where tankers could offload. It was Arthur Harley, chief of the Anglo-Iranian Oil Company, who suggested that the solution was to run a flexible four-inch hose encased in a dozen reinforced layers across the bottom of the Channel from Britain to France. By the eve of D-Day it was in position and ready to deploy.[28]

There were other, less ambitious innovations, many of which sprang from the mind of a British major general named Percy Hobart, the erstwhile commander of the British 79th Armored Division, and coincidentally Montgomery's brother-in-law. Hobart, who sported owlish glasses and a brush mustache, developed a whole series of unconventional weapons that collectively came to be known as "Hobart's Funnies." Many of them were contraptions added to either a Sherman or Churchill tank to give it special capabilities. One, called an AVRE (for Assault Vehicle, Royal Engineers) mounted an oversize short-barreled gun capable of firing a huge 40-pound shell for blasting German pillboxes. Another, called a "flail tank," carried a fantastical rotating cylinder of chains that pummeled the ground to its front to detonate mines in its path. Still another fired self-propelled Bangalore torpedoes, and one, appropriately nicknamed "Bobbin," boasted a giant spool of matting that unfurled as it advanced so that it could traverse boggy ground. There was even one with no turret at all whose function was to act as a movable ramp so that tanks behind it could drive over the top of it to scale walls and other impediments. To one American officer, it seemed that nearly every vehicle "had some kind of Rube Goldberg contraption hooked up to it." The Americans were intrigued by some of these innovations but on the whole preferred to rely on more conventional weaponry applied with overwhelming force. There was one device, however, that the Americans found interesting enough to adopt in large numbers. It was called the duplex drive tank.[29]

Conceived by an Austrian immigrant to Britain, Nicholas Straussler, the duplex drive (or DD) tank was supposed to solve the problem of getting armor ashore with the first wave of infantry. To do that, thirty-four-ton Sherman M4 tanks were equipped with giant waterproof canvas shrouds, like water wings, that wrapped all the way around the tank, virtually obscuring it. When deployed, the shroud was so high that the tank driver, standing on a platform behind the turret, could not see over the rim without a periscope. When inflated, the shroud contained enough air to keep the tank afloat, or, more accurately, to keep it from sinking, since the tank itself was suspended below the waterline with only about nine inches of canvas showing above the water. The tank's engine was connected to drive shafts that turned twin propellers astern. In theory at least, a tank so equipped could drive off the ramp of an LCT several miles offshore—beyond the range of German artillery—and swim to the beach on its own without attracting the heavy gunfire that would be directed at an amphibious ship. Essentially an amphibious stealth weapon, the DD tanks would crawl up onto the beach "like a big bug coming out of the water," as one sailor put it. Once ashore, the shroud collapsed and the tank resumed its terrestrial character. Eisenhower and Bradley witnessed a demonstration of some duplex drive tanks in February, and they were sufficiently impressed to include them in the planning for D-Day. Soon enough, the DD tanks became part of the regular landing exercises.[30]

Their performance was mixed. They worked satisfactorily as long as the seas were relatively calm, but they were slow and cumbersome, and steering by periscope was problematic. At one rehearsal, attended not only by Montgomery, Ramsay, and Leigh-Mallory but also by King George himself, the DD tanks arrived both twenty minutes late and in the wrong place. On other occasions a DD's propellers broke down and an LCT had to be dispatched to tow it in. The tanks were so heavy, however, that even with all three of the LCT's 225-horsepower engines running flat out, they could hardly be moved. "We just had to wrestle with it and keep pulling," an LCT skipper recalled, and eventually he got it close enough to the beach that a bulldozer could tow it onto dry land. Sometimes they couldn't be saved. During Exercise Fox, two of them swamped and went to the bottom. Long after the war was over, one of them was salvaged, and it remains on Slapton Sands today as a memorial.[31]

Superficially similar but in fact quite different from the DD tanks were the DUKWs, which were essentially amphibious trucks used to carry cargo, especially ammunition, to the beach.* While the DD tanks were land vehicles with water wings, the DUKWs (which everyone called "ducks") were essentially boats with wheels, and therefore far more reliable as vessels and also more nimble ashore. Built by General Motors and powered by Chevrolet engines, they weighed six and a half tons each and could make five and a half knots afloat and fifty miles per hour ashore. They had been used successfully during the landings on Sicily and in Italy and were therefore less of a gimmick than most of Hobart's "Funnies." Even so, with only about a foot of freeboard when fully loaded, they, too, could take on water in rough seas and lose their marginal buoyancy.[32]

IN LATE APRIL, Don Moon and "Lightning Joe" Collins prepared to conduct "Exercise Tiger," the last full scale rehearsal of Force U before the invasion. The plan was for Moon's amphibians to put the bulk of Collins's VII Corps ashore at Slapton Sands, from which it would advance to "capture" the town of Oakhampton, twenty-five miles inland. In order to duplicate as closely as possible the actual Utah Beach landings, now only five weeks away, the beach was prepared with two lines of steel tetrahedrons and barbed wire; even live mines were put in place.[33]

---

* DUKW" was not an acronym. Instead, the letters indicated its model type. *D* indicated that it had been built in 1942; *U* stood for "utility"; *K* meant that it had front-wheel drive; and *W* indicated that it had two rear axles. Since the DUKWs were considered trucks that could float rather than boats with wheels, they were assigned to motor transport and operated, for the most part, by African American drivers.

Moon's force involved a mix of American landing craft and Royal Navy warships. Such an arrangement was no longer novel or even noteworthy, though there were some awkward aspects to it. One was that in the Royal Navy, the flag officers serving as Commander in Chief, Plymouth and Commander in Chief, Portsmouth had full authority over all vessels, of any nationality, when they were in port. Only when the ships cleared the harbor did command authority shift to the task force commanders. In addition, Kirk was concerned that his zone of authority did not extend to the French city of Cherbourg at the end of the Cotentin Peninsula, which remained the responsibility of the C in C Plymouth. That worried him, because it was from Cherbourg that any German surface units would sortie to assail his right flank. Some weeks before, Kirk had sent his chief of staff, Rear Admiral Arthur Struble, to ask Ramsay to change that. Struble may have picked a bad day, for there was a palpable sense of annoyance in Ramsay's reaction. Ramsay listened to Kirk's request to change the command boundaries, then blurted out: "You Yanks want everything. No, I won't do it. They're going to stay where they are." And they did. These arrangements created a certain ambiguity about the Allied naval command structure and a potential for confusion—even, as it proved, catastrophe.[34]

Almost all of Moon's Force U took part in Exercise Tiger. That included twenty-one LSTs, twenty-eight LCI(L)s, and sixty-five LCTs, plus nearly a hundred smaller vessels and the usual escort of warships. Moon and Collins watched the exercise from Moon's flagship, the attack transport *Bayfield*. Other interested viewers watched from shore. That audience included much of the top brass at both SHAEF and ANCXF. Even Eisenhower attended, bringing Tedder, Leigh-Mallory, and Omar Bradley with him from London on a special train called "Bayonet." Kirk sent Moon a short note to let him know that Eisenhower was coming, and like all naval messages, it contained what was called padding at the beginning and the end of the message to confuse enemy code breakers. Such padding consisted of nonsense phrases picked at random by the radioman from a thick book. Ominously, the padding that was added to the end of Kirk's message was: "No luck."[35]

As the various elements of Force U gathered off Slapton Sands early on the morning of April 27, Moon learned that at least one LCT flotilla was behind schedule. Careful as always, he decided to postpone the landing by an hour to ensure that all the pieces of the invasion force were in place. But Moon made that call at 6:25 for a landing that was scheduled to begin at 6:30. In a complex exercise with army, naval, and air elements, that invited confusion. Some of the Higgins boats began heading for the beach in accordance with the original schedule when the British heavy cruiser *Hawkins* opened fire on the beach. Shells fell among the landing craft and caused a number of friendly-fire casualties. It was quickly straightened out and the forces eventually got ashore, but it was not an especially good showing. And it was about to get much worse.[36]

The second-wave assault force for Exercise Tiger, scheduled to land the next day, consisted of eight fully loaded LSTs collectively dubbed convoy T-4. The commodore of the convoy was U.S. Navy Commander Bernard Skahill, from New York City, a prim, neat man with a thin neck that protruded stalk-like from his crisp uniform collar. At forty-six, Skahill was a Naval Academy grad from the class of 1921, and to the young officers and men of the amphibious force, he seemed positively ancient. The Royal Navy escort for the convoy consisted of one small Flower-class corvette, the *Azalea*, which at just over two hundred feet in length was even smaller than an American destroyer escort, plus the larger but much older destroyer *Scimitar*. The *Azalea* would lead, and the *Scimitar* would screen the convoy's right flank, which was the likely avenue of approach for any German naval force seeking to interfere with the exercise.

In the jostling of ships inside Plymouth Harbor just prior to departure, the *Scimitar* was struck by an American landing craft in a collision that gouged a two-foot hole in her starboard side some twenty feet back from the bow. Such collisions were not altogether unusual in a crowded harbor, and the damage was not significant, but the C in C Plymouth, Rear Admiral Sir Ralph Leatham, nevertheless ordered the *Scimitar* into the yards for repair. Neither Leatham nor the captain of the *Scimitar*, however, notified Commander Skahill, who, after all, was not in the Royal Navy chain of command. Skahill saw the *Scimitar* going in the wrong direction as it headed for the repair yard, but he assumed it was part of the complicated maneuvering necessary to get all the ships out of port and into formation. As a result, convoy T-4 went to sea that evening with only a single escort, the tiny *Azalea*, and no flank guard. After joining up off Berry Head, the eight LSTs headed out into the Channel. The idea was for them to spend as much time at sea as it would take to cross the Channel to Normandy, thus emulating the experience of an actual assault.[37]

Several hours after Skahill and the LSTs left Plymouth, at about 10:00 p.m., nine small German warships sortied from Cherbourg. Called E-boats by the Allies, the German designation for these craft was *Schnellboote* (S-boat) or "fast boat"—a particularly apt designation. With their 7,500-horsepower Daimler-Benz engines, they could make up to forty knots. Built of wood on a light metal alloy frame with a thin sheath of mahogany, they were about a hundred feet long (about twenty feet longer than an American PT boat) and armed with 40 mm guns, though their principal weapon was the four torpedoes they carried amidships that had a range of seven to eight thousand yards—about four miles. The E-boats operated almost exclusively at night and were painted either gray or in a mottled camouflage pattern, which made them very hard to see. Their sortie from Cherbourg on the night of April 27 was noted by British radar technicians ashore, but in the dual communication system, no word of it got to Skahill or to the captain of the *Azalea*, Commander George C. Geddes, RNVR, until after midnight. The news did, however, concern Admiral Leatham, who realized belatedly that convoy T-4 was at sea with only a single escort. At 1:37 a.m. he dispatched the destroyer HMS *Saladin*, a sister ship of the damaged *Scimitar*, as a relief escort.[38]

Like the German E-boats, the LSTs of convoy T-4 were running blacked out. They were approaching Lyme Bay at a few minutes past 1:00 in the morning on April 28 when crewmen and the embarked soldiers on LST-507 heard what one described as "a scraping and dragging noise" under the ship. In hindsight it is evident that this was a German torpedo passing just under the shallow-draft LST. Lieutenant J. S. Swarts, skipper of the 507, sounded general quarters, though most of the sailors who dutifully headed for their combat stations assumed, quite naturally, that this was simply part of the exercise. Only minutes later, bright green tracer rounds from the E-boats lit up the darkness. Even then, most of the men on board the 507 and the other ships in the convoy assumed this was another, quite realistic part of the drill.[39]

All doubt evaporated at 2:07 a.m. when the first torpedo exploded. It struck the 507 amidships in the auxiliary engine room, knocking out both the ship's electricity and its communications and starting several fires. The dozens of vehicles on the tank deck had all been topped off with gasoline, and as the fires reached them, they burst into flame one by one. The 507 also began taking on water. Because of their large open tank deck, LSTs had no transverse bulkheads or watertight compartments that could be used to limit the flooding. The only thing that could be done was to close off as many hatches as possible in the hope of controlling the inundation of water. Meanwhile, the fires produced "a dull roar," as one sailor recalled, "punctuated by the crackling and sputtering of small arms ammunition" cooking off. Lieutenant (j.g.) Gene Eckstam, the ship's doctor, looked into the tank deck to see "a huge, roaring blast furnace...Trucks were burning; gasoline was burning; and small-arms ammunition was exploding." He could hear the screams of men being consumed by the flames, but he knew there was nothing he could do for them; smoke inhalation would soon overcome any who were still alive. "So I closed the hatches into the tank deck and dogged them tightly shut."[40]

Crowded as the ship was, with nearly five hundred soldiers on board as well as more than a hundred crewmen, the men got in one another's way as they reacted to the crisis. They found that the metal pins holding the life rafts to the bulkheads had rusted in place and couldn't be pried loose. Crewmen tried to lower the Higgins boats alongside, but the LST was listing so badly the hydraulic gear jammed. A soldier used his rifle to shoot the cable holding one of them, and it finally dropped into the water. Men panicked and began jumping over the side. Soon the sea around the 507 was filled with struggling men, some who could swim and many who could not.[41]

Eleven minutes after the 507 was struck, a torpedo hit LST-531, and less than a minute later it was hit again. The result was "a gigantic orange ball" of flame, and the 531 began to sink almost at once. Sailors and soldiers simply leaped over the side into the chill water, trusting to their life vests. The water was so cold it drove the breath from their bodies. Moreover, the life vests that had been issued to the soldiers proved worse than useless. Unlike the kapok vests that were standard in the Navy, the soldiers had been issued something that resembled a bicycle inner tube that wrapped around their chests. Most wore them at their waist so they didn't interfere with their packs. As a result, when men triggered the CO_2 cartridges and inflated them, the vests tipped them over onto their heads. Those who could clung to one of the small two-man rafts, which soon became overcrowded. One raft had more than twenty men clinging to it and to each other in concentric circles. As the frigid cold overcame them and they lost consciousness, they let go and drifted away into the dark.[42]

Then LST-289 was hit. The skipper, Lieutenant Henry A. Mettler, saw the torpedo coming and ordered, "Right full rudder." The maneuver may have saved the ship, because the torpedo struck the ship's stern rather than its broadside. It blew off the after section of the 289, containing the crew's quarters and the galley, while the rest of the ship remained afloat; this time, the fact that LSTs were shaped like a bathtub proved an advantage. By now both the 507 and 531 were gone. The 507 had broken in half, with the bow and stern sections rising up to form what one sailor described as "a fiery jackknife" before it went under. The 531, hit by two torpedoes, had gone down in only six minutes. Gunners on the remaining LSTs fired at the swift, dark shadows in the night as red (American) and green (German) tracer bullets filled the air. German tracers had a delayed illumination, so it was difficult to determine their point of origin, and in the confusion and poor visibility, many of the American shells struck other LSTs.[43]

Commander Geddes, in the *Azalea*, heard the explosions from his position a mile ahead of the convoy and circled back at flank speed. He was reluctant to fire a star shell that would illuminate the scene, for he knew that it would also expose the LSTs. He did not even know from which direction the attacks had come or whether the attacker was a U-boat or an E-boat. For his part, Commander Skahill in LST-515 ordered the remaining ships of the convoy to head toward shore. This was the correct and well-established protocol when a convoy came under attack. But the order did not sit well with the captain of Skahill's flagship, Lieutenant John Doyle.[44]

Doyle was much younger than Skahill and was what was called a "mustang"—that is, a prior enlisted sailor. Thickset, bluff, hearty, and short-necked, he was a bulldog to Skahill's aging greyhound. Doyle objected vociferously to Skahill's decision to turn shoreward while two, and perhaps three, of his ships were sinking. Doyle wanted to go back and pick up the survivors. Skahill knew not only that this was a violation of standing orders but also that trying to pick up survivors more often than not resulted in yet another ship being sunk. Doyle didn't care. In an act of near mutiny, he got on the 1-MC loudspeaker and explained the situation to the men on board. Their shipmates and fellow soldiers were dying out there, he announced. Who wanted to go back to get them? A rousing cheer went up, and Skahill capitulated. The 515 returned to the scene.[45]

It was too late. With the sun coming up, the E-boats had retreated, but it had been more than two hours since the first men had gone into the frigid water. Even most of those who could swim or who had found something to cling to had lost functionality in their limbs. The *Saladin* arrived to help, and men on Doyle's 515 and on the *Saladin* began retrieving those who were left alive. Most of the bodies in the water, however, were not moving. After rescuing the few survivors, the 515 and the *Saladin* began retrieving the lifeless forms from the water with the intent, no doubt, of giving them a proper burial. Then orders arrived from shore to leave them where they were. There were complaints about that, too, but this time the orders held, and the ships left the scene. Hours later, crewmen on LCT-271 passing through the area en route to Portland Harbor noted that the sea around them was filled with hundreds of small floating objects. "As we got closer," a sailor recalled, "we noted that they were American GI's." Crewmen used a boat hook to pull one of the bodies alongside. It was a U.S. Army soldier, "in a sort of sitting position with all his clothes on … His eyes were wide open and staring." He looked, a sailor recalled, like he had known he was going to die. After reporting the discovery, they, too, got orders to leave the bodies where they were, and LCT-271 continued on to Portland, though it had to zigzag "to keep from running over the bodies."[46]

The final death toll from Exercise Tiger was 198 sailors and 441 soldiers killed, which was more, as it happened, than died during the actual landings on Utah Beach five weeks later.[47] But no one was to know about the slaughter that had occurred in Lyme Bay. The news, after all, would be a crushing blow to morale and cast a pall over the other major rehearsal scheduled to take place only five days later. Indeed, if news of the disaster became public, it might even undermine support for the D-Day landings themselves. Certainly the Germans would take increased confidence from knowing how badly the Allies had been hurt. So the decision was made at the very top—very likely by Eisenhower himself—that the incident would remain a secret. When Skahill, Doyle, and LST-515 arrived in Portland late on the afternoon of April 28, they saw that every U.S. Navy ship in the harbor flew its flag at half staff. Naturally, they assumed that this was in honor of the hundreds of men who had died in the Channel that morning. It was not. By coincidence, Secretary of the Navy Frank Knox had died that same day, and the flags had been lowered in his honor. In an effort to keep news of the debacle in Lyme Bay from spreading, the survivors were placed in hospitals. Officially they were under observation, but to some it felt like incarceration, and the entire incident remained largely unknown until well after the war was over.

Terrible as the death toll was, Eisenhower and Ramsay were almost as concerned about the loss of those three LSTs.* The Allied operational margin of safety in terms of LSTs was so narrow that the loss of three of them threatened the viability of Neptune itself. Stark wired King that three replacement LSTs must be sent from America at once. King advised Stark that the only way replacements could get there in time was to bring them from the Mediterranean, but Admiral Cunningham, who commanded in the Med, said he had no LSTs to spare. King promised that he would send

---

* Eisenhower also worried about the security of the D-Day plans because he knew that at least one of the officers reported as missing after Exercise Tiger had been thoroughly briefed about Neptune-Overlord. If that officer had been pulled from the water by one of the E-boats and interrogated, it could jeopardize the entire operation. In the end, however, the Allies recovered the bodies of all those who had access to the invasion plans.

three replacements to the Med in June. Once again, the Allies were forced to shift naval assets around from theater to theater like a slide puzzle.[48]

━━━━

PUTTING A LID ON THE CATASTROPHE did not mean there were no repercussions. Ernest King ordered eight more destroyers from the U.S. Navy to join Ramsay's command, adding, "Experience against E boats desirable." Kirk did not think that was sufficient. He wanted to use the battleship *Nevada* and her big 14-inch guns to blast the E-boat pens in Cherbourg. Ramsay was cool to the idea, partly because it might alert the Germans that something was up, but also because it deviated from the carefully structured Neptune operational plan. To Kirk, this was simply another example of British unwillingness to depart from the script. Kirk was annoyed that his previous attempt to obtain operational control over the waters around Cherbourg had been rejected, and angry that the cumbersome command structure in Plymouth had resulted in the convoy having an inadequate escort. In an official letter to Ramsay, he expressed himself rather strongly on both issues. Ramsay took umbrage at Kirk's tone and thought Kirk had "quite lost his sense of proportion." He concluded that Kirk "is not a big enough man to hold the position he does." For his part, Kirk attributed Ramsay's attitude to the British tendency to view all operations as "a set piece" in which "no initiative was possible." The relationship got testy on May 7 when Ramsay met with the command teams of both of his naval task forces. After meeting with Vian and his force commanders in the morning, Ramsay met with Kirk, Hall, and Moon in the afternoon. There, Kirk again brought up the question of attacking the German E-boat sanctuary in Cherbourg. Ramsay thought Kirk was being "stupid," and admitted that "I somewhat lost my patience with him." Ramsay's final verdict on Kirk was that he was "a poor fish." They had come a long way from being "Alan" and "Bertie."[49]

Still Kirk wouldn't let it go. Getting no satisfaction from Ramsay, he ensured that his concerns found their way through back channels to Eisenhower's chief of staff, Beetle Smith. That irritated Ramsay even more, and he briefly considered an official reprimand of Kirk for violating the chain of command. At a meeting with both Eisenhower and Ramsay on May 8, Kirk again argued the importance of "blasting the German E-boats out of their nests." Eisenhower asked Ramsay what he thought about the idea, and Ramsay explained why he thought a naval attack on Cherbourg was unnecessary and perhaps even harmful. Then, to Ramsay's horror, Ike turned back to Kirk to ask what he thought of Ramsay's argument. To Ramsay, that was outrageous. In his view, it didn't matter what Kirk thought. Ramsay was the naval C in C, and Kirk was his subordinate. He was appalled that Eisenhower acted as if their views had equal merit. Ramsay kept quiet at the time, but he was furious. "It was a bad meeting," he wrote in his diary, "& made me cross."[50]

On an official level, Stark ordered an "immediate investigation" of the events in Lyme Bay, and the ensuing report cited several failures that could be taken as lessons. The first was obvious: American-British communications had failed. The existence of an independent command for the C in C Plymouth, as distinct from the operational command, had made possible the kind of confusion that led to the absence of HMS *Scimitar*. Another failure was that almost everyone involved with Exercise Tiger had conceived of it as another rehearsal and had behaved accordingly. There had been so many practice landings that the sailors and soldiers—even the officers—had trouble making the mental adjustment to actual combat. Despite the tracer fire in the night and even the exploding torpedoes, many clung to the idea that this was a rehearsal right up to the moment they found themselves in the water.[51]

Like Kirk, many of the Americans blamed the British, especially Leatham. But in the U.S. Navy, responsibility for every event belongs, rightly or wrongly, to the commanding officer. An old saw in the U.S. Navy was that you could delegate authority, but you could not delegate responsibility. Though Moon might properly have been held accountable for his questionable decision to postpone the practice landing on Slapton Sands on the morning of April 27, he had had no hand at all in the circumstances that led to the disaster in Lyme Bay in the early morning hours of April 28. Nevertheless, he was the man in overall command, and so it did not surprise him when he received an order to report on board Kirk's flagship, the heavy cruiser *Augusta*. Instead of Kirk, however, Moon found Kirk's chief of staff, Rear Admiral Arthur Struble, waiting for him.

Though Moon was close to Hall (who was godfather to Moon's son), he had an awkward relationship with Struble. For one thing, Struble had graduated a year ahead of Moon at the academy and resented the fact that Moon had a fleet command while he had a staff position. When Moon arrived in Struble's cabin on the *Augusta*, Struble was standing with his back to the hatchway, looking out a porthole, and he did not immediately turn around to acknowledge Moon's arrival. Some moments passed in awkward silence. When a British submarine passed within Struble's vision with a broom lashed to its periscope to signal that it had made a clean sweep, he muttered, "Well, I see somebody did his duty." Only then did he turn to face Moon and, with a cold expression, ask, "All right, Moon, what happened?" Moon offered a full oral report of the events as he understood them, but the atmosphere in the room remained chilly. Struble responded only that Admiral King in Washington was not going to be pleased. Eventually Moon made his escape and returned to his flagship, no doubt determined to work even harder.[52]

NOT QUITE A WEEK LATER, on May 3, the Allies began a series of exercises, called Fabius, that lasted for six days. Hall's Force O carried elements of Gerow's V Corps from Portland and Weymouth to Slapton Sands, and the British conducted full-scale landings of Dempsey's Second British Army on the beaches east of Portsmouth. This time there was no interference from the enemy—indeed, few problems of any kind. Ramsay, watching the British landings from Vian's flagship, the cruiser *Scylla*, was "very favorably impressed." Despite lingering concerns over what he perceived as Kirk's "wilful stupidity" about the E-boat threat, Ramsay informed Eisenhower that the Neptune force was ready.[53]

Perhaps it would have been more accurate to say that it was as ready as could reasonably have been expected given the circumstances. The destroyer squadron that King had dispatched after the debacle of Exercise Tiger was still en route, and although May 1944 was the most prolific month of the entire war for LST production, only a few of the new LSTs made it from the shipyards on the Ohio River, down the Mississippi, and across the Atlantic in time to join the Neptune force. Moreover, those that did arrive had novice crews with no amphibious training whatsoever. A handful of veterans were transferred into them from other landing craft to provide some experienced leadership, but the rest were neophytes, "literally jumping from boot camp to combat," in the words of one. For the new arrivals, the assault on the beaches of Normandy would be the first beach landing of any kind they had ever made. Nevertheless, the operation could be put off no longer. As one LCT skipper put it, "Our training was about as good as could be done given the shortness of time available," adding, "What we lacked in expertise, we made up for in enthusiasm." It remained to be seen if that would be enough.[54]

At the last full-scale briefing, held at St. Paul's School on May 15, all of the principal commanders from Eisenhower on down delivered detailed oral summaries of the forthcoming operation. It was a star-studded audience filled with admirals, generals, and air vice marshals as well as the prime minister and King George himself. On the stage was a giant three-dimensional map of the target beaches, angled so the audience could see it, and as each of the principal commanders spoke, he walked around the map pointing out the key sites. In spite of himself, Churchill was impressed. When at last it was his turn, he gave what Eisenhower called "one of his typical fighting speeches," but then the prime minister added this: "Gentlemen, I am hardening toward this enterprise." Eisenhower was taken aback. It was as if Churchill was only then becoming reconciled to the operation that had dominated Allied planning for a full year.[55]

On May 28, Ramsay sent an order to all hands: "Carry out Operation Neptune." In response, battleships and cruisers set out from ports in Northern Ireland and Scotland, landing ships and landing craft moved along the Channel coast to their assigned ports, and trucks filled to capacity with soldiers in full kit made their way in an endless stream along the narrow roads of southern England to ports of embarkation from Falmouth in Cornwall to Newhaven in East Sussex.

D-Day was eight days away.

CHAPTER 10

"A HUM THROUGHOUT
THE COUNTRY"

I T WAS HAPPENING AT LAST, and all over England people could sense it. As hard as Allied leaders tried to conceal the timing of the invasion, the acceleration of events at the end of May created an almost palpable sense of anticipation. On May 26, one resident of southern England recorded in his diary, "England is expectant, almost hushed." The weighted stillness did not last. Within days, there was hectic, even frenetic, activity at each of the 171 embarkation ports located along the southern coast, up on the Bristol Channel, in the Thames estuary, and as far north as Scotland. Much of the equipment and supplies for the invasion had been pre-positioned near these ports, and locals had grown used to seeing camouflaged piles of military hardware and car parks filled with military vehicles. That proved to be only the beginning, however, for as the day of departure drew near, vehicles began moving shoreward in long caravans along Britain's narrow roads. They did so mostly at night to keep hidden from German reconnaissance aircraft, but they could not be concealed from the local population. A resident of Dorset recalled, "Our nights echoed to the ceaseless clatter of heavy tanks lumbering down the Bournemouth-Southampton Road." Aware that something special was happening, people in the small villages came down to the road to watch, flashing the V-for-victory sign as the tanks and trucks rolled past.[1]

Just after midnight on June 2, Seaman George Hackett was sleeping in his tent near Dartmouth when he was awakened by the commanding officer of LCT Flotilla 17 and told to get the jeep. The CO had to go to Torquay, east of Dartmouth, to meet with the other commanders for a briefing. As he drove the lieutenant through the dark with his headlights partially obscured by black tape, Hackett became aware of "a strange sound" that filled the air. It was a kind of deep, persistent drone, and it grew louder as he drove, until the very air seemed to throb with it. When he joined the main road south, he realized its source: hundreds of diesel trucks were on the move, one after another in an endless caravan, all heading south. As he joined that caravan, Hackett speculated that this was probably happening all along the Channel coast, at Falmouth, Plymouth, Exmouth, and elsewhere, creating "a hum throughout the country."[2]

At the same time, hundreds of amphibious ships assembled at the embarkation sites. They, too, moved mostly at night, and as furtively as possible, though near-absolute Allied command of the air made them relatively secure from enemy discovery. Once on site, most of the ships' officers attended briefing sessions ashore. Those commanding the LCTs and LCIs in the Dart River received their briefing on the large parquet quarterdeck of the Britannia Royal Naval College. After listening to the details of the operation, they were told what they should expect during the invasion. It was a pretty grim recital. The first menace was the mines, and the skippers were cautioned to take special care to stay within the swept lanes, passages eight hundred yards wide marked by red and green dan buoys, as they crossed the Channel. In addition, they were told that "strong and persistent attacks by enemy E-boats and submarines are to be expected," as well as "heavy and persistent enemy air attacks with bombs, glider bombs, aerial mines, and possibly torpedoes." Finally, it was possible—perhaps even likely—that the Germans would use poison gas. The briefing officer concluded that they should not worry, however, because the Allies had a comfortable margin of superiority and could absorb very heavy casualties and still succeed. That last bit of information was probably less comforting than the briefer intended.[3]

Some had more reason to worry than most. That certainly included the men who would go in first to clear the mines and obstacles on the assault beaches. In the U.S. Navy these men belonged to Naval Combat Demolition Units (NCDUs); in the Royal Navy they were part of the Landing Craft Obstacle Clearing Units (LCOCUs). In either service, their jobs were among the most perilous in the entire operation. Just behind them would come the men of the Special Engineer Brigades, whose job it was to construct passages through the cleared minefields using bulldozers, road graders, and tractors landed from the LCTs. Then there were the beach masters who acted as traffic cops, supervising the landing and off-loading of the vessels bringing the infantry and the tanks ashore. At one of the preinvasion briefings, a designated beach master in the audience asked about how he was to get food and drinking water during his extended stay ashore. "Not to worry," the briefer replied matter-of-factly. "If any of you beach officers are still alive after the invasion, we'll take care of you and find a way to supply you."[4]

The marshaling areas around the Channel ports were known as "sausage camps" because their locations were indicated on the maps by sausage-shaped symbols. To disguise the military buildup, the trucks, tanks, and jeeps were parked, whenever possible, in wooded areas where they could not be easily identified from the air. Forested areas from Cornwall to East Sussex soon filled up with a wide variety of camouflaged vehicles and equipment. Even the woods around the athletic fields at the British Naval Academy at Dartmouth were crowded with parked vehicles. That caused a bit of a flutter when some of the old guard protested that driving tanks over the cricket pitch was just too much. Surely some things were sacred! As diplomatically as possible, local commanders explained that painful sacrifices were necessary to ensure victory.[5]

Though the buildup was unceasing, those who arrived first in the marshaling areas confronted the old story of "hurry up and wait"—and the waiting was agonizing. Robert Miller, a member of the 149th Combat

Engineer Brigade, scheduled to go ashore in the first wave, recalled that time "hung heavy" on him and the rest of his team. Like many others, he wondered what his fate would be on the other side of the Channel. "We made pacts with our best buddies," he recalled, "to contact each other's family after the war," should they be killed, and to tell them how they had died. Others repeatedly, even compulsively, cleaned their rifles and checked and double-checked their equipment. Members of the demolition teams carefully measured out two-pound explosive charges and put them into Navy socks, tying off the ends so they could be quickly affixed to the obstructions ashore. Given that half a million men were now crowding up to the embarkation sites, much of their time was spent standing in long chow lines. The sailors were weary of waiting, too. Ensign Curtis Hansen of LST-315 recalled, "We were tired of the training and of the boredom, and wanted to get it over with no matter what the outcome personally would be."[6]

Even now, at nearly the last minute, there were some jitters within the high command. Leigh-Mallory went to Eisenhower to urge the cancellation of the air drop behind the beaches. Given the uncertain weather and the difficult terrain, he was convinced that the casualty rates among the paratroopers would be unacceptable. It was one more burden for Ike to shoulder as he queried others at SHAEF about the impact such a cancellation would have. In the end, he told Leigh-Mallory that the air drop would take place as planned, and that he—Eisenhower—would accept the responsibility.

AFTER THE LONG WAIT, the moment came suddenly. As George Goodspeed remembered it, "One morning we were told to pack our sea bags, stack them in a building, and take with us what we actually needed." Army platoon commanders were told to ensure that all the men were "freshly bathed, shaved, and wearing warm underclothing." Some filled their pockets with candy bars, uncertain when they would have another chance to eat a regular meal. Divided into "boat teams" of 220 men each—roughly the capacity of an LCI(L)—they were loaded into trucks that drove them to the harbors, where they lined up on the quay. At 171 different sites all over

England and Scotland, some 176,000 men, more than 20,000 vehicles, and uncounted tons of equipment was embarked into thousands of transports and landing craft. Harried junior officers bearing clipboards sought to ensure that every soldier, vehicle, and crate was brought to the correct site, placed on the proper vessel, and stowed in the necessary order.[7]

Of course, the Allies had been preparing for this moment for more than a year, and part of that preparation involved the construction of more than two hundred special embarkation platforms, known as "hards": broad, paved ramps that sloped down from the roadway into and well below the waterline, giant cousins to the small launching ramps used by pleasure boaters today. To construct these hards, the area was first graded into a gently sloping beach, then covered with thousands of pre-formed reinforced concrete rectangles weighing 350 pounds apiece. Laid out across the loading area, these giant concrete tiles formed a pattern that resembled a segmented Hershey bar, which led some to refer to them as "chocolate." The hards were more useful than conventional piers for loading the landing ships because several LSTs and LCTs at a time could nose up to them and drop their ramps right onto the chocolate, allowing the tanks, trucks, and jeeps to make their way down the concrete slope and up the ship's ramp into the hold.[8]

Of the five invasion forces, the 865 ships of Moon's Force U had the longest voyage, from the West Country of England to the assembly area south of the Isle of Wight, so they would be the first of the five groups to leave port. The ships began to embark the men and equipment of Major General Raymond "Tubby" Barton's 4th Infantry Division at ports along the south coast of Devon from Salcombe to Torquay on Thursday, June 1. The character of a ship's cargo varied depending on its specific assignment, but a typical LST might carry twenty tanks, twenty trucks, a dozen jeeps with trailers or artillery pieces, plus some 350 officers and men who were assigned to vertical racks of bunks running along the port side of the ship. Officially, their scheduled departure time was 8:00 p.m. on Saturday, June 3, though some vessels began to depart as early as noon that day.

Further up the Channel at Weymouth and Portland, the amphibs of Hall's Force O also began to load up, though they were not scheduled to depart until 7:00 a.m. on June 4. Hall's fifteen large transport ships, two dozen LSTs, thirty-seven LCI(L)s, and more than 140 LCTs took on board men of Major General Clarence Huebner's 1st Infantry Division, plus two Regimental Combat Teams (the 115th and 116th) of the 29th Division. In some cases the loading process reunited Navy crews with infantry units they had carried during one or more of the many rehearsals. A sailor on LST-498 at Weymouth peering over the bow to watch the soldiers marching up the ramp noticed the patches on the men's shoulders that marked them as belonging to the 29th Division. It was somehow comforting to him that they were boarding old comrades, though he also felt that it was different this time. "Everybody knew what was up," he insisted.[9]

Still further east, at Southampton, Portsmouth, and Newhaven, British LSTs boarded the Tommies of the British Second Army, for the invasions of Sword and Gold Beaches, and men of the Canadian Third Division, who would assail Juno Beach. The British soldiers were outfitted with studded boots, and many of them found walking on the steel decks of an LCT or LST a precarious undertaking. The shiploads varied only slightly from the American LSTs. LST-543, for example, part of Force J, for Juno Beach, took on sixty-six vehicles that included both light and heavy trucks, two artillery pieces, and twelve tracked armored vehicles known as Bren gun carriers, plus 354 Canadian officers and men. Other LSTs swallowed up some of the big 40-ton Churchill tanks that had steel treads which scarred up the decks of the LCTs "like they were sand papered."[10]

At all of these sites, vessels had to be combat loaded, which meant not only that the items that would be needed first had to be loaded last, but also that the tanks and trucks had to be backed in, reversing gingerly up the ramps so that they would all be facing forward when the LSTs reached the target beaches. Then each vehicle had to be carefully positioned to ensure that everything fit and that the weight distribution would leave the ship on an even keel. Once that was done, crewmen crawled under the vehicles to secure them to the deck with chains so that they did not careen about and smash into one another during the expected rough crossing.

The whole process of loading, positioning, and securing the vehicles, plus boarding the men and assigning them to their respective billets, took about two and a half hours for each ship. When that was completed, a two-man team of officers, one each from the Army and Navy, certified that the load was both complete and accurate. The LST captain signaled his readiness to the port captain by flag hoist, and upon receiving clearance, he ordered the ramp raised and the bow doors closed, then backed the packed vessel out into the harbor, where it dropped anchor at a previously assigned position. As soon as it cleared the hard, another LST came in to take its place. Once a loaded ship was at anchor, no further communication with the shore was permitted.[11]

By June 2, it had become evident to all that this was no mere rehearsal. Not only was it simply too large for an exercise, but in addition almost everyone noted that during all the previous exercises the weather had been at least tolerable. More than once when the Channel was rough, a rehearsal had been postponed until the weather moderated. Now, despite whitecaps in the Channel and a strong gusting wind, the work never paused. On the other hand, the weather was so bad that some wondered if a crossing was even possible. The fully laden LSTs, riding low in the water, rolled dizzyingly even in the protected harbors, and many of the embarked soldiers were already puking over the side. On board LST-530, Armond Barth was sure "we weren't going anywhere."[12]

Loading the smaller LCTs took less time simply because they could hold only four or five vehicles each, though the process was prolonged because there were so many of them—142 of them in Moon's force alone. Like the bigger LSTs, they were packed to the thwarts. George Hackett watched with growing alarm as his vessel settled lower and lower in the water while the Sherman tanks and "deuce and a half" Dodge trucks backed slowly into the well deck. By the time the skipper pulled up the ramp, the vessel rode so low in the water that Hackett wondered if it might not be swamped by the four-foot Channel swells.[13]

Unlike the big LSTs, which would remain offshore during the initial assault, the LCTs would actually run right up onto the beaches just behind the first wave, and given the uncertainties of amphibious landings, it was not impossible that they could be stranded there. Because of that, the LCT crewmen were issued shoulder arms, though what they got were World

War I–vintage .30 caliber bolt-action rifles still packed in greasy cosmoline, a box of ammunition, an eight-inch knife, and a helmet. The prospect of having to do battle with the Wehrmacht with such weapons was sobering. The LCT crewmen were also required to wear special chemically treated overalls that were supposed to protect them from a gas attack. Upon donning them, many sailors wondered if poison gas might not be preferable. The treated clothing smelled like rotten eggs, and the stench was so powerful that some sailors gagged. "These clothes covered all of our bodies from the neck down," a sailor recalled, "and they were hot as hell, itchy, and the odor was unbearable." The treated material did not breathe at all, and one sailor described it "like walking around in a steam bath all day and in a suit of ice at night." Even the sailors' traditional white hats were dyed blue, presumably to make them less visible at sea, though many of the sailors resented having to sacrifice this particular tradition to some planner's notion of security.[14]

The LCT officers also wore the malodorous gas outfits. Their orders instructed them to ensure that they had a full supply of "foul weather gear, rain gear, combat boots, overshoes, gloves, [and] mittens." As a result, they looked more like well-padded North Sea fishermen than naval officers—and smelled like them, too. The briefing officers on shore had impressed upon them that this gear could save their lives, but it was somewhat embarrassing during the subsequent crossing when a U.S. Navy LCT passed a Royal Navy ship and the Americans saw that the British had not bothered with any of this. With characteristic sangfroid, the Royal Navy officers were wearing double-breasted service dress blue uniforms with white officer's caps. A bit chagrinned, perhaps, many of the Americans discarded their smelly gas suits as soon as they could. Once the LCTs were loaded, they, too, backed away from the hards one by one to anchor in the outer harbor, their open cargo holds covered by camouflage nets to make it more difficult for enemy aircraft to determine if they were full or empty.[15]

The huge 492-foot attack transport ships that could carry fifteen hundred soldiers at a time were too big to come into the hards and anchored further out. To board them, soldiers with sixty-pound packs strapped to their backs and M-1 rifles slung over their shoulders trooped aboard the LCTs at the hards, and after a brisk ride across the wind-tossed harbor they climbed up cargo nets hung over the side. Several days later, on the other side of the English Channel, they would reverse the process, climbing down those nets into the LCTs or the smaller Higgins boats to make their way to the invasion beaches.[16]

For many of the embarked soldiers, the on-board waiting was worse than waiting in the sausage camps. Even more than the big LSTs, the smaller LCTs bounced around energetically in the blustery weather, rising and swooping with the wind and waves. Keyed up by the prospect of imminent action, the soldiers and crewmen now had to endure a period of unknown duration waiting for the "go" order. There was little to do but to look around the harbor, exchange small talk with their buddies, and think about the forthcoming operation. On a number of ships, chaplains held religious services, which were well attended. On his flagship, the *Bayfield*, Moon authorized showing a film to help pass the time, and the soldiers sat down to watch George Sanders and Herbert Marshall in *The Moon and Sixpence*, a 1942 drama about a middle-aged stockbroker who, like Paul Gauguin, settles on a South Sea island to paint and go native. This naturally led some sailors to make jokes about the old man showing a movie about himself and his salary.[17]

At least there was plenty to eat. This was especially true on the big attack transport ships and the LSTs, both of which were well equipped with galleys designed to feed hundreds of men at a time. On some of the LSTs, the cooks served up a full steak dinner on June 3. While it was much appreciated, a number of men wondered at the symbolism. Was this the last meal of the condemned man? The fare was more Spartan on the LCTs. Each LCT had been stocked with fifteen days' of food, but much of it consisted of K rations, which came in small cardboard boxes containing a can of meat or cheese, four crackers, some malted milk balls, a pack of coffee, four cigarettes, and a candy bar. It was not uncommon for a soldier to put the cigarettes in his pocket, eat the candy bar, and throw the rest away. Slightly more tolerable were C rations, which included a canned entree of hash or stew. Curtis Hansen, on LST-315, tried to heat up a can of stew from a C ration pack by placing it on the engine manifold. That worked just fine, but such was the state of his constitution that when he took the first bite, his stomach rebelled, and he threw up over the side.[18]

Some tried to sleep, though with so many men on board, space to stretch out was at a premium. A few soldiers "hot-bunked" in the available racks. Others climbed into the back of the trucks and sought to find room amidst the crates and equipment, ignoring the fact that much of it consisted of ammunition. Still others climbed on top of the trucks, making a hammock out of the swale of canvas between the metal supports. They found that if they wriggled down deep enough in the truck's canvas top, it would block the wind and the stinging sea spray. Then it began to rain. To escape it, they sought refuge below deck. That proved to be a problem for some of the nonswimmers on board, who, suspicious of being at sea at all, had inflated their inner-tube-style life vests as soon as the LCT backed away from the hard. Now they discovered that they were unable to go below because the hatches on an LCT were not wide enough to accommodate a man wearing an inflated life preserver. Before very long, almost everyone on board was, in the words of one, "wet and miserable."[19]

During the lengthy loading process, senior officers occasionally dropped by one or another of the embarkation sites to ensure that things were progressing satisfactorily. Both Eisenhower and Ramsay visited Portsmouth to chat with the soldiers and sailors and offer encouragement. Even King George showed up. Robert Evans was busy loading jeeps and other equipment onto LCT-271 when a black Rolls-Royce pulled up on the hard and King George VI stepped out wearing the uniform of a five-star admiral in the Royal Navy. Evans knew the proper protocol was for him to come to attention and salute, but instead he, and everyone else in the immediate area, started cheering and waving. The king took it all in good spirit and waved back. At another site, the king strode toward the ramp of a ship that was being loaded, only to be confronted by a young American quartermaster, clipboard in hand, who had been told not to let anyone on board without first checking his identity and recording his name. That led to this curious exchange:

"What is your name, Admiral?"

"Windsor."

"First name?"

"George."

The quartermaster dutifully recorded on his clipboard that the ship had been visited by Admiral George Windsor.[20]

Churchill, too, could not resist inserting himself into the frenzy of preparations. He was a regular visitor to Southwick House, where Eisenhower, Ramsay, and others felt obliged to provide him with updated briefings, and the prime minister also visited several of the embarkation sites. More problematically, he announced to Ramsay his plan to cross the Channel himself on the British cruiser HMS *Belfast* so that he could be present when Allied guns opened on the French coast. When Eisenhower expressed his opposition to this idea, Churchill overrode him. Churchill conceded that Eisenhower had command authority over the invasion force, but he insisted that the American general did not have the right "to regulate the complement of the British ships in the Royal Navy." Ike backed down, but Churchill still had King George to contend with. At first the king was enthusiastic about the idea and suggested that he, too, should board the *Belfast* and take part in the invasion. Soon enough, however, he appreciated how reckless it was to create a situation where a chance bomb or shell could produce an inestimable psychological victory for the Axis. He told Churchill that neither of them should go. Churchill was a dutiful and even enthusiastic monarchist, but he rebelled at being told that he could not go to sea, even by the king. He was, after all (as Roosevelt often called him in their correspondence), a "former naval person." When George VI reminded Churchill that the prime minister required the king's permission to leave the country, Churchill replied that being on a king's ship was technically not "out of the country." George VI saw that the key to resolving this impasse was not an authoritarian declaration but an appeal to Churchill's sense of duty. On June 2, even as the invasion fleet prepared to depart, he demonstrated his sensitivity and political skill in a letter to his prime minister:

Please consider my own position. I am a younger man than you, I am a sailor, and as King I am the head of all these Services. There is nothing I would like better than to go to sea, but I have agreed to stay at home; is it fair that you should then do exactly what I should have liked to do myself? I ask you most earnestly to consider the whole question again, and not let your personal wishes, which I very well understand, lead you to depart from your own high standard of duty to the State.[21]

Churchill stayed behind.

AS THE MOMENT OF DEPARTURE NEARED, many men in the invasion armada, sensing the imminence of action, took the opportunity to write a last letter home professing their love to their families, asserting their willingness to die if necessary, and asking to be remembered. Some wrote their parents, others their wives. In this, there was little difference between the ranks. Ensign Edwin Gale assured his father that he was proud to be "one of the chosen thousands who are going to strike the blow that is going to win the war." Admiral Don Moon wrote his wife that he would do his best to "carry the country's banner high and apply all power to the enemy's defeat." Both pledged their "devotion and love" to their families.[22]

The time of departure varied from port to port, and even from ship to ship, with the more distant and slower vessels leaving first. Indeed, some elements of the Allied armada were already at sea well before the amphibious ships began to load their cargoes. The first to leave port were the "corncobs"—the derelict ships that would be sunk off the target beaches to form the "gooseberry" breakwater. They had left the small port of Oban, in northern Scotland, under tow on May 31. Traveling at only three to four knots, it would take them ten days to get to Normandy, by which time, presumably, the beaches would be secured. The next to depart were a pair of four-man midget submarines, the X-20 and the X-23, which left Portsmouth under tow on June 2 to take up positions off the British beaches, where they would act as beacons and guides for the invaders.

Of the actual landing forces, Moon's Force U was the first to sortie. The LCTs in the Dart River began unmooring from their nests and heading out into the lower anchorage off Dartmouth Castle at noon on June 3. By the afternoon, it was evident to even a casual observer that they were all getting under way. Edwin Gale, on LCT-853, found it "quite a moving spectacle," not the least because the townspeople of Dartmouth, aware of what was happening, gathered in large numbers along the riverbank, where they stood silently waving goodbye. Cliff Underwood, skipper of the 853, turned to Gale and said, "Edwin, you know we may not do anything as worthwhile as this again in our lives. But it is a fine thing to be here." Gale was moved by Underwood's words, though it did not stop him from wondering, as their vessel passed out through the submarine net and into the open Channel, if "we might not ever come back again."[23]

June days are long in the northern latitudes, and the sun did not set that night until after ten o'clock. Throughout the long afternoon and into the evening, hundreds of Allied ships exited from Plymouth, Salcombe, and Brixham, as well as from Dartmouth. They moved into the Channel and formed up into twelve separate convoys, which then turned south by southeast, with the English coast off their port side. They crossed Lyme Bay, where three LSTs had come to grief during Exercise Tiger in April, and headed for a position south of the Isle of Wight designated as Area Zebra, where they would rendezvous with the four other invasion forces due to sortie the next morning. Providentially, there were no German air reconnaissance missions during these crucial hours. Very likely this was due to the unsettled weather, though at least one senior U.S. officer found it "simply incredible."[24]

The weather remained a concern, for as soon as Moon's vessels left their several harbors, they were hit with four-to-six-foot seas, strong winds, and intermittent rain. The smaller ships suffered the most. That included the several fifty-six-foot-long landing craft control ships, intended primarily for use as navigational aids to mark the eventual line of departure. An officer on one of these (the LCC-60) recalled that the sea was "abusively choppy and disagreeable." It was particularly nasty on the open bridge, where the "bitter winds and raw salt spray" challenged the enthusiasm of officers and crew alike. These conditions also affected the Seabees on the rhino ferries being towed by the LSTs. The wind and current tended to slew the rhino barges off to one side, so they proceeded crab-like, acting like a kind of sea anchor for the ships towing them. The big hemp towlines would lie slack on the water, then jerk taut, sometimes knocking the Seabees off their feet. It also put a great strain on the towlines and made it difficult for the towing ships to maintain their position in the formation. Soon the careful structure of the convoys began to unravel. Moreover, since the rhinos were essentially flat metal barges, they offered no protection at all from the waves that sloshed across their decks or the cold winds that whipped around them. The Seabees had to stamp their feet to keep their lower legs from going numb.[25]

That same night, three hundred miles to the north, the gunfire support ships for the invasion left Belfast, in Northern Ireland, and the Firth of Clyde, in Scotland. Even after the sun eventually set, there was a full moon whose light struggled to pierce the heavy cloud cover. According to U.S. Navy Rear Admiral Carleton F. Bryant, who commanded the Omaha Beach bombardment group, the result was "a kind of half twilight" that struck him as "eerie." Bryant led a mixed command of two American battleships (*Texas* and *Arkansas*) plus two British and two French cruisers. Another American, Rear Admiral Morton Deyo, commanded the bombardment group for Utah Beach, which consisted of the battleship *Nevada* (a Pearl Harbor survivor) and three heavy cruisers. The bombardment groups for Gold, Juno, and Sword Beaches were made up entirely of Royal Navy warships, including the battleships *Warspite* and *Ramillies,* and all these ships headed south through the Irish Sea on a course to clear Land's End before dawn on June 4. The captain of a Royal Navy destroyer operating in the Irish Sea looked out over the starboard quarter of his ship that night to see the fighting tops of several battleships and heavy cruisers coming up over the horizon. He identified most of the British ships, which were followed by others with the distinctive higher freeboard of American warships. *Here are the lions of the great armada,* he thought, *and the flags of two nations bent together.* The very sight of them erased any doubt he had about the success of the forthcoming operation.[26]

By midnight on June 3, several of the tightly scheduled elements of the complex invasion plan had been set in motion, but there was one aspect of the plan that could not be scripted.

THE SHIPS OF MOON'S FORCE U were still emerging from their several harbors at 9:30 p.m. on June 3, when Eisenhower and his principal deputies met at Southwick House near Portsmouth to hear the latest weather forecast from Group Captain James M. Stagg, the Royal Air Force officer who was Ike's chief meteorologist. The day before, Stagg had reported that the forecast for June 5 was "full of menace," and that the weather was likely to turn worse before it got better. Ike had decided to wait a day before deciding what, if anything, to do about it. Now, twenty-four hours later, Stagg's updated forecast was even more dire. A low-pressure area was moving in, and the weather stations in Northern Ireland were reporting large waves and winds of thirty miles per hour. Eisenhower asked his trio of commanders what they thought. Ramsay, who had spent the day visiting the hards in Portsmouth, replied that he believed the initial assault force would be able to get ashore but that the worsening weather would make it difficult, perhaps even impossible, to provide follow-up support. Leigh-Mallory was similarly cautious, suggesting that even if his planes could fly, the pilots would not be able to see well enough to be sure of their targets. Only Montgomery announced himself ready to go, a statement that provoked a few sidelong glances from others in the room who wondered if this was just Monty being Monty. The decision, of course, was Eisenhower's. To send the invasion force into the teeth of a bad storm could prove disastrous, but a postponement might prove almost as bad. A delay risked losing the element of surprise and would utterly disrupt the intricate invasion timetable, with potentially catastrophic results. There seemed to be no good option. Eisenhower announced that the circumstances seemed to require a twenty-four-hour postponement but that he would wait until four-fifteen the next morning to hear one more weather report before making a final decision. In the meantime, the original schedule would be maintained, and Moon's Force U continued on its southeasterly course, battling the elements.[27]

By 4:15 a.m. on June 4, the winds had moderated, and when the SHAEF command team gathered again at Southwick House, there was a surge of cautious hope. As he entered, Captain Stagg felt an almost physical tension in the room. Ike nodded to him meaningfully, and Stagg presented his updated forecast. It was not good. Clouds and winds would continue to increase all day, he reported, and bring the cloud ceiling down to a mere three hundred feet. Ramsay spoke up to observe that it was clear and calm outside at the moment, but Stagg assured him that the weather would worsen over the next several hours. Eisenhower again queried his commanders. Ramsay feared that the low cloud ceiling "would prohibit use of airborne troops" and most other air action, "including air spotting" for naval gunfire support. Ramsay had agreed to a daylight attack in the first place only because of assurances that air and gunfire support would be "overwhelming." Given the conditions described by Captain Stagg, it seemed unlikely now that there could be any significant air or naval support. Ramsay believed the invasion should be delayed. Eisenhower concurred. "If the air cannot operate," he said, "we must postpone." He looked around the room and asked if everyone was in agreement. No one spoke; even Montgomery remained silent. Eisenhower thereupon announced that the landings would be postponed for twenty-four hours. In fact, the postponement would be twenty-four and a half hours, since the original H-Hour was 6:00 a.m. on June 5 but had now been changed to 6:30 a.m. on June 6 to accommodate the tide.[28]

Ramsay at once notified his task force commanders by phone. Vian's three task groups, though fully loaded and ready to go, had not yet left port, so for them, while the news was irksome, it was not dire. Kirk's two task groups were more of a problem. Hall's Force O had been scheduled to depart at 7:00 a.m., now just over two hours away, which meant that his ships had already begun their departure routines. And of course most of Moon's Force U had been at sea since the night before. Nevertheless, when Ramsay called Kirk to ask, "Can you hold up?" Kirk at once replied, "Yes we can." Kirk's confidence derived from his knowledge that there was an annex to the operational plan dedicated to precisely these circumstances. All that was necessary, Kirk believed, was to broadcast the preestablished code phrase for a twenty-four-hour delay, and all the elements of his Western Task Force would adjust accordingly.[29]

For the most part, Kirk's confidence proved well founded. The signal ("One Mike Post") went out over the radio at 5:15 a.m., and hundreds of ships from the Irish Sea to the Thames Estuary adjusted as necessary. The battleships and cruisers from Scotland and Ireland reversed course. As Admiral Deyo put it, "We merely countermarched up the Irish Sea during the day, got some sleep, and countermarched again that evening." The "corncobs," proceeding under tow at a leisurely three to four knots, adjusted similarly.[30]

The problem, of course, was Moon's Force U. Moon had been up all night ensuring that the various elements of his eclectic command successfully got to sea in accordance with the detailed timetable. So far he had managed it, though during the transit eastward, near-gale-force winds and high waves had scattered elements of his command over a wide swath of the western Channel. Now with the postponement, Moon not only had to consolidate his literally far-flung command, he also had to redirect the ships into nearby ports. They could not remain at sea like the cruisers and destroyers, for they were already in mid-Channel where daylight (sunrise was at 5:58 that morning) would soon expose them to German reconnaissance aircraft if any bothered to overfly the Channel. Moreover, the smaller vessels, including the LCTs, LCIs, and Mike boats, did not have the fuel capacity to stay at sea for another twenty-four hours and still have enough left to carry out the operation. They had to find a safe harbor for the night, one with substantial refueling capability. Most of Moon's ships headed into Weymouth and Portland, though one of the convoy groups, designated as U-2A, was beyond the reach of the short-range TBS (talk-between-ships) radio and unwilling to break radio silence, Moon sent the destroyer Forrest (DD-461) speeding at better than thirty knots to find it and turn it around.[31]

Unsurprisingly, the recall dampened morale. Though most of the sailors and soldiers had correctly guessed that this was the actual invasion, the ship captains had waited until their vessels had cleared the harbor before making a formal announcement. On many ships that announcement had provoked cheers; on others, thoughtful solemnity. Then, only hours later, came the "One Mike Post" radio message, and the captains came back on the speaker system to announce, essentially, never mind. For some it was relief; for many it was disappointment. For almost everyone it was frustrating. Having steeled themselves to make the supreme effort of their lives, their adrenaline crashed and left behind a curious lethargy. "When we departed...we were ready to go, and in a high state of excitement," one sailor remembered later. The recall announcement "was a real letdown, and it exhausted the crew."[32]

Not all of Moon's command was at sea when the postponement order came through. Those forces designated for the follow-up assaults, including most of the personnel-carrying LCIs, were still loading in the several West Country ports. Captain James Arnold was supervising the embarkation of soldiers at Dartmouth when a courier handed him a flimsy with the new orders. Arnold secured the work details, but he was too keyed up to sleep, so he got a cup of coffee from the galley and went out on the starboard wing of one of the ships. There he "gazed at the silent, eerie waters of the Dart River, watching the incoming tide slack the mooring lines." Like ghostly shadows in the dark, sailors took in the lines to keep the ship secure, carefully stepping over and around the sleeping bodies of hundreds of soldiers lying on the deck.[33]

Meanwhile, the recalled elements of Moon's command were discovering that the harbors at Weymouth and Portland were already crowded with the ships of Hall's Force O. They worked their way cautiously into the harbors seeking an open stretch of water where they could drop anchor, and in doing so many inevitably became separated from the other vessels in their unit. Those lowest on fuel made their way to the fueling docks to top off their tanks. Moon and his various flotilla commanders tried to keep track of all the vessels in their charge, but in the chaos of the moment, with each ship captain looking out for his particular command, that became all but impossible. "We were never again in the proper order in the convoy," Edwin Gale remembered. An additional burden was that all the ships were operating under strict radio silence. The short-range TBS radio could be used, but only for emergencies, and most communication took place by flag hoist, by blinker light, or even by shouting and gesticulating from ship to ship. At one point two LCT flotillas, one from Force U and one from Force O, became intermingled. Seeking to restore order, the commander of one flotilla found himself reduced to yelling and waving, recalling later that "we could not do anything but curse and swear at one another until the whole thing got sorted out."³⁴

Though they had reached safe harbor, the crews and the embarked soldiers remained confined to their ships, and by now the men were no longer "freshly bathed, shaved, and wearing warm underclothing," as the operational order had specified. As one sailor put it, "we were exhausted, saltwater soaked, and hungry long before we got back to England and tied up at Weymouth." Besides the physical exhaustion and the anticlimax of the recall, there was now another period of apprehensive waiting. The thoughts of many turned to home, family, and their own mortality. Some prayed. Richard G. "Jack" Laine recalled making a private vow that if he lived through the invasion, he would strive to be a better Christian. He assumed others were making similar pledges, for he could see men in various corners with their beads bent and their lips moving silently. Others played cards, read, passed along rumors, and waited in lines to use the limited number of heads on board. Nearly all wondered "what the dawn would bring."³⁵

Once it was full dark, their reveries were broken by a routine Luftwaffe raid. The planes dropped mainly mines, and with the harbors as crowded as they were, they could hardly miss. Though no ships were sunk, several were damaged. When a mine exploded near LCT-271, it threw everyone out of their bunks and severed the anchor cable. Unable to operate without an anchor, the 271 made a quick trip to the repair yard for a new one so that it would not miss the sortie.³⁶

THAT NIGHT AT 9:00, Eisenhower met yet again with his command team. His decision to postpone the landing from June 5 to June 6 had been difficult, but it was not evident that the operation could be launched even on June 6. Unless the weather moderated, it might have to be postponed again, perhaps even until the next moon and tide cycle, which was not until June 19–21. If that happened, the ships would all have to return to their original ports, the men disembark, and the loading process be restarted.* Aware of that, the men who gathered at Southwick House that night were solemn. As Stagg had foretold, a storm was raging outside, the sound of it clearly evident in the room as rain beat against the windows and wind whistled around the corners. This time, however, Stagg had a glimmer of good news. It appeared likely, he reported, that the storm would moderate on June 6. That provoked cheers from the assembled officers, though Tedder, Ike's deputy, leaned in to ask for specifics. He wanted to know exactly what the weather would be like over the landing beaches on June 6. Stagg was quiet for a long breathless moment before he replied, "To answer that question would make me a guesser, not a meteorologist." The weather was likely to improve, he said, but there remained a huge element of uncertainty—and therefore of risk.[37]

Once again, Eisenhower surveyed opinion in the room. Ramsay was willing to go, though he made it clear that because of the lead time necessary to get his armada back to sea, he had to know Eisenhower's decision soon, within the next half hour. Both Tedder and Leigh-Mallory were cautious, but Monty, as always, was game. "I would say—Go!" he declared pugnaciously. Ike agreed. "I don't see how we could do anything else," he said. As he had the night before, however, Eisenhower declared that they would meet again at four-fifteen in the morning to hear Stagg's latest report, at which time he would make the final and irrevocable decision one way or another. The decision could be recalled if Stagg came in with bad news, but for now, Ramsay should tell his force commanders that it was a go. When Ramsay called them, Vian and Kirk "showed great concern," for the storm was then at its peak. Nevertheless, they both passed the orders to their task group commanders, and the five invasion fleets—two of them now intermingled in Weymouth and Portland—again prepared to sortie. Some left immediately.[38]

---

* With hindsight, it is evident that a postponement until June 19 would have been catastrophic. Though Eisenhower could not have known it, June 19 was the date a massive summer storm came churning up the English Channel. (See Chapter 14.) That would have made any invasion during the June 19–21 window impossible and might have scuttled the invasion entirely.

After a sleepless night, the SHAEF command team met again at South-wick House at 4:00 a.m. While the weather had begun to improve, it was hardly ideal. Nevertheless, Stagg came into the room smiling. The wind would remain "fresh," he said, and while it was evident that the crossing would be "uncomfortable," the weather would improve throughout the day, and indeed for the next several days. Eisenhower got up from his chair and walked about the room, his head bent forward and his hands clasped be-hind his back. No one spoke. Everyone understood that the decision was his alone. His next words would decide the fate of thousands, and quite possibly change the course of history.

"O.K.," he said. "We'll go."[39]

The various commanders left to pass the news. Eisenhower headed down to Portsmouth to watch men boarding the LCI(L)s and to chat informally with some of the soldiers. Now that the decision had been made, a weight was lifted from his shoulders and he talked easily and confidently. After-ward, he met briefly with members of the press, and as he did so, the morn-ing clouds parted just enough to allow "a quick flash" of sunlight. If Monty had been there, he might have made some remark about "the sun of Auster-litz," the gleam of light that presaged Napoleon's greatest victory back in 1805. Since it was Ike, he merely said, "By George, there *is* some sun."[40]

CHAPTER 11

D-DAY: THE INVASION

MONG THE FIRST CRAFT to sortie on June 5 were the minesweepers that would clear channels for the invasion forces. Though less glamorous than combat, and too often underappreciated, minesweeping was (and is) a complicated and dangerous business. Stark believed that "minesweeping is one of the most vital and critical parts of our forthcoming operation," and Ramsay insisted that "the mine is our greatest obstacle to success." Despite the advent of advanced sweeping gear, minesweeping remained an imperfect science. The mines were not merely cleared away or "swept," the way one might sweep a kitchen floor; they were deliberately detonated, hopefully in a way that did not also sink the minesweepers, though occasionally they did.[1]

The German mines off the Normandy beaches were not as numerous as the Allies feared, mainly because Hitler had decreed that a full deployment of mines should be postponed until it was clear where the Allies were coming ashore. Still, the mines that were there proved particularly challenging because they relied on a variety of technologies. So-called Katie mines rested on tripods that bent out of the way when contacted by minesweeping gear, then rocked back into place to detonate only when a ship passed overhead. German "oyster" mines rested on the bottom and detonated when they sensed a change in water pressure caused by a vessel that was at least 120 feet long passing overhead. The only effective Allied countermeasure for this type of mine was to tow a sled that mimicked the signature of a passing ship. But since the sled was towed astern, the minesweeper itself remained vulnerable, as was evident when the minesweeper USS *Osprey* was lost during the sweeping operations on June 5. Another problem was that some of the mines had "counters," which meant that they would ignore the first one or two vessels that passed overhead and then detonate under the third. The Germans also deployed anti-sweeping devices that could cut the sweeping gear and temporarily put a minesweeper out of action until it could be repaired.[2]

All but thirty-two of the more than three hundred minesweepers assigned to the operation were Royal Navy vessels. Ramsay had appealed to Ernest King to increase the American contribution, but without success. Ramsay's appeal did, however, result in the assignment of an American PT boat squadron to protect the minesweepers from E-boat attacks, though that decision had as much to do with the disastrous events during Exercise Tiger as with Ramsay's request. As it happened, the PT boat squadron King sent was under the command of Lieutenant Commander John Bulkeley, who had been awarded the Medal of Honor two years before for his role in the Philippine campaign, including extracting Douglas MacArthur from Corregidor. Bulkeley's squadron arrived in England only two days before the invasion, and Jimmy Hall told him to "get those minesweepers in and get those lines swept, then get out by 5:15 in the morning."[3]

The minesweepers left port on the afternoon of June 5 and began sweeping at 8:00 p.m., while it was still daylight. They worked in flotillas of six, steaming en echelon to cover the desired channel width, while smaller vessels followed them to deploy red and green buoys on either side of the cleared channel. Charged to clear ten channels to the invasion beaches— two for each beach—they steamed in toward the coast for four hours, then turned around and swept back again on a parallel track. Once they had swept and marked the ten channels, they began sweeping the area off the landing beaches where the big transports would anchor. They did not complete their work until only minutes before dawn on June 6, after more than sixteen hours of nonstop labor. Not every mine was detected, and mines remained "a constant source of worry," but the role of the minesweepers was crucial. Captain Powell Rhea, who commanded the American battleship *Nevada*, declared in his official report that the minesweepers "deserve the lion's share of the credit for the successful accomplishment of the mission." In an unusual testimonial, he added: "They not only swept and buoyed a remarkably clear and geographically accurate channel through the German mine fields, but did so at night, unescorted, in severe cross currents, in mine-infested waters, and in the face of possible enemy attack."[4]

While the minesweepers did their work, the invasion forces sortied from their several harbors. The LCTs carrying the men and equipment for the first wave left within minutes of Eisenhower's preliminary "go" decision at 9:45 p.m. on June 4. The bigger troop transports, LSTs and LCI(L)s, joined the exodus the next morning. By midday on June 5, most of the vast Allied armada was at sea, and once again for thousands of men, the butterflies of uncertainty mixed with the adrenaline of anticipation.

British ships made up well over half of the invasion armada of more than six thousand vessels, and they offered a remarkable spectacle as they filed out of Southampton and Portsmouth. English ships had put to sea from those ancient ports for nine centuries, and the channels that led from them to the open sea were household names. Those leaving Southampton passed through the Solent, which separated the Isle of Wight from the mainland, and into a broad open roadstead known as Spithead for the long spit of sand that protected it from the Channel. This was the historic anchorage of the Royal Navy and the scene of formal reviews of the fleet by monarchs since Elizabeth I. Yet familiar as these roadsteads were to generations of British seamen since Drake and Frobisher, Spithead had never seen an armada like this one. To Vian, watching from his flagship, the cruiser *Scylla*, "the constant stream of landing craft and ships" coming down the Solent and into Spithead was "a heartening sight."[5]

As Captain Stagg had promised, it was an "uncomfortable" crossing. Four-foot waves smacked into the blunt bows of the LCTs, and green water washed over the thwarts and sluiced across their crowded decks. One LCT officer recalled that "the water would come in over the top front of the boat and flush out the back." Occasionally when an LCT nosed into a trough in the waves, its stern would rise out of the water and, lacking any resistance, its propellers would spin out of control as the engines emitted a high-pitched whine. Then the LCT pushed up into the next wave, the stern settled back into the sea, and the engine noise returned to normal. There was no place to escape the elements, and the embarked soldiers "huddled together in their trucks and kept as warm as possible." Navy crewmen tried to keep them supplied with hot coffee, but even that proved difficult. Unlike the steak-and-eggs breakfasts served on some of the larger ships, men on the smaller LCTs got only more boxes of the despised K rations.[6]

It was even worse for the men on the rhino ferries. In order to make their way into the overcrowded harbors the night before, many of them had uncoupled from their tows, and they now proceeded to the rendezvous site on their own, "chugging along," as Arthur Struble put it, at two or three knots, propelled by their twin outboard motors. A few of the rhinos had been designated as repair barges, and those had a Nissen hut in the middle of the deck that offered some refuge from the elements. On others, enterprising Seabees had cut a hatchway into one of the pontoons and set up Spartan quarters inside, though because the rhinos had only two feet of freeboard, the Channel's four-foot swells washed over the flush deck and down through the contrived hatch, rendering those ersatz quarters unusable. There was nothing for it but to huddle together in the middle of the rafts and endure the discomfort. Kirk and Struble, moving swiftly past them in the commodious *Augusta*, noted that on some of the rhinos, the Seabees had built open fires on the deck to fight off the cold or to warm their rations. To Kirk, they were "just like Robinson Crusoe," and they reminded Struble of Boy Scouts on a campout, though Bill O'Neill, passing by on an LCT, felt sorry for the men who were "leaning into the wind and spray" and "undoubtedly completely miserable."[7]

After nightfall, a prerecorded message from Eisenhower was played on board all the invasion ships. The 1-MCs squawked to life, and the men heard the voice of the Supreme Allied Commander speaking in his flat,

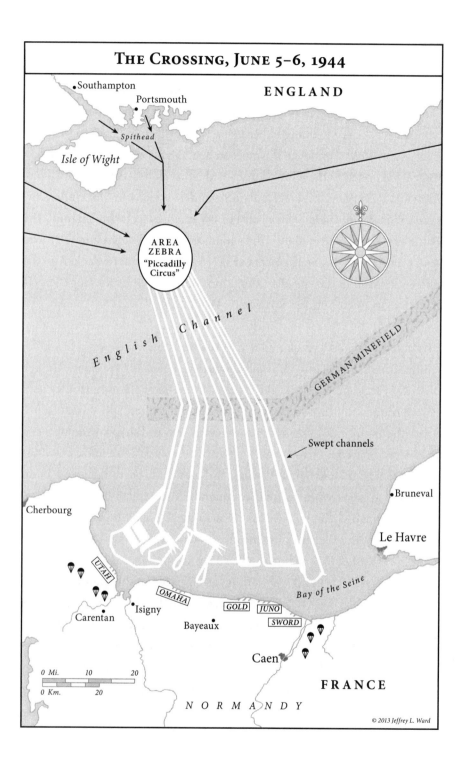

THE CROSSING, JUNE 5-6, 1944

Southampton

ENGLAND

Portsmouth

Spithead

Isle of Wight

AREA
ZEBRA
"Piccadilly
Circus"

English Channel

GERMAN MINEFIELD

Swept channels

Cherbourg

Bruneval

Le Havre

UTAH

OMAHA

Bay of the Seine

Isigny

GOLD

JUNO

Carentan

SWORD

Bayeaux

Caen

0 Mi.   10   20

FRANCE

0 Km.   20

NORMANDY

© 2013 Jeffrey L. Ward

midwestern American accent: "Soldiers, Sailors, and Airmen of the Allied Expeditionary Forces! You are about to embark upon the Great Crusade, toward which we have striven for many months." Ike acknowledged that "your task will not be an easy one," though he also assured them that they would have "overwhelming superiority in weapons and munitions," and that he had "full confidence in your courage, devotion to duty, and skill in battle." He ended with: "Good Luck! And let us all beseech the blessing of Almighty God upon this great and noble undertaking." On Moon's flagship, that inspired hundreds of men on the open decks to begin singing "The Battle Hymn of the Republic." The sound of it filtered down into the lower decks, where men lay on their cots or sat cross-legged on the deck. A junior officer on Moon's staff recalled the lump in his throat as he sang: "As He died to make men holy, let us die to make men free."[8]

THE RENDEZVOUS SITE for all five of the invasion forces was a few miles south of the Isle of Wight. Officially it was designated as Area Zebra, though virtually everyone called it "Piccadilly Circus" after the notoriously congested roundabout in the middle of London. It was an appropriate sobriquet. The thousands of ships of nearly every size and shape made up a city on the sea. The congestion was so great that it was difficult for some of the vessels to find their assigned flotillas, and inevitably there was some intermingling of ships from various commands. Lieutenant Dean Rockwell, who commanded the sixteen LCTs carrying the sixty-four duplex drive tanks for Omaha Beach, counted noses—or rather masts—and came up one short. Ensign F. S. White's LCT-713 was missing. Like the proverbial good shepherd, Rockwell went off in search of it, and he found it maneuvering among the LCTs of Moon's Force U. Rockwell came alongside the 713 and called out to White: had he noticed that while his vessel had a large white *O* painted on its conning tower, every other vessel in this area was marked with a *U*? White looked around and with dawning comprehension, though no apparent sense of irony, responded, "Oh."[9]

By midnight on June 5, the Piccadilly Circus rendezvous in mid-Channel was far more congested than the original ever had been. The assembled armada included between four thousand and six thousand vessels depending on whether one counted the minesweepers, patrol craft, tugs, rhino ferries, and other auxiliaries. Among them were 284 warships, a number that includes five battleships, two monitors, twenty-three cruisers, and more than a hundred destroyers and destroyer escorts, plus 142 smaller gunships. Adding armed patrol craft and PT boats to the list boosts the number of warships to nearly seven hundred. In addition to that, there were 311 LSTs, two hundred LCIs, eight hundred LCTs, nearly five hundred Mike boats (LCMs), and more than fifteen hundred of the small landing craft: Higgins boats and LCAs. Of all the memories that soldiers and sailors carried with them in the years afterward, the most pervasive was the one of "thousands and thousands of ships of all classes stretched from horizon to horizon."[10]

Because the galley fires had to be put out at midnight, many of these ships served the last hot meal the men would have for some time. After that, all the ships went to general quarters and set Condition Zebra, which required dogging down the watertight hatches. Paint cans and other inflammable materials were thrown over the side; firefighting and damage-repair equipment was broken out. On the destroyers, men pulled the plugs from the muzzles of the 5-inch guns and stacked shells in the ammunition hoists from the magazines. On some ships, the captain gave a short speech over the 1-MC. Then the invasion groups began to sort themselves out and move ship by ship into the marked channels.

There were two swept channels to each beach—a fast channel for ships moving at twelve knots, mostly the big transports and destroyers, and a slow channel for those traveling at five knots, which included all the landing craft. Small sub chasers acted as guide ships for long lines of LCTs, all of them blacked out save for a single small blue light on the fantail to serve as a beacon for the ship behind it. To men on the guide ships out in front, the illuminated dan buoys—red on the right, green on the left—seemed "like a highway leading us to our own section of beach." On Sub Chaser 1282, George Hackett looked astern to see hundreds of LCTs, one after another, in a line that stretched as far as he could see. One officer thought it looked like "a gigantic, twisting dragon."[11]

Most of the skippers focused on the blue light of the vessel in front of them rather than the red and green dan buoys. That was an imperfect navigating system since the high waves often obscured the blue lights. At one point, the executive officer of an LCT turned to the skipper to ask if the green buoys were supposed to be on the right side or the left side! To their horror they saw that their entire line of LCTs was outside the lane.

In another case, a line of landing craft passed directly across the bow of some transport ships, and last-second "radical course changes were necessary to avoid them." Inevitably, some ships broke down: more than a few had engine trouble, others leaked and began taking on water, still others had fuel problems. LCT-852 reported that its ramp "fell off," offering no further explanation. All of these ships had to return to port.[12]

For most of the men, however, the three-hour crossing was routine. "The hours crept slowly by," one recalled, and men passed the time in different ways. On LST-315, a large poker game began soon after midnight and lasted throughout the crossing. Chaplains on some of the larger ships hosted brief religious services. On one British destroyer, men stood "bare headed and drenched with spray…, holding on to anything they could find which would steady them against the violent movements of the ship," as the chaplain recited the traditional Royal Navy prayer, written by Lord Nelson on the eve of the Battle of Trafalgar in 1805: "May the Great God whom I worship grant to my Country and to the benefit of Europe in general a great and glorious victory. Amen." On other ships, men kept to themselves, thinking of family, sweethearts, and friends. To many the silence seemed "terrible," and at least one man thought, "The ripple of the bow wave sounded like Niagara Falls in the tense silence."[13]

So far there had been no reaction from the enemy, or any indication that the Germans even knew what was about to descend on them. At about 1:00 a.m., most of those on board the ships of Force O and Force U who were topside could hear, even if they could not see, hundreds of airplanes passing overhead. They were C-47 transport planes towing gliders filled with men of the 82nd and 101st Airborne divisions who would land behind the American beaches that night. Other planes carried the paratroopers of the British 6th Airborne Division toward their drop zone behind Sword Beach near Caen. As the Allied ships approached the French coast, the navigators were astonished to see that the 236-foot gray stone lighthouse on Cape

Barfleur was still operating, its powerful beam of light blinking as usual, almost as if the Germans disdained the whole idea of a sea assault. The big troop transports dropped anchor at their designated positions eighteen thousand yards (just over ten miles) off the coast at about 2:30 a.m., well ahead of the slower and more numerous LCTs and LCIs, and they had barely dropped anchor when they began to lower their Higgins boats alongside. Kirk, Hall, and Moon all agreed that, packed as they were with American soldiers, the transports were far too valuable and vulnerable to risk taking them within range of the German shore batteries, and for the soldiers that meant a long and dizzying ride to the assault beaches in the tiny Higgins boats. At 3:00 a.m., the 1-MC loudspeakers on the transports squawked to life: "Now hear this. Stand by all troops."[14]

Ashore on the high ground behind what the Allies called Omaha Beach, near Colleville-sur-Mer, German Lance Corporal Hein Severloh was anticipating his breakfast of bread, cheese, and butter when he paused to look out over the sea. With the morning haze lifting, several dark objects slowly came into focus, hundreds of them—thousands! "Holy smoke!" he said aloud. "Here they are."[15]

DUE TO THE TIDE DIFFERENTIAL and the curious geography of the Normandy coastline, the Americans would land sixty to eighty minutes ahead of the British and Canadians. There had been a lot of discussion about this. The Normandy beach gradients were very gradual—on much of the shoreline there is only about a foot of vertical rise in fifty feet of horizontal beach. Combined with tides of eighteen to twenty-four feet, that meant that the width of the beach changed dramatically from high tide to low tide. The generals had argued for making the attack at high tide, when the killing zone of the beach was relatively narrow, but the admirals wanted to attack at low tide so that the beach obstructions, most of them wired with mines, would be exposed. That would allow the landing craft to avoid them en route to the beach and would give the Navy Combat Demolition Units an opportunity to neutralize at least some of them before the second and third waves came ashore. In the end, the compromise decision was to attack two hours after low tide, which on June 6 was 6:30 a.m. That would give the demolition teams a brief window to attack the obstructions, and the swiftly rising tide would narrow the width of the beach as subsequent waves of infantry came ashore.[16]

A problem with this solution was that at two hours after low tide, the sand bars off Sword Beach near Caen did not provide sufficient deep water to allow the British LCTs to pass over them; not for another hour would there be enough water to provide clearance. Thus while H-Hour was 6:30 on the American beaches, it was 7:25 on Sword Beach. The asymmetry of the landings concerned Eisenhower, who would have preferred to strike all five beaches at once, but in the end he bowed to the tyranny of the coastal geography.

Nervous but confident, the soldiers on the American transports lugged their oversized packs and their nine-and-a-half-pound Garand M1 rifles onto the weather deck and lined up to board the Higgins boats. On a few ships, the soldiers climbed into landing craft that were suspended at the rail and were lowered along with the boats; on most, however, the Higgins boats were lowered empty save for their three-man Navy crews, and the soldiers climbed down into them on the scramble nets. Each soldier had to remember to hold the vertical supports on the nets rather than the horizontal ropes so that the man coming down after him did not step on his hands. Then, near the bottom of the net, he had to time his last-second jump into the Higgins boat carefully since the boats were rising and falling dramatically with the Channel swells. Some mistimed their jump and suffered lacerations and the occasional broken leg. The injured were brought back on board bearing the dubious distinction of being the first to be wounded during the invasion. As soon as the boats filled up with their designated complement, the Navy coxswains cast off and motored away to join boats from other transports that were circling in a holding pattern nearby. This process took about an hour; on the *Thomas Jefferson* (APA-30), for example, it took exactly sixty-six minutes.[17]

Not all the soldiers disembarked at once. Even with twenty or more Higgins boats per ship, the big transports could land only about five hundred men at a time—roughly a third of their onboard total. The rest would have to wait until the boats returned several hours later to carry them ashore in a subsequent wave. The invasion of occupied France was not to be accomplished in a single dash shoreward, but in a series of waves ten to fifteen minutes apart all day long, and indeed over the next several weeks. For more than nineteen hours, from before dawn until after ten that night, the coxswains in their Higgins boats and LCAs and the ensigns in their LCTs shuttled back and forth from the transports and the LSTs to the beach carrying troops and equipment ashore. For them, as much as for the soldiers they carried, June 6 was truly the longest day.[18]

Once inside the Higgins boats, the soldiers could see nothing. The high sides of the boat were above their heads and, heavily burdened as they were, they stood uncomfortably and precariously side by side, jostling up against one another as the boat lurched shoreward through the severe chop. Sea spray smacked them in the face and drizzled down into their clothing. Some who had avoided seasickness during the Channel crossing succumbed to it now, and the smell of *mal de mer* on the deck and on their boot tops added to the general discomfort of all. To many, the circling seemed endless. Then, just after 4:00 a.m., with the sky turning from full dark to dove gray, the landing craft were taken in charge by a small patrol boat or an escorting destroyer and led shoreward at a leisurely five knots. At that rate, the journey would take another two and a half hours, and they would arrive at their target beaches precisely at H-Hour. By then, however, many of the soldiers were so worn out from the journey and from seasickness that their battleworthiness was questionable. As one Higgins boat approached the beach, a soldier hoisted himself out over the thwarts to vomit into the roiling sea, provoking his sergeant to order him, "Get your head down. You'll be killed." The soldier didn't move, answering, "I'm dying anyway."[19]

FROM THE START, the planners had wrestled with the question of how to get at least some of the tanks ashore with the first wave of infantry so that the attackers would have armored support. Sending in the scarce LSTs with the first wave would subject them to unacceptable risk. Not until the enemy's big coastal guns had been neutralized could the LSTs run up onto the beach and spew out their massive cargoes of tanks and trucks. For the initial assault, therefore, the Allies relied on a few score specialized LCTs.

One version was an armored variant, designated LCT(A). These vessels were to go ashore with the infantry, ground themselves on the beach, and unload their Sherman tanks, including some equipped with bulldozer blades so they could help clear the beach obstacles. Another group of LCTs carried the experimental duplex drive tanks that would be launched from offshore and swim into the beach under their own power. Since the DD tanks were considerably slower than the Higgins boats, they would launch early, around 3:00 a.m., to give them time to motor to the beach at a painstaking two or three knots.

The problem, of course, was the weather. The inflatable canvas shrouds on the DD tanks had only about nine inches of freeboard when deployed, and it seemed unlikely that they could survive very long in the four-foot waves. The Neptune orders specified that "if state of sea is such as to prevent their being launched...land them with the first wave." The responsibility of judging the "state of sea" lay with the commanding officers of the LCT flotillas. Thus the first life-and-death decisions off the Normandy beaches on June 6 fell to a handful of ensigns and lieutenants.[20]

Off Omaha Beach, that responsibility belonged to Navy Lieutenant Dean Rockwell. A tall, dark, and robust individual with an oversized personality, Rockwell was a former athlete at Eastern Michigan University and a sometime professional wrestler. He had been teaching high school in Michigan and coaching the school's football team when he heard about Pearl Harbor and immediately enlisted in the Navy. Now, on D-Day, he was in charge of LCT Flotilla 12, consisting of sixteen vessels, each commanded by an ensign, and each carrying four DD tanks, half of them from the 741st Tank Battalion and half from the 743rd.[21]

In the predawn darkness, Rockwell led his sixteen LCTs in a long single file past the looming shadows of the big transports, battleships, and cruisers off Omaha Beach to take up their assigned positions six thousand yards (a little over three miles) off the beach. At the designated line of departure, Rockwell deployed his flotilla into two groups of eight in a line abreast facing Omaha Beach. It was just past 3:00 a.m., and the soldiers in the Higgins boats had not yet begun their slow journey toward the beach. Nevertheless, according to the plan, this was the moment for Rockwell's LCTs to open their bow doors, drop their ramps, and send the amphibious DD tanks on their way. It was evident to Rockwell, however, that doing so in such a violent sea would be tantamount to murder. He talked it over with Army Captain Ned Elder, the senior Army officer on board, and between them they decided "it would be insane" to launch the DD tanks into that volatile sea. Rockwell concluded that it was his duty to carry the tanks all the way to the beach.[22]

The problem was how to communicate that decision to the other vessels in his flotilla. Rockwell doubted that flag signals were sufficient. Nor could he use flashing lights, which would alert the enemy, and of course the Allies were operating under radio silence. But with the eastern sky already beginning to lighten in anticipation of dawn and the coast now visible to the naked eye, Rockwell decided to break the rules. *What the hell,* he thought. *By now the Germans know what is about to happen.* Rather than use the ship's long-range radio, however, he employed the shorter-range radio in one of the tanks, calling the other LCTs in his flotilla to order them *not* to launch.[23]

Not all the LCT skippers got the word. The eight vessels that were under Rockwell's immediate supervision did, but the other eight, carrying the thirty-two tanks of Companies B and C of the 741st Tank Battalion under Army Captain James G. Thornton, did not. On those vessels, there was uncertainty and confusion as the young and mostly inexperienced Army and Navy officers grappled with the distinction between duty and judgment. According to protocol, until the men and equipment were ashore, operational authority and responsibility belonged to the senior naval officer on board. But in this case those naval officers were ensigns in their early twenties, and quite naturally they felt some diffidence in making such a decision on behalf of the tank men. The Army officers were young, too, and they were eager to go—after all, they had spent months in rigorous training for just this moment. On LCT-600, Ensign Henry Sullivan discussed the circumstances with Second Lieutenant Patrick J. O'Shaughnessy. Even though they agreed "it was a little too rough to launch," O'Shaughnessy was cognizant of the historic immensity of the moment. Driven by a powerful sense of duty, he told Sullivan that he wanted go anyway, and Sullivan deferred to him. At 5:35 a.m. O'Shaughnessy drove the first DD tank off the bow ramp.[24]

As the second tank prepared to follow, a near miss from a German artillery shell caused LCT-600 to rock violently. The tanks jostled against one another, and the motion tore a hole in the canvas shroud of the second tank in line. That may have been providential, for with its shroud compromised, it could not be launched at all, nor could the two tanks behind it. Like Rockwell, Sullivan concluded that he had to take the other three tanks all the way to the beach. As for O'Shaughnessy's tank, it swam about a hundred yards under its own power, then disappeared from sight. Worse was to come. Without the fortunate accident of a torn shroud, all seven of the other LCTs in the group launched their DD tanks as prescribed in the op order. Captain Thornton went first. Then, one after another, twenty-seven more DD tanks rolled off the ramps and into the tossing sea. As on the 600, one of the tanks on board LCT-537 had a tear in its canvas shroud, but the tank driver, Staff Sergeant John R. Sertell, insisted that the tank's bilge pump could manage the leak. Ensign Robert J. McKee declined to overrule him, and all four tanks went into the water. Sertell's tank sank almost immediately. The other three struggled forward through the severe chop for a few hundred yards before they, too, went down. In the end, of the twenty-nine tanks launched off Omaha Beach that morning, only two made it to dry land. It was horrifying to watch. "They just went down to the bottom like rocks," a crewman on one of the LCTs recalled. "Some men were able to jump out in time, but not all." The rest, trapped inside a thirty-four-ton tank, went to the bottom with it. The LCTs and other nearby vessels hastened to pull bodies from the water, both living and dead. Joe Esclavon was one of those so engaged, and as he worked, he recognized the bodies of some of those he had trained with at Slapton Sands. He was deeply affected by the sight of them stacked "like cordwood" on the deck. Recalling it forty years later, he paused in the midst of his description and muttered: "They were real nice people on those tanks."[25]

The survival rates of the DD tanks varied from beach to beach. Off Utah Beach, U.S. Navy Lieutenant (j.g.) John B. Richer, commanding one of the tiny patrol craft whose job it was to mark the landing zones, saw that the sea conditions made launching the DD tanks from six thousand yards impossible. On his own, he moved his patrol craft to within two thousand yards of the beach to establish a new departure line. There the LCTs were not only closer to shore but also in the lee of the protruding headland of Cape Barfleur. One of them, LCT-597, was hit by a German artillery shell and sank with all four tanks still on board, but twenty-seven of the remaining twenty-eight DD tanks made it safely to shore.[26]

Some fifty miles to the east, off Sword Beach, the British LCT skippers closed to fifteen hundred yards, less than a mile, before launching their swimming tanks. Consequently, of the forty DD tanks there, thirty-four of them launched successfully, and thirty-one made it ashore, where, according to Vian, they did "sterling work." At Gold Beach, the LCTs brought their tanks to within a half mile of the shore before launching, though eight were lost anyway. At the Canadian Juno Beach, many of the DD tanks could not be launched at all, but of those that were, twenty-one of twenty-nine made it ashore. Though the tanks that survived the journey did good work, the disaster off Omaha Beach meant that the soldiers there had relatively little tank support.[27]

Almost as disastrous was the fate of the DUKWs. The Allies had more than twenty-five hundred of these little wheeled amphibians, which were entrusted with carrying some of the Army's artillery pieces to the beach. They, too, were launched from well offshore, and though they had performed flawlessly during the exercises at Slapton Sands, some of them now suffered a fate similar to the DD tanks, shipping water until they lost buoyancy. Though their crews were rescued, twenty-six field pieces were lost. One crewmember, hauled up onto a rhino ferry after his DUKW sank beneath him, was thoroughly disgusted. After practicing for most of three years "to be in the spearhead of the invasion," he said, "when the time comes, the God Damn boat sinks from under us."[28]

WHILE THE HIGGINS BOATS chugged shoreward and the LCTs sought with decidedly mixed results to launch the DD tanks, the Allies unleashed a carefully coordinated air and sea bombardment of the target beaches. This consisted of three phases: a massive air assault by thousands of heavy and medium bombers from England, a naval barrage by the battleships and cruisers, and a last-minute rocket attack by specially equipped LCTs. The idea was that the application of so much ordnance in so short a time frame would, at the very least, utterly demoralize the defenders, if not actually stun them into submission.

Though Allied bombers had been busy over Europe for months, they had focused relatively little attention on the Normandy beaches in order to avoid tipping their hand. Instead, in accordance with Eisenhower's "transportation strategy," they had targeted the railroad network in northern France to make it difficult for the Germans to rush reinforcements to the threatened spot. Churchill had worried that this approach would result in heavy civilian casualties, but Ike had insisted on it, writing Churchill that "casualties to civilian personnel are inherent in any plan for the full use of Air power to prepare for the assault." In the end, this transportation strategy proved remarkably effective, though of course it also meant that the preparation of the landing beaches themselves was limited to a relatively short bombardment in the brief half hour of twilight just before the landings. Moreover, because senior Army officers worried that dropping 500- and 1,000-pound bombs on the beach would create craters that could impede Allied tanks, the ordnance packages on many of the Allied bombers consisted of 100-pound antipersonnel bombs. These would make no craters on the beach, but neither would they seriously damage even modest concrete fortifications.[29]

More than two thousand bombers took off from half a dozen airfields in East Anglia late on the evening of June 5. As the planes circled to gain altitude, darkness closed in around them and made assembling into formations a dangerous undertaking. Just as the Allied ships in the invasion force maintained their positions during the Channel crossing by watching the blue light on the fantail of the ship in front of them, so, too, did the pilots hold their position in the formations by watching the blue lights on the wingtips of the other planes.[30]

After assembling over the English Midlands, the bombers flew south in several enormous formations. While they did so, the battleships and cruisers of the bombardment groups took their assigned positions off the coast. According to the operation order, the ships were to open fire at 5:50 a.m., just minutes before official dawn at 5:58. On the American beaches, they were to maintain a steady and concentrated fire against designated targets for exactly half an hour, then lift fire in time for the men and the tanks to storm ashore at 6:30 amid the dust and smoke. Due to the later landings on the British and Canadian beaches, the bombarding ships there would have an extra hour to soften the defenses.

Without doubt, a longer pre-invasion naval bombardment would have been more effective. The Americans had learned from operations in the Pacific, at Tarawa and elsewhere, that extended bombardments, often lasting several days, were needed to knock out hardened defensive positions. But in the Pacific, the Americans were attacking islands where the defenders could not expect any reinforcements. Army leaders argued that a lengthy bombardment of the Normandy coast would alert the Germans and provide them time to dispatch reinforcements to the threatened area. In the end, the Neptune planners decided that surprise was crucial, and so they opted for a short but concentrated pre-invasion blitz that they hoped would knock the defenders back on their heels while the invaders came ashore. Rear Admiral Morton Deyo, who commanded the bombardment group off Utah Beach, recalled, "We hoped that by sending our crashing salvos into the midst of all the known enemy positions, we could sufficiently terrorize their none-too-patriotic crews enough to distract and drive them from their posts." It proved a vain hope.[31]

Deyo directed his ships into position off Utah Beach between St. Martin de Varreville and St. Vaast-la Hougue at 5:00 a.m. There they were only eleven thousand yards (just over six miles) off the beach, and silhouetted as they were against a rising sun, they made an irresistible target. At 5:05 a.m., the 170 mm (6.7-inch) German guns in the battery at St. Vaast-la Hougue opened fire, the first enemy shots of the day. The Germans directed most of their fire at the still-active minesweepers and at the Royal Navy cruiser *Black Prince*, which was closest, though shell splashes also erupted around the American cruisers *Quincy* and *Tuscaloosa*, the latter of which Deyo was using as his flagship.*

---

* Deyo used the same cabin on the *Tuscaloosa* that President Roosevelt had used during a vacation trip to the Caribbean in December 1940. It was in that cabin that Roosevelt came up with the idea for Lend-Lease.

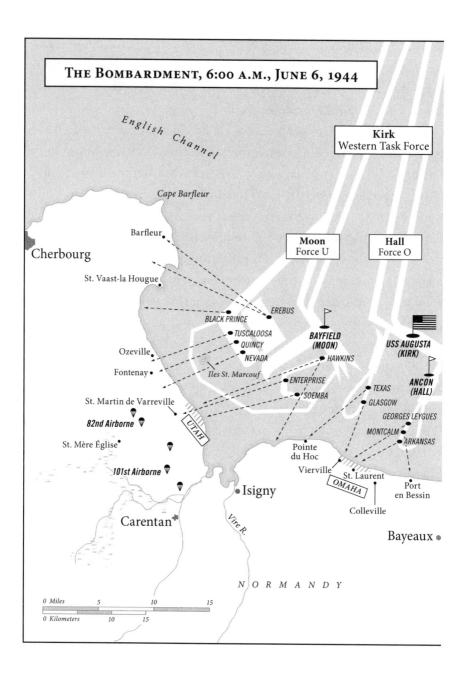

THE BOMBARDMENT, 6:00 A.M., JUNE 6, 1944

English Channel

Cape Barfleur

Barfleur

Cherbourg

St. Vaast-la Hougue

Kirk
Western Task Force

Moon
Force U

Hall
Force O

EREBUS

BLACK PRINCE

TUSCALOOSA

QUINCY

Ozeville

NEVADA

Fontenay

Iles St. Marcouf

BAYFIELD
(MOON)

HAWKINS

ENTERPRISE

SOEMBA

USS AUGUSTA
(KIRK)

ANCON
(HALL)

TEXAS

St. Martin de Varreville

82nd Airborne

St. Mère Église

101st Airborne

UTAH

GLASGOW

GEORGES LEYGUES

MONTCALM

ARKANSAS

Pointe
du Hoc

Vierville

St. Laurent

OMAHA

Port
en Bessin

Isigny

Colleville

Carentan

Vire R.

Bayeaux

NORMANDY

0 Miles   5   10   15

0 Kilometers   10   15

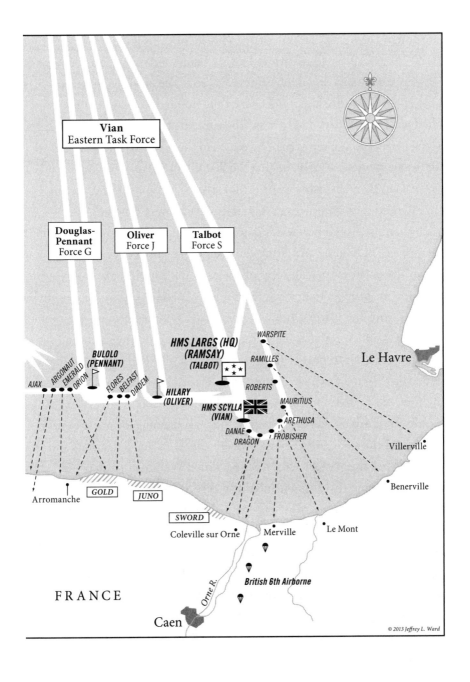

Vian
Eastern Task Force

Douglas-
Pennant
Force G

Oliver
Force J

Talbot
Force S

WARSPITE

HMS LARGS (HQ)
(RAMSAY)
(TALBOT)

RAMILLES

Le Havre

AJAX ARGONAUT EMERALD ORION

BULOLO
(PENNANT)

FLORES BELFAST DIADEM

HILARY
(OLIVER)

ROBERTS

HMS SCYLLA
(VIAN)

MAURITIUS

ARETHUSA

DANAE

DRAGON

FROBISHER

Villerville

Beneville

Arromanche

GOLD

JUNO

SWORD

Coleville sur Orne

Merville

Le Mont

British 6th Airborne

Orne R.

FRANCE

Caen

© 2013 Jeffrey L. Ward

Though Deyo's orders were to open fire at 5:50, his gunners were getting antsy. "Shells splashed all around us," a boatswain's mate on the *Quincy* remembered, "and shrapnel skittered across the deck." One near miss opened a hole in the skin of the *Quincy* and flooded a storage compartment filled with Oh Henry! candy bars. The captains of the various Allied ships asked permission to reply, but Deyo turned them down; he wanted to wait for the air spotters to arrive so that the first salvos had maximum effect. But as German marksmanship improved, Deyo changed his mind. At 5:36 he gave the order to "commence counter-battery bombardment."[32]

In an unpublished postwar memoir, Deyo offered a vivid description of the process of loading and firing the 8-inch guns on a heavy cruiser. First came "the shrill ascending song of the ammunition car speeding upward from the magazine." That was followed by "a metallic thump" as the shells dropped into the loading trays. A pneumatic rammer shoved the rounds into place, and soon afterward the three turrets, each with three 8-inch guns, pivoted out to port to face the target. All nine barrels rose gracefully in response to the calculated target data. Two quick buzzes signaled "stand by," then one buzz, then, as Deyo put it: "Flash! Jar! Lurch!" and twenty-four hundred pounds of high explosives were sent screaming toward the beach.[33]

Among the early Allied targets were the German radar stations: big metal dishes, twenty feet across, called "Giant Würzburgs," that could scan out to sea some forty-three miles and direct the fire of artillery ashore. Even before the bombardment began, ships in the Allied fleet had intercepted electronic emissions as the Giant Würzburgs sought to obtain targeting coordinates for the German gunners. Until the radar sites could be destroyed by gunfire, the Americans used onboard transmitters that sent out bursts of electrical energy designed to jam and deflect the radar beams. While employing this technology, the electronics technicians on *Tuscaloosa* were much relieved to see the enemy radar sweep past them and then "wander off."[34]

The *Nevada* added her big guns to the assault at 5:47. Giant black and red fireballs roiled from the muzzles of her 14-inch guns, the big ship lurched sideways, and fifteen thousand pounds of high-explosive shells flew in a single ten-gun salvo toward the German batteries behind Utah Beach. The concussion created by the firing of those big guns was so powerful that one sailor on board thought it would pull his clothes off; several suffered nosebleeds. Men on LCTs miles away felt their ship's hull move beneath them. It was particularly daunting for the soldiers in the Higgins boats already headed shoreward since the shells passed directly over their heads, sounding like a freight train that was about to run them down. Many instinctively ducked. The shells could not be seen as they streaked toward the targets, but the air friction they created generated a small red light that allowed witnesses to follow the line of shot through the predawn twilight.[35]

The biggest naval guns off Utah Beach belonged to a curious vessel officially dubbed a "monitor." It was HMS *Erebus*, essentially a fat-bodied light cruiser with an oversized turret on its foredeck that boasted two 15-inch guns. Those guns fired shells weighing 1,920 pounds each and had a range of nearly twenty miles. Early in the bombardment, the *Erebus* targeted the German batteries on the Iles Saint-Marcouf, the small islands off the coast above Utah Beach south of St. Vaast-la Hougue. There, the German guns were encased in bunkers with concrete walls thirteen feet thick. Nevertheless, the big guns on the *Erebus* silenced them before they could be used to enfilade the landing beaches.

Off Omaha Beach, RADM Carleton Bryant commanded the bombardment ships of Force O, led by the battleships *Texas* and *Arkansas*. Both were older vessels, laid down in 1910–11; indeed, the *Arkansas* was the oldest American battleship still in service. She was so old, there were no showers or toilets on board—the men washed from buckets, and the toilet facilities consisted of a metal trough with salt water flowing through it. Both ships had been built using rivets instead of welds, and occasionally when they fired a full salvo, a rivet or two would pop loose. Despite their age, however, they were superb gun platforms, and they fired their big shells at a low, almost flat trajectory into the high ground behind Omaha Beach. Ensign Donald Irwin was driving LCT-614 toward Omaha Beach when his ears were assailed by "the most ear-splitting, deafening, horrendous sound I have ever heard" as the big shells passed overhead. He looked back at the *Texas*, her guns still wreathed in smoke, and from his vantage point it looked as if those big 14-inch guns "were pointed right at us." To Ensign Victor

Hicken, commanding LCT(A) 2227, the *Texas*'s guns sounded "like a giant door slamming," and another recalled that the very air vibrated with the sound and set everyone on board trembling.[36]

The American battleships off Omaha Beach were supported by two French cruisers, *Montcalm* and *Georges Leygues*, as well as the British heavy cruiser *Glasgow* and the light cruiser *Bellona*. It is easy to imagine the mixed emotions of the sailors on the French warships as they opened fire on French soil. The skipper of the *Montcalm*, Captain E. J. H. L. Deprez, mused that "it is a monstrous thing to have to fire on our homeland." From his ship, he flew a giant French tricolor flag, sixty by one hundred feet in size, that could be seen from the shore.[37]

The greatest firepower in the Allied armada was off Sword Beach. There, two British battleships each carried a battery of eight 15-inch guns. These were the *Warspite*, known as the "grand old lady" of the Royal Navy, and *Ramillies*, named for the 1706 battle during the War of the Spanish Succession that had been won by Churchill's ancestor, John Churchill, the first Duke of Marlborough. This group also included HMS *Roberts*, another so-called monitor with two more 15-inch guns. That gave the Allies a total of eighteen 15-inch guns at Sword Beach, and from those guns the British could fire nearly thirty-five thousand pounds of high explosives in a single salvo. To that was added the firepower of five cruisers and fifteen destroyers. And because the Sword Beach landings would not take place until later that morning, these ships had an extra hour to prepare the beach. The heavy guns, the sheer number of them, and the extended time on target all had an impact. The commander of Force S, British Rear Admiral Arthur George Talbot, believed that "the enemy was obviously stunned by the sheer weight of [gunfire] support we were meting out."[38]

There were no Allied battleships off Gold or Juno Beaches, though there were half a dozen cruisers and two dozen destroyers. The cruisers off Juno Beach included HMS *Belfast*, which, if King George had not intervened, would have included the prime minister among the ship's company. As it happened, the *Belfast* escaped harm during the operation, and Churchill afterward made a point of saying, in effect, "See, it would have been all right."[39]

There had been plenty of discussion about the best way to direct the naval gunfire. The Army preferred to rely on shore-based fire control parties (SFCPs), while the Navy wanted to use air spotters. In the end, the Allies did both, which proved invaluable when the fire control parties on shore were decimated by the unexpectedly heavy enemy fire on Omaha Beach, and in any case, shore spotting could not begin until the troops landed. Air spotting was best conducted by slow, two-seater aircraft that could linger over a target. Since the Normandy beaches were blanketed with anti-aircraft batteries, that was not realistic on June 6. As Deyo put it, "Slow sea-planes such as we normally used would not long survive over that country." Instead, the Allies used British Spitfires, which, over the American beaches, were piloted by U.S. Navy volunteers. The Spitfires worked in pairs, with one pilot reporting the fall of the shot, while the other scanned the skies for potential Luftwaffe interference, though given Allied mastery of the air, such a precaution was probably unnecessary. The Germans did, however, put up an impressive amount of anti-air ground fire. An observer on the *Texas* thought that the German tracer fire looked like someone "taking a garden hose and wiggling it back and forth." The fire came up from several sites at once, so it "kind of crocheted the AA fire" across the sky.[40]

The long flight from airfields in Britain meant that the Spitfires could remain over the beach for only about forty minutes, but when one pair had to depart, another pair arrived to take its place. At any given moment, there were at least six spotter planes aloft for each beach: two overhead, two returning, and two en route. Spotting remained problematic, however, because the high speed of the fighter planes made them imperfect for the task, and because the clouds of smoke and dust generated by the fall of thousands of rounds of high-explosive shells made for poor visibility. Then, too, Allied radio communications were disappointing. Deyo's flagship, *Tuscaloosa*, established contact with its spotter plane at 5:38 but lost it ten minutes later and did not regain contact for over half an hour.[41]

The Allies sought to make up for imperfect spotting with sheer volume. In the half hour dedicated to the naval gunfire off Utah Beach, the *Nevada* alone fired 337 rounds of 14-inch shells and 2,693 rounds of 5-inch shells. The gun barrels grew so hot they had to be hosed down with seawater.[42]

More than sixty destroyers added thousands more rounds of 4-inch and 5-inch ammunition to the bombardment. Initially, the newer and larger American *Gleaves*-class destroyers were assigned to the bombardment mission, while the lighter British destroyers and American destroyer escorts carried out screening duties to fend off German E-boats. The main reason for this was that the *Gleaves*-class destroyers had radar fire control that allowed them to target German gun emplacements by map coordinates even through heavy smoke. As one destroyerman put it, "The Brits had to be able to see their targets, while the Americans could deliver blind fire."[43]

Then, in the midst of the naval bombardment, more than two thousand Allied bombers converged on the five beaches. Their impact was significantly weakened, however, by the weather conditions. Though the storm that had delayed the invasion was moderating, the cloud layer above the beach remained thick enough that the pilots and bombardiers were unable to see their targets. Consequently, they had to bomb by radar from above the clouds. With so many planes operating in so small a space, each group was assigned a very specific flight path. The pilots of the 450 high-flying B-24 Liberator bombers assigned to Omaha Beach had the most difficult mission, for their flight path was almost due south, directly over the invading fleet, and they would strike Omaha Beach perpendicularly. Unable to see their targets, and desperate to avoid dropping their bombs on the Allied landing craft already heading for the beach, the pilots waited an extra five to twenty seconds before releasing their ordnance. The B-24s dropped more than thirteen thousand bombs, but due to the conditions and their determination to avoid friendly casualties, all of them fell uselessly into the French countryside behind Omaha Beach. While the spectacular pyrotechnics boosted the morale of the men in the approaching landing craft, who cheered the explosions ashore, the historian Joseph Balkoski has noted that "not a single bomb fell anywhere near Omaha Beach."[44]

Bombing on the other beaches was more successful. The B-26 Marauders assigned to Utah Beach flew lower than the B-24s, so pilot visibility was better. Even more important, however, their flight path took them along the length of Utah Beach, so bombs that fell either long or short still had a good chance of hitting a target. The 276 Marauders dropped nearly five thousand bombs, most of them weighing 250 pounds each, though a few carried giant 2,000-pound "blockbuster" bombs, which, even if they did not hit a specific target, left both attackers and defenders momentarily stunned. Utah Beach was completely obscured by the resulting smoke, dust, and debris. In addition, Allied destroyers just off the beach generated more smoke to screen the approaching Higgins boats from German artillery ashore. The consequence was that neither the gunners on the Allied warships nor the coxswains driving the Higgins boats could see much of anything through the thick pall of smoke.[45]

Once the Allied planes departed, the naval gunfire resumed, though the smoke and dust were now so thick that gunners were reduced to firing blindly. Allied destroyers close to shore sought to pick out targets of opportunity, but there were so many ships off the coast they literally got in one another's way. Lieutenant Commander G. J. Marshall, on the destroyer USS *Doyle* (DD-494), spent much of his time "avoiding collision" amidst the wind and currents of the crowded seafront, though his ship still managed to fire 364 rounds of 5-inch ammunition.[46]

The third element of the Allied effort to soften the beaches relied on a novel and somewhat experimental weapon: rocket-firing LCTs. Designated as LCT(R)s, these vessels carried two layers of rocket launchers that entirely filled their well decks. The launching racks were loaded with 1,080 three-foot-long rockets. Since the rockets weighed sixty pounds each, an LCT(R) could hurl nearly 65,000 pounds of ordnance toward the enemy in about ninety seconds, and there were thirty-six of them dedicated to the bombardment mission, eight of them off Omaha Beach. The problem was that the rockets could be aimed only by pointing the vessel itself in the general direction of the target, and the range could be adjusted only by changing the angle of the racks. Once the commanding officer made the best estimate he could of the target and distance, the crew headed below and the CO retreated into an armored bolt-hole. When he triggered the launch, the rockets fired off automatically in a programmed sequence without any further human involvement. There was no disputing the visual impact of it. A crewman recalled that "the ship seemed to explode" as hundreds of rockets whooshed off the racks in a virtual stream of fire, leaving trails of black smoke as they streaked through the sky. Smoke rose up all around the ship "like a dense fog," and small fires broke out on board. In the aftermath of the launch, "everyone was cursing and screaming and fighting the flames." Impressive as it was, however, most of the rockets off Omaha Beach fell short, hissing harmlessly into the sea. Those that reached the beach did some damage to the barbed wire and the obstructions, but not as much as might have been guessed from the pyrotechnic display. At least none of them struck a Higgins boat.[47]

All of this meant that for just over an hour between 5:37 and 6:40 a.m., thousands of bombs, shells, and rockets filled the air over the two American beaches on the Normandy coast. It was stunning, indeed all but overwhelming, to the senses. The men in the Higgins boats, now within minutes of landing, crouched down and covered their ears, glad that their enemies and not they were on the receiving end of such awesome firepower. Alas, all that sound and fury disguised the fact that on Omaha Beach at least, the bombs fell too long, the rockets fell too short, and the naval gunfire was too brief. Ashore, the Germans crouched down in their bombproof shelters, many with concrete walls five feet thick, and they too covered their ears, but none of the Allied ordnance penetrated their bunkers and pillboxes.

The gunners on the battleships and cruisers maintained a beach-drenching fire until just before the first Higgins boat reached the shore. It was a fine calculation. If they stopped too soon, the defenders would have a chance to recover; if they continued too long, they might hit their own men. Deyo and Bryant agonized over the proper moment. Then an escorting destroyer signaled that the men were landing, and the big ships lifted fire. It was 6:40 a.m., H-Hour on Omaha and Utah Beaches.

CHAPTER 12

D-DAY: THE BEACHES

I T IS AN APHORISM among military professionals that no plan survives first contact with the enemy. That may be especially true when the plan is as detailed and complex as the eleven-hundred-page, four-inch-thick plan for Operation Neptune. Crafted with so much care and effort by hundreds of men over months of close study, it specified the D-Day assignments of every ship, every landing craft, every vehicle, and nearly every Allied sailor and soldier on almost a minute-by-minute schedule. As Samuel Eliot Morison wrote in 1957: "This scheme was a little too neat." It was perhaps inevitable that it would not play out exactly as scripted. Moreover, with so many working parts, and a timetable that made each element dependent on so many others, early miscues created a cascading series of difficulties that threatened to wreck the invasion altogether, especially on Omaha Beach. In the end, what saved the day was the ability of the men both afloat and ashore to adapt and adjust.[1]

There were many heroes on June 6, 1944, but surely among the most consequential were those who served at the point of the spear. That certainly included the Navy and Coast Guard coxswains who took their fragile Higgins boats through the coastal obstacles. It included as well the lieutenants and ensigns who drove their LCTs and LCIs onto the crowded beaches even after it became evident that the elegant plan was going spectacularly awry. It included the Army captains and lieutenants who led their small tank and infantry units into the slaughterhouse ashore, and it included the sergeants and other noncommissioned officers who assumed responsibility on the beach after their officers fell in the first burst of relentless gunfire. Finally—indeed, most of all—it included the enlisted sailors and soldiers, who though terrified to the core, executed their assignments as best they could for as long as they could. In the end, it was the training and instinct of those soldiers and sailors, more than the carefully prepared script, that produced the Allied victory on the Normandy beaches.

THE FIRST ALLIED LANDING CRAFT arrived on the American beaches within minutes of the moment indicated on the timetable. The Navy and Coast Guard coxswains jammed their Higgins boats up onto the beach, or as close to it as the uneven sub-aqueous terrain and still-visible mined obstacles would allow. The coxswains had been guided to the departure points by patrol craft, but for the final run in to the smoke-enshrouded beach, they simply aimed their craft shoreward and opened the throttles, going "hell bent for election as fast as we could go," as one put it. More than a few of the boats, running flat out and pushed on by the rising tide, were virtually lifted up by the surf and slammed down violently onto the sand. One sailor remembered that the wooden boats "would just bounce up and down, up and down, until finally they were hard aground." Some of them "split wide open" and the men had to swim or crawl away. Those not wrecked on the beach became targets of the German artillery which immediately opened fire.[2]

Most of the Higgins boats had to thread their way through the obstacles, sometimes with only a few feet to spare on either side. Due to the shallow gradient of the beach, many grounded while they were still well off the surf line. A few of the coxswains backed out and tried to find another section of beach where they could get closer. Others toggled their engines forward and back, trying to force their way over the sandbars. Sooner or later,

Roosevelt and Churchill get acquainted prior to a joint religious service on board HMS *Prince of Wales* on August 10, 1941. Behind them are many of the men who would play central roles in the development of Anglo-American strategy during the war. At left, Harry Hopkins chats with Averell Harriman; in the center, Ernest King talks with George Marshall; Sir John Dill is behind Churchill's left shoulder; and at right Harold "Betty" Stark stands with Dudley Pound. (FDR Library)

George Marshall, seen here in a January 1945 photo wearing five stars, was the U.S. Army Chief of Staff and a principal architect of Allied strategy. Despite a calm and reserved temperament, he was a fierce advocate of an early invasion of occupied Europe, and in pursuit of that goal, he fought a lengthy verbal war with his British counterpart, Alan Brooke. (U.S. Army Photo)

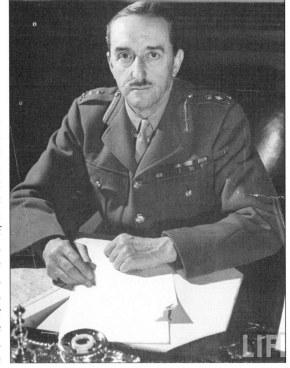

As Chief of the Imperial General Staff, British General Alan Brooke fought two battles: on the one hand he sought to dampen or deflect American enthusiasm for an early invasion of occupied France, and, at the same time, he attempted to control, or at least to moderate, Churchill's penchant for peripheral and even bizarre operational gambits. (U.S. Army Photo)

George Patton (left) and Kent Hewitt share a laugh on board Hewitt's flagship the heavy cruiser *Augusta* during Operation TORCH in November 1942. Despite Patton's cheerful demeanor here, he was unsure that the easy-going and unpretentious Hewitt was sufficiently ferocious. Patton's controversial behavior and statements kept him out of the D-Day operation, but he assumed command of the American Third Army in in August 1944 and participated in the Allied breakout. (U.S. Naval Institute)

A portion of the trans-Atlantic convoy for Operation TORCH photographed from the air. (U.S. Naval Institute)

One of Eisenhower's great assets as an Allied commander was his deftness in dealing with political issues. In North Africa, however, he found himself overmatched by the complexity of French wartime loyalties and rivalries. Unable to convince French General Henri Giraud to embrace a public role as an ally, he made an arrangement with French Admiral Jean François Darlan, a former Nazi collaborator. Here, Ike appears to regret his decision as a pleased Darlan looks on. (U.S. Army Photo)

Another aspect of Eisenhower's leadership was his ready smile, which Rear Admiral Morton Deyo believed was worth twenty divisions. Here he reacts to a witticism from Churchill, who worked unceasingly to convince Eisenhower to extend Allied operations in the Mediterranean through 1943. In the end, Churchill got his way, though it was as much the momentum of events as Churchill's charm and persistence that led the Allies into Sicily and Italy. (U.S. Naval Institute)

Roosevelt and Churchill at the Casablanca Conference in January of 1943. Behind them are most of the members of the Combined Chiefs of Staff (left to right): Ernest King, George Marshall, Dudley Pound, Charles Portal, Alan Brooke, John Dill, and Louis Mountbatten. (U.S. Navy Photo)

The SHAEF commanders pose for a group photo in Southwick House near Portsmouth. Seated in the front row are (left to right) Eisenhower's Deputy, Air Marshal Sir Arthur Tedder, Eisenhower, and General Bernard Montgomery, who commanded Allied ground troops. Standing behind them are Lieutenant General Omar Bradley, commander of the U.S. First Army; Admiral Sir Bertram Ramsay who commanded the naval forces as ANCXF; Air Marshal Sir Trafford Leigh-Mallory who commanded the air forces; and Major General Walter "Beetle" Smith, who was Ike's Chief of Staff. (U.S. Naval Institute)

Shipbuilding was a central, indeed decisive, element of Allied strategy and planning. In this photo, long lines of workers enter the Henry J. Kaiser Shipyard near Portland, Oregon, one of eighteen Kaiser Shipyards that built mostly Liberty Ships. A banner over the entrance gate reads: "REMEMBER PEARL HARBOR." (U.S. Naval Institute)

Landing Craft, Vehicle and Personnel (LCVP), commonly known as Higgins boats, were the workhorses of all amphibious landings in World War II. They could carry either thirty-six soldiers or one or two small vehicles at a time. (U.S. Navy Photo)

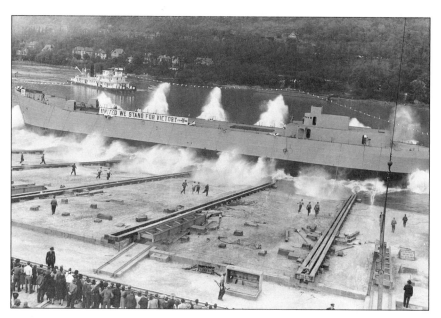

A new LST is launched sideways into the Ohio River at the Neville Island Shipyard below Pittsburgh early in 1943. Before the end of the war, this shipyard would employ 16,000 workers and produce 147 LSTs. Other LST construction sites included Seneca, Illinois, and Evansville, Indiana. By mid-1944, workers at these yards could build an LST in just over two months. Despite that, competition for resources, especially steel, meant that production never fully caught up with need. (U.S. Naval Institute)

Landing Craft Infantry (LCI), called "Elsies" by their crewmen, were larger than Higgins boats but could not carry vehicles. The most common was the LCI(L), with the second "L" standing for "large." These vessels could carry up to 200 soldiers at a time, who disembarked along twin ramps deployed on either side of the bow. (U.S. Coast Guard Photo)

A Rhino Ferry hardly looked like a vessel at all. Manned by Seabees, they were essentially rafts powered by twin outboard motors. Many of them were towed across the Channel by LSTs. Here a fully-loaded Rhino Ferry heads for the beach on D-Day. (U.S. Navy Photo)

Many of the rehearsal landings for D-Day occurred during the spring of 1944, and were conducted along a stretch of beach called Slapton Sands on Devon's south coast just west of Dartmouth. The pebbly beach, marshy Slapton Ley, and the rising ground behind the beach were all superficially similar to the terrain in Normandy. Here a group of soldiers rushes out of an LCVP (Higgins boat) onto the beach during an early exercise. (U.S. Navy Photo)

The early exercises were sometimes disappointing. Here some GIs, having successfully landed from some LCTs, appear to be loitering about the beach with little sense of purpose or urgency. Such behavior prompted the American V Corps commander, Leonard Gerow, to wonder if, in a real invasion, any of them would get off the beach alive. (Britannia Museum Collection)

One of the Allied landing rehearsals turned tragic in April of 1944 when German *Schnellbooten*, literally fast boats, though often called S-boats or E-boats by the Allies, attacked a convoy of LSTs heading for Slapton Sands during Exercise Tiger. The E-boats managed to sink two LSTs and severely damage another. The LST 289, seen here, was badly mauled when a torpedo struck its stern. The 289 managed to make it back into port but could not be repaired in time for the invasion. The loss of three LSTs this late in the planning was a severe blow. (U.S. Naval Institute)

A group of LSTs loads an artillery unit across a "hard" at Brixham, just north of Dartmouth, on June 1, 1944. Seen here are LSTs 382, 499, 384, and 380. The 499 was destroyed by a German mine off the invasion beaches on June 8. (U.S. Naval Institute)

The Allied bombardment of the target beaches began at 5:36 a.m. on June 6. Here guns of the American battleship *Nevada* (BB-36) fire on Utah Beach. In just over an hour, the *Nevada* fired 337 rounds of 14-inch shells and 2,693 rounds of 5-inch shells. Other American and Allied ships also punished the invasion beaches, but only on Sword Beach did the preliminary bombardment by Royal Navy warships have a significant effect. (U.S. Navy Photo)

A long line of LCI(L) vessels, manned by U.S. Coast Guard crews and loaded with soldiers of Group B, the follow-up invasion force for Omaha Beach, cross the English Channel during the daylight hours of June 6. The barrage balloons above them were to prevent strafing by German aircraft, though complete Allied command of the air made that an unlikely threat. (U.S. Coast Guard Photo)

American GIs headed for Omaha Beach steel themselves for the assault. The point of view in this photograph is that of the coxswain who is driving the Higgins boat. Packed into the craft like cattle, the soldiers could see little beyond the back of the soldier in front of them, though an officer peers out over the port bow for a look at the beach. (U.S. Army Photo)

This drawing by U.S. Coast Guard artist H. B. Vestal depicts the American destroyer USS *Doyle* (DD-494) firing onto the bluffs above Omaha Beach at about 9:00 a.m. on June 6. The close-in gunfire support that morning from a handful of destroyers was critical in turning the tide on Omaha Beach. (U.S. Coast Guard Photo)

An aerial view of the British Mulberry (Mulberry B) off Arrowmanche near Gold Beach a week after the invasion. Four Liberty ships are moored inside the line of Phoenix units, and the floating "whale" roadways can be seen leading from the Lobnitz Piers to the beach. (U.S. Naval Institute)

A portion of the wrecked "whale" roadway of the American Mulberry (Mulberry A) off Omaha Beach after the storm of June 19–21. The "spuds" of the Lobnitz piers are visible in the background. After a survey of the damage, the American supervisor of salvage recommended that the American Mulberry be shut down. (U.S. Naval Institute)

The cruisers USS *Quincy* (foreground) and HMS *Glasgow* fire on the Querqueville batteries west of Cherbourg on June 25, 1944. Though the Allied naval task force was able to silence the smaller (6-inch) German batteries, the bigger 11-inch guns east of Cherbourg managed to hold their own. (U.S. Army Photo)

British, American, and Canadian salvage experts struggle to clear the wreckage in Cherbourg Harbor, where the Germans blew up piers, scuttled ships, and sowed 133 mines. It would take more than a month before the port was again fully functioning. (U.S. Naval Institute)

A long row of LSTs discharge their cargoes onto Omaha Beach. Unloading across a beach was more time-consuming than at a pier, especially if the LSTs "dried out" through a tide cycle. On the other hand, the broad beach allowed many more LSTs to come ashore simultaneously, and despite the loss of Mulberry A at Omaha Beach, the Allies were able to sustain both the troop buildup and the logistic supply line for the armies in Normandy. (U.S. Navy Photo)

however, they concluded that this was as close as they were likely to get, and they dropped their ramps into the water. The coxswains hollered, "Everybody out," and, released at last from their long purgatory inside the claustrophobic confines of a Higgins boat, the soldiers staggered out into the hell of the beach itself.[3]

Though they were on time, their company and platoon leaders saw almost at once that they were in the wrong place. A steady three-knot southeasterly current had pushed most of the landing craft well to the left of their intended targets, especially on Utah Beach. The boat drivers had been supplied with composite photographs assembled painstakingly over many weeks from pictures taken by Army Air Forces pilots who had swooped in low over the beach to photograph the terrain. The idea was that the coxswains could use the photo images to guide them into the proper landing area. But with the ubiquitous smoke and dust over the beach, picking out recognizable landmarks was all but impossible, especially on Utah Beach, where the terrain was unrelievedly flat. During the approach of LCT-853, the skipper kept asking his exec if they were headed for the right beach. The exec examined the composite photograph, glancing up from it regularly to study the beach, but he was "totally unable to see anything because of the smoke." Like almost everyone else, the skipper of the 853 simply headed for the closest piece of open beach he could see. Consequently, when the soldiers finally staggered ashore, their officers looked about them in vain for any of the landmarks they had studied so carefully for all those weeks back in England.[4]

The set of the current was strongest off Utah Beach, where the men came ashore more than half a mile south of their intended objectives. Now what? Rejecting the notion that they should work their way back to the right to reconnect to the careful minute-by-minute timetable of the invasion plan, Colonel James Van Fleet, commanding the 8th Infantry, and Brigadier General Theodore Roosevelt Jr. instead made the commonsense decision to go forward from where they were. Like his father, who had encountered his "crowded hour" at Kettle Hill in Cuba some forty-six years earlier, Teddy Roosevelt sought to lead from the front, and had convinced Eisenhower to let him land with the first wave at Utah Beach. Almost at once he validated that decision by approving the reorientation of the Utah Beach invasion plan to accommodate the reality on the ground. It required adjusting both the timetable of subsequent waves as well as the logistical support plan, but it got the soldiers off the beach sooner and unquestionably saved many lives. Indeed, the accidental reorientation of the Allied assault on Utah Beach was fortuitous in several ways. The German defenses were somewhat weaker where the men actually landed than where they were supposed to have landed, and the access to routes inland was easier, too. For this and for his other activities that day, Roosevelt was subsequently (and posthumously) awarded the Medal of Honor.[5]

The offshore current was less assertive at Omaha Beach, but there were other, far more serious problems there. The most salient was geography. Omaha was the only landing beach that was overlooked by high bluffs that ranged from 100 to 150 feet in height. On those bluffs the Germans had erected thirty antitank and field guns as well as an astonishing eighty-five machine gun positions, four times as many as on any of the other invasion beaches. And almost all of their positions were so cleverly camouflaged that it was all but impossible to see them. Worse, the crescent shape of the beach allowed the Germans to fire not only down from the bluffs but also from both flanks. Though the preliminary bombing and gunfire had forced the defenders to keep their heads down, none of the German gun emplacements had suffered a direct hit. As a result, when the first wave of Allied infantry rushed out onto the beach, the men were struck almost at once by an intense crossfire of artillery, mortars, and machine guns. And finally, unknown to the Allies, the Germans had recently reinforced that sector of beach with the 352nd Division, which had been sent there for training. Thus as a result of geography, weaponry, and manpower, Omaha was a much tougher objective than any of the other targeted beaches.[6]

Among the first to land on Omaha Beach that morning were the men of the Gap Assault Teams (GATs), composed of a Navy Combat Demolition Unit and an Army Combat Engineer group. Technically, all of the men in an NCDU team were volunteers, though many had volunteered in the time-honored military way: when not enough men raised their hands for this hazardous duty in one particular shipload of new arrivals in England, an ensign simply declared that all the men whose names began with the letters *A* through *C* had just volunteered. On the other hand, none of them objected or tried to escape the duty.[7]

On Omaha Beach there were sixteen of these teams, each charged with clearing a path, fifty yards wide, through the beach obstructions. Those obstructions took several forms. One type, which the Allies called hedge-hogs, consisted of steel sculptures created by welding three steel beams together into free-standing tetrahedrons five or six feet across. They resembled enormous steel jacks, almost as if the children of giants had been interrupted in a game and walked off leaving their toys scattered on the beach. Placed between high and low tide, they could tear the bottom out of small craft at high tide. Another common type was made up of wooden poles resembling telegraph or telephone poles, most of which had plate-like Teller mines affixed to them, so if the pole was jarred, the mine would explode. Even if a vessel successfully navigated between two of the poles, many were connected by wires that would trigger the nearest mine. The Allied decision to land two hours after low tide was to provide an opportunity, however brief, for the NCDU teams to clear at least some of these obstacles. The initial expectation was that by landing immediately after the fury of the pre-invasion bombardment, they would face little if any resistance, though that proved not to be the case.[8]

Each member of an NCDU team carried a double-sided canvas bag, much like those used by newspaper boys back home, though instead of newspapers, they were filled with sixty pounds of C-2 explosives divided up into two-pound blocks. Struggling ashore through the surf with such a burden was difficult enough, and it became much more so when machine gun and mortar fire erupted from the high ground behind the beach and on both flanks. Since few of the landing craft could maneuver all the way to the surf line, the men in the GAT teams had to disembark well off the beach and wade ashore. Worse, while the water might be only a foot or two deep just off the bow where the vessel grounded, deep runnels scattered unpredictably along the beachfront meant that many of the men took only a few steps shoreward before they floundered into water that was over their heads. Robert Miller of the 149th Combat Engineers would "never forget the feeling of panic" as he stepped off into a runnel and went straight to the bottom, dragged down by the weight of his pack. He shucked off the pack, pushed hard against the sandy bottom, and struggled up to the surface, gasping for air. Half swimming and half flailing, he managed to make it to the beach. "I was near exhaustion by this time," he remembered, "and felt as though my body weighed at least three hundred pounds." NCDU team member Orval Wakefield made it ashore still in possession of his pack, but when he got there he noted with alarm that his legs were so weak he could hardly stand. He wondered briefly if that meant he was a coward, until he realized that his canvas sack had filled with seawater. He used his knife to cut holes in the bottom of each bag so the water could drain out, and found that he could stand up after all.[9]

Because so many, like Miller, lost their explosives and detonators in their desperate scramble ashore, some waded back out to the boats to retrieve the rubber rafts filled with the team's reserve explosives. Alas, the rafts, too, had filled with water and were too heavy to move. So the men grabbed as many satchels as they could carry and breasted their way back through the water to the beach. All the while, machine gun bullets churned up the sea around them, making little *zip zip* sounds as they hit the water. On shore, the bullets kicked up the sand when they didn't find a more yielding target. Many men fell—the casualty rate among the NCDU teams on Omaha Beach that morning was 70 percent. The survivors took cover behind the beach obstacles and, lying prone, began to affix prima cord and C-2 explosives to the poles. Using enemy mines as cover while deploying highly volatile prima cord was extraordinarily hazardous, but there were few activities on Omaha Beach that morning that were not.

Several of the NCDU teams managed to place charges on the obstacles, called out "Fire in the hole!" and exploded them one by one. One team, assigned to the Dog White sector of Omaha Beach near Les Moulins, managed to clear a fifty-yard-wide gap in a mere twenty minutes. Elsewhere, however, the teams were slowed by ferocious enemy fire. One team was wiped out entirely when the LCT taking them ashore was hit by an artillery shell. Another was obliterated when a shell hit their raft loaded with explosives. Elsewhere, the men had to cut their work short when the infantry began coming ashore—one recalled that "the infantry was right on top of us." Amid the heavy fire from the bluffs, the arriving soldiers instinctively took cover behind obstacles that had already been wired for demolition, and the men of the NCDU teams had to chase them away in order to trigger the charges. Soon they had to stop altogether, for any more explosions would endanger the arriving GIs. In the end, the sixteen GAT teams on Omaha Beach managed to create only five gaps through the obstacles. Consequently, when the second and third waves got to the beach, they found most of the mined impediments still in place.[10]

The men in the first several waves had been told that the bombing and naval gunfire would knock out the enemy defensive positions, and many also expected that the beach would be pockmarked with ready-made bomb craters that they could use as foxholes, but of course neither of those expectations was validated. Some of the German machine guns fired at the astonishing rate of twenty rounds per second, and that created a virtual wall of fire that could not be avoided. Those who made it through the surf to the beach staggered forward to find imperfect cover behind a slight rise in the sand some two hundred yards inland from the surf line. Along part of the beach there was a low concrete seawall that offered additional protection, but elsewhere there was only this slight rise in the shingle—the product of several centuries' worth of high tides. The men could advance no further due to the ubiquitous fire across the beach, nor could they go back, since any landing craft that had not been wrecked on the beach or hit by German gunfire had already retracted.

Indeed, the destruction of so many landing craft was nearly as disastrous to the Allied invasion plan as the casualties to the soldiers. As one example, the USS *Thurston* (AP-77) lowered a total of twenty-five Higgins boats that morning. One sank when it collided with a submerged tank just off the beach; two others broached during the landing; five were smashed up by hard landings or enemy fire and had to be abandoned; the rest succeeded in landing their soldiers and retracting, but of those, nine were so badly damaged they had to be hoisted back on board the *Thurston* for repairs. As a result of these and other incidents, of the twenty-five boats employed in the first wave, only three remained available for subsequent ones.[11]

THE SECOND AND THIRD WAVES heading for Omaha Beach were only minutes behind the first. In addition to the Higgins boats, these included a large number of the bigger and stouter LCTs. As the men on board them got close enough to peer through the smoke to see what was happening ashore, they were horrified. "For Christ's sake, they're pinned down," a soldier on one LCT called out to no one in particular. Of more immediate concern to the boat drivers was the fact that there was almost no place for them to go. The few gaps between the obstacles created by the NCDU teams were clogged with sunken tanks and wrecked and damaged Higgins boats, as well as other, more grisly impediments. Ensign Karl Everitt, driving his LCT toward the beach, felt compelled to throttle down to avoid running over the many bodies floating in the water. He did not want "to cut them up with my screws," so he stationed men in the bow with boathooks to push the bodies out of the way. Coxswain George Poe, driving a Higgins boat, also saw that "the water was full of men, some dead," but he did not slow down, fearing that if he did, his boat would not be able to clear the sand bar.[12]

The congestion along the beachfront and the artillery fire from the bluffs played havoc with the prescribed formations of the approaching landing craft. Guide ships had escorted them to the departure line. After that, the beach masters were supposed to direct them to appropriate landing sites. But the beach masters—those who were still alive—were no more in control of the situation than anyone else. Coxswains and LCT captains maneuvered back and forth off the shoreline, often getting in one another's way as they searched desperately for an open section of beach. The result was that, as Hall put it in his subsequent report, "all semblance of wave organization was lost." More prosaically, a sailor on one of the landing craft recalled that "we ran into one another like little Dodgem cars."[13]

Ensign Bill O'Neill, executive officer of LCT-544, lay prone atop the wheelhouse as his ship approached Omaha Beach as part of the second wave at about 6:45. He was watching the chaos ashore when he spotted a beach master signaling frantically. O'Neill stood up to give him the go-ahead signal, the letter *K*, then read the ensuing message, which was: "Stay low. Keep your head down." Muttering furiously at such useless advice, O'Neill flattened himself back onto the deck plates atop the wheelhouse. As he scanned the shore, however, he saw that there were no openings—only mined obstacles and wrecked landing craft. His skipper was just a few feet away, standing on the ladder down into the wheelhouse where he could both see and give helm orders. O'Neill looked over at him and, disregarding the niceties of rank in the excitement of the moment, said, "What the hell are you doing here? You'll get us all killed!" He suggested that they try further off to the right, and the skipper ordered an abrupt turn to starboard. The 544 cruised west-ward along the beachfront for more than a mile before finding a likely gap in the obstructions and turning for shore.[14]

Other LCTs did the same. One of them, LCT-305, made several attempts to land. During the first, she was raked by machine gun fire that severely wounded her commanding officer; during the second, the Army captain in command of the embarked tanks declared the site too dangerous. On her third try, with her executive officer now in command, she nudged up onto the beach just to the right of the 544. As she did so, she struck a mine that broke her in half, and at almost the same moment, two German shells hit her, one forward and one aft, smashing up what was left of her hull. On the other side of the 544, LCT-25 also struck a mine that flooded her engine room, and soon afterward she was hit by a phosphorus shell, after which the whole ship "erupted in flames." That caused the onboard ammunition to cook off, and within minutes the LCT-25, too, was a total wreck.[15]

Amazingly, with all this going on around her, the 544 was able to land her cargo, which consisted of a bulldozer leading half a dozen jeeps all tied together like a child's pull toy. The bulldozer clawed its way ashore, drag-ging the mostly submerged jeeps. But of course they were nowhere near their assigned beach and completely separated from the rest of their unit. Despite orders to retract at once, the crew of the 544 stayed long enough to gather up some of the wounded. With the sailors at the 20 mm guns pro-viding what cover they could, members of the crew ran out onto the sand to drag wounded men back aboard, and only then did the 544 successfully retract.

The fire was so intense on Omaha Beach that on some of the LCTs, the soldiers balked at leaving the ship at all. Beach master Joel Smith watched one LCT come ashore, and noted that the minute it dropped the ramp, "a German machine gun or two opened up, and you could see the sand kick up right in front of the boat." The soldiers could see it, too, and, as Smith noted, "no one moved." The Navy ensign in command of the boat "stood up and yelled" at the same moment that, for whatever reason, everything suddenly got quiet, so Smith clearly heard his plaintive entreaty: "For Christ's sake, fellas, get out! I've got to go and get another load."[16]

It was not an isolated case. Don Irwin, commanding LCT-614, which was carrying five jeeps, two bulldozers, and sixty-five men, approached the beach under heavy fire. When the 614 grounded and Irwin dropped the ramp, the first two soldiers who stepped forward were immediately shot and had to be pulled back into the well of the boat. After that, the rest of the soldiers simply refused to leave. During the pre-invasion briefing, Irwin had been told that if the men hesitated to disembark, he was to compel them to do so, "at gunpoint if necessary." But Irwin was unwilling to do that. Bullets were "pinging and ricocheting off the ship," he recalled, and it was evident to him as well as to them that walking out into that fire was a death sentence. His own crewmen begged him to retract: "Skipper, let's get out of here!" they pleaded. Irwin tried to comply, but the anchor needed to winch the boat off the beach had snagged on something, and the LCT would not budge. Irwin ordered all engines back full, then all ahead full, then back again, but the 614 was well and truly stuck. For almost ninety minutes the 614 remained on the beach, fully loaded and under nearly constant fire, unable to move. Not until high tide, near ten o'clock, did it manage to retract. When the crew of the 614 finally got the anchor up, they found that it was hooked into a sunken Higgins boat.[17]

Other LCTs were stranded on the beach due to damage from mines or gunfire or, like the 614, encumbered by wrecked and sunken vessels, jeeps, and even tanks. One Mike boat attempting to retract found its propellers had snagged on something in the water. Two men jumped over the side to clear the obstruction, which turned out to be "the bottom half of a man entangled in the screws." Even when there were no obstructions, withdrawal was not an easy matter. When LCT-612 was ready to retract, Ensign Horace "Skip" Shaw ordered a young sailor, whom he remembered only as "Helpy," to "wind up on that winch and get us off the beach." The young sailor hung his life vest on the exhaust pipe next to him to have more freedom of movement, and engaged the lever to wind in the stern anchor. A German machine gun had the range, and a storm of bullets "just blew that life jacket to a million pieces." More bullets flew all around the sailor, thudding into the wheelhouse of the LCT only inches away. Shaw was amazed. "He didn't bat an eye, that guy," Shaw remembered. "He just plain wound up that winch, got that anchor up, and got us off the beach."[18]

NOT FAR BEHIND THE LCTS were the troop-carrying LCIs, each of them packed with two hundred or more soldiers. Because the LCIs were lightly armored, they had been assigned to later waves, when, presumably, the beach would be relatively secure. During the approach, "spray over the bow kept the men wiping their faces," and they could see very little beyond "a smoky haze over the approaching land," as one sailor recalled. When the beach finally became visible, the men began to discern "shattered Higgins boats on the beach and men running to take cover." Obviously, the beach was not secure at all.[19]

The first LCI to land on Omaha Beach was LCI(L)-91, commanded by Coast Guard Lieutenant (j.g.) Armend Vyn. As he approached the beach, Vyn saw that his assigned channel was neither cleared nor marked, and that in any case it was "blocked by what appeared to be a sunken tank." Maneuvering around the tank and then though "a maze of stakes topped with teller mines," he nudged his vessel aground at 7:40. Though there was still nearly a hundred yards of water between the ship and the beach, he dropped the twin ramps on either side of the bow so the soldiers could disembark. With machine gun bullets smacking into the ship's bow and clanking against the twin ladders, the soldiers were naturally reluctant to venture down the ramps, and disembarkation was excruciatingly slow.[20]

Because of that, and because of the swiftly rising tide, Vyn continuously pushed forward with the engines "to keep grounded." Soon, however, it was impossible to go further "without detonating mines on the stakes" on both sides of the ship. One mine off the port bow did explode, blowing a two-foot hole in the forward hull and injuring two soldiers. Going further would endanger the ship itself. Even though he had offloaded only 60 of the 201 soldiers on board, Vyn backed away from the beach and hoisted the signal Baker Queen to notify nearby Higgins boats that they should come alongside to assist in landing troops. But those Higgins boats that were still afloat were all on missions of their own, and Vyn saw that he would have to find another landing site. He spotted one further along the beach and again pushed his ship ashore. As he did so, a mine exploded under the ship, and almost simultaneously a German artillery shell struck the bow. "Within seconds," Vyn reported, "the entire well deck was a mass of flames." There was not enough water pressure in the hoses for the crew to fight the fires, and the ship could not retract without sinking. Reluctantly Vyn gave the order to abandon ship.[21]

At that moment, the 91's sister ship, LCI(L)-92, was also headed for the beach. Though crewmen on the bow could see that the 91 was "enveloped in flames and smoke," the 92 pushed on nonetheless. The men on board could feel the concussion of near misses as tall funnels of water erupted on both sides. Then "a terrifying blast lifted the whole ship upward with a sudden lurch." The concussion threw men to the deck, and the heat was so powerful that one crewman felt like he was in "the midst of a blast furnace." Only seconds later, "another shattering explosion shook the ship like a toy boat." Like the 91, the 92 had been struck by an enemy shell only seconds after hitting a mine. The mine "blew out a hole in the starboard side big enough to drive a Higgins boat through," and the shell landed among the soldiers who were bunched forward preparing to disembark. Forty-one of them were killed instantly. Another shell hit the starboard ramp, and soldiers and sailors began jumping over the side, though others stayed on board and tried to fight the fires. The rising tide pushed the crippled LCI(L)-92 sideways up onto the beach, a complete wreck. Like the survivors of the 91, the crew of the 92 and those soldiers who made it off the ship joined the growing mass of humanity on the beach.[22]

It was a mess. Lieutenant (j.g.) Harry Montgomery, skipper of LCI(L)-489, reported that "craft of all description were maneuvering in all directions," making it impossible for him, or anyone else, to steer a straight course. He could not get to the beach because it was completely congested with "debris, wreckage, broached and sunken boats, burning tanks and vehicles." Those soldiers who had landed, and those sailors forced to join them when their ships were wrecked, sheltered precariously behind that low ridge of shingle, pressed facedown into the sand as they sought to avoid the machine gun bullets passing only inches over their heads. Soon German mortar fire would erase even that limited protection. And all the while, the relentless tide continued to mount the beach, faster than some of the wounded could crawl, reducing slowly but inexorably the narrow strip of land where men could still live. At eight-thirty, the beach master on Omaha notified Admiral Hall that "they were stopping the advance of follow up waves." Only two hours after it had started, the invasion of Omaha Beach had stalled.[23]

BY THEN, THE BRITISH AND CANADIAN FORCES had landed on Sword, Juno, and Gold Beaches. The British version of the Higgins boats, the wooden-hulled LCAs, which carried thirty men each, began heading for the beach at 6:00 a.m., and they crunched up onto the sand at 7:25, not quite an hour after the Americans. The British and Canadians also faced ferocious resistance, but they had several advantages that the Americans on Omaha Beach did not. First, the naval bombardment there had been far more effective, especially on Sword Beach. Second, the German defenders at Sword and Juno Beaches lacked the advantage of occupying high ground and the ability to create a crossfire over the beach. Finally, the assaulting troops had better tank support, since far more of the swimming DD tanks had made it successfully to shore. Several of the DD tank crews at Sword Beach found that their engines had been compromised with seawater while en route to the beach, though that did not prevent them from playing a role in the attack. Using their stern propellers, they pushed their tanks as close to shore as they could, and then, with most of the tank still awash in the surf and only the turret exposed, they opened fire on the German gun positions. One coxswain of an LCA returning from Sword Beach for a second load, shouted up to the deck of the transport: "It's a piece of cake!"[24]

Behind the tanks and the infantry came the British obstacle-clearing teams. As on Omaha Beach, they worked feverishly to clear as many mines and obstructions as possible before the high tide covered them up. British commandos also came ashore, most notably the First Special Service Brigade, commanded by Brigadier General Simon Fraser, known by his Scottish title as Lord Lovat. As the commandos splashed ashore, Lovat's piper, Bill Millin, played "Blue Bonnets" on the bagpipes. Lovat then led his commandos in a dash across country to relieve the British paratroopers who were holding Pegasus Bridge over the Caen Canal. Other units conducted house-to-house fighting in Ouistreham, the first urban fighting of the invasion. One element of that assault was a French unit led by Captain Philippe Kieffer. Assigned to secure a German strongpoint outside the city, the French commandos encountered fierce German resistance until Kieffer rounded up a few of the DD tanks; with their support, he routed the Germans out of their position and entered the city.[25]

The Germans defending the beaches recognized their peril, even if the high command in Berlin and Paris did not. The 84th Corps commander, General Erich Marcks, who was celebrating his fifty-third birthday that day, begged permission to use his tanks in a counterattack. Headquarters, however, remained convinced that this was a mere diversion and denied his request, which prompted the normally restrained Marcks to growl that the decision was "a disgrace." Not until the British and Canadians were well established ashore and moving inland did Marcks get permission to release his tanks. He organized forty of them into a strike force and ordered the commander to drive a wedge between the British on Sword Beach and the Canadians on Juno. He told the officer in charge, "If you don't succeed in throwing the British back into the sea, we shall have lost the war." Though this belated attack had some initial success, the British blunted it with effective antitank fire and then hurled it back. Nevertheless, the ferocity of the German counterattack helped convince the Allied commanders that rather than dash inland at once to seize the city of Caen, they should instead consolidate the front and dig in.[26]

BACK ACROSS THE ENGLISH CHANNEL the invasion's commanders waited anxiously for battle reports. Eisenhower had gone to bed late on June 5, though he had slept little. He was particularly concerned about the fate of the paratroopers of the airborne divisions. Leigh-Mallory had predicted disaster if the drops went ahead as scheduled, and Eisenhower had over-ruled him. Now the SHAEF commander awaited reports from the returning transport planes about the fate of those paratroopers. Leigh-Mallory himself called headquarters at 6:40 a.m., just as the first American sol-diers were pushing up onto Omaha Beach in their Higgins boats. Ike's naval aide, Harry Butcher, took the call, and he ran to Eisenhower's trailer with the report. Butcher found the Allied Supreme Commander sitting up in bed with a western novel in his hands and a filled ashtray next to him. Butcher relayed Leigh-Mallory's information: twenty of the 850 American transport planes had been lost, and only eight of the 400 Brit-ish planes. There had been no enemy fighter opposition, and little flak. The drops had been a success. Then Ramsay called. He reported a sortie by a few German E-boats from Le Havre and that the landings were pro-ceeding. Beyond that he had little news. Ike had no choice but to wait helplessly for further reports of the battle he had set in motion. He drafted a quick note to Marshall in Washington: "I have as yet no information concerning the actual landings," he wrote, adding, "preliminary reports are satisfactory."[27]

Churchill, too, was eager for news. He had remained in the vicinity of the Channel ports, "making a pest of himself" according to Brooke, until June 5 when Eisenhower had postponed the invasion for a day. He had then returned to London to await events. Never as sanguine about the outcome of the invasion as the Americans, he bade his wife Clementine goodnight that evening with the comment: "Do you realize that by the time you wake up in the morning, twenty thousand young men may have been killed?" As she retired, Churchill went down to his Map Room to read the reports as they arrived, moving the little pins on the maps as necessary. At noon he left to address the House of Commons. He announced the liberation of Rome, which had coincidentally taken place two days before, but as to the Normandy landings, he was unable to tell them anything beyond the fact that the battle was "proceeding according to plan."[28]

Roosevelt had originally planned to fly to London to be alongside Churchill during the invasion, but to his and Churchill's great disappointment, his declining health made that impossible. ("How I wish you were here," the prime minister cabled the president.) Instead, Roosevelt went to Charlottesville, Virginia, to be with his daughter Anna and her husband. He went to bed on June 5 aware that the invasion was likely to be under way before he awoke. George Marshall called from Washington at 3:00 a.m. (It was 8:00 a.m. in Normandy, and Vyn's LCI(L)-91 was burning on Omaha Beach.) Marshall told the president that the landings had taken place on schedule. Roosevelt authorized a public announcement a half hour later, and those who heard it also heard Eisenhower's recorded message to the invading force from the night before: "Soldiers, sailors and airmen of the Allied Expeditionary Force! You are about to embark upon the great crusade . . . ." As the sun rose and the news spread, church bells began to ring, and factories sounded their whistles. Even as the celebrations began, however, the outcome of the fighting on Omaha Beach remained in doubt.[29]

OFF THE AMERICAN BEACHES, the American generals who commanded the men who were pinned down on Omaha Beach were nearly wild with frustration. Omar Bradley, commander of the American First Army, stared shoreward at the smoke-enshrouded coastline from Kirk's flagship, the heavy cruiser *Augusta*. Off Utah Beach, Joe Collins, the VII Corps commander, and Raymond O. "Tubby" Barton, the 4th Division commander, watched from Moon's flagship, the transport *Bayfield*, while off Omaha Beach, Leonard T. Gerow, who commanded V Corps, and Clarence R. Huebner, who commanded the 1st Division, were on board USS *Ancon*, the converted ocean liner that Jimmy Hall used as his command ship. All these generals agonized about the circumstances ashore, and they chafed at their enforced absence from the battlefield. The command protocol for the American invasion beaches was that Kirk and the Navy retained full operational authority and control until the generals landed on the beach to assume command. That made the generals little more than high-ranking but largely impotent passengers, at least until they got their boots onto

French soil. It was maddening. They had spent most of their adult lives training for a moment such as this, and they had spent months honing their commands to a hard edge. Yet even as their men were dying, here they were a dozen miles offshore, unable to do much of anything to affect the course of events.[30]

The *Augusta* was a grand old lady of a warship. Laid down as a so-called Treaty cruiser in 1930, she had been designed to squeeze in just under the 1922 Naval Arms Limitation Treaty's definition of a battleship. She served from 1933 to 1940 as the flagship of the U.S. Asiatic Fleet, and then, transferred to the Atlantic in 1941, she had carried Franklin Roosevelt to Newfoundland to meet Churchill in the first of the Anglo-American strategy conferences. Now she was the flagship of the Western Task Force and the hub of much of the frenetic activity off the American beaches on D-Day.

Kirk and Bradley got on well. They had served together during the landings in Sicily, and they trusted and genuinely liked each other—from the beginning they had called each other "Alan" and "Brad." Now, at 8:00 a.m. on June 6, 1944, they were both deeply concerned. The forces on Utah Beach seemed to be doing all right, even if they had landed too far to the south. Though resistance there continued, "jeeps and tanks with their human cargoes seemed to be spilling out on[to] the sands without trouble," as one witness recalled. It was Omaha that was the problem. Kirk confessed to being "worried, very much worried, about Omaha," and Bradley wrote later of his "grave personal anxiety and frustration." The few reports that arrived on board *Augusta* from the beach suggested nothing less than a mounting disaster. Those who had landed were pinned down on the beach and not moving, and the clogged shoreline meant that the ensuing waves of landing craft had no place to go. Vessels offshore were jockeying about in obvious and increasing disorder. "I gained the impression," Bradley wrote, "that our forces had suffered an irreversible catastrophe, that there was little hope we could force the beach."[31]

Both Kirk and Bradley knew the old military adage "Never reinforce failure," and Bradley in particular wondered if instead of sending more soldiers to be slaughtered on Omaha, he and Kirk should direct ensuing waves to one of the other beaches where there was measurable progress. Of course, such a momentous decision would utterly shatter the carefully scripted inva-sion plan, and in any case it would be difficult to do, since successive waves of landing craft, only ten or fifteen minutes apart, were already heading shoreward, and recalling them now would only introduce more chaos. Nev-ertheless, Kirk alerted Moon that some of the Omaha force might be shifted over to Utah, and Moon told his senior beach officer, Captain James Arnold, that "the show on Omaha didn't go quite according to plan" and that they might have to "take on a little extra burden." To prepare for that, Moon ordered the LSTs of Force U to move to within four miles of the beach.[32]

On Jimmy Hall's flagship, USS *Ancon*, a mile or two inshore of the *Augusta*, both Gerow and Huebner were finding their enforced idleness all but intolerable. The few reports from Omaha Beach came in with agonizing slowness. This was largely due to the fact that three-quarters of the radios belonging to the landing teams had been smashed or water-soaked in the initial landings. Then, too, the radiomen themselves were either dead, wounded, or too busy trying to stay alive to submit regular reports. Des-perate for information, Gerow sent his assistant chief of staff, Colonel Ben-jamin Talley, in a DUKW to investigate. Talley maneuvered back and forth across the beachfront, closing to only five hundred yards off the beach, and reported to Gerow that things were very bad indeed. He confirmed that the men ashore were pinned down by heavy fire from the high ground, and that the beachfront was so congested that the LCTs were milling around like "a herd of cattle."[33]

Gerow went up onto the bridge of the *Ancon* and confronted Hall in what the latter described as "a state of alarm." Wasn't there something more that could be done? Gerow asked. Hall, the big, lantern-jawed, three-sport athlete who had felt no qualms in lecturing both Savvy Cooke and Freddy Guingand, was unperturbed, or at least he projected a demeanor of uncon-cern. He explained that the attack was still developing, and even if it had temporarily stalled, the way to fix it was simply to continue with the land-ings. He assured Gerow that it was all going to work out. Perhaps in an effort to get him off the bridge, Hall told Gerow that he could probably get a better understanding of what was happening ashore by reading the incoming message traffic down in the operations room.[34]

Navy Captain Lorenzo Sabin, who witnessed their conversation, offered the unsolicited suggestion that perhaps Hall could employ the two remaining rocket-firing LCTs that had been held in reserve. Gerow seized on that idea and urged Hall to do it, but Hall shook his head. The slapdash aiming protocols on the LCT(R)s would put too many Allied soldiers at risk, he said, and was unlikely to do much good anyway. The way to change the tide of battle, Hall repeated, was to continue landing more men and equipment. He assured both Gerow and Sabin that "the enemy was not going to [be able to] stop the landings" and that eventual victory was "only a matter of time." Sabin thought that "everyone except Admiral Hall seemed to be tense, worried, and disturbed." For his part, Gerow could not simply wait and do nothing, and he decided to commit the 115th Combat Infantry Team ahead of schedule. While that contributed to the growing American power ashore, it also added to the confusion and congestion on the beach.[35]

General Huebner, the strict, no-nonsense commander of the 1st Division, which was known as the "Big Red One," was also on board the *Ancon*, and he was worried, too; after all, those were his men being slaughtered on the beach. Huebner was busy doing what Hall had suggested to Gerow: reading the battle reports in the operations room as they came off the teletype machine on thin strips of paper, much like the tape from a stock ticker. Huebner spread the strips of paper out on a table and read them eagerly. By eight-thirty he concluded that the situation on the Omaha beaches was dire, and he sent his chief of staff, Colonel Stanhope Mason, up to the bridge to express his concern. Once again, Hall adopted a patient, confident demeanor. Mason listened, but he was not the one who needed convincing, and he urged Hall to go down and talk to Huebner. Perhaps in an effort to communicate the seriousness of the moment, Mason hinted that Huebner was considering a withdrawal.

Hall had no intention of leaving the bridge, nor did he have any notion of sanctioning a withdrawal. He reminded Mason that until Huebner established his headquarters ashore, the general did not have the authority to consider a withdrawal, much less order one. Only the naval commander could do that, and Hall had no intention of doing so. "I don't want to leave the bridge because there's so much that I can see and do up here that I can't do down there," he told Mason. If General Huebner wanted to talk to him, Hall said, Mason should "go down and bring General Huebner up here." When Huebner arrived, Hall asserted again that the situation, precarious as it was, was not dire, and he expressed his belief that, in time, the weight of Allied men and matériel would shift the balance of power on the invasion beaches. Hall insisted later that "there was never a time that I had any apprehension that we would not succeed." Meanwhile, he told Huebner in no uncertain terms: "I'm in command, and I'm not worried."[36]

Hall may not have been worried, but fifty miles to the east on the headquarters command ship HMS *Largs*, Ramsay was. The *Largs* was a former French vessel that had been docked in Gibraltar when France fell back in 1940. Taken into the Royal Navy, she had been renamed in honor of Mountbatten's Scottish estate. Redesigned with advanced communications equipment to serve as a command ship, she had so many antennae and radio wires strung about her that at least one member of the crew thought she looked "like a Monday morning wash line." It was thanks to all that electronic equipment that Ramsay could monitor all five beaches at once, and on June 6 it was the news from Omaha Beach that alarmed him. Leaving Rear Admiral Talbot to supervise the landings on Sword Beach, Ramsay quit the *Largs* and boarded a British destroyer that carried him over to the American sector, where he summoned Kirk on board.[37]

Kirk found Ramsay visibly agitated, and, much as Hall had done with Gerow and Huebner, he offered assurances. "We'll straighten it out," Kirk told Ramsay, "don't worry." In fact, Kirk was much less confident than his words suggested, but he was loath to confess such a thing to a British admiral with whom he had recently exchanged heated words. So he assumed a confident air and assured Ramsay that it was all going to work out. Ramsay was not entirely reassured. He blamed the mess on the "really bad" state of American communications—the product of all those smashed radios. Still, having made his point by coming over to see Kirk, there was little more that he could do. Because they were on a Royal Navy ship, where such things were permitted, the two men indulged in a quick glass of whiskey, then each returned to his post.[38]

There was no disguising the seriousness of the moment. Despite Hall's repeated assertions of confidence, the situation ashore was genuinely precarious. Omar Bradley confessed later that he was contemplating "evacuating the beachhead and directing the follow up troops to Utah Beach or the British beaches." Horrified by the prospect of failure, he asked Kirk if there wasn't something more the Navy could do to break the bloody stalemate on Omaha Beach.[39]

In fact, there was.

D-DAY: THE CRISIS

SEVERAL OF THE AMERICAN DESTROYERS that had participated in the early-morning bombardment had pulled off the invasion beaches prior to H-Hour. They did so partly to make room for the landing craft and partly to take up screening positions to seaward. Nevertheless, the destroyer skippers could see for themselves that the situation on Omaha Beach was deteriorating, and even without orders, some of them returned to the beachfront to open fire on the high ground behind the beach. Now, just past eight-thirty, Hall recalled the rest of them, ordering them to "maintain as heavy a volume of fire on beach target[s] as possible." In support of that, Admiral Bryant radioed a general message from the USS *Texas*: "Get on them, men! Get on them! They are raising hell with the men on the beach, and we can't have any more of that! We must stop it!"[1]

The destroyer captains responded with enthusiasm—indeed, almost too much enthusiasm. Most of the ships were American *Gleaves*-class destroyers that drew more than thirteen feet of water, and the gradual slope of Omaha

Beach made close-in fire support extremely hazardous.* It was self-evident that if a destroyer grounded in the shallows, the German gunners could blast it to pieces at their leisure. Nevertheless, they now came speeding shoreward at twenty knots or more into water that was both shallow and outside the swept channels. One sailor on an LCT approaching the beach was shocked to see "a destroyer ahead of us with heavy smoke pouring from its stack." To him, the ship appeared to be out of control and headed directly for the beach. *My God*, he thought, *they're going to run aground and be disabled right in front of the German artillery.* At the last minute, the destroyer made a sudden hard left, turned its starboard side parallel to the beach, and began "blazing away with every gun it had, point blank at the defensive positions." The sailor was thrilled to see "puffs of smoke and mounds of dirt" flying "everywhere on the hillside as the destroyer passed swiftly by."[2]

More than a dozen Allied destroyers responded to the call that morning, nine of them from Destroyer Squadron (DESRON) 18, under the command of U.S. Navy Captain Harry Sanders, who, like King's planning officer, Charles Cooke, had earned the nickname "Savvy" for his academic brilliance at the Naval Academy. Two of Sanders's destroyers, USS *Satterlee* (DD-626) and USS *Thompson* (DD-627), along with HMS *Talybont*, supported the U.S. Army Rangers assigned to assault the nearly vertical cliff at Pointe du Hoc, west of Omaha Beach. Two more, *Carmick* (DD-493) and *McCook* (DD-496), joined later by the USS *Harding* (DD-625), took up positions near the center of Omaha Beach, off St. Laurent-sur-Mer, and five others, led by the squadron flagship *Frankford* (DD-497) with Sanders on board, steamed for the eastern end of the beach near Colleville-sur-Mer. Most of them took up positions only eight hundred to a thousand yards off the beach, so close that, as a witness reported, "Germans were hitting them with rifle bullets." Though gradients varied across the beachfront, at that distance the water depth was only about twelve to eighteen feet. Sanders later speculated that there were

---

* The American *Gleaves* class destroyers, which carried five 5-inch guns, were modified during the war to carry one fewer 5-inch gun in order to accommodate additional anti-aircraft batteries. These wartime versions were dubbed *Bristol* class destroyers. A total of ninety-six vessels variously dubbed *Gleaves* or *Bristol* class were commissioned during the war. To avoid confusion, all these vessels will be referred to here as *Gleaves* class.

OMAHA BEACH, 9:00 A.M., JUNE 6, 1944

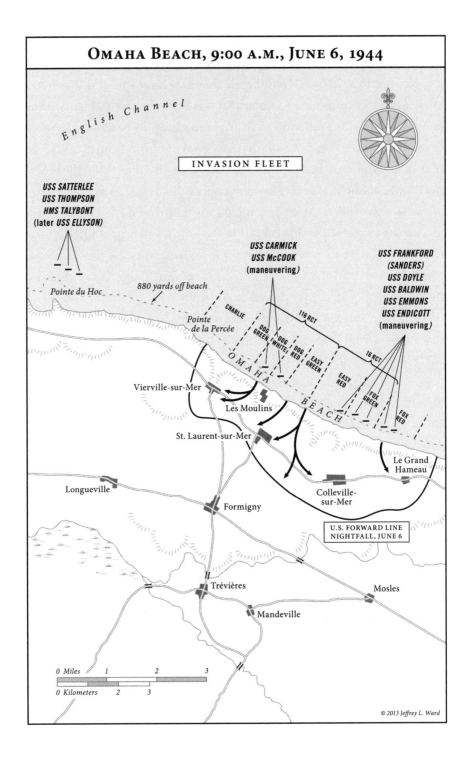

English Channel

INVASION FLEET

USS SATTERLEE
USS THOMPSON
HMS TALYBONT
(later USS ELLYSON)

USS CARMICK
USS McCOOK
(maneuvering)

USS FRANKFORD
(SANDERS)
USS DOYLE
USS BALDWIN
USS EMMONS
USS ENDICOTT
(maneuvering)

Pointe du Hoc

880 yards off beach

Pointe
de la Percée

CHARLIE

116 RCT

DOG
GREEN
DOG
WHITE
DOG
RED
EASY
GREEN

16 RCT

O M A H A

EASY
RED

Vierville-sur-Mer

B E A C H

FOX
GREEN

FOX
RED

Les Moulins

St. Laurent-sur-Mer

Le Grand
Hameau

Longueville

Colleville-
sur-Mer

Formigny

U.S. FORWARD LINE
NIGHTFALL, JUNE 6

Trévières

Mosles

Mandeville

0 Miles   1   2   3
0 Kilometers   2   3

© 2013 Jeffrey L. Ward

moments when the *Frankford* had only a few inches of water under her keel, and Kirk later asserted that "they had their bows against the bottom." Even if that was not literally true, it suggested the willingness of the destroyer captains to put their ships at risk in an obvious emergency. These dozen or so destroyers constituted only a tiny fraction of the more than five thousand ships that participated in the invasion, but over the ensuing ninety minutes, they turned the tide of battle on Omaha Beach.[3]

Several destroyers played a key role in what was perhaps the most daunting assignment of the entire invasion: the assault by 225 U.S. Army Rangers under Lieutenant Colonel James A. Rudder on Pointe du Hoc. Atop this promontory west of Omaha Beach, the Germans were believed to have placed several heavy guns that could reach both American beaches. To eliminate this threat, the Rangers would have to land on a narrow rocky beach at the base of the cliff, then scale the nearly vertical cliff with ropes and ladders. They boarded ten Royal Navy landing craft before dawn, but like almost every other vessel that morning, the boats were swept well to the left of their intended landing site by the current, and the coxswains initially aimed their boats not at Pointe du Hoc but Pointe de la Percée, slightly west of Vierville. Recognizing their error at about six-thirty, just as the first landings on Omaha and Utah Beach were taking place, the coxswains sought guidance and direction from one of the tiny (fifty-six-foot) landing control craft off Omaha Beach.

U.S. Navy Lieutenant William Steel commanded the control craft off Charlie Beach that morning, and he was fully engaged in trying to establish order amid the emerging chaos onshore when the group of landing craft carrying Rudder's men closed on his position. One of the boats eased up to the starboard side of Steel's little vessel, and a Royal Navy officer stood up with a megaphone in his hand. "I say," he called out, "can you tell me the way to Pointe du Hoc?" Steel was astonished; the question was delivered with the kind of casual diffidence a tourist might employ "standing on a street in New York City saying, 'How do you get to Times Square?'" Steel recovered quickly and, consulting the chart, gave the officer a bearing to Pointe du Hoc. The British officer took up the megaphone again: "Thank you very much," he called out, and with a wave, off they went.[4]

Despite this evident sangfroid, the delay did affect the Rangers' mission. Instead of landing at 6:30 and on both sides of the promontory as planned, they landed at 7:10 and only on the eastern side. On the other hand, that was precisely where several 14-inch shells from the USS *Texas* had collapsed a section of the cliff onto the narrow beach, creating a spoil of rocks forty feet high. The Rangers clambered up the pile of fallen rock, triggered their rocket-fired grappling hooks, and began to ascend the cliff face. The Germans sprayed them with machine gun fire and dropped grenades over the cliff, but the men kept climbing. The first of them to reach the top dropped ropes for the others, then turned to take on the German defenders. Of the 225 men who began the climb, 108 made it to the top. With so few of them, and arriving piecemeal as they did, it was touch and go.[5]

A crucial factor in their eventual success was gunfire support from the destroyers. Hard pressed by German light artillery, the Rangers used a blinker light to send target coordinates to the destroyers offshore. *Satterlee* responded first, joined by *Thompson* at 8:30 and by *Ellyson* (DD-454) an hour later. Unable to see the target, the destroyers had to rely on indirect fire, stopping after each salvo to receive a report from the Rangers about the fall of shot. At 9:52 the Rangers called for the destroyers to cease fire, and at 11:30 lookouts in the destroyers saw an American flag flying over the position. Having scaled the cliffs, driven off the defenders, and seized the high ground, however, the Rangers soon discovered that the reported big guns on Pointe du Hoc had been removed, replaced by wooden dummies. They moved inland and set up a defensive perimeter, which they held for the rest of the day and into the night.[6]

The other destroyers of Sanders's squadron, operating off Omaha Beach itself, had great initial difficulty identifying appropriate targets. The poor visibility along the beachfront and the excellent German camouflage made it all but impossible to figure out where the German guns were. Some of those guns retracted into underground bombproofs; others were so well hidden that, as one sailor put it, "you couldn't see it if you was ten feet from them." In theory, the ships were supposed to coordinate with shore-based fire control parties that would identify the targets and report the fall of the shot, as the Rangers did on Pointe du Hoc. But there was such chaos on the beach that morning, and such a dearth of working radios, that not until the afternoon did the destroyers establish regular radio communication with spotters ashore. In the meantime, the destroyer skippers were compelled to seek "targets of opportunity." There was one immediate benefit of their arrival, however: many of the German gunners, fearful of disclosing their location, briefly held their fire, while others shifted their fire to target the destroyers. In both cases that created a blessed, if temporary, respite for the soldiers on the beach.[7]

Near the center of Omaha Beach, just off the beachfront village of Les Moulins, Commander Robert Beer, the tall, lanky captain of the *Carmick*, scanned the bluffs looking for telltale "puffs of smoke or flashes from enemy gun emplacements." Because the Germans were using smokeless powder, he saw none, and Beer became impatient, finding the process "slow and unreliable." As he studied the beach through his binoculars, however, he noted a few Allied tanks trying vainly to fight their way up the draw, or gully, in the cliffs near Vierville-sur-Mer. It was evident to him that they were being held up by heavy gunfire from above, though he could not identify the source of that fire. Several of the Allied tanks were shooting at a particular spot on the bluffs, and, carefully noting the fall of their shot, Beer directed his ship's guns to target those same positions. The *Carmick* fired a series of rapid-fire salvos from her 5-inch guns into the suspicious area. After a few minutes, Beer noted that the tank gunners had shifted their fire to another site, and Beer directed his gunnery officer to follow suit. "It became evident," Beer reported afterward, "that the Army was using tank fire in [the] hope that fire support vessels would see the target and take it under fire." In a kind of deadly pas de deux, the tank men used their shells to point out enemy gun positions, and the destroyer men aimed accordingly.[8]

Near the *Carmick*, Lieutenant Commander Ralph Ramey, in USS *McCook*, opened fire on two strongly fortified German guns set into the cliff face. Many of Ramey's friends thought he was the spitting image of the comedian Will Rogers, and Ramey often sprinkled his conversation with country aphorisms, but he was all business now. Ramey and the *McCook* maintained an unremitting fire at the German battery for more than fifteen minutes, and eventually that concentrated bombardment undermined the rock strata on which the enemy guns rested. The cliff crumbled away; one of the guns flew up into the air and the other plunged down the cliff face.[9]

A mile or two further east, Commander Clarence Boyd, captain of the *Doyle* (DD-494), maneuvered his ship among the landing craft that were swarming off the Fox Green sector of Omaha Beach. From only eight hundred yards off the surf line, Boyd could see the men ashore "dug in behind a hummock of sand along the beach, and the boats of the second wave [actually the third] milling around offshore." Absent contact with fire control parties ashore, he posted lookouts to scan the high ground behind the beach for evidence of enemy gun positions, though visibility was "very difficult because of smoke and dust in the target area." One lookout reported a machine gun emplacement on a steep hill at the west end of Fox Red Beach between Colleville-sur-Mer and Le Grand Hameau, and the *Doyle* fired two salvos onto the site. The *Doyle* then shifted fire to a casemate at the top of the hill and fired two more salvos, and in both cases Boyd was able to report "target destroyed." More often, however, the results were less conclusive. Lacking other clear sightings, Boyd simply picked out what seemed to him to be logical places for gun positions to be and opened fire on them even if he could not see anything there. Having completed its assignment off Point du Hoc, the *Thompson* joined the *Doyle* off Fox Green beach, and there her commander, Albert Gebelin, whose darkly handsome features reminded some of "a cigar store Indian," directed his ship's fire into "a clump of trees" that he thought might be "cover for a field battery." Whether it was or not, the trees got a thorough pounding.[10]

Other ships got into the act. A sailor on an LCT happened to be looking at the vegetation along the line of bluffs when he noticed a tiny movement among the bushes, and a second later a shell exploded on the beach. He kept his eye focused on those bushes, and soon another small movement of the brush was followed by another explosion on the beach. He called the skipper over and pointed it out. The officer watched as the pattern was repeated, and he noted the coordinates on his chart. He then got on the short-range TBS radio and called the nearest of the destroyers. Almost at once a destroyer "came barreling in there, popped over sideways, port side to the beach, and turned loose about eight rounds of 5-inch projectiles" into the German gun position.[11]

Compared to the aerial bombs dropped from high altitude and the big shells fired from ten or fifteen miles offshore, the smaller-caliber destroyer fire was more accurate and therefore far more effective. The bigger 8-, 12-, and 14-inch shells from the cruisers and battleships had made the ground shake, but they had left the German gun positions largely intact. Now those positions were pounded with hundreds of 5-inch shells and knocked out one by one. One witness recalled seeing three 5-inch shells hit within twenty inches of a narrow gun slit on a pillbox, and in at least one case a German artillery piece was hit directly on the muzzle and split wide open. A beach master on Omaha watching the tin cans fire into the cliff later claimed, "You could see the trenches, guns, and men blowing up where they were hit." There was no doubt in his mind that "the few Navy destroyers that we had there probably saved the invasion." With more enthusiasm than precision, he insisted that the handful of American ships "destroyed practically the entire German defense line at Omaha Beach." If they didn't quite do that, they did change the trajectory of the battle. Inside an artillery bunker behind Omaha Beach, a German regimental commander phoned headquarters to report, "Naval guns are smashing up our strongpoints. We are running short of ammunition. We urgently need supplies." There was no answer because the line had gone dead.[12]

For more than an hour, from shortly before nine o'clock until well past ten, the destroyer gunfire was virtually nonstop. And it needed to be. As the commanding officer of LCI(L)-408 noted while heading for the beach just before ten o'clock, "If a destroyer ceased shelling a shore battery for even a very brief time, the battery resumed fire on the craft along the beach." Of course, the constant firing soon depleted the ammunition stores on the destroyers. To ensure that they retained sufficient capability for emergencies, the Neptune invasion order had specified that the destroyers were to expend no more than 50 to 60 percent of their ammunition before going back to England to replenish. In this crisis, however, the destroyer skippers disregarded that injunction. *Gleaves*-class destroyers carried between fifteen hundred and two thousand rounds of general-purpose 5-inch ammunition. Most of the ships in Sanders's squadron had fired off between a quarter and a third of that during the early morning bombardment, and now they expended most of what was left. Between 8:50 and 10:15 that morning, USS *Emmons* (DD-457) fired 767 rounds, *McCook* 975, and *Carmick* 1,127. Kirk became sufficiently nervous about this that he issued an order that "destroyers must husband [their] ammunition," reminding them that "our resources are limited." When the gunners on the *Herndon* (DD-638) ran out of high-explosive ammunition, they began firing star shells that were primarily used for illumination. On USS *Butler* (DD-636), Petty Officer Felix Podolak remembered that the firing was so hot "we had to hook up one-and-a-half-inch fire hoses to hydrants to spray water on our gun mount," and even then, "the barrels were running red hot."[13]

The German gunners fired back, mostly with their mobile 88 mm field guns, but the swift destroyers were difficult targets, even in the shallow and crowded waters off Omaha Beach. The Germans had already claimed one destroyer that morning when USS *Corry* (DD-463) hit a mine and virtually broke in half, going down in less than thirty minutes. The Germans were less successful in targeting the destroyers with gunfire. The skippers used their engines "in spurts," ordering them alternately "ahead and astern, to throw off the enemy gunners." There were some close calls. A German battery behind Fox Red Beach straddled the *Emmons*, and USS *Baldwin* (DD-624) was hit twice in rapid succession, the first shell striking her whaleboat on the starboard side and the second blowing an eight-by-twelve-inch hole in her main deck. But the *Emmons* escaped injury, and *Baldwin* responded with accurate counterbattery fire, silencing its tormentor after several salvos. No other destroyer was hit during this crucial and decisive ninety-minute period.[14]

Shortly before noon, the accuracy of the destroyer gunfire improved when the ships finally established contact with some of the fire control parties ashore. At 11:24, Army spotters directed the fire of the *Frankford* into a concentration of German troops behind the beach and therefore beyond the sightline of the destroyers. After two salvos, the spotters called a ceasefire because the soldiers had scattered. Occasionally it worked exactly as it was supposed to, as it did, for example, two days later, on June 8, when the *Ellyson* got target coordinates from a shore fire control party for a German artillery position. After one salvo, the spotters reported, "Up four hundred yards"; after the next, "Up fifty yards"; and after the third, "Mission success-ful." Of course, shore spotting had limits, too. An exchange recorded later that same day suggested why. Receiving a request for fire support, the gun-nery officer on the USS *Laffey* (DD-724) asked for coordinates. The answer came back: "We're lying on our stomachs in a ditch under enemy fire. Can-not furnish spots." The *Laffey* opened fire nonetheless, and after several sal-vos, the shore spotter radioed back: "Whoever was shooting at us has stopped, so you must have done alright."[15]

Given the dearth of working radios ashore and the complications of inter-service communication, it is not surprising that there were errors. Late that afternoon, several of the American destroyers received reports that the Ger-mans were using the church steeples in both Colleville-sur-Mer and Vierville-sur-Mer as observation posts. USS *Emmons* took on the task of taking down the steeple in Colleville, and after a few salvoes, it did, smashing it, as one sailor recalled, "just like you'd hit it with a big ax." A few miles to the west, off Vierville, USS *Harding* took the church there under fire. From offshore the results looked spectacular. The *Harding*'s first salvo clipped off the cross at the peak, the second hit the steeple about ten feet from the top, and the third hit ten feet below that. From seaward it looked like the *Harding* was slicing off the steeple ten feet at a time, and Admiral Bryant, watching from the bridge of the *Texas*, thought it was "a beautiful sight." The reality on the ground was much different. Not only did the shelling cause a lot of collateral damage, but, far worse, American troops had already captured the town, and the *Harding*'s shells killed and wounded a number of Americans. Army Captain Joseph Dawson of the 16th Infantry thought it was "totally disgraceful."[16]

Despite such errors, the cumulative effect of the close-in naval gunfire support was decisive. For the first time since they had landed, the men lying facedown behind the low rise of sand and shingle at the high tide mark were able to lift their heads and look around them for a way off the beach. As early as 10:36, lookouts on the *Frankford* noted that some Allied troops were beginning to advance, mov-ing forward from that low hillock of sand toward the base of the cliffs. And an hour later, at 11:37, some of the German defenders began coming out of their positions with their hands up. While much of this was the result of incredible bravery and determination by the soldiers themselves, the destroyers played a critical role. In his postwar memoir, Bradley acknowledged that "the Navy saved our hides." Colonel Mason, who several hours earlier had tried to convince Hall to quit the bridge and go down and talk to Huebner on the *Ancon*, declared that "without that gunfire, we positively could not have crossed the beaches."[17]

BUT CROSS THEY DID. When every instinct was telling the soldiers to stay down and keep still, their officers insisted that they needed to get up and get moving. Among them was the assistant commander of the 29th Division, Brigadier General Norman "Dutch" Cota, who had landed with the second wave at seven-thirty. Cota worked his way along the line of men behind the seawall telling every officer he saw: "We've got to get these men off this Goddammed beach." Another was Colonel George A. Taylor, commander of the 16th Infantry Regiment, who made the choice clear. "There are two kinds of people who are staying on this beach," he told the men. "Those who are dead and those who are going to die. Now let's get the hell out of here." Thanks to the destroyers, and emboldened by the zeal and passion of their officers, the soldiers began to move forward.[18]

The original plan called for them to advance up the several gullies, or draws, that cut narrow valleys through the cliff line. The Germans had anticipated that and heavily fortified the draws. To escape the killing ground of the beach, many of the solders now ran forward to the base of the cliff itself. There they were shielded from the German artillery, but they were hardly safe. German infantry crept to the lip of the bluffs, held their machine guns out over the edge, and fired blindly down onto the Americans below. Their aim was erratic, yet it was evident that the base of the cliff was only marginally less deadly than the beach itself. Resolving this tactical dilemma was complicated by the fact that many of the GIs crowding up to the base of the cliff had become separated from their commands, and the units were hopelessly intermingled. In some respects, the mass of men at the base of the cliff was less an organized military force than a collection of survivors: men who had, against the odds, somehow lived through the long passage to the beach, the struggle from the surf line to the hillock of beach sand at the high tide mark, and the move from there to the cliff face. There were sailors as well as soldiers among these survivors: a handful of NCDU team members who had been cut off from their teams, and sailors who had been forced to abandon their vessels when they were wrecked on the beach. All of them recognized that they now depended on each other, and amid the chaos, they formed up into ersatz teams led by majors, captains, lieutenants, and sergeants. And then, in an act rivaling the Union Army's ascent of Missionary Ridge in the Civil War, they began to climb the cliffs, working their way upward, hand over hand, using rifle fire and grenades against the startled defenders.[19]

In this, too, they received help from the destroyers offshore. Still patrolling the beachfront between Vierville and St. Laurent, Beer saw some GIs pinned down "behind a big house in the Dog Green area." It was, in fact, a group of soldiers that had been collected by U.S. Army Major Sidney Bingham. The men had captured a large three-story stone house on the beach near the Les Moulins draw, but they could not advance beyond it. Beer could not see what was keeping them pinned down. Still, he directed the *Carmick*'s fire into the cliff face above them, and after a few salvos he saw the GIs charge forward and begin to ascend the bluffs. Beer then elevated the *Carmick*'s guns to the top of the bluffs, and he maintained a supporting fire ahead of them as the men scrambled up the cliff's face.[20]

Among them was Robert Giguere, a seventeen-year-old seaman who had lied about his age in order to join the Navy and who had been stranded on the beach with his NCDU team since early that morning. Cut off from his shipmates, he had sought cover behind the low seawall along with everyone else who could still move. After enduring what seemed an eternity of machine gun and artillery fire, he heard an Army officer say, "Let's ... knock out some of these pill boxes. We might as well get killed inland [as] here on the beach." The men responded and began to run forward. Giguere went with them. "At this point," he recalled later, "I never thought I'd see my eighteenth birthday."[21]

While Giguere and hundreds of others scrambled up the cliffs, others sought to fight their way up through the draws. Among them was Navy Ensign Karl Everitt. His LCT had wrecked on a beach obstacle during the landing, and he and his crew had been forced to abandon ship, joining the hundreds of others who took cover behind that low rise of sand and stones, though Everitt had to roll several dead soldiers out of the way to find room. He saw some Army engineers attempting to screw several lengths of Bangalore torpedo tubes together in an effort to blow a hole through the thick coils of barbed wire that obstructed the Vierville draw. Rather than sit and watch, Everitt and his crewmen "started screwing those tubes together." When they had fifty to sixty feet of it assembled, they tried sliding it forward, but it got entangled in the wire and they had to pull it back and start over. All the time they endured heavy machine-gun fire. Eventually they got the tubing in position and pressed the plunger, and the subsequent explosion folded the barbed wire "back right up against that cliff and [it] stayed there." Everitt remembered what happened next: "Well, boy, those guys went out of there like a stampede.... They just come off that ground and they headed for that opening." Everitt and his boat crew went with them, advancing all the way to the top of the ridge, where they met up with those who had climbed the face of the cliff. After that, having had enough of Army life for one day, Everitt and his men returned back down to the beach where they saw that the tide had gone out and left their LCT sitting high and dry impaled on a beach obstruction. They had to wait for the next high tide to get it off the beach.[22]

THE TIDE WAS CHANGING ON SHORE, TOO. The fighting was still intense, but it was no longer one-sided. As Hall had foreseen, the influx of more and more Allied men and equipment, aided by the accurate destroyer fire, finally tipped the balance ashore. The seventeenth wave landed around noon, and even if the line of landing craft did not resemble the neat formation envisioned by the planners, the boats managed to discharge their men and vehicles. Meanwhile, soldiers from the 116th Regimental Combat Team (RCT) who had successfully assailed the bluffs west of Vierville found their way into the town from above. Other soldiers from the 115th RCT that Gerow had decided to commit early made their way to the top of the bluffs near St. Laurent, and men from the 16th RCT ascended the bluffs between Colleville and Le Grand Hameau. By one o'clock that afternoon they had captured Colleville itself. At about the same time, shellfire from the *Texas* took out the last German strongpoint in the Vierville draw, which allowed seventeen tanks from the 743rd tank battalion to push their way up the gap and into Vierville itself. At one-thirty Gerow reported to Bradley that the men were off the beaches and advancing onto the high ground.[23]

An hour later, the first elements of Force B, carrying the rest of the 29th Division, arrived off Omaha Beach. In addition to a dozen LCI(L)s packed with infantry, it included HMS *Oceanway*, a former U.S. Navy Landing Ship, Dock (LSD) that had been turned over to the British under Lend-Lease only two months earlier. Hall sent her to Fox Green Beach near Colleville, and there she flooded her well deck and disgorged her twenty Mike boats, each preloaded with one M4 Sherman tank. By five o'clock the men and the tanks were ashore and backing up the move inland. The commander of the 29th Division, Major General Charles Gerhardt, also went ashore. Gerhardt was something of a showman who wore twin pearl-handled revolvers. En route to the beach in an LCT, he was annoyed when the boat's commander, Ensign Curtis Hansen, turned away to look for a better landing site. Gerhardt exploded. "Get ashore!" he yelled. "I've got work I've got to do in there and run this invasion." Hansen, however, had been briefed on exactly this issue, and he recited the prescribed statement: "General, I'm in charge of this small boat until we hit the beach, and then you are in charge." Gerhardt was stymied, for he, too, knew the protocols. "You are right, Ensign," he said, and he remained uncharacteristically silent until they landed some ten or fifteen minutes later.[24]

By then, General Huebner was also ashore. He found that the morning assault had separated many of his officers from their commands, and that many of his 1st Division units were intermingled. He therefore focused most of his energies on restoring order, and at midnight he reported to Hall that he had established a continuous front line "from Vierville through St. Laurent to about a mile south of Colleville." (See Map, page 292.) Though well short of the official objective for D-Day, it was a significant accomplishment in light of all that had gone wrong.[25]

By 6:00 p.m. on June 6, while Omaha Beach remained a dangerous place, the momentum had clearly shifted. German long-range artillery continued to lob shells onto the beach, and fighting—some of it hand-to-hand—still raged on the high ground behind it, but it no longer seemed likely that the

Allies would be driven into the sea. Higgins boats and LCTs carrying men, vehicles, and equipment shuttled back and forth in a nearly continuous stream between the transports and LSTs offshore and the beach. Though the initial Neptune plan had assigned specific roles for these landing craft, most of them simply went up to whatever vessel was nearby, took on whatever cargo was available, and headed for whatever piece of beach was open. When one Higgins boat driver reported to an officer on an LCI to ask for orders, the officer said simply, "Just continue shuttling material ashore."[26]

With the division commanders now on the beach, control of the ensuing operations transferred formally from the Navy to the Army. That did not mean the Navy had finished its work. As soon as the tide receded, the surviving members of the NCDU teams got busy again attacking the beach obstacles to clear more paths for subsequent waves of men and equipment. The loss of so much of their equipment compelled Hall to send an urgent request to Commander Service Forces back in England for "additional explosives and demolition equipment...by the quickest available means." The quickest means proved to be Bulkeley's PT boats. Speeding at forty knots, they completed the round trip across the Channel by nine the next morning. As the NCDU teams cleared the mines, the bulldozers of the Combat Engineer Brigades began shoving aside the wrecked Higgins boats, the disabled jeeps, and even the Allied dead. Seaman Second Class Jackson Hoffler, who at age fourteen was almost certainly the youngest warrior on Omaha Beach that day, was sure he would "never forget seeing vehicles driving over bodies."[27]

Though Omaha Beach was now in Allied hands, it was evident to nearly everyone that the assault had not gone according to plan. As the historian Adrian Lewis bluntly put it, "The plan for the assault at Omaha Beach failed." The list of disappointments was long. The preliminary air attack and naval bombardment had failed to knock out the German strongpoints; too few of the DD tanks had made it to the shore; the NCDU teams had insufficient time to clear the obstacles; most of the troops had come ashore in the wrong places; too many of the landing craft had been wrecked or disabled; and the advance inland, when it finally happened, had been largely a product of initiative and determination by brave and desperate men rather than the neat and structured offensive detailed in the operational plan. And, of course, the losses had been heavy. The most commonly cited number of Allied killed, wounded, and missing for June 6, 1944, is around ten thousand, with 60 percent of them American. Nearly half of those casualties were incurred by the airborne troops behind the beaches, but nearly three thousand of them resulted from the fighting on Omaha Beach, which was greater than the losses on all four of the other invasion beaches combined. In spite of that, the Allies were ashore, and by nightfall it was evident that they would stay there. No small part of the credit for that belonged to the sea forces: the ships and men of the Royal Navy, the U.S. Navy, and the U.S. Coast Guard. Gerow himself finally got ashore between seven and eight that evening, and his first message to Bradley, still on board the *Augusta*, was: "Thank God for the United States Navy."[28]

The news from the other beaches was better. Utah Beach was well in hand, with the men of Collins's VII Corps already moving inland for an eventual link-up with the airborne troops. West of Omaha Beach, the British—and alongside them the Canadians—were established ashore and already attracting the attention of several furious German counterattacks. Off Sword Beach, the Germans mounted their only naval counterattack of the day when German torpedo boats out of Le Havre stumbled into the invasion force. Awestruck by the spectacle, and no doubt assuming that it would be all but impossible to miss in such a target-rich environment, the E-boats had fired off their torpedoes in the general direction of the Allied fleet and then fled. One torpedo passed between the *Warspite* and *Ramillies*, and another headed directly toward Ramsay's headquarters ship, *Largs*. The officer of the deck on the *Largs* ordered full astern, and the torpedo passed across its bow, missing by only a matter of feet. The Norwegian destroyer *Svenner* was less fortunate. A torpedo struck her boiler room, and the ensuing explosion lifted her out of the water, breaking her in half. Like the *Corry*, she sank within minutes. That, however, proved to be the only Allied loss of the day to enemy surface action.[29]

THE SUN FINALLY SET AT 10:06. Even then, a bright, full moon cast a silver glow over the beaches, offering good visibility through thinning clouds, though it also bled the color out of the landscape, turning everything into shades of black and white. The detritus on Omaha Beach offered mute testimony to an apparent catastrophe. Despite the ongoing work of the combat engineers, the beachfront remained littered with scores of wrecked landing craft, tanks, trucks, and jeeps. Though a dozen lanes had been cleared through the obstructions, many of those obstacles remained in place—obscene black sculptures scarring the silvered sheen of the beach.

Yet thanks to the sheer will of the officers and men who had fought the battle, and in part at least to the close-in fire support of a handful of destroyers, by nightfall on June 6 the Allies had landed 132,450 American, British, and Canadian soldiers on French soil.* To the east, British Tommies advanced gingerly from Sword Beach toward Caen; to the west, American GIs moved inland from Utah Beach toward the village of Sainte-Mère-Eglise; and on Omaha, the men were at last off the beach and in possession of the high ground, including the villages of Vierville, St. Laurent, and Colleville. In the end, it was less the detailed invasion plan, labored over for so many months, that provided the margin of success than it was the desperate ferocity of the men themselves. If the plan had failed, the men had triumphed; if they had not quite established a foothold, they had at least secured a toehold. The question now was whether they could maintain the buildup of men, vehicles, and supplies needed to keep that toehold and to expand it.

---

* Among the American, British, and Canadian forces was a battalion of Inter-Allied Commandos that included Dutch, Belgian, Norwegian, Polish, and of course French troops. There were even a few expatriate Germans.

CHAPTER 14

"THE SHORELINE WAS JUST
A SHAMBLES"

THE OFFICIAL OBJECTIVE of Operation Neptune was "to secure a lodgment on the Continent from which further offensive operations can be developed." By midnight on June 6, it might have been argued that this objective had been achieved. But as Frederick Morgan had noted back in 1943 when he was still COSSAC: "The surprise assault...would no doubt win the first round." The far more important question, the one that would ultimately decide the campaign, was whether the Allies could bring in reinforcements and equipment over the assault beaches faster than the Germans could direct their mobile divisions there—as Morgan put it in a rough paraphrase of Confederate General Nathan Bedford Forrest, "who could get the mostest men there fustest."[1]

In that race, the D-Day landings were only the first lap. The Allied soldiers who had seized the beaches had to be fed and supplied with ammunition. Then thousands more men—tens of thousands, hundreds of thousands—had to be brought ashore in a never-ending stream to support and expand the beachhead, and those men, too, had to be fed and supplied.

The tanks, trucks, jeeps, and artillery pieces that had been lost during the assault had to be replaced, and thousands more had to come ashore to provide mobility and firepower to the invading army. And all of this had to be accomplished swiftly so that the Allied force in Normandy would be strong enough to withstand the German counteroffensive when it came, as it inevitably would. Not to be forgotten were the displaced French civilians of Normandy cowering in their basements or driven from their homes altogether; they, too, had to be fed and supplied. Fulfilling all these essential needs constituted a logistical challenge of the greatest magnitude. As Eisenhower had put it in a letter to Marshall in February, "From D day to D plus 60 this thing is going to absorb everything the United Nations can possibly pour into it."[2]

IT GOT OFF TO A POOR START, especially on Omaha Beach. In spite of all that had gone wrong, the Allies had managed to land an impressive number of men and vehicles on D-Day, but the delivery of stores and supplies fell far short of the pre-invasion goal. According to the original schedule, the first loads of military cargo were supposed to start coming ashore by H plus three hours, that is, at about 9:30 a.m. That schedule was exploded almost at once, for at 9:30 on the morning of D-Day, virtually nothing at all was moving on Omaha Beach. Consequently, instead of the 2,400 tons of supplies that were supposed to be landed that day, the actual total was only about 100 tons. Moreover, the buildup over the ensuing several days also fell significantly short of the official targets. The goal was 8,000 tons per day, but during the first four days of the invasion, the Allies landed a *total* of only 4,581 tons on Omaha Beach. One reason for this was the obvious reality that, as Hall put it rather laconically, "obstacles still impeded access to the beach," and because of that, ships of the follow-up supply convoys from England had to loiter offshore waiting to be unloaded. Not until the evening of June 9 was the beachfront sufficiently cleared of obstacles and wreckage to allow unrestricted use of the waterfront. As a result, the movement of supplies across the beach fell so far behind schedule that even Hall's famous equanimity was tested. "The general progress of unloading," he wrote, was "far too slow."[3]

A second factor that affected the offloading process was that the Army commanders who were fighting the Germans inland sent back urgent—and sometimes frantic—requests for particular items, especially ammunition. In an effort to respond to those requests, beach officers had to first figure out which ships contained the needed supplies and then resequence the landing schedule to give them priority. Ships that were in position and ready to offload were ordered to stand off while others containing the needed items were brought in, and this, too, caused delays. Hall complained that this slowed down delivery, but Army commanders insisted that "unloading must be done according to priorities." Hall appealed to Bradley, and on June 10 he got permission from Bradley's chief of staff, Major General William Benjamin Kean, to unload all ships "as fast as possible regardless of priorities." As Ramsay put it, "Empty the ships and [the] priorities will take care of themselves." After that, the pace of unloading picked up significantly, though periodic demands to prioritize certain kinds of supplies caused occasional difficulties.[4]

A third factor that impeded the offloading schedule during those first few days was Ramsay's decision that on Omaha Beach at least, the big and valuable LSTs were not to go ashore to discharge their cargoes until the beaches were no longer within range of enemy artillery. Two LSTs had attempted to land on D-Day and had been badly battered—the 133 was stranded on the beach, and the 309 had to back away and offload into smaller craft. Though Ramsay did authorize sending the LSTs onto the British beaches, and even onto Utah Beach, as early as June 7, he insisted that this should not be done on Omaha Beach "except in an emergency." As serious as things were, Hall could not in good conscience label a slowdown in offloading an "emergency," and so for the first several days almost everything headed for Omaha Beach initially had to be unloaded into smaller craft offshore. This was already standard procedure for the transports and Liberty ships, and including the LSTs in this protocol put an additional strain on the small craft and consumed both time and manpower.[5]

While the LCTs and Higgins boats carried the soldiers, the work of transporting the vehicles and heavy cargo fell mainly on the big, flat, barge-like rhino ferries, which had six times the capacity of an LCT, and ten times that of a Higgins boat. Most of the rhinos and their Seabee crews had come across the Channel under tow, and when they arrived off the invasion beaches, they first had to cast loose and motor around to the bow of the LST to load up. Some found that difficult to do—the violent sea state had so strained the towing shackles that many of them had bent. On one rhino ferry, the Seabees labored for more than an hour, "cursing, sweating, and scrambling," trying to unshackle the disfigured couplings. All that time, the skipper of the LST stood at the stern of his ship, megaphone in hand, yelling at them to get on with it.[6]

After the rhinos liberated themselves, they then had to maneuver around to the bow of the LSTs, and that, too, proved difficult. The rhino barges were particularly unwieldy, and the heavy sea state made the approach hazardous as well as difficult. Some of the steel cables used to connect the two vessels snapped "like kite cord," as one sailor put it. In at least one case, a Seabee jumped into the chill water to retrieve the loose end of a parted chain. Once the rhino was finally in place, the LST lowered its ramp, and the tanks and fully loaded trucks drove out of the ship's tank deck onto the rhino's flat, exposed surface. As they did so, the rhino settled deeper and deeper in the water until sometimes there was only a few inches of freeboard. Water "began to wash over the stern," as one Seabee recalled, and soon everyone on the rhino was "wet from the knees down."[7]

Once divorced from the LSTs, the rhinos then made their painstaking way the ten or eleven miles to the beach. Occasionally a tug might be assigned to assist them, but the cumbersome rhinos were so ungainly that the tugs were overmatched. As one Seabee put it, "It was like the tail trying to wag the dog." After the rhinos got to within a mile or two of the beach, the beach masters often ordered them to wait their turn before going ashore. When they finally got the go-ahead signal, they had to contend with the eastward-flowing current, which kept trying to push them to the left. As one Seabee put it, "We kept sliding down the beach with the current." All in all, it was a difficult and sometimes precarious process that contributed to the disappointing totals of tonnage delivered ashore.[8]

One of the biggest Allied logistical concerns during those first several days was ammunition. As the historian Russell Weigley has noted, a salient characteristic of the "American way of war" is the application of over-whelming firepower. The British viewed this with a mixture of amuse-ment and disapproval. To them, the American profligacy with ordnance only underscored their indifferent military skills. Here was one more as-pect of the cultural differences between the Anglo-American partners. Having been forced all their lives to make do with limited resources, the British shook their collective heads at the American tendency to "use a sledgehammer to crack nuts," as one British officer put it. To the Americans, the application of overwhelming firepower was simply the most effective and efficient way to defeat the enemy while minimizing their own casual-ties. That view, however, also meant that the American front-line troops had to be supplied with prodigious quantities of bullets and artillery shells. To do this, the initial plan was for ammunition ships to provide afloat stowage offshore while the small amphibious DUKWs ferried am-munition to the beach. They seemed especially appropriate for such a mission because after motoring ashore with their supply of ordnance, they could then simply keep going and drive inland to wherever the am-munition was needed.[9]

From the beginning, however, Bradley had worried that a U-boat tor-pedo or Luftwaffe bomb might blow an ammunition ship to kingdom come and thereby interrupt the delivery of ordnance to his men. A few weeks before the invasion, therefore, he had approached Kirk with the idea of acquiring several car ferries and filling them up with what were called "units of fire"—prepackaged containers of bullets, machine gun belts, bazooka rockets, and artillery shells. The car ferries could be towed across the Chan-nel, Bradley explained, and deposited onto the beach at high tide, where they would serve as permanent ammunition depots. They would still be subject to a lucky shot by long-range German artillery, but at least they could not be sunk. As a result of that conversation, in the days after the ini-tial landings several LCIs towed eight ammunition barges across the Chan-nel and landed them on the invasion beaches just past midnight on June 8. In at least one case a beach master strenuously objected to the placement of the barges, but once they were well and firmly aground it was too late to reposition them.[10]

The Allied beaches were relatively secure from air attack during the daytime, when Allied planes ruled the skies, though one bold German plane did manage to land a 550-pound phosphorus bomb on HMS *Bulolo*, the headquarters ship for Force G. The more serious danger was at night, when German bombers flew regularly over the beaches dropping flares (to illuminate the targets), bombs, and mines. Though these Luftwaffe raids were less ferocious than the Allied planners had feared, the Germans did have several weapons that, had they been employed in large numbers, might have changed the course of the battle. One was the pressure-sensitive oyster mine, for which the Allies had no effective countermeasure. German planes dropped these into the waters off the Normandy beaches in their nightly raids, and while those mines claimed several ships, there were simply not enough of them to halt the invasion.

Another weapon with the potential to change the course of history was the rocket-propelled Henschel H.S. 293 radio-guided aerial bomb, the forerunner of air-launched guided missiles. German bombers could carry two of these, one under each wing, and launch them miles away, guiding them into the target by radio signals. The Allies were aware of the threat and had developed a countermeasure. When a ship recognized the tone emitted by these radio-guided bombs, it sent out a one-word warning to the fleet: "Vermin!" Thus alerted, the ships employed radio jammers designed to throw the bomb off its course. This was generally effective, though several radio-guided bombs did find their mark. The brand-new *Sumner*-class destroyer USS *Meredith* may have been a victim of such a weapon. At an hour past midnight on June 7–8, the *Meredith* was rocked by "a violent explosion" that "appeared to lift her up and throw her forward." She began to list to starboard almost immediately and, dead in the water, drifted shoreward. With the main deck awash, her captain, Commander George Knuepfer, ordered abandon ship. Curiously, though, the *Meredith* did not sink, and the next morning two salvage tugs began to tow her back to England. En route there, she was rocked by a near miss from a 2,000-pound bomb that shook the ship so violently she broke in half. She went to the bottom having suffered the loss of thirty-five killed and another twenty-seven wounded.[11]

A third German anti-ship weapon, one of an especially desperate character, was the so-called human torpedo. A pilot drove a modified torpedo on the surface that carried another torpedo, this one with a warhead, slung underneath. It was not a suicide weapon; the pilot would release the torpedo at a ship and then turn away. The Germans deployed forty-seven of these off the Normandy beaches, but they succeeded in sinking only three minesweepers. Of course, there were also losses from more conventional weapons. Only a few hours after the *Meredith* was hit, a mine exploded under the USS *Glennon* (DD-620), and when the destroyer escort USS *Rich* (DE-695) came to her aid, she, too, hit a mine. Both vessels were lost.

During the nightly air attacks, gunners on the Allied ships responded with a fury. There were literally thousands of anti-aircraft guns in the Allied armada, and, confident that planes flying at night were almost certainly hostile, whenever the gunners heard the sound of aircraft overhead, they simply aimed skyward and pulled the trigger. So much flak was hurled into the night skies that spent rounds fell back to earth as if it were raining bullets. Admiral Bryant, on USS *Texas*, recalled that "shrapnel fell on our decks like snow." Inevitably, some of that spent ordnance inflicted casualties on Allied sailors. One Seabee on a rhino ferry felt a slight thump on the collar of his life vest, followed by a fierce burning sensation all down his front. Ripping open his life vest, he saw that a spent tracer round had entered his collar and burned an ugly welt all the way down his chest. Soon enough, orders came down that the relatively inexperienced gunners on the amphibious ships should hold their fire, not only to reduce friendly-fire incidents but also because all those tracer rounds going up into the sky actually assisted the Germans in locating Allied shipping. It proved much safer simply to darken ship and hold fire. As one sailor put it, "We hid."[12]

Off Utah Beach, Moon ordered the gunners on the *Bayfield* not to fire at all lest they expose their position. Nevertheless, one night when a German bomber got closer and closer, the gunners could not restrain themselves. When they opened up, the pilot of the bomber followed the line of tracer fire to land a 500-pound bomb only fifty yards off the stern of the *Bayfield*. The big ship "shook like a rag doll." Men were knocked to the deck and clouds of dust fell from the overheads. Moon himself was bounced around on the bridge, and he was furious about the lack of fire discipline. According to one witness, "angry words were spoken to the captain."[13]

Another threat was the E-boats out of Le Havre and Cherbourg. For the most part, these were easily fended off, though one of them did manage to put a torpedo into the USS *Nelson* (DD-623) on June 12, and two LSTs (314 and 376) were torpedoed and sunk, presumably by E-boats. Due to these threats from air and sea, the men on the Allied ships offshore remained at general quarters around the clock throughout the first week. Stewards carried coffee, soup, and sandwiches to the men at their stations, and only one man at a time was allowed to visit the head. When there was a lull, half the men were allowed to sleep on the deck near their stations, but no one was to go below.[14]

THINGS BEGAN TO IMPROVE on D-Day plus four—that is, June 10. Ramsay concluded that Omaha Beach was now sufficiently secure that the LSTs could begin to go ashore without having to discharge their cargoes onto the LCTs or rhinos. Because Moon had authorized LSTs to run up onto the beach on the afternoon of June 7, the tonnage delivered to Utah Beach exceeded the totals for Omaha Beach on both June 8 and 9. Now, with the LSTs going ashore on Omaha Beach as well, the totals there quickly mounted. Offloading was relatively swift for those LSTs loaded solely with vehicles because they could discharge their tanks and trucks and retract again before the retreating tide stranded them. Those LSTs carrying cargo, however, took much longer to unload, and in most cases that meant remaining on the beach, thoroughly aground, throughout a full tide cycle—a process known as "drying out." If the big flat-bottomed LSTs came ashore near the high-water mark, the retreating tide left them sitting so high up on the beach that crewmembers could walk all the way around the ship without getting their feet wet. Even the smaller LCTs occasionally had to "dry out" on the beach, and more than a few LCT crews actually sought a "dry load" so that after they landed, they could remain on the beach and get eight to ten hours of rest before going back to work.[15]

For the LST crewmembers, the biggest inconvenience during these drying-out periods was that because the ship's generator required a constant circulation of water, there was no electricity on board. Rather than just sit it out, sailors often went ashore to assist in the unloading of their own or other vessels, or even to do a little sightseeing or souvenir collecting. In at least one case, some crewmen tried to organize a baseball game, though they had to call it off when the ball rolled under the ship. Of course, Omaha Beach was still a dangerous place. On one occasion when an artillery shell whistled overhead, some sailors from LST-75 who had been sent ashore to help unload a nearby LCT took shelter against the cliff. They were standing there when the beach master came over to ask them what they were supposed to be doing. They explained about unloading the LCT, and the beach master told them: "Well then, get the hell over there and unload it, or pick up one of these rifles and get up the hill and start shooting them damn Germans." Given that choice, they decided the stevedore work was preferable.[16]

The beach masters were the choreographers of the Allied supply effort, and it was difficult work. They and the Navy signalmen who worked with them stayed on the beach for weeks, living in foxholes with canvas roofs or inside wrecked ships, and surviving on cold K rations while directing traffic both offshore and on the beach. A few skippers resented their authority, especially when, after maneuvering for hours, they finally found a likely landing spot only to be ordered away from it by a beach master. One LCT skipper later described his initial reaction to receiving such an order: "Hey, this is my ship and you aren't going to tell me what to do." He kept that view to himself, however, and did as he was told. There was additional friction when American skippers sought to land on a British beach. While most Americans found British speech patterns amusing, at least one ground his teeth with annoyance when a British beach master told him: "Skipper, don't come in there.... Over here, old chap."[17]

On the other hand, there could be advantages to landing on a British beach. When Ensign Don Irwin landed LCT-614 on Gold Beach, the beach master invited him and his exec over to his "headquarters" while the vessel was being unloaded. Those headquarters turned out to be a wrecked British LCT. It was a place for the beach master to rest when he could, and to sleep whenever possible. It was also stocked with, among other things, British rum. After his American visitors climbed aboard, the beach master poured out three generous tumblers and handed them around. The two Americans sipped cautiously and found the rum alarmingly potent. Irwin felt it burn "like a red hot poker all the way down." Not wanting to be thought either unappreciative or unmanly, he waited until the beach master turned away, then poured the contents over the side. Afterward, he wondered if that explained why so many of the British beach masters seemed to have such a "ruddy glow."[18]

Other sailors sought to effect repairs to their wrecked and stranded vessels. Many of the Higgins and Mike boats that had been shot up during the initial landings were so full of holes that they looked like sieves. To effect repairs, each vessel came equipped with a sack of tapered wooden plugs, and the crewmen began hammering these into the holes from the outside, leaving half-inch-long stubs sticking out. By the time they finished, one sailor thought "the old boat looked like it was growing something."[19]

Food was a problem for many. The sailors had each been issued K rations when they left England, though many had simply tossed them over the side after extracting the cigarettes and the candy bars. Now, after several days on the beach, even K rations sounded pretty good. They soon learned that while most of the small boats were out of food, the larger LSTs and transports were still well stocked, and some of them, at least, were willing to share. One of the Royal Navy LSTs was, in effect, a floating bakery; when smaller vessels came alongside, the British tars handed over a few loaves of bread. Once the word got around, there was nearly always a long queue of small boats nearby, though at least one U.S. Navy sailor complained that "the bread was so hard you could hardly chew it."[20]

Those boat crews that had been stranded on the beach and were unable to visit well-stocked ships offshore had to improvise. On June 9, a crewmember from a grounded Mike boat stumbled across a wooden crate filled with cans of beef and chicken stew. He alerted his shipmates, and they dug a shallow pit in the sand, used diesel fuel to start a fire, and heated the cans on top of a .50 caliber machine gun sight, which they used as a grate. Not all crews were so fortunate, and some simply went without. One boat's crew survived for two days on nothing but canned tomato juice.[21]

Once the LSTs had been emptied, they retracted during the next high tide and headed back across the Channel in convoys to take on another load. In a representative example, LST-543 discharged its cargo on D-Day, came back across the Channel on June 7, loaded up again at Southampton on the eighth, delivered that cargo on the tenth, recrossed the Channel on the thirteenth, and made another delivery on the fifteenth. It was exhausting work. At ten knots, a round trip from Spithead to Normandy took eighteen hours. That meant that to sustain this schedule, the ships had to be constantly steaming, loading, or unloading. Most LSTs made at least forty or fifty such round trips, and one crewmember was sure that his ship had made the crossing "at least a hundred times." No wonder they looked forward to drying out. Inevitably, confusion crept into this frenetic schedule, but when it did, the ships and their crews simply muddled through. As an example of that, Admiral Morison tells the story of an American LCI that off-loaded at Utah Beach, then returned to Portsmouth for more. Once it had loaded up, however, no orders were forthcoming, so on his own the skipper joined an outbound British convoy. As the ship left the Solent, a signal station on shore flashed the message "Where do you think you are going?" to which the skipper replied, "I don't know." After a short pause, the response came: "Proceed."[22]

As chaotic and frenzied as it seemed, the delivery of men, vehicles, and supplies over the beach became increasingly efficient after June 10. The pre-invasion goal of 8,000 tons per day on Omaha Beach was reached and surpassed on June 12 when some 8,529 tons came ashore. By June 15, the backlog of unloaded ships had been cleared, and Hall noted with some pride that "all previous records for stores landed on the Force O beaches was broken on each successive day." In the five-day period from June 12 to June 16, the Allies landed a total of 75,383 men, 10,926 vehicles, and 66,571 tons of supplies on Omaha Beach. That was roughly the equivalent of a fully equipped infantry division every day—and there were five Allied beaches where this was happening. If the Allies could maintain that pace, it would overmatch anything the Germans could do.[23]

Bringing men and supplies in over the beach remained precarious, however. Nightly raids from the Luftwaffe and occasional sorties by E-boats from Cherbourg were never severe enough to imperil the invasion, though accidents, enemy mines, and weather did cause occasional interruptions. At seven in the morning of June 7, the USS *Susan B. Anthony* (APA-72), formerly the passenger liner *Santa Clara* and known as the "Susie Bee," loaded with more than twenty-three hundred men of the Fourth Infantry Division, hit a mine, very likely one of the pressure-sensitive oyster mines that had been dropped overnight by a German bomber. All power went out, and the big ship began to settle. Without power, damage control was impossible. Once it was clear that the ship could not be saved, her captain, Commander T. L. Gray, sent out a signal to all vessels: "Come alongside, we need help." Assuming he wanted help with unloading, a nearby LCT responded: "Sorry, we have other orders," to which Gray replied: "We are sinking." That brought every ship in the area to her aid, including the British frigate *Narbrough*. The crew of the "Susie Bee" threw the boarding nets over the side, and the soldiers climbed down into the sea, where rescuing vessels picked them up. Not a single soldier or sailor was lost, but the incident underscored the Allied assumption that it was essential to capture a major seaport early in the campaign so that offloading could be more reliable and efficient. To accomplish that, the men of "Lightning Joe" Collins's VII Corps were already fighting their way northward from Utah Beach to target the seaport city of Cherbourg. Until Cherbourg fell, however, the Allies had a backup plan.[24]

THE SAME DAY the "Susie Bee" went down, men on Omaha Beach who looked seaward witnessed a curious sight, described by one as "several large barges, loaded with long, steel pylons and huge, odd forms made of concrete, and two rusty, old freighters being pulled and pushed toward the land by tugs." The freighters were the first of the so-called corncobs—the derelict blockships that would be sunk to form breakwaters—and the "odd forms made of concrete" were the giant Phoenix units, each of them as big as a city office building. Here were the first elements of Project Mulberry, the artificial harbors to be constructed off Omaha Beach near St. Laurent-sur-Mer and off Gold Beach near Arromanche.[25]

The very existence of this program was nearly as great a secret as the invasion itself. Yet the Phoenix caissons were so enormous that complete concealment was impossible. In May, the men who were to make up the crews of the Phoenix units were startled to hear Lord Haw Haw* announce on Nazi Germany's propaganda radio station, "We know exactly what you intend to do with these concrete units. You intend to sink them off our coast in the assault." Then Haw Haw promised that the German navy would be happy to do that for them: sinking them well before they ever made it to the coast.[26]

Not everyone in the Allied high command was enthusiastic about the Mulberry project. One of the officers who helped supervise it wrote later that "Force Mulberry was an unwanted orphan." Ramsay, Kirk, Hall, and many of the other operational commanders were openly dubious, even scornful, about whether it could be done at all, and even if it could, whether it would be worth the effort. The candid-to-a-fault Hall told Admiral Cunningham, "One storm will wash them all away." Still, the skeptics knew better than to get in the way of a project supported by Churchill, and they were happy to leave the management of it to others while they focused on more conventional issues. This lack of institutional enthusiasm made obtaining materials for the project an uphill struggle. Because of that, for the men who ran the Mulberry program, the postponement of the invasion from May to June was critical.[27]

Then, as D-Day approached, it became evident that the British simply did not have the towing capacity needed to move all the various parts of the Mulberry project across the Channel. Somewhat grudgingly, the Americans agreed to contribute 25 tugs out of the 132 that were required, though when they arrived, 11 of them proved to be relatively small yard tugs that lacked the horsepower to move the giant Phoenix caissons through the water. Yet somehow, in spite of skepticism from the admirals, a scarcity of resources, an almost impossible schedule, and an insufficiency of tugs, the

---

* Like "Tokyo Rose" in the Pacific, "Lord Haw Haw" was a generic term applied to a number of English-speaking radio broadcasters used by the Axis in an attempt to undermine the morale of Allied soldiers and sailors. Many if not most of the broadcasts of Lord Haw Haw were the work of an American-born British citizen named William Joyce. After the war, Joyce was arrested, tried for treason, and hanged.

work got done, the components got to sea, and on the day after the landings, the first elements of this vast project appeared off Omaha and Gold Beaches.[28]

All five of the invasion beaches were to be protected by the artificial breakwaters called gooseberries, but two of them—Omaha and Gold—were to host complete artificial harbors composed of several elements. First, some two thousand yards off the coast, the Allies would position so-called bombardons: enormous floating steel pontoons, each of them more than two hundred feet long, that were strung together end to end, like a Brobdingnagian pool float. Then, another thousand yards closer to the beach, the tugs would maneuver the giant Phoenix units into place and sink them in a long row. Inside the protection of these concrete structures, several steel pier heads, known as Lobnitz piers for their designer, Henry Pearson Lobnitz, would be connected to the beach by "whales," which were long, floating roadways. These causeways required more than thirteen thousand steel pontoons that would be anchored to the sea floor by more than two thousand special anchors called kites. The roadway sections would float on the surface and rise and fall with the tide. In theory, at least, once all these elements were in place, fully loaded ships could maneuver into the sheltered harbor created by the Phoenix units, nose up to the Lobnitz piers at either high or low tide, quickly disgorge their tanks, trucks, or cargo onto the floating roadway, and then immediately back off again for another trip. The whole project was a marvel of imagination and engineering—if it worked.

The first elements to be put in place were the corncobs that made up the gooseberry breakwaters. Off Omaha Beach, the gooseberry was anchored at its western end by the former Royal Navy dreadnaught HMS *Centurion*, which was wrestled into place by the tugs early on the afternoon of June 7. The Germans immediately opened fire on this battleship, which in their view had been foolish enough to come within artillery range. When the pre-positioned charges on the *Centurion* were detonated and the big ship settled to the bottom, the Germans thought they had sunk her. That night, Goebbels himself announced this triumph of German coastal defense forces on the radio.[29]

THE PLAN FOR THE MULBERRY HARBOR
OFF OMAHA BEACH

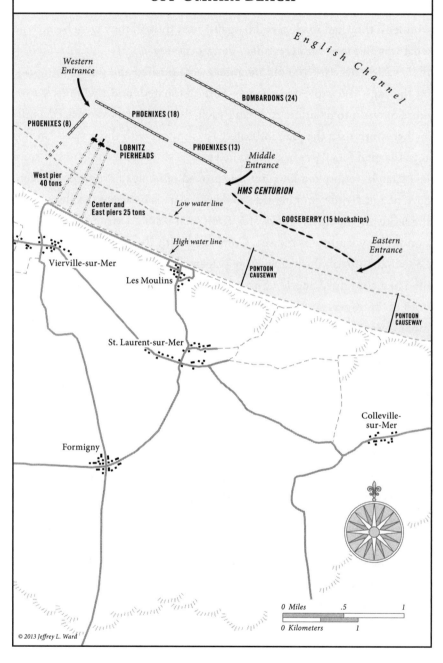

English Channel

Western
Entrance

BOMBARDONS (24)

PHOENIXES (18)

PHOENIXES (8)

LOBNITZ
PIERHEADS

PHOENIXES (13)

*Middle
Entrance*

West pier
40 tons

Center and
East piers 25 tons

Low water line

HMS CENTURION

GOOSEBERRY (15 blockships)

High water line

*Eastern
Entrance*

Vierville-sur-Mer

Les Moulins

PONTOON
CAUSEWAY

St. Laurent-sur-Mer

PONTOON
CAUSEWAY

Colleville-
sur-Mer

Formigny

0 Miles   .5   1

0 Kilometers   1

Two more of the corncob blockships were pushed into place and sunk astern of the *Centurion* that same afternoon. The German gunners continued their barrage, and the civilian crews of the derelict ships began to wonder if they had made a bad bargain, even though they were being paid what was all too accurately called "danger money" for the job. At all five of the invasion beaches, the old freighters were pushed and pulled into place by the tugs, the explosive charges were detonated, and the ships settled more or less into position. At Utah Beach, the corncobs were placed a mile farther south than the plan indicated, to comport with the revised landing site. The plan for all five beaches called for the ships to be sunk bow to stern in a straight, unbroken line, but this proved difficult to do in the insistent current and swiftly running tide, and several gaps between the ships made the result an imperfect breakwater. Even so, it resulted in a dramatic reduction in the volatility of the sea. Combined with the decision to allow the LSTs to dry out on the beaches, the placement of the gooseberries contributed to a continued acceleration of the supply effort. The gooseberries off both of the American beaches were completed by June 12, and on June 14 more than 27,000 men, nearly 2,000 vehicles, and another 7,752 tons of supplies came ashore on Omaha Beach in a single day.[30]

Even before the gooseberries were completed, the giant concrete Phoenix units were being towed into place off Vierville on Omaha Beach and Arromanche near Gold Beach. Huge and balky as they were, and with the tide and current so assertive, the tugs struggled to nudge the Phoenix units into the proper place and keep them there while the men on board them opened the sea cocks and the units settled to the bottom. Even with four ocean tugs pushing all at once, the Phoenix units were difficult to hold in place against the current. Occasionally one would drift away on its own no matter what the tugs did. As with the corncobs, the eventual alignment of the Phoenix units only superficially resembled the straight lines drawn on the planning maps.[31]

Then the Lobnitz pier heads had to be set in position inside the protected anchorage. These were big, complex structures, two hundred feet long, sixty feet wide, and ten feet high, with giant metal posts called "spuds," sixty feet long, sticking up at each corner. To at least one observer, they resembled "a huge water bug with its four retracted spud legs sticking up like giant feelers into the sky." Once the pier head was in position, the "spuds" were lowered to the seabed to become its legs, and the steel platform on the Lobnitz pier hung suspended from steel cables attached to the top of the spuds. Unlike the "whale" roadway, it did not float. Rather, diesel engines raised or lowered the pier with the tide, and a permanent crew of fifteen managed the "maze of complicated diesel electric hoisting gear."[32]

To transport the tanks, trucks, and other equipment from the pier heads to the shore nearly a mile away, the Allies constructed a floating steel roadway—the "whale"—composed of hundreds of eighty-foot-long prefabricated sections. To keep the whales stable, the Americans anchored every other section to the ocean floor. The more careful British anchored every section of their whale roadways. The Americans thought that, as usual, the British were being overly careful, though as it happened, the British would have the last laugh. For now, however, it allowed the Americans to complete the Mulberry off Omaha Beach three days ahead of schedule.

At 4:43 p.m. on June 16, the entire Mulberry workforce at Omaha Beach paused to watch as LST-342 eased up to the end of the middle Lobnitz pier. The ship dropped its ramp onto the metal platform, and one by one, seventy-eight vehicles rolled out of the LST onto the pier and then drove along the whale to the beach at a steady fifteen miles an hour, emptying the ship in a mere thirty-eight minutes. Soldiers and sailors cheered lustily, and the exhausted managers of the Mulberry project congratulated one another on a remarkable engineering triumph. Over the next thirty-six hours, ten more LSTs unloaded at the Lobnitz pier, and the average unloading time per ship was only sixty-four minutes. The visionary champions of the Mulberry project had been vindicated. Or so it seemed.

Though each LST unloaded quickly—much more quickly than they could over the beach, especially if they were drying out—each Lobnitz pier head could accommodate only two LSTs at a time, whereas the beach could, theoretically at least, host dozens of them. It was a trade-off between the swift unloading of a few ships and the slow unloading of many ships. It was not immediately clear which would prove more efficient. After the Mulberry was opened for business on June 16, the daily tonnage of cargo delivered to Omaha Beach increased slightly, from 8,500 tons to 8,700 tons, but at the same time, the landing of personnel actually dropped from an average of 17,843 per day (June 13 to 16) to only 11,686 per day (June 17 to 19). (See Table 3, page 328.) Either way, the flood of men, vehicles, and supplies into Normandy was remarkable. In the two weeks after D-Day, the Allies landed a total of 618,855 men, 93,986 vehicles, and 245,133 tons of supplies over the five Normandy beaches, even though most of the unloading at Sword Beach had to be halted due to continuing German artillery fire. Only a small percentage of the total came in via the Mulberries, and given that, it was not yet evident that the great effort put into the Mulberry project was yielding a significant return. To validate the wisdom of the project, the next several days would be crucial.[33]

THE STORM THAT ARRIVED on June 19 caught almost everyone by surprise. Indeed, after the inclement weather on June 5 that had forced the initial postponement of the invasion, the weather in the Channel had been relatively benign, and all predictions were that it would remain that way. On June 18, the official weather report for the next day was: "Cloudy to partly cloudy. Visibility fair, 4–6 miles. Wind NE, velocity gentle—8–13 knots." Even as that forecast was distributed to the fleet, however, the wind was gusting in excess of twenty knots. On June 19, a southward-moving cold front from Ireland collided with a depression moving north from the Mediterranean to produce a summer gale of historic ferocity. The barometer dropped to 29.92 inches, and the wind increased to thirty knots. By ten o'clock that night, waves were crashing over the top of the Phoenix units, and the British gun crews in the anti-aircraft batteries atop each of the units had to be evacuated. When the Mike boats arrived to do that, the British soldiers were "hanging onto the gun for dear life." Even inside the breakwater, the seas were so rough that the Mike boats rose and fell as much as fifteen feet, soaring up to the top of the Phoenix units at the crest of a wave, then suddenly swooping down again. In one Mike boat, the men took off their kapok life jackets and threw them into the open deck space to create a cushion for the soldiers to land on, and then encouraged the men on the Phoenix to jump. Of the five men in one gun crew who did so, two were severely injured.[34]

Meanwhile, the floating metal roadways from the Lobnitz piers to the beach began to heave wildly, undulating, as one put it, "like writhing pythons." The Seabees worked furiously to secure them, holding on with one hand to avoid being swept into the sea while they sought to double up the lines on both the Lobnitz pier and the floating roadway with eight-inch hawsers. The whales off Arromanche were less vulnerable, partly because they were more protected by the coastal geography, but also because of the British decision to anchor both ends of every section.[35]

Allied shipping also suffered from the wrath of the storm, and the smaller vessels were particularly at risk. The bigger ships put out heavy anchors to both port and starboard, but the LCTs, Higgins boats, and Mike boats carried only a single anchor, and they were not equipped with spring lines that could ease the strain. As these smaller vessels were buffeted by seven-foot seas and thirty-knot winds, their anchor lines stretched "taut as bowstrings," and inevitably some of those lines snapped and sent the vessels careening helplessly before the wind. Many were driven ashore and broached sideways on the sand, where they were pounded by the heavy surf. One witness claimed they were "piled six deep against the shore." On some vessels, the skippers deliberately ran their boats up onto the beach, concluding that it was better to go aground than to go under.[36]

The storm lasted all night, and the next day even the big ships began to drag their anchors as a powerful north-by-northeast wind pushed them shoreward. Many got up steam and headed out to gain sea room off what was now a lee shore. Even so, that afternoon a salvage barge and five British LCTs whose anchor lines gave way crashed violently into the whale off Omaha Beach. Their steel hulls punctured the pontoons that kept the roadway afloat, and several sections of the whale were wrecked; other sections simply disappeared.

On the morning of June 20, there were glimpses of blue skies through the gray clouds, and many hoped that the worst had passed. Instead, the storm worked its way up to a full-blown gale—the worst June storm in the English Channel in forty years. Those LCTs that had gotten under way to avoid being blown ashore now began to run low on fuel, and they sought a safe place to tie up. With so many vessels seeking shelter, such places were hard to find.

The big ships were already virtually surrounded by smaller vessels tied up alongside, and there was no more room. Often when an LCT or a Mike boat sought to tie up, it was warned off, first with shouts, then with threats, and in a few cases with gunfire. When one British LCT requested permission to tie up to a large American ship that was already surrounded by scores of small Higgins boats all tied together, the American officer of the deck, Ensign Clifford Sinnett, shouted back that there was no room. The British LCT skipper was desperate, however, and after a moment of silence, he announced: "We're coming in to tie up." This time Sinnett responded more emphatically, announcing "in no uncertain terms that he was *not* going to come in and tie up," and using some sailor's language for emphasis. The British officer replied: "I don't know who you are, sir, but you are no gentleman."[37]

By now, "the whole Baie de la Seine was a mass of dirty yellow-gray water streaked and flecked with white foam and cresting seas." The cables securing the Lobnitz piers to the bottom began to snap, and though the legs, or spuds, remained intact and in place, the whole structure swayed dramatically with the huge swells, some of them a hundred feet long. Fearing that the strain would be too much, the crew released the clutch holding the platform in place so that it could ride up and down with the swells. That eased the strain on the platform, but it multiplied the discomfort level for the men on the pier heads, who had to hold on with both hands as the platform rose and fell dramatically and unpredictably. Worse yet, the two-hundred-foot-long bombardons a thousand yards out to sea broke loose from their anchors and hurtled down on the artificial harbor like so many battering rams. They smashed into the Mulberry with such velocity that some of the Phoenix units actually broke in half. Before it was over, twenty of the thirty-one Phoenix units off Omaha Beach were wrecked. By now, a total of seventeen ships had collided with the floating metal roadway, turning it into "a tangled heaving mass."[38]

The winds finally began to abate on the evening of June 22, and on the morning of the twenty-third it was possible to assess the damage. Kirk was appalled. "Landing craft were piled up on the beach," he recalled later, and "the shoreline was just a shambles." Kirk's chief of staff, Arthur Struble, estimated that there were between twenty-two hundred and twenty-four hundred vessels wrecked on the beach, though many of them had grounded there on purpose and would later be salvaged. The actual total of destroyed vessels came to about three hundred, which was bad enough. That morning there were only twelve LCTs and one rhino ferry in operating condition off Omaha Beach.[39]

The damage to the artificial harbors was harder to assess. Though a few of the corncobs had been shifted out of place, the gooseberries remained mostly intact. The barrier of Phoenix units, the key element of the Mulberry harbors, had suffered serious damage, and off Omaha Beach, at least, the whale roadways were all but destroyed. Some of those who had worked on the Mulberry program from the beginning thought it could all be repaired. But Commodore William A. Sullivan, the U.S. Navy's supervisor of salvage, decided otherwise. He recommended to Eisenhower that the Mulberry off Omaha Beach should be shut down and that salvageable elements of it should be towed over to effect repairs on Mulberry B, off Arromanche, which had fared much better. Eisenhower agreed. The gooseberries would be repaired and even reinforced, but the complicated Lobnitz piers and whale roadways off Omaha Beach were abandoned.[40]

At the time, no one knew what impact this would have on Allied plans; whether without the artificial harbors it would even be possible to maintain the buildup of men and equipment needed to sustain the invasion. There were a few rays of hope. Bradley's idea of beaching ammunition ships ashore proved a godsend, for they had been largely unaffected by the storm. Bradley worried nonetheless, and on June 22, as the storm abated, he urged Kirk to land more ammunition barges on the beach. Though at one point the stockpile of ammunition ashore got down to only three days' supply, the delivery of both men and supplies to the beach never stopped entirely. The daily totals dropped from 8,700 tons before the storm to only 676 tons on June 21, when the storm was at its height. But then the numbers rose to 1,077 tons the next day and to 4,595 on June 23. On the twenty-fourth, they actually topped 10,000 tons for the first time—more than when the Mulberry was in full operation. On that one day, 22,630 men, 3,513 vehicles, and 10,974 tons of supplies landed on Omaha Beach, all of it over the beach, and mostly by the LSTs. Moreover, the LSTs were able to sustain these levels over the next several weeks. That confirmed what should have been

| Table 3 | Unloading of Men and Supplies on Omaha Beach, June 6–26, 1944 | | |

Date	Personnel	Vehicles	Stores (in tons)
June 6–11: The Initial Landings: Average 1,075 tons			
June 6–9	73,667	8,538	4,581
June 10	5,000	—	—
June 11	15,250	2,030	2,472
June 12–16: LSTs Allowed to Dry Out: Average 8,502 tons			
June 12	4,010	2,369	8,529
June 13	12,444	2,270	7,500
June 14	27,060	1,881	7,752
June 15	19,554	2,836	9,352
June 16	12,315	1,570	9,380
June 17–19: Mulberry A Functioning: Average 8,700 tons			
June 17	11,538	2,228	8,535
June 18	10,791	2,515	8,876
June 19	12,729	2,087	8,690
June 20–23: During the Storm: Average 3,028 tons			
June 20	8,318	1,902	5,764
June 21	3,299	533	676
June 22	1,498	243	1,077
June 23	10,915	541	4,595
June 24–30: Landings over the Beach: Average 13,321 tons			
June 24	22,630	3,513	10,974
June 25	11,948	2,470	12,708
June 26	10,400	2,781	13,689
Totals	273,366	40,307	126,479

Source: Hall to Wilkes, July 9, 1944, John Lesslie Hall Papers, box 1, Swem Library, W&M.

evident in the five days before the Mulberry opened for business: that while the Mulberry project was unquestionably a testament to Anglo-American, and especially British, imagination, creativity, and determination, it was not, after all, essential to the maintenance of the Allied invasion.[41]

THE SHIPS BRINGING MEN AND SUPPLIES to the invasion beaches did not return to England empty. Back in January, Ramsay had suggested that because the LSTs were so scarce and valuable, they should not be used to evacuate casualties because that was likely to slow their turnaround time and thereby risk the rapid and continuous delivery of reinforcements and supplies. That may have been a ploy to demonstrate how important it was to increase LST availability, because for the actual invasion a number of LSTs were specially staffed with Navy doctors and pharmacist's mates to take care of casualties. A few ships even had ersatz operating rooms. Vessels so equipped performed a kind of shuttle service, carrying troops and vehicles in one direction and wounded men in the other.[42]

There were so many wounded men on Omaha Beach that first day that relatively few could be evacuated at all. Far too many had to survive one or even two cold nights lying on the sand. As the soldiers fought their way inland and the threat of German artillery was reduced, the Allies established aid stations on the beaches. For the first several days, these were little more than foxholes with sandbag walls and a canvas roof, but at least the Navy pharmacist's mates who manned them had bandages and (critically) morphine. Many of the wounded were assisted down to the aid stations by their buddies. Others arrived in specially configured ambulance trucks, modified from the nearly ubiquitous two-and-a-half-ton Dodge trucks. Still others were carried down from the bluffs in Stokes stretchers, a kind of wire basket in a metal frame. Occasionally a wounded soldier staggered in on his own.[43]

Many of them were wounded psychically as well as physically. Post-traumatic stress disorder had not yet acquired its current designation, and the commonly used term was "battle fatigue." Whatever name it bore, its victims were unmistakable. Pharmacist's Mate Bill Milne, off LST-491, treated one wounded American airborne soldier who had somehow made it down to the aid station unassisted. He had parachuted out over enemy territory in the middle of the night, endured conditions that only he knew for certain, and though he had been shot through the leg, he had nevertheless walked all the way to Omaha Beach. By the time he arrived at the aid station, he was a grisly apparition, and Milne saw at once that he was in shock. "He had his .45 in one hand, and a combat knife in the other," Milne recalled. "I remember specifically that we could not get his pistol or knife away from him until we had given him morphine." Survivors of sinkings reacted similarly. One man who was pulled from the water onto a rhino ferry seemed not to know where he was or what was happening. Someone put a coat in his hands, but he stood there dripping, apparently confused by what he was supposed to do with it. After a minute or two, someone put it around his shoulders. The man never moved.[44]

After triage at the aid station, the wounded were loaded onto LCTs or Mike boats, or in a few cases into DUKWs, for the trip out to a waiting LST. It proved possible to lay twenty wounded men, end to end and side by side, on the open cargo deck of a Mike boat. The boats then retracted from the beach and ferried the wounded out to empty LSTs, where cranes hoisted those who were not ambulatory on board in their Stokes stretchers. Carried down into the tank deck, either they were placed on racks arrayed along the bulkhead or their stretchers were chained down to the deck using the same tie-downs that had secured the tanks during the passage from England. Navy pharmacist's mates and others cut away their damp and filthy clothing, often clotted with dried blood, and covered them with fresh blankets.

For the most serious cases, several of the LSTs had makeshift operating rooms at the far end of the tank deck below the galley. There, Navy doctors performed hundreds of operations, many of them involving amputations. Afterward, the removed limb was affixed to a piece of iron and dropped over the side. Despite the conditions and the circumstances, the doctors did remarkable work. A pharmacist's mate on board one LST remembered that the doctors "worked for hours…removing shrapnel, patching bullet wounds, and trying to calm down some men that were completely out of their minds."[45]

Not every ship had a doctor. Off Sword Beach, a leaking DUKW filled with several badly wounded British soldiers had to go to four different ships before it found one that had a doctor on board. Five minutes after the last man was taken off the DUKW, it sank alongside. As a result of the doctor shortage, pharmacist's mates often found themselves not only setting splints and administering plasma transfusions but also performing operations, even when the task was well beyond their training. On Moon's command ship *Bayfield*, Pharmacist's Mate Second Class Vince del Guidice was in charge of head wounds. When he removed the helmet from one U.S.

Army Ranger, he saw that a shell fragment had cut off the crown of the man's skull, so his brains were spilling out. Instinctively, he tried to push them back into place, but the wound was mortal and the soldier soon died.[46]

In addition to wounded Allied soldiers, the returning LSTs also carried prisoners of war. Many of these prisoners turned out not to be Germans at all, but rather men—boys, really—from one or more of Hitler's conquered eastern European nations: Poles, Lithuanians, and Russian-speaking Georgians. More than once, a prisoner was startled when an American of Polish extraction spoke to him in his native language. By the third day of the campaign, these men were surrendering in large numbers, and the beach masters had difficulty accommodating all of them. When a platoon of GIs marched more than two hundred prisoners down to Omaha Beach, a Navy lieutenant asked them, "What in hell am I supposed to do with them?" The American soldiers essentially shrugged—they had fulfilled their assignment to deliver them to the beach, and they prepared to return to the front. The Navy lieutenant assigned four sailors with old carbines to guard the two hundred men, but he need not have worried, for they were "meek as lambs," though one of the men assigned to guard them, Navy Signalman Second Class Bill DeFrates, was haunted for years afterward by "the blank stare in the eyes of a defeated soldier."[47]

Most of the prisoners were embarked in LSTs dedicated to that purpose. In such cases, the men were simply herded into the tank deck until no more would fit. Vernon Paul on LST-983 estimated that there "must have been a thousand of them" packed "like sardines" into the tank deck of his ship. They were fed K rations, and probably were happy to get them. Most of the prisoners were utterly submissive, lining up when and where they were told, and obeying orders without murmur. There were exceptions, however. On one occasion, when a Navy officer ordered a group of prisoners to embark onto an LCT by walking out through the surf, a German officer objected that his men would get their feet wet. The American in charge was utterly unsympathetic. We got our feet wet when we came ashore, he told the German; you can get your feet wet going the other way.[48]

Occasionally German prisoners and wounded American soldiers shared passage on the same ship, and that sometimes proved awkward. Some of the wounded Americans objected to sharing passage with enemy soldiers, even wounded enemy soldiers. On one LST, Pharmacist's Mate Ralph Crenshaw noticed that when he provided medical treatment to a wounded German, the Americans nearby muttered aloud that he should let the man die. Sensitive to the mood on board, when a boat came alongside with another load of prisoners, Crenshaw refused to let them board. The American officer in the boat objected, insisting that he had orders. But Crenshaw told him he would not be responsible for their safety if the officer persisted in putting them on the ship.[49]

The one group that neither the Allies nor the prisoners wanted anything to do with was the SS troops. That, apparently, was just fine with the SS troops. An American sailor on LST-371 noted that the SS soldiers "were all well dressed, with very good uniforms." When they were herded into the tank deck of an LST, they "immediately set up an area separate from the other German troops," even posting a guard detail to keep others away from their little corner of the ship. One observer believed that the SS soldiers showed as much disdain for the other Germans as they did for the Allies.[50]

Like the ships that carried the wounded back to England, those LSTs assigned to carry prisoners operated a kind of shuttle service, as these terse entries from one crewmember's journal testify:

Sunday: To France with American GI's and heavy equipment.
Monday: Back to Portland with prisoners.
Thursday: Back to France with American troops.
Sunday: To Southampton with prisoners. [51]

TWO WEEKS AFTER THE INITIAL LANDINGS, Ramsay, Kirk, and the other Neptune commanders could be generally satisfied. The crossing had been virtually bloodless, and the landings, while confused and costly, had been ultimately successful. The U.S. Navy and Coast Guard had played the central role in getting the troops ashore on the American beaches, and the

Royal Navy had performed flawlessly off the British and Canadian beaches. The ships had sustained the soldiers with naval gunfire support and maintained a robust line of supply even in the face of bad weather and furious opposition. Despite the loss of the Mulberry harbor at Omaha Beach, the supplies continued to pour in, meeting and even exceeding expectations. The Allies had lost one major troop carrier (the "Susie Bee") and several destroyers as well as hundreds of small landing craft, but the losses had been less than projected. Only one task now remained for the men and the ships of Operation Neptune: seizing a major seaport.

CHAPTER 15

"A FIELD OF RUINS"

FROM THE BEGINNING, Allied planners had assumed that even after obtaining a foothold on the beach, sustaining the kind of massive buildup needed to conquer a continent required seizing a major port on the French coast. The Neptune operational plan called for the deployment ashore of eighteen fully equipped divisions during the first two weeks, and almost no one believed it would be possible to do that over an open beach. Even if that proved feasible, surely it would be impossible to maintain such a pace during the long period the Allies needed to build their force up to a million men or more without a working seaport. The Allies made effective use of the small Norman ports of Courseulles-sur-Mer on Juno Beach and Port-en-Bessin on Gold Beach, but they were both small harbors incapable of handling deep draft ships. For that, the Allies needed to seize a major seaport. The selection of Normandy as the Allied objective necessarily meant that the harbor in question had to be Cherbourg, the city at the tip of the Cotentin Peninsula. Consequently, one of the first Allied goals once the beaches were secure was for the VII Corps of "Lightning Joe" Collins, including both the 4th Infantry Division and the scattered and much-bloodied 82nd Airborne, to push northward up the east coast of the peninsula to seize Cherbourg in a swift coup de main.[1]

It didn't happen. Cherbourg remained in German hands for three weeks after D-Day, and when the Allies finally did seize it on June 27, its value as a seaport had been all but eliminated thanks to the Nazi penchant for smashing and wrecking anything they could not possess. The campaign for Cherbourg was the capstone of Operation Neptune, and though it was eventually successful, in the end it did not allow the Allies to shift the logistical focus of the invasion from the Normandy beaches to a functioning seaport. Instead, in this, as in so many aspects of the invasion, the key to Allied success was the ability of the participants to adjust, adapt, and get on with it.

EISENHOWER VISITED THE BEACHHEAD on June 8. Accompanied by Ramsay and Montgomery, he crossed the Channel on the British minelayer *Apollo* and surveyed all five of the landing beaches. He was concerned by the slow progress of Montgomery's forces toward Caen, where the Germans were focusing their counterattacks, and he also worried about the situation on Omaha Beach. He met with Bradley, who by now had established his headquarters ashore, and expressed his unease that the American enclaves on Utah and Omaha Beach were still separated from each other. Four regiments had already begun an advance northward along the coast toward Cherbourg, but Eisenhower decided that it was more important to unify and stabilize the beachhead before continuing that drive, and Bradley concurred. It is possible to imagine them in Bradley's headquarters bending over a map as Eisenhower pointed out the revised objectives. First he wanted to eliminate the pocket of German resistance near Sainte-Mère-Eglise, which would unify the 4th Division with elements of the 82nd Airborne, and then he wanted Bradley to seize the city of Carentan, on the Taute River. That would unify Omaha and Utah Beaches and make both beaches more secure. Only then would it be possible to turn north toward Cherbourg.[2]

Navy warships provided gunfire support for both of these efforts, firing their big guns ten or fifteen miles inland in response to requests from fire control parties ashore. The cruiser *Quincy* sent her 8-inch shells smashing into bridges over the Douve River above Carentan, and the other heavy gunships fired their shells against enemy troop concentrations, tank parks, artillery positions, and even a railroad train parked on a siding. The Army's advance toward Carentan and Isigny allowed Kirk to consider opening those cites as possible seaports, though because of the narrow channels that connected them to the sea, they could be used only by small coasters and barges. For oceangoing ships, the seizure of Cherbourg remained critical.[3]

The going was tough in the *bocage* country with its thick hedgerows and numerous waterways, but by June 14 the Allies had secured Carentan and established a continuous front from Quineville, north of Utah Beach, to Ouistreham, on the Orne River east of Sword Beach. By then, however, it was a full week after the initial landings, and the opportunity for a quick thrust up the peninsula to Cherbourg had passed. Instead, it now seemed more important to cut off the Cotentin Peninsula at its base in order to isolate the city and prevent the Germans from sending reinforcements there. Collins assigned the task to the veteran 9th Infantry Division, which began a westward drive on June 15 in company with elements of the 82nd Airborne. Advance units reached St.-Saveur-le-Vicomte on the sixteenth and pushed on rapidly overnight, and a tank company attached to the 9th Division reached Barneville-sur-Mer, overlooking the sea, before dawn on the seventeenth. Now that they had cut off the peninsula, it was time to turn north for Cherbourg.

Collins reorganized his command so that the newly designated VIII Corps under Major General Troy Middleton faced southward to ensure the isolation of the peninsula, while three divisions of his own VII Corps (the 9th, 79th, and 4th) turned north on parallel fronts to close in on Cherbourg. As his nickname suggested, Lightning Joe Collins was an aggressive commander, "independent, vigorous, heady, capable, and full of vinegar," according to one fellow officer. He had served on Guadalcanal in the Pacific War, where he became known for his highly personal, hands-on command style. Now he was often to be found in the front lines as his three divisions headed northward. The advance began on June 19, the same day the storm struck the ships off the Normandy beaches.[4]

THE CAMPAIGN FOR CHERBOURG, JUNE 19–25, 1944

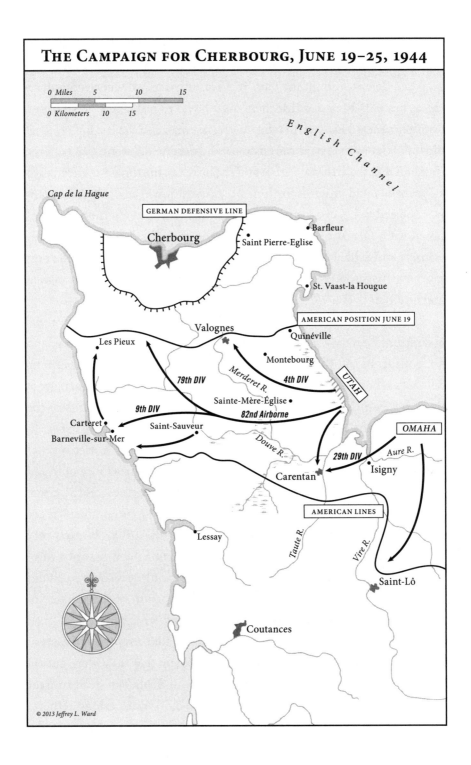

0 Miles   5   10   15

0 Kilometers   10   15

English Channel

Cap de la Hague

GERMAN DEFENSIVE LINE

Cherbourg

• Barfleur

• Saint Pierre-Eglise

• St. Vaast-la Hougue

AMERICAN POSITION JUNE 19

Valognes

Les Pieux •

• Quinéville

• Montebourg

Merderet R.

79th DIV

4th DIV

UTAH

Sainte-Mère-Église •

9th DIV

82nd Airborne

Carteret •

Saint-Sauveur •

Barneville-sur-Mer •

Douve R.

OMAHA

29th DIV

Aure R.

• Isigny

Carentan

AMERICAN LINES

• Lessay

Taute R.

Vire R.

Saint-Lô

Coutances

© 2013 Jeffrey L. Ward

The commander of the German defenders, General Karl von Schlieben, requested permission from headquarters to withdraw his forces into the prepared defenses about the city. That was obviously the correct military move, but Hitler insisted that there must be no retreat, and von Schlieben dutifully ordered his men to fight "to the last man and the last bullet." That did little to slow the American advance, and despite the storm that battered the ships and the artificial harbors off the beaches, the three American divisions made rapid progress. By June 21, as the storm abated, the Americans were poised to begin a general assault on the city. That afternoon, Collins broadcast a formal request for surrender in several languages, essentially warning von Schlieben that if he did not capitulate by nine o'clock the next morning, his forces would be annihilated. Collins did not expect an answer, and he did not get one.[5]

Shortly after 9:00 a.m. on June 22, the Allies initiated a massive aerial assault on the city's defenses. Four squadrons of RAF Typhoons and six squadrons of RAF Mustangs bombed and strafed the German defenses. They were followed by twelve groups of fighter-bombers from the American IX Tactical Air Command. Once again the results of the air assault were disappointing. As on Omaha Beach, the German fortifications proved stubbornly resistant to aerial bombing. Moreover, the fluidity of the front lines outside Cherbourg and the proximity of friend to foe meant that Allied troops occasionally found themselves the target of Allied bombs. Men in both the 9th and 4th Divisions complained angrily that they had been strafed by friendly aircraft. Collins himself very nearly became a casualty when Typhoons strafed a position not a hundred yards from him. But if the bombing did little physical damage, it did depress the morale of the defenders. A large portion of the soldiers in von Schlieben's command were non-Germans who had been forced into service from one or another of the subjugated countries of eastern Europe, including the Soviet Union. They knew that they were cut off from support, and few of them embraced von Schlieben's call to fight to the death. As von Schlieben himself noted, "We are asking rather a lot if we expect Russians to fight in France for Germany against the Americans."[6]

Still, the defenses of Cherbourg remained formidable. The city and its harbor sat in a kind of bowl surrounded by a series of ridges that commanded the lines of approach. On the western side of the city was the old Citadel, and on the east was Forte des Flamands. In the center was the powerful Forte du Roule, built on a high bluff overlooking the city. Between these strongpoints, the Germans were dug deep into the ground. The Americans would have to target each defensive position individually, with the infantry maintaining a steady covering fire while engineers crept around to the flanks with satchel charges. It could be done, but it would take time as well as lives, and time was now of the essence. Von Schlieben had received orders to begin destruction of the harbor facilities as early as June 10, even before the campaign for Cherbourg began. Hitler told him that it was his duty "to defend [Cherbourg] to the last bunker and leave to the enemy not a harbor but a field of ruins." Von Schlieben's objective, therefore, was not so much to defend the city as to delay its fall long enough for his engineers to thoroughly destroy the harbor facilities. Every day that the Germans remained in control gave them another day to continue their ruthless sabotage.[7]

To speed the fall of the city and minimize damage to the harbor, Bradley asked Ramsay if the Navy could use its long-range guns to target the German strongpoints. The biggest guns that Collins had were 155 mm (6-inch) artillery pieces, and he did not have enough of them. But the Navy had 8-inch guns on the heavy cruisers, and 12- and 14-inch guns on the battleships. Perhaps the Navy could hit the German positions from seaward.

Though Ramsay was less than enthusiastic about pitting ships against coastal fortifications, he asked Kirk to work up a plan. Two months before, in the wake of Exercise Tiger off Slapton Sands, Kirk had urged Ramsay to use the American battleships to destroy the German E-boat pens at Cherbourg. On that occasion, Ramsay had turned him down, and the decision had provoked some bitter words and lingering resentment. Now Kirk saw this as a chance to show what those big battleships might have done—and still could do—to hardened German defenses.[8]

FOR THE NAVAL ASSAULT on Cherbourg, Kirk formed Task Force 129 under Rear Admiral Morton Deyo, the fifty-seven-year-old career officer who had commanded the bombardment group off Utah Beach on D-Day and who bore a passing resemblance to John Wayne. Deyo divided his task force into two groups. Group One, under his direct supervision, included many of the same ships he had commanded on D-Day: the battleship *Nevada*, the heavy cruisers *Tuscaloosa* and *Quincy*, and the British light cruisers *Enterprise* and *Glasgow*, plus six destroyers. Group Two, with Rear Admiral Carleton F. Bryant in command, consisted of the battleships *Texas* and *Arkansas* plus five destroyers. Their overall mission was not to capture Cherbourg or even to smash it up. After all, the whole point of the campaign was to seize the port facilities intact—or as intact as possible. Rather, their job was to support Collins's ground attack by eliminating some of the hardened defensive positions and suppressing the enemy's heavy guns.

To do that, Deyo proposed first to attack the German coastal batteries that protected the seaward approaches to the harbor. Allied intelligence reported that these consisted of twenty concrete casemates housing guns that ranged in size from 155 mm (6 inches) all the way up to 280 mm (11 inches), and for the security of his command, these would have to be suppressed before the ships could turn their attention to the landward defenses. The Germans had only four of the big 280 mm guns, all of them in Battery Hamburg behind Cap Lévi, about six miles east of the city, and they would be the responsibility of Bryant's two battleships. Many of the smaller 6-inch guns were clustered around the village of Querqueville, three miles west of the city, and Deyo expected that his cruisers should be able to take care of them. Once the coastal batteries were silenced, the task force would take positions off the city to respond to call-fire requests from Collins's men ashore. Deyo planned to stay there for at least three hours, from noon to 3:00 p.m. on June 25.[9]

At almost the last moment, however, Bradley and Collins decided that they did not want Deyo's ships to shoot at all except in response to specific requests from spotters ashore, and even then, they were not to fire more than two thousand yards inland. Recalling the friendly-fire casualties during the air assault three days before, Collins wanted to ensure that none of those big 12- and 14-inch shells came crashing into his own front lines, which were now less than a mile from the city. As Deyo put it, employing

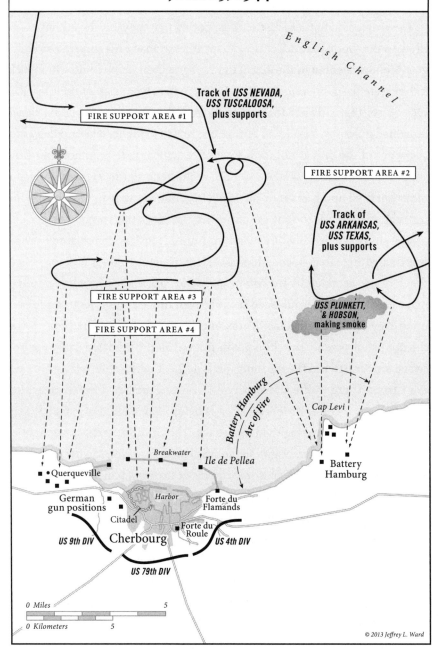

THE NAVAL BOMBARDMENT OF CHERBOURG,
JUNE 25, 1944

English Channel

Track of **USS NEVADA,
USS TUSCALOOSA,**
plus supports

FIRE SUPPORT AREA #1

FIRE SUPPORT AREA #2

Track of
**USS ARKANSAS,
USS TEXAS,**
plus supports

FIRE SUPPORT AREA #3

**USS PLUNKETT,
& HOBSON,** making smoke

FIRE SUPPORT AREA #4

Battery Hamburg

Arc of Fire

Cap Levi

Breakwater

Ile de Pellea

Battery
Hamburg

•Querqueville

German
gun positions

Harbor

Forte du
Flamands

Citadel

Forte du
Roule

US 9th DIV

Cherbourg

US 4th DIV

US 79th DIV

0 Miles   5

0 Kilometers   5

© 2013 Jeffrey L. Ward

the passive voice, "Concern was felt lest we fire into our own troops." In addition, Bradley and Collins decided that the Navy ships should fire for only ninety minutes, not the three hours Deyo suggested.[10]

Deyo objected to these restrictions, noting that they left the initiative entirely to the Germans and, at the outset at least, made his ships passive targets. Collins relented to the extent that he agreed the ships could shoot back if they were fired on, as long as the Navy gunners were sure of their targets. Of course, that still left the initiative to the defenders, and while Deyo remained unhappy, he had no option but to carry out his orders. He was to show up off the city at noon on June 25, establish radio contact with fire-support parties ashore, and respond to requested call fire. He could defend himself if fired upon, as surely he would be, but otherwise he was to wait for instructions. He was to stay for only ninety minutes, then withdraw.[11]

The ships assembled at Portland on June 22, just as the Channel storm was dissipating. That storm added a certain urgency to their mission, since the damage sustained by the Mulberry harbor off Omaha Beach seemed to make the capture of a full-sized seaport even more urgent. Kirk impressed upon Deyo and Bryant that "it was necessary to capture Cherbourg with the utmost dispatch." The ships got under way in the predawn darkness, between four and five in the morning, on June 25. The sun rose as they crossed the Channel, and in the aftermath of the storm, the day dawned clear and bright over a sea one witness recalled as being "like a piece of glass."[12]

There would be no stealth in this attack. The whole operation would take place at midday under bright sunshine. The only cover for the big ships would be provided by the accompanying destroyers, which were to "dash between the cruisers and battleships and the beach and lay a thick smoke-screen." The men went to general quarters at nine-thirty that morning, and an hour later the two task groups approached the shore separately, slowing to five knots in order to follow the British minesweepers to their firing positions. Deyo's *Nevada* group took up its initial position in Fire Support Area #1 about twenty-eight thousand yards (sixteen miles) due north of Cherbourg. At noon, he moved up to Fire Support Position #3, only twelve thousand yards from the city. Meanwhile, Bryant's *Texas-Arkansas* group moved into Fire Support Area #2, east of Cap Lévi.[13]

Despite the restrictions imposed by the Army, Deyo and Bryant were confident of success. They were certainly aware that guns ashore had a number of inherent advantages over guns afloat. Shore batteries sat on a stable firing platform; they did not have to maneuver or worry about their engines being hit; and of course they were much less vulnerable since they constituted a smaller target, were often protected by thick walls of steel and concrete, and could not sink. These were the factors that initially fed Ramsay's reluctance to accept the assignment. Yet in the twelve months prior to D-Day, U.S. Navy gunners had grown increasingly confident, not only in their ability to put heavy ordnance on target but also in their superiority over shore batteries—even batteries of large-caliber guns. At Sicily, Salerno, Anzio, and elsewhere, Allied naval guns had demonstrated their ability to suppress and even dominate the shore batteries of the defenders. This newfound confidence would be severely tested at Cherbourg, however, mainly because the four 280 mm guns in the Hamburg Battery were bigger than any the Navy had faced so far, they were housed in heavy concrete and steel casemates, and they were manned by sailors from the German navy, the Kriegsmarine, who were equally confident of their ability to sink ships.[14]

The Allied ships were all in position by noon. Because of the requirement to withhold fire until the Army requested it, the Germans opened the battle, firing on the ships of Deyo's Group One from the batteries in and around Querqueville at 12:06. From the very first salvos, the German gunners proved to be remarkably—even alarmingly—accurate. The first salvo straddled the destroyer *Murphy* (DD-603), and one 6-inch shell hit the *Walke* (DD-723). That shell shattered the *Walke*'s glass windshield on the open bridge and sent large pieces of broken glass flying almost the entire length of the ship. A sailor manning a 40 mm mount amidships was outraged when the glass shards flew past him, and he hollered: "Those dirty ——— are shooting glass at us!" Only minutes later, shells landed all around the USS *Quincy*, and HMS *Glasgow* was hit twice. The *Nevada* herself was bracketed by a three-gun salvo, with one shell landing only a hundred yards off her starboard quarter. At 12:09, just three minutes into the battle, the deck officer on the *Nevada* noted dryly in the ship's log: "Enemy is getting the range rapidly."[15]

Deyo ordered counterbattery fire, but it seemed to have little immediate effect, for the *Nevada* was straddled six times in the five minutes between 12:40 and 12:45. An ensign on board insisted later that the *Nevada* was straddled by enemy salvos a total of twenty-seven times that afternoon. A sailor whose battle station was in an AA mount on the superstructure recalled seeing the shells arcing in toward the ship through the clear blue sky. He watched as one shell passed "between the Nevada's masts" and landed only a few yards off the side, "sending up a huge geyser of water and scattering shell fragments against the ship's hull." The *Nevada's* captain, Powell Rhea, maneuvered radically in an effort to throw off the German gunners, calling down to the engine room for emergency speed that allowed the old battlewagon to work herself up to twenty-one knots, a turn of speed she had not shown since before Pearl Harbor.[16]

MEANWHILE, BRYANT WITH THE SHIPS of Group Two, including the battleships *Texas* and *Arkansas*, approached Cherbourg from the east. Bryant's assignment was to neutralize the big guns at Battery Hamburg behind Cap Lévi, then join Deyo off the city. Bryant knew that Battery Hamburg had been positioned to cover the seaward approach to Cherbourg Harbor, and as a result, its guns could track only to a point about thirty-five degrees east of due north. (See Map, page 341.) His plan, therefore, was to open fire while his ships were still east of that arc and slowly hammer the battery to pieces. That plan was undone at the last minute by the order not to open fire until fired upon or until contacted by a fire control party ashore. As it happened, however, the *Arkansas* established early radio contact with spotters ashore who had the Hamburg Battery under direct observation. That allowed the *Arkansas* to close to eighteen thousand yards (ten miles) and open a "slow deliberate fire" on the Hamburg Battery at 12:08. Explosions from her 12-inch guns erupted all around the target, but there was no response from the enemy. Some in the American battleships wondered whether the German gun positions had been abandoned.[17]

The Germans were merely biding their time. Bryant's ships crept westward until they were inside Hamburg's arc of fire, and then at 12:29 the Germans opened up. The guns in Battery Hamburg significantly outranged those on the *Arkansas* and *Texas*, and as at Querqueville, their marksman-ship was "extremely accurate." The destroyer *Barton* (DD-722) was hit on the second salvo at 12:30 when a 9.4-inch shell ricocheted off the water and crashed into her hull, smashing through several bulkheads and coming to rest inside the ship. But it did not explode. Then, only seconds later, an-other salvo landed just in front of USS *Laffey* (DD-724). Again, one of the shells ricocheted off the water and smashed into the hull of the American destroyer, and it, too, failed to explode. Ordinarily an 11-inch shell, or even a 9.4-inch shell, could break a destroyer in half, sinking her almost at once, and to some the fact that neither of these shells exploded was nothing less than providential. Bryant later speculated that the shells may have been manufactured at the famous Skoda Arms Works in Pilson, Czechoslovakia, where anti-Nazi patriots risked their lives to sabotage them. If so, the Amer-icans off Cherbourg were much in their debt.[18]

Despite their flawed shells, German marksmanship was unnervingly ac-curate. They fired in three-gun salvos, and they proved very adept at adjust-ing fire. A salvo aimed at the destroyer *O'Brien* at 12:51 landed six hundred yards long; only seconds later, a second salvo was three hundred yards long; a third straddled her; and at 12:53 she was hit—and this shell *did* explode. Thirteen men were killed outright, and nineteen more were wounded. That shell also knocked out the *O'Brien's* radar, leaving her blind in heavy smoke amid several radically maneuvering vessels. To avoid a col-lision, the *O'Brien's* skipper, Commander W. W. Outerbridge, temporarily retired northward. When he returned to the fight later, he shifted his ord-nance to air-burst shells in the hope of forcing the German gunners to keep their heads down.[19]

Just as the gunners at Querqueville focused on the *Nevada*, those in Bat-tery Hamburg concentrated much of their attention on the *Texas*. The *Texas* was bracketed on the third salvo, and as Bryant put it, "They had us pretty well pinpointed." The salvos came in at unrelenting intervals every twenty to thirty seconds while the *Texas* maneuvered radically. Bryant thought the incoming shells had a kind of "seductive sound—a soft swish, almost a caress" while they were en route. Then they hit the water with "the most ungodly smack you ever heard—sharper than that of your own guns firing." Alas, not all of them hit the water. One 9.4-inch shell struck the *Texas*, plowed through several deck levels, and came to rest in the warrant officers' stateroom directly above the ship's magazine for 14-inch ammunition. It, too, was a dud.* Another shell hit the top of the *Texas*'s armored conning tower, and this one did explode, smashing up the bridge area, killing the helmsman, and wounding eleven others. Captain Charles Baker, having just ordered a turn to starboard, had left the bridge to watch the maneuver when the shell struck, or he, too, would have been a casualty.[20]

At 1:10, under the impetus of this rapid and accurate fire, Bryant ordered the task group to turn away northward while the destroyers *Plunkett* and *Hobson* made smoke to cover their withdrawal. The small minesweeper *Chickadee* also ran the gauntlet of enemy fire to lay a protective smokescreen. *Texas* and *Arkansas* circled to starboard and continued to fire from twenty thousand yards (just over eleven miles), but the guns in the Hamburg Battery had a range of forty thousand yards, and Bryant's maneuver did little to retard either the frequency or the accuracy of their shelling.[21]

While they dueled with the German batteries, the Navy ships also responded as best they could to call-fire requests from Collins's forces. The smaller batteries near Querqueville received a lot of attention, since those guns could be turned to face landward as well as out to sea. The destroyer *Ellyson* closed to within a mile of one battery and fired twenty-seven rounds of 5-inch ordnance "full salvos and rapid fire" in a single minute. The *Ellyson* ceased fire only because the ensuing smoke so obscured the target that the spotters could no longer see it. Either the object of the *Ellyson*'s fury was wrecked or the German gunners decided to lie low for a while, because the battery ceased firing.[22]

By 1:20, the ships had been on station for eighty minutes, and according to their orders they were supposed to retire at 1:30. It was obvious, however, that the German defenses had not been suppressed, and Deyo radioed Collins to ask, "Do you wish more gunfire?" Collins may have been away from his headquarters when the query came in, for he did not reply until

---

* That shell remains on board the USS *Texas* to this day and can be seen by visitors to the battleship, which is anchored off Houston as a museum ship.

2:05, when he answered, in effect, "Yes, please." He asked if the Navy ships could continue firing until 3:00, as Deyo had initially suggested.[23]

Because most of the Querqueville batteries had been silenced by now, at least temporarily, Deyo ordered the *Quincy* to steam eastward and join Bryant in the ongoing battle against Battery Hamburg. Some of the smaller batteries near Cap Lévi had been suppressed, but the Hamburg Battery remained defiantly active even though it was now the target of nearly every ship in Bryant's group, plus the *Quincy*. With eight ships firing at once, their shells created great clouds of smoke and dust around the target, and the spotters could not tell which ship had fired which shell, making corrections impossible. The Navy gunners simply fired into a curtain of smoke. Only when they spotted the bright orange stab of a muzzle flash could they determine the location of an enemy battery, and even that provided merely a bearing to the target. In spite of these difficulties, at 1:35 the *Texas* finally landed a 14-inch shell directly on one of the big German guns, putting it out of action. The other three, however, continued to fire, and soon the *Texas* was bracketed again. At 2:51, Bryant ordered the task group to turn away for the second time while the destroyers again made smoke.[24]

Before it was over, the *Texas* fired more than two hundred 14-inch shells and the *Arkansas* fired fifty-eight 12-inch shells at the Hamburg Battery. *Quincy* and the five destroyers added more than six hundred 8-inch and 5-inch rounds. Yet at three o'clock, when Deyo ordered a general withdrawal, three of the big guns there were still in action. The *Tuscaloosa* continued to fire until she was beyond range, but so did the Germans, and because their range was longer, they got the last word. At 3:10 a shell that was almost a taunt landed just twenty-five feet from the *Texas*, flinging seawater and shrapnel across her deck. Again Bryant ordered the destroyers to make smoke. As the Kriegsmarine gunners in Battery Hamburg watched the Allied task force disappear over the northern horizon, they may well have congratulated one another on having driven off the enemy.[25]

Bryant put the best face he could on the operation in his official report, writing that although his ships were "hopelessly outranged and continually harassed by enemy fire over a period of two hours and twenty minutes," they were "smartly handled and continued the engagement until ordered to withdraw." Ramsay, too, was complimentary, praising the "skill and determination" of Deyo's command. Yet in the aftermath of the naval assault on Cherbourg, it was evident to nearly everyone that despite recent experiences in the Mediterranean, heavy-caliber coastal artillery, strongly fortified and well served by trained crews, remained a very tough opponent for guns afloat. After the war, Bryant himself wondered if the naval attack had "advanced the surrender [of Cherbourg] one hour."[26]

It may well have. Though the naval assault on June 25 did not cause the Germans to throw up their hands, it almost certainly had an impact, however indeterminate, on the defenders. Like the aerial assault three days before, the naval bombardment further eroded the already flagging morale of the German garrison. Even von Schlieben was losing his nerve, and he wired Rommel to ask, "Is the destruction of the remaining troops necessary?" Seeking permission to negotiate, he declared, "I must state in the line of duty that further sacrifices cannot alter anything." It didn't matter. Rommel wired him back: "You will continue to fight until the last cartridge in accordance with the order from the Fuehrer." Von Schlieben would obey, however reluctantly, though both he and the men he commanded fully appreciated the hopelessness of their situation. Surrounded on three sides by Collins's ground troops, bombarded from the air, and now assailed from the sea, many—perhaps most—looked only for a swift end to the battle. And a swift end to the battle was exactly what Collins had in mind.[27]

IN THE END, CHERBOURG FELL to the soldiers on the ground. The men of Tubby Barton's Fourth Division sealed off the city to the west, and on June 25 the men of the 9th and 79th Divisions fought their way into the outskirts of the city, even as Deyo's and Bryant's ships continued their bombardment. The final assault was a collage of small-unit actions, many of them marked by astonishing individual heroism. Forte du Roule surrendered when GIs who had clambered up onto the ramparts lowered explosives down the ventilation shafts and the Germans inside rapidly appreciated their vulnerability.[28]

When the Allies learned that von Schlieben himself was in a nearby underground bunker, they blocked the tunnel entrance and sent in a German prisoner with a demand for his surrender. Obedient to Hitler's order to fight to the last, von Schlieben refused. The Americans then brought up a few tank destroyers—tracked artillery vehicles with 3-inch guns—and fired a half dozen rounds into the mouth of the tunnel. That was enough. A German voice called out for a cease-fire, and a German-speaking American officer went into the tunnel to tell von Schlieben he had two minutes to surrender. He didn't need two minutes. Within seconds, hundreds of German soldiers were streaming out of the tunnel under a huge white flag—very likely a bedsheet. Von Schlieben had hoped to stage a formal surrender, but he was swept along with the others in the general stampede, his dignity in shambles. The American officer on the scene, the bespectacled and cherubic Major General Manton Eddy, was stunned to find himself addressing not only von Schlieben but also the German naval commander at Cherbourg, Admiral Walther Hennecke.[29]

Eddy sent both men to see Collins, who pointedly asked von Schlieben if he was surrendering on behalf of his entire command. Fearful even now of provoking Hitler's wrath, he answered no, he surrendered only himself. Collins was furious and asked von Schlieben how he could justify "having his soldiers fight on when he saved himself by giving up." Von Schlieben made some remark about how small groups operating independently might still delay the American victory. A disgusted Collins made sure that the news was broadcast to the defenders of the city that their commanding general had saved his own skin by capitulating while condemning his men to die in the last ditch.[30]

Other strongpoints capitulated one by one. The final obstacle was the naval arsenal, where the German commander, Major General Robert Sattler, wanted only to ensure that he could assert he was compelled to bow to overwhelming force. When Collins sent in a flag of truce, Sattler indicated that he would surrender if the Americans fired a few shells at the fortress for show. The shells were duly fired, and Sattler and four hundred men marched out with their bags packed. The forts on the outer breakwater held out for two more days. Kirk sent the destroyer *Shubrick* and six of Bulkeley's PT boats to test their resolve, but the Germans there still had some fight in them, and once again shore batteries proved more resilient than expected. They finally surrendered on June 29 after being repeatedly strafed by American aircraft. By then, Collins had already presided over a ceremony at city hall in which a homemade French flag made of parachute cloth was raised over the Hôtel de Ville.[31]

Even before that ceremony, a Coast Guard advance team under Lieutenant Commander Quentin Walsh had begun to investigate the condition of the harbor facilities. Walsh and his team had accompanied the 79th Division during its overland campaign, and as they worked their way through the ruined city to the dock area, they encountered occasional pockets of continuing resistance. Dodging snipers and taking prisoners, they made their way to the harbor, where they found that the Germans, with their usual efficiency, had wrecked virtually everything. What they had not smashed, they had booby-trapped with mines and explosives. They had used an entire freight train filled with explosives to demolish the railroad pier, and the inner harbor was choked with dozens of scuttled ships and sown with 133 mines. The Germans had even blown up the E-boat pens that had been the object of Kirk's keen interest since April. The steel-reinforced concrete overheads of those pens turned out to be eight feet thick, and as Walsh and his men arrived, the E-boats inside them were still burning. Walsh reported to Kirk that the harbor was useless.[32]

Nevertheless, American, Canadian, and British salvage teams got to work almost immediately to clear the wreckage, sweep the mines, and repair the facilities. It was slow going. For more than two weeks, into mid-July, no Allied ships could use the harbor piers at all, and it was August before deep-draft supply ships could come into Cherbourg to unload at the rebuilt piers. Of course that meant that the Allies remained dependent on the beaches in Normandy. Thankfully, the steady delivery of supplies there continued to exceed expectations. On July 29, the day that the last pockets of resistance in Cherbourg were cleaned out, the Allies landed more than 23,000 tons of supplies on Omaha and Utah Beaches, and they sustained that level of efficiency through the next several weeks while Cherbourg Harbor was being repaired. On August 1, Allied ships landed 16,000 tons on Omaha Beach alone, an amount exactly double the pre-invasion daily goal.[33]

ON JUNE 30, RAMSAY DECLARED that Operation Neptune was officially over. For more than two and a half years, ever since the ABC conversations in Washington back in March 1941, nine months before Pearl Harbor, the Anglo-Americans had wrestled with the concept of invading Europe. Their strategic negotiating had been marked by often contentious and sometimes angry disputes about when and where to land. If the conversations at times grew sharp and many of the principals cursed one another privately in their diaries and letters, they never let their disagreements scuttle the alliance. George Marshall, Dwight Eisenhower, and the Americans had been proven correct in identifying northern Europe—and in particular France—as the strategic center of gravity, and Churchill, Alan Brooke, and the British had been correct in asserting that a premature invasion would have been catastrophic. From Bolero and Roundup to Neptune and Overlord, the plans underwent numerous revisions. Neptune was confirmed in May 1943 at Quebec, and it then took thirteen more months to plan, assemble, and execute the biggest maritime expedition in history. In those thirteen months, the Allies defeated the U-boat menace in the Atlantic and secured command of the air over France; they brought more than a million American GIs to Britain and conducted numberless training exercises on British beaches; they built the thousands of ships—the destroyers, Liberty ships, landing ships, and especially the LSTs—needed to conduct the invasion, and they brought them all together in British ports. It was an astonishing chronicle of perseverance and productivity, and on June 6, 1944, the greatest armada in the history of the planet assembled off the Normandy beaches.

Yet despite all that has been rightly said about the importance of Allied manpower and superior material assets, it was not merely the overwhelming numbers that made Neptune possible. Nor was it the creative but often dubious gimmick weapons: the DD tanks, the rocket-firing LCTs, or even the Mulberry harbors, all of which proved disappointing at some level. It was, instead, the commitment and the dedication of the men themselves. From the stalwart and unflagging determination of Winston Churchill to the pragmatic flexibility and cheerful congeniality of Franklin Roosevelt, from the dispassionate clear-eyed professionalism of George Marshall to the flamboyant self-assurance of Bernard Montgomery, from the political sensitivity and quiet competence of Dwight Eisenhower to the patrician and highly professional Bertram Ramsay, it was the people involved who made

Neptune possible. The planners sought to account for every eventuality, though in the end the factor that produced the Allied victory was human judgment applied at a crisis moment, often instinctively and selflessly. That certainly included Ike's courageous decision to go ahead with the operation despite the storm that was raging around Southwick House on June 5. It included the grim determination of the young Navy and Coast Guard officers and coxswains who pushed their landing craft onto the target beaches through the hedgehogs and the teller mines. It included the close-in gunfire support provided by the destroyers off Omaha Beach, which all but put their bows on the bottom to suppress the German guns ashore. It included the soldiers themselves, trapped on that deadly beach, who scaled the bluffs hand over hand and seized the high ground. It included the British commandos who held Pegasus Bridge, as well as the Rangers who seized Pointe du Hoc. And it included thousands of others, officers and men, who had to make life-and-death decisions in the midst of furious combat on all the beaches. Back in their hometowns, the newspapers and radio reports announced the names of the Allied commanders in large boldface type. Most of those engaged in Neptune, however, did their jobs anonymously: the ensigns and lieutenants, coxswains, enginemen, boatswain's mates, line handlers, demolition specialists, gunners, Seabees, and medics—indeed, all the varied ratings of a vast and complex maritime organization, American, British, and Canadian, both Navy and Coast Guard. They made Neptune a success.

EPILOGUE

On June 22, the day the storm off the Normandy beaches began to abate, and while Collins's three divisions prepared to launch their final assault on Cherbourg, Russian forces on the Eastern Front initiated Operation Bagration, a massive ground offensive along a three-hundred-mile front that involved 2.3 million men and 2,700 tanks in 146 divisions. Initially, that offensive was to have taken place simultaneously with the Normandy landings, but Stalin waited until two weeks after D-Day because June 22 was the third anniversary of the German invasion of Russia. Here at last was a double envelopment of the enemy on a continental scale. Nazi Germany now confronted a two-front war with a million American, British, Canadian, and French soldiers attacking in the west and more than two million Russians attacking in the east.

Hitler refused to accept reality. Just as he had ordered von Schlieben to die in the last ditch at Cherbourg, so now he ordered all his armies to stand and fight where they were, insisting that there should be no retreat. That, of course, simply condemned most of them to die. And die they did, by the tens of thousands. Officers who suggested any other tactical solution were sacked. Field Marshal Karl von Rundstedt, commanding German armies in the west, felt obligated to tell Hitler that the strategic situation in France was hopeless. Hitler responded by replacing him with Gunther Hans von Kluge.

Throughout the rest of June and into July, the principal fighting in Normandy continued to swirl around Caen, which allowed Montgomery to assert, with justification, that his forces were bearing the brunt of the enemy's counterattacks. It also allowed the Royal Navy battleships and cruisers to hammer away at German positions in and around the city, doing so with such effectiveness that Major General Leo Geyr von Schweppenberg, commander of Panzer Group West, appealed to Berlin for permission to withdraw beyond the range of the Allied naval guns. Hitler denied the request and fired von Schweppenberg.[1]

All that time, the Allies continued to pour men, vehicles, and equipment into France. With Cherbourg harbor still not fully operational, the LSTs and smaller landing craft brought men and supplies over the Normandy beaches as well as the British Mulberry pier off Arromanche. On July 4, the millionth Allied soldier came ashore, and two days later George Patton, who up to then had been cooling his heels in England as a decoy, landed at a small airstrip behind Omaha Beach. Once off the plane, he told the soldiers who crowded around him that they were going to Berlin, where, he insisted, "I am going to personally shoot that paper-hanging goddammed son of a bitch."[2]

Three weeks later, on July 25, the Americans initiated Operation Cobra, a plan to break out of their enclave in Brittany and Normandy. Early gains were incremental and costly. Then on August 1, two armored divisions of Collins's VII Corps opened a hole in the German lines, and Patton's newly activated Third Army burst through into the French countryside. Hitler ordered an immediate counterattack, and though his lieutenants attempted to obey, their assaults were blunted and then hurled back. With unchallenged command of the air and dominant superiority on the ground, Allied columns raced across France the way the Germans had done back in 1940. The Allies very nearly trapped two full German armies in a double envelopment in what was known as the Falaise pocket south of Caen, and while the Germans managed to escape by the narrowest of margins, they nevertheless fled eastward all the way to the Seine River.[3]

AS THE FIGHTING MOVED INLAND, away from the beaches, the Neptune forces were dispersed. Ramsay himself continued to cooperate with Montgomery's Second Army in the campaign for the lowlands and especially the capture of Antwerp in September, but both Vian and Kirk returned to England for reassignment. Kirk's Western Naval Task Force was officially dissolved on July 10, and he became Commander, U.S. Naval Forces in France. Vian, elevated to a Knight Commander of the Bath and the rank of vice admiral, went to the Pacific, where he assumed command of a fleet of aircraft carriers. In that capacity, he supervised the attack Churchill had long advocated against Japanese-held Sumatra. Both Jimmy Hall and Morton Deyo also got orders to the Pacific, where in the spring of 1945 they participated in the American invasion of Okinawa, for which each of them received the Navy's Distinguished Service Medal. Leigh-Mallory, too, was assigned to the Pacific as the Air Commander-in-Chief for South East Asia, though while en route there his plane crashed over the French Alps in poor weather and everyone on board was killed.[4]

Don Moon got orders to the Mediterranean to command the invasion force for the attack on southern France, initially code-named Anvil but now renamed Dragoon, supposedly because Churchill claimed that he had been dragooned into it. Arriving in Naples in July, Moon reported to Kent Hewitt, the overall commander of Dragoon, who had been his math professor at the Naval Academy and a kind of mentor. Moon was uneasy about the short interval he had to absorb all the various elements of this new operation. He urged Hewitt to postpone the landings. Hewitt turned him down. The invasion had been postponed once before, Hewitt reminded him, and too many factors, political as well as logistical, were involved.[5]

Moon had been working fifteen-hour days, seven days a week for months and now suffered from a physical tiredness that bordered on exhaustion. Much of that was due to his work ethic. Throughout the planning period for Neptune, then during the crisis of Exercise Tiger, and all through the invasion itself, he had worked fifteen-hour days, seven days a week. Reluctant to delegate even the smallest detail to his subordinates, he sought to manage everything personally. Commander Frank Lowe, the medical officer on the *Bayfield*, had told him repeatedly that he needed to get more rest and exercise, warning him that, "no individual can work those long hours over an indefinite period and stand up under the work." Lowe insisted that Moon meet with the Eighth Fleet medical officer, Captain Frederick Greaves.[6]

To Greaves, Moon acknowledged that he was working hard, but, he insisted, "it was necessary for him to work too many hours a day." Greaves later testified that during their interview, Moon was clear and focused and betrayed no evidence of mental confusion or uncertainty. Nevertheless, every man has a breaking point, and by August 5, 1944, Rear Admiral Don Pardee Moon had reached his.[7]

At 7:00 a.m., Moon sat down at the desk in his cabin on the *Bayfield*. "The mind is gone," he wrote in a clear steady hand. "With the mind stalled & crazy...things once easy are not in sight." The fact that he was still in his underwear and that he wrote in uncharacteristically jumbled syntax evidenced that he was struggling with a severe mental crisis he could not control. "Command is wrong under such a condition.... Overwork thru the years—I have given the Navy everything I had—too much—it has broken me." "My country," he wrote, "what am I doing to you. My wife & dear children...I am sick, so sick." He signed with his initials, then, meticulous as always, he wrapped his .45 caliber sidearm in a towel to minimize the mess, put the gun to his head, and pulled the trigger.[8]

The war went on without him. Ten days later, Operation Dragoon took place as scheduled when three divisions of Lucian Truscott's VI Corps went ashore on the French Riviera against what turned out to be light opposition. Ten days after that, on August 25, the Allies entered Paris, led by the French 2nd Armored Division, which was accorded pride of place in the liberation of the city. A week later, elements of the American Third Army crossed the Meuse, and on September 3, the British Second Army liberated Brussels.

For a moment, it seemed the war might end soon—perhaps before winter. But the moment passed. There would be many more battles before the end, including the sanguinary Battle of the Bulge in December, when

Hitler sought to turn the war around with a desperate ground offensive into the Ardennes Forest. When the Germans began that counteroffensive, Ramsay decided to fly from his headquarters northwest of Paris to Montgomery's headquarters in Brussels to talk face-to-face about the defense of Antwerp. In soggy weather, his small two-engine plane took off successfully, then suddenly plummeted to the ground and exploded. Along with his chief of staff and his flag lieutenant, Ramsay died instantly.

The surprise assault in the Ardennes allowed the Germans to seize a broad salient in the front line—the famous "bulge"—but their offensive stalled after only a week, and the British and Americans counterattacked. By Christmas the German gambit had failed, and it was clear to all, or at least to everyone except Hitler, that the end of the war was only a matter of time. By spring, the Anglo-Americans were just 250 miles west of Berlin, and the Russians were in the outskirts of the city. Though many more men would die while Hitler clung to power for a few more days, the Allied triumph in Europe was now inevitable. The war in the Pacific continued until August, terminated at last by the deus ex machina of the atomic bombs.

Franklin Roosevelt did not live to see it. In spite of the good news from the various fighting fronts, the president was worn down from his exertions. On January 20, 1945, he took the oath of office for a fourth term, and in February he left for yet another conference, this one at Yalta in the Russian Crimea. There he sought to play the role of mediator between Churchill and Stalin, a delicate and trying balancing act that left him even more exhausted. His skin, unnaturally gray, sagged on his once robust frame, and though he still occasionally flashed his famous smile for the cameras, it was too often the rictus of a game but obviously very ill man.

At the end of March, Roosevelt traveled south to Warm Springs, Georgia, where he often went for the sake of his crippled legs to swim in what he was convinced were the healing waters of the local spring. He had agreed to have his portrait painted while he was there, and he was posing for it early on the afternoon of April 12, when he told the artist, "I have a terrific pain in the back of my head." Then he slumped in his chair. He never regained consciousness, and within hours he was pronounced dead of a cerebral hemorrhage. Having restored American optimism during the Depression, sustained Britain in its darkest days, and shepherded the anti-fascist alliance through four years of war, his work was finally at an end. He was sixty-three years old.

George Marshall was promoted to the rank of General of the Army (five stars) in December 1944 even as the Battle of the Bulge was raging in the Ardennes, although he never exercised the field command that he coveted and which many of his colleagues felt was his due. After the war, he resigned as chief of staff, though because his new rank was a life tenure, he technically remained on active duty. In 1947, he accepted President Harry Truman's invitation to serve as secretary of state, in which capacity he made what was arguably his greatest contribution to history by sponsoring the European Recovery Program, better known as the Marshall Plan. In recognition of that, he was awarded the 1953 Nobel Peace Prize. Though Marshall resigned as secretary of state in 1949, he was called back to service a year later as secretary of defense upon the outbreak of the Korean War. He was disappointed and very likely hurt during the 1952 presidential campaign when Eisenhower, his former protégé, publicly supported those who criticized Marshall's tenure of leadership in both cabinet positions. True to his character, however, Marshall never responded to those charges or spoke an unkind word about Eisenhower or any of his other wartime associates. He died in Walter Reed Army Hospital in Washington on October 16, 1959, at the age of seventy-eight.

Alan Brooke outlived Marshall by four years. After retirement, Brooke became the First Viscount Alanbrooke and indulged his passion for bird watching, becoming vice president of the Royal Society for the Protection of Birds and president of the Zoological Society of London. He held several ceremonial positions, including Lord Lieutenant of the County of London. As Constable of England, he played a key role in the ceremonies surrounding the 1953 coronation of Elizabeth II, an event also attended by his former counterpart, George Marshall. Four years later, in 1957, there was a flurry of public interest and titillation upon the publication of his edited, though still quite candid, diaries that contained sharp criticisms of Churchill, Marshall, Eisenhower, and others. Alanbrooke suffered a fatal heart attack in June 1963, a month short of his eightieth birthday.

Winston Churchill outlived all of them. A month after Roosevelt's death, he was the featured speaker at a huge outdoor rally in London to celebrate the German surrender, which was announced on May 8, 1945. Churchill told the crowd, "This is your victory," and almost to a man they shouted back: "No, it is yours." In many ways, that was true enough, for it was Churchill more than anyone who had held the beleaguered nation together in those dark days during 1940 and 1941. Ironically, however, the very strengths that made him an unrivaled wartime leader—his unconquerable will, his love of king and country, and his reverence for the old Empire—did not resonate in the same way in the postwar era. By 1945, Britons were tired of "blood, tears, toil, and sweat," and despite their gratitude for all that he had done for them, they voted his party out of office in the first postwar election later that year. Churchill felt the blow keenly and resigned at once, but he was never one to withdraw quietly into the shadows, and he remained an active and voluble member of Parliament. As ever, he was also a prolific author, producing his magisterial six-volume history, *The Second World War*, which won him the Nobel Prize for Literature in 1953, the same year that George Marshall won the Nobel Peace Prize. Churchill returned to office in 1951, but poor health, including a severe stroke, convinced him to resign again in 1955, at the age of eighty. Despite lifelong habits of heavy drinking, heavy smoking, and absurdly late hours, he lived to the age of ninety and died at his home in Hyde Park Gate, London, in January 1965.

Dwight Eisenhower returned to the United States in November 1945 to succeed his mentor George Marshall as Army chief of staff. In 1948, he declined offers from both political parties to run for president of the United States and instead became president of Columbia University in New York City. Two years later he became Supreme Allied Commander of NATO forces, and in 1952 he accepted the Republican nomination for president. Elected twice by wide margins, he presided over a period of relative stability both at home and abroad, and stepped down in 1961 a much-beloved national figure. He retired to his farm near Gettysburg, Pennsylvania, where he had spent much of World War I, and indulged his interest in golf. Having suffered from heart disease for much of his later life, he succumbed to a massive heart attack in March 1969, dying at Walter Reed Army Hospital on March 28, at the age of seventy-eight.

Bernard Montgomery proved nearly as resilient as Churchill. He had insisted to all who would listen that after the Normandy landings he would spearhead a drive into the heart of Germany and win the war before winter set in. Instead his forces bogged down almost at once. The city of Caen, which was supposed to have fallen on D-Day, held out for more than two months. Monty's attempt to atone for this disappointment, a thrust into the lowlands code-named Operation Market Garden, also went awry. Because he was Monty, however, none of this dampened his hearty self-confidence, and he was at his best in responding to the emergency of the Battle of the Bulge. After the war, he succeeded Brooke (now Viscount Alanbrooke) as chief of the Imperial General Staff, though he was out of his depth in dealing with the political and strategic elements of the job, and it was not a successful tour. He retired from the Army in 1958 at age seventy-one, was made Viscount Montgomery of Alamein, and wrote his memoirs. An ardent Tory, he supported and defended apartheid in South Africa, and campaigned against the decriminalization of homosexuality in Britain. As abstemious in his personal habits as Churchill was self-indulgent, he nevertheless did not quite match Churchill's longevity, dying in 1976 at the age of eighty-nine.

AS FOR THE REST, those thousands of largely anonymous junior officers and enlisted men who took part in Operation Neptune from its conception in the spring of 1943 to its culmination in the summer of 1944, nearly all of them were changed by their experience. The British returned to a nation where the scars of war lingered for many years. They would rebuild, but shortages—including food shortages—continued for nearly a decade. The Americans returned to a country with few visible scars. They were reluctant to talk about the war, at least with their families. Many tried to behave as if the war had not happened at all. They went back to school on the GI Bill, or they got jobs building houses, refrigerators, and automobiles. They got married, bought homes, had children, mowed the grass, and built America.

But they never forgot. Karl Bischoff had spent more than a year as the "motor mac," a machinist's mate, on LCI(L)-489, including a landing on Omaha Beach on D-Day. His main job had been to ensure that the engines were working and in good repair. One night he woke up in pitch darkness with the chilling awareness that he could not hear the engines. He threw off the covers and raced to the door. Yanking it open, he was completely befuddled to see his father standing there holding a cup of coffee. It made no sense: what was his father doing in the engine room? It took him several seconds to process it. And then he knew. He was home.[9]

ACKNOWLEDGMENTS

A S IN EVERY PROJECT, I am indebted to the many people who went out of their way to help me find resource materials, provide information and insight, and make valuable suggestions about the remarkable story of Operation Neptune and the Allied invasion of Europe.

At the National Archives (Archives II) in College Park, Maryland, Nathaniel Patch directed me to U.S. Navy and Allied sources; Timothy Mulligan brought my attention to German sources I would otherwise have overlooked, and even translated them for me. John Hodges of the Naval History and Heritage Command (NHHC) in the Washington Navy Yard was helpful with both sources and logistics during my visits, and managed to dig up Rear Admiral Morton Deyo's description of the naval bombardment of Utah Beach out of Samuel Eliot Morison's old files. Evelyn Cherpak, archivist at the U.S. Naval War College and editor of Hewitt's memoirs, assisted me with the Kent Hewitt Papers. Both Jennifer Bryan and David D'Onofrio were unflaggingly cheerful and welcoming during my visits to the Special Collections Room of Nimitz Library at the U.S. Naval Academy. The late Stephen Ambrose spent years collecting hundreds of oral histories of D-Day veterans, which he then had transcribed and which are now deposited with the Eisenhower Center (which he created) at the National World War II Museum in New Orleans. All students of World War II are indebted to Ambrose, and I am grateful as well to Lindsey Barnes, the senior archivist and digital projects manager at the museum, who was gracious and generous when my wife, Marylou, and I conducted research there. Similarly, I am grateful to Reagan Grau, archivist at the National Museum of the Pacific War in Fredericksburg, Texas, who made available not only the museum's oral history collection but also the extensive and valuable papers of the LCI Association, which are archived there. Janis Jorgenson at the U.S. Naval Institute was once again an invaluable aid in helping me find and identify suitable photographs, as was Richard Porter, the museum director at the Britannia Royal Naval College in Dartmouth, England.

I am grateful to Otis Bingemer, who served on LST-325 at Normandy and who gave me a tour of his former ship at Evansville, Indiana. Of the more than a thousand LSTs built during the war, LST-325 is the only one still in operational condition. Sold to the Greek navy after the war, the 325 was decommissioned by the Greeks in the 1970s. A handful of U.S. Navy World War II veterans, by then in their seventies, determined that their ship should not be sold for scrap. They raised the money to buy it, flew to Athens, and sailed it back across the Atlantic, an adventure worthy of a major motion picture. The ship is moored today in the Ohio River at Evansville, where it was built. I am also grateful to Dr. Meredith Moon, daughter of Rear Admiral Don P. Moon, and to her cousin, also named Don Moon, both of whom were generous with their time and their materials, and helped me understand the circumstances and character of their admiral ancestor. I offer thanks as well to Navy Captain William Garrett (Ret.), who took a particular interest in this project from the start, and Rev. John R. Kenny, who served off the Normandy beaches in 1944.

Finally, I am deeply indebted to those who helped me look at the events in different ways or who offered both substantive and editorial help. The idea for this book came from my editor at Oxford University Press, Tim Bent, who provided just the right amount of direction, encouragement, and license to allow me to engage fully with the topic. It has been wonderful to work again with the team of professionals at Oxford, including Keely Latcham, Joellyn Ausanka, and Sue Warga. I am thankful to Evan Davies, my former colleague at Britannia Royal Naval College in Dartmouth, England, with whom I first toured the Normandy beaches. I am particularly indebted to two friends who read the entire manuscript, made me rethink some aspects of the story, corrected more than a few errors, and offered enthusiastic encouragement. These two worthies are Richard B. Frank, whose knowledge of the Second World War is unmatched, and Paul Stillwell, whom I have known for more than thirty years and to whom every historian of naval history owes an enormous debt for his leadership of the Oral History Program at the U.S. Naval Institute, as well as for his many books and articles. If some gaffes have nonetheless survived the careful scrutiny of these two scholars, it is not because they did not make every effort to save me from myself. I am grateful, too, to Jeffrey Ward, who rendered the maps and charts in this book with exceptional care and accuracy, and tolerated my repeated pleas for just one more addition or correction.

Finally, as always, my greatest debt is to my wife, Marylou, who remains my most exacting and sympathetic editor as well as my indispensable partner in all things. This book is dedicated to Jeff Symonds and Susan Witt, both of them exceptional teachers and exceptional parents to our two grandchildren, William and Beatrice, and to my big sister Carol who claims to have read all my books, including "The Professor General," which I wrote at age eight.

ABBREVIATIONS USED IN NOTES

ANCXF	Allied Naval Commander, Expeditionary Force (Ramsay)
BAOR	World War II Battle Action and Operational Reports (Mss 416), Nimitz Library, Special Collections, U.S. Naval Academy
Brooke Diary	Alanbrooke, Field Marshall Lord [General Alan Brooke]. *War Diaries, 1939–1945*. Alex Danchev and Daniel Todman, editors. London: Weidenfeld & Nicholson, 2001.
CCS	Combined Chiefs of Staff
ComUSNavEu or COMNAVEU	Commander, U.S. Naval Forces, Europe (Stark)
COS	Chiefs of Staff (British)
DDE	Dwight D. Eisenhower
FDR	Franklin D. Roosevelt
FDRL	Franklin D. Roosevelt Library, Hyde Park, New York
FRUS	U.S. Department of State, *Foreign Relations of the United States*. Washington, DC: Government Printing Office, various dates by volume and series.
GCM	George C. Marshall
JCS	Joint Chiefs of Staff (American)
NA	National Archives and Records Administration (Archives II), College Park, Maryland
NHHC	Naval History and Heritage Command, Washington Navy Yard, Washington, DC
NMPW	The National Museum of the Pacific War, Fredericksburg, Texas
NWWIIM-EC	The National World War II Museum, New Orleans, Louisiana (Eisenhower Center)
PGCM	*The Papers of George Catlett Marshall*. Larry I. Bland, editor. Baltimore: Johns Hopkins University Press, 1996.
PDDE	*The Papers of Dwight David Eisenhower*. Alfred D. Chandler, editor. Baltimore: Johns Hopkins University Press, 1970.
Ramsay Diary	*The Year of D-Day: The 1944 Diary of Admiral Sir Bertram Ramsay*. Robert W. Love Jr. and John Major, editors. Hull, England: University of Hull Press, 1994.

RG	Record Group (at the National Archives)
USNA	United States Naval Academy (Nimitz Library), Annapolis, Maryland
USNI	United States Naval Institute, Annapolis, Maryland
W&M	William and Mary University
WSC	Winston S. Churchill

NOTES

Chapter 1: Germany First

1. Robert E. Sherwood, *Roosevelt and Hopkins: An Intimate History* (New York: Harper, 1948; reprinted, Enigma Books, 2008), 337–80 (all page references are to the 2008 edition); Richard Ketcham, "Yesterday, December 7, 1941," *American Heritage*, November 1989, 54.

2. Harold Ickes, *The Secret Diary of Harold Ickes* (New York: Simon & Schuster, 1953–54), 662 (entry of December 14, 1941); Frances Perkins, *The Roosevelt I Knew* (New York: Viking Press, 1946; reprinted, Penguin Press, 2011), 364 (page references are to the 2011 edition).

3. Mark Harrison, ed., *The Economies of World War II: Six Great Powers in International Comparison* (Cambridge: Cambridge University Press, 1998), 10.

4. FDR press conference, November 3, 1941, in *The Complete Presidential Press Conferences* (New York: DaCapo Press, 1972), 18:280.

5. Ickes, *Secret Diary* (entry of April 20, 1941), 485; Henry Morgenthau, *The Presidential Dairies of Henry Morgenthau, Jr.* (New York: Clearwater, 1984), 2:253–54.

6. Sherwood, *Roosevelt and Hopkins*, 349.

7. Ibid.

8. Edward Miller, *War Plan Orange: The U.S. Strategy to Defeat Japan, 1897–1945* (Annapolis, MD: Naval Institute Press, 1991); Craig C. Felker, *Testing American Sea Power: U.S. Navy Strategic Exercises, 1923–1940* (College Station: Texas A&M University Press, 2007).

9. Ingersoll's testimony, April 21, 1939, is quoted in Mark S. Watson, *Chief of Staff: Prewar Plans and Preparations* (Washington, DC: Historical Division, Department of the Army, 1950), 98.

10. From Marshall's notes at the June 22 meeting, quoted in Watson, *Chief of Staff*, 111.

11. Watson, *Chief of Staff*, 111–12, 114.

12. Ibid., 108.

13. Stark to Knox, November 12, 1940, available at www.fdrlibrary.marist.edu.

14. Ibid.

15. Memo of the Joint Planning Commission to the Joint Board, January 13, 1941, in Watson, *Chief of Staff*, 371.

16. Watson, *Chief of Staff*, 372–73.
17. "United States–British Staff Conversations Report," March 27, 1941, printed as exhibit #49 (copy No. 98 of 125), U.S. Congress, *Pearl Harbor Attack Hearings* (Washington, DC: Government Printing Office, 1946), 15:1487–96. The passages referring to assumed U.S. participation in the war are on 1489 and 1524.
18. Ibid., 1490–91.
19. Ibid., 1491.
20. Ibid.
21. Ibid., 1493.
22. Ibid., 1497.
23. Ibid., 1485.
24. Sherwood, *Roosevelt and Hopkins*, 230.
25. Thomas A. Bailey and Paul B. Ryan, *Hitler vs. Roosevelt: The Undeclared Naval War* (New York: Free Press, 1979), 138–40.
26. Sherwood, *Roosevelt and Hopkins*, 242; Kenneth R. Davis, *FDR: The War President, 1940–1943* (New York: Random House, 2000), 229, 232.
27. Robert F. Cross, *Sailor in the White House: The Seafaring Life of FDR* (Annapolis, MD: Naval Institute Press, 2003), 90–92.
28. Jean Edward Smith, *FDR* (New York: Random House, 2008), 499n; Jon Meacham, *Franklin and Winston: An Intimate Portrait of an Epic Friendship* (New York: Random House, 2004), 105–6.
29. Sherwood, *Roosevelt and Hopkins*, 276–77.
30. Ibid., 276.
31. Ibid., 276–78.
32. British Strategy Review, July 31, 1941, in Watson, *Chief of Staff*, 403.
33. Memo to the Joint Board, September 25, 1941, in Watson, *Chief of Staff*, 408.
34. Winston Churchill, *The Grand Alliance* (Boston: Houghton Mifflin, 1950), 433–37. A facsimile of this document is on 235.
35. Sherwood, *Roosevelt and Hopkins*, 338.
36. Knox to ALNAV (all Navy personnel), December 7, 1941, Nimitz Papers, NHHC, box 1, folder 5.
37. Grace Tully, *F.D.R.: My Boss* (New York: Charles Scribner's Sons, 1949), 256–57. A facsimile copy of FDR's hand-edited speech is available at www.archives.gov/education/lessons/day-of-infamy.

Chapter 2: Arcadia

1. Robert E. Sherwood, *Roosevelt and Hopkins: An Intimate History* (New York: Harper, 1948; reprinted, Enigma Books, 2008), 347 (page references are to the 2008 edition); Winston Churchill, *The Grand Alliance* (Boston: Houghton Mifflin, 1950), 603–4; Lynne Olson, *Citizens of London* (New York: Random House, 2010), 143–44.
2. Churchill, *The Grand Alliance*, 606–8.
3. Ibid., 641.
4. Sherwood, *Roosevelt and Hopkins*, 347–49. A transcript of the telephone conversation between Beaverbrook and Hopkins is on 348.

5. WSC to George VI, December 8, 1941, in Churchill, *The Grand Alliance*, 608; WSC to FDR, December 10, 1941, in Francis L. Lowenstein et al., *Roosevelt and Churchill: Their Secret Wartime Correspondence* (New York: Saturday Review Press/E. P. Dutton, 1975), 169–70.

6. The text of Hitler's speech is available at several online sites including the Jewish Virtual Library at www.jewishvirtuallibrary.org.

7. Churchill, *The Grand Alliance*, 606.

8. Ibid., 620.

9. Forrest C. Pogue, *George C. Marshall: Ordeal and Hope* (New York: Viking Press, 1965), 271–72.

10. Ibid.

11. See WSC to Smuts, December 20, 1941, in Churchill, *The Grand Alliance*, 632–33. See also 641–43.

12. Churchill's briefing memo is in FRUS (Special Conferences Series), 1:21–37. Part II is also printed in Churchill, *The Grand Alliance*, 652–55.

13. Memorandum by WSC, December 16–20, 1941, FRUS (Special Conferences Series), 1:30.

14. Quotations in this paragraph are from Ibid., 25.

15. Churchill, *The Grand Alliance*, 662.

16. Sherwood, *Roosevelt and Hopkins*, 349; Churchill, *The Grand Alliance*, 603.

17. George Elsey, "Strategy and Secrecy," in Paul Stillwell, ed., *Assault on Normandy: First-Person Accounts from the Sea Services* (Annapolis, MD: Naval Institute Press, 1994), 14.

18. Sherwood, *Roosevelt and Hopkins*, 351.

19. Ernest J. King and Walter Muir Whitehill, *Fleet Admiral King: A Naval Record* (New York: W. W. Norton, 1952), 360.

20. Churchill, *The Grand Alliance*, 646; WSC Memo to War Cabinet, December 23, 1941, in Ibid., 665. See also Minutes of Meeting between FDR and WSC, December 22, 1941, FRUS (Special Conferences Series), 1:63–65.

21. Minutes of Conference in the White House, December 23, 1941, FRUS (Special Conferences Series), 1:77–80. See also Churchill, *The Grand Alliance*, 663, and Pogue, *Ordeal and Hope*, chapter 12.

22. Roosevelt relied in part on a briefing paper Stimson had prepared. It is printed in FRUS (Special Conferences Series), 1:44–47. WSC memo to War Cabinet, December 23, 1941, in Churchill, *The Grand Alliance*, 665; Eisenhower, Notes, December 23, 1941, PDDE, 1:19. See also J. M. A. Gwyer, *Grand Strategy* (London: Her Majesty's Stationery Office, 1964), 2:354.

23. Minutes of Chiefs of Staff meeting, December 24, 1941, FRUS (Special Conferences Series), 1:82–90.

24. Ibid., 82; Dill to Brooke, January 3, 1942, in Arthur Bryant, *The Turn of the Tide: A History of the War Years Based on the Diaries of Field Marshall Lord Alanbrooke* (Garden City, NY: Doubleday, 1957), 2:234. The dispute over diverting U.S. ships to Singapore is in Hollis to Smith, December 24, 1941, FRUS (Special Conferences Series), 1:267–68. See also Pogue, *Ordeal and Hope*, 264.

25. Meeting minutes, December 24, 1941, are in FRUS (Special Conferences Series), 1:90–94. The "grinding away" comment was Eisenhower's in DDE to Lucian Booth, January 14, 1942, PDDE, 1:55–56. See also Eisenhower's Memorandum for file, December 28, 1941, in PDDE, 1:25–26.

26. Pogue, *Ordeal and Hope*, 277–79.

27. Sherwood, *Roosevelt and Hopkins*, 358; Eisenhower, Memorandum for File, December 28, 1941, PDDE, 1:25.

28. Eisenhower initially designated the combined forces as ABDU (Australian, British, Dutch, and United States), though this was later changed to ABDA, in which "America" replaced "United States" in the acronym. The draft of Eisenhower's proposal is in PDDE, 1:28–30.

29. George C. Marshall, *Interviews and Reminiscences for Forrest C. Pogue*, ed. Larry I. Bland (Lexington: George C. Marshall Foundation,1996), 357; King and Whitehill, *Fleet Admiral King*, 363.

30. Marshall, *Interviews and Reminiscences*, 357; Sherwood, *Roosevelt and Hopkins*, 358; Churchill, *The Grand Alliance*, 673.

31. Philip Ziegler, *Mountbatten* (New York: Alfred A. Knopf, 1985), 183–85; Marshall, *Interviews and Reminiscences*, 358, 595, 600–601; Pogue, *Ordeal and Hope*, 279–80; Sherwood, *Roosevelt and Hopkins*, 368–69; Churchill, *The Grand Alliance*, 674.

32. GCM to FDR, December 26, 1941, FRUS (Special Conferences Series), 1:239. The minutes of the December 26 meeting are in Ibid., 100–104. See also notes taken by General Gerow, Ibid., 104–106. Churchill, *The Grand Alliance*, 647; Sherwood, *Roosevelt and Hopkins*, 364.

33. Minutes of the Chiefs of Staff meeting, January 12, 1942, FRUS (Special Conferences Series), 1:182–91. The Marshall quotation is from 190. See also Sherwood, *Roosevelt and Hopkins*, 361–66.

34. Sherwood, *Roosevelt and Hopkins*, 366; William Hardy McNeill, *America, Britain, and Russia: Their Cooperation and Conflict, 1941–1946* (New York: Oxford University Press, 1953), 108.

35. Sherwood, *Roosevelt and Hopkins*, 367–68; Thomas Parrish, *Roosevelt and Marshall: Partners in Politics and War* (New York William Morrow, 1989), 227–31.

36. Sherwood, *Hopkins and Roosevelt*, 368–70.

37. Ibid., 353–57.

38. Ibid., 375.

39. Churchill, *The Grand Alliance*, 686.

Chapter 3: "We've Got to Go to Europe and Fight"

1. George Marshall, *Interviews and Reminiscences for Forrest C. Pogue*, ed. Larry I. Bland (Lexington, VA: George C. Marshall Foundation, 1996), 108–9. See also Thomas Parrish, *Roosevelt and Marshall: Partners in Politics and War* (New York: William Morrow, 1989), 15–18.

2. Brooke Diary (entry of April 15, 1942), 249.

3. Ernest J. King and Walter Muir Whitehill, *Fleet Admiral King: A Naval Record* (New York: W. W. Norton, 1952), 368.

4. Eisenhower, Notes for Diary, January 22, 1942, PDDE, 1:66.

5. FDR to WSC, March 7 and 9, 1942, Francis L. Lowenstein et al., eds., *Roosevelt and Churchill: Their Secret Wartime Correspondence* (New York: Saturday Review/E. P. Dutton, 1975), 188, 190. Hereafter *Correspondence*.

6. Memo for the Chief of Staff, March 25, 1942, PDDE, 1:205–7.

7. Henry L. Stimson with McGeorge Bundy, *On Active Service in Peace and War* (New York: Harper & Brothers, 1947) 416–17 (entry of March 25, 1942). Hereafter Stimson Diary. A complete text of Marshall's plan as drafted by Eisenhower is in Appendix III of J. R. M. Butler, *Grand Strategy II*, vol. 3 of *History of the Second World War* (London: Her Majesty's Stationery Office, 1964), 675–81.

8. FDR to WSC, March 9, 1942, is not in Lowenstein's edited volume. Instead, see Warren F. Kimball, ed., *Churchill & Roosevelt: The Complete Correspondence* (Princeton: Princeton University Press, 1984), 1:298–99.

9. Brooke Diary (April 8, 1942), 246.

10. Robert E. Sherwood, *Roosevelt and Hopkins: An Intimate History* (New York: Enigma Books, 1948, 2008), 408–9; Memo, March 25, 1942, PDDE, 1:205–7; Forrest C. Pogue, *George C. Marshall: Ordeal and Hope* (New York: Viking, 1965), 305–6; Stimson Diary (March 25, 1942), 417.

11. FDR to WSC, April 1 and 3, 1942, Lowenstein et al., *Correspondence*, 200, 202.

12. Sherwood, *Roosevelt and Hopkins*, 407–8.

13. The estimates are from a report by Richmond Kelly Turner to the CCS, May 12, 1942, ComUSNavEu, Subject File, RG 313, box 9, NA. The Marshall quotation is from GCM to FDR, May 4, 1942, PDDE, 1:280.

14. DDE to Sommerville, April 10, 1942, PDDE, 1:240; CCS minutes, April 28, 1942, ComUSNavEu, Subject Files, RG 313, box 9, NA.

15. Marshall, *Interviews and Reminiscences* (October 5, 1956), 587. The "senior British officer" was Hastings "Pug" Ismay, who is quoted in Pogue, *Ordeal and Hope*, 320.

16. For details of the British planning, see Joseph L. Strange, "Cross Channel Attack, 1942: The British Rejection of Operation SLEDGEHAMMER and the Cherbourg Alternative," Ph.D. dissertation, University of Maryland, 1984, 146–210.

17. Brooke Diary (April 9 and 15, 1942), 246, 249.

18. GCM to FDR, May 4, 1942, PDDE, 1:280–81.

19. Brooke Diary (April 9, 1942), 246.

20. Ibid. (April 10, 1942), 287.

21. Ibid. (April 13, 14, and 15, 1942), 247–49; GCM to McNarney, April 13, 1942, quoted in Pogue, *Ordeal and Hope*, 318.

22. WSC to FDR, April 17, 1942, Lowenstein et al., *Correspondence*, 206–7; Brooke Diary (May 27, 1942), 261. See also Arthur Bryant, *The Turn of the Tide* (Garden City, NY: Doubleday, 1957), 287.

23. FDR to WSC, April 22, 1942, Lowenstein et al., *Correspondence*, 209.

24. Eisenhower, Notes for Diary, May 5, 1942, PDDE, 1:282.

25. "Memorandum of Conference Held at the White House," May 30, 1942, in FRUS (1942), 3:575–77.

26. Marshall's remarks are from notes taken by Hopkins and are printed in Sherwood, *Roosevelt and Hopkins*, 442. Italics added here to Roosevelt's comment.

27. "Memorandum of Conference," May 30, 1942, FRUS (1942), 3:578–83.

28. Sherwood, *Roosevelt and Hopkins*, 454; Winston S. Churchill, *The Hinge of Fate* (Boston: Houghton Mifflin, 1950), 341–42.

29. FDR to WSC, May 31, 1942, Lowenstein et al., *Correspondence*, 218.

30. Pogue, *Ordeal and Hope*, 312; Albert C. Wedemeyer, *Wedemeyer Reports!* (New York: Henry Holt, 1958), 109.

31. Mountbatten's report on the conversation is printed in Sherwood, *Roosevelt and Hopkins*, 458–59; WSC to FDR, June 13, 1942, Lowenstein et al., *Correspondence*, 220.

32. Churchill, *Hinge of Fate*, 377.

33. Marshall's mood is from Stimson Diary (July 10, 1942), 424. Other quotations are from CCS minutes, June 19 and 20, 1942, FRUS (Special Conferences Series), 1:422–26, 429–31, and from "Informal Meeting of Military Leaders," June 19, 1941, in Ibid., 1:426–28.

34. CCS minutes, June 20, 1942, FRUS (Special Conference Series), 1:430; Eisenhower notes, June 19, 1492 [*sic*], PDDE, 1:346–47; Thomas B. Buell, *Master of Sea Power: A Biography of Fleet Admiral Ernest J. King* (Boston: Little, Brown, 1995), 223.

35. Churchill, *Hinge of Fate*, 379, 381–82.

36. Ibid., 382.

37. Ibid., 382–83.

38. Pogue, *Ordeal and Hope*, 333.

39. Brooke Diary (June 21, 1942), 268.

40. Memorandum, June 21, 1942, FRUS (Special Conferences Series), 1:434–35; Churchill, *Hinge of Fate*, 385–86.

41. Churchill, *Hinge of Fate*, 386.

42. Marshall conceding the impracticality of Sledgehammer is in the CCS minutes for June 10, 1942, ComUSNavEu, Subject File, RG 313, box 9, NA; Churchill's letter to Roosevelt, July 8, 1942, is in Lowenstein et al., *Correspondence*, 222.

43. Stimson Diary (July 10, 1942), 424; Pogue, *Ordeal and Hope*, 340. See also David L. Roll, *The Hopkins Touch: Harry Hopkins and the Forging of the Alliance to Defeat Hitler* (New York: Oxford, 2013), 207–9.

44. Marshall, *Interviews and Reminiscences*, 593 (October 5, 1956); FDR to Hopkins, Marshall, and King, July 16, 1942, in Sherwood, *Roosevelt and Hopkins*, 471–73.

45. Roll, *The Hopkins Touch*, 215.

46. Sherwood, *Roosevelt and Hopkins*, 476.

47. Roll, *The Hopkins Touch*, 217–18; Maurice Matloff and Edwin M. Snell, *Strategic Planning for Coalition Warfare* (Washington, DC: Department of the Army, 1953), 278; Samuel Eliot Morison, *Operations in North African Waters* (New York: Little, Brown, 1947), 15.

48. Roll, *The Hopkins Touch*, 218; Churchill's astonishment is in DDE to GCM, September 21,1942, PDDE, 1:570. His comments to Stalin are in Churchill, *Hinge of Fate*, 478–83. FDR is quoted in Matloff and Snell, *Strategic Planning*, 282.

49. DDE to Ismay, August 4, 1942, PDDE, 1:441; Matloff and Snell, *Strategic Planning*, 283.

Chapter 4: The Mediterranean Tar Baby

1. DDE to GCM, June 26, July 29, and August 17, 1942, PDDE, 1:359–61, 425, 476. Eisenhower's memorandum is dated July 17, 1942, and is in PDDE, 1:378–91. The quotation is from 189.
2. On Eisenhower, see Stephen E. Ambrose, *Eisenhower: Soldier and President* (New York: Simon and Schuster, 1990), esp. 63–82, and Carlo D'Este, *Eisenhower, A Soldier's Life* (New York: Henry Holt, 2002). For a more intimate assessment see John S. D. Eisenhower, *General Ike: A Personal Reminiscence* (New York: Free Press, 2003). It was Rear Admiral Morton Deyo who opined that Eisenhower's smile was worth "twenty divisions." The quotation is from Stephen Ambrose, *D-Day: June 6, 1944, The Climactic Battle of World War II* (New York: Simon & Schuster, 1994), 128. The Eisenhower quotation is from DDE, Notes for Diary, February 23, 1942, PDDE, 1:129.
3. Mark W. Clark, *Calculated Risk* (New York: Harper & Brothers, 1950), 65; DDE to GCM, August 17, 1942, and DDE to Hartle, Clark, and Lee, August 25, 1942, both in PDDE, 1:496–97 (italics in original); Ambrose, *Eisenhower*, 76.
4. For a discussion of the political factors in North Africa, a useful source is Francois Kersaudy, *Churchill and De Gaulle* (London: Collins, 1981). See also D'Este, *Eisenhower*, 343ff.
5. Maurice Matloff and Edwin M. Snell, *Strategic Planning for Coalition Warfare, 1941–1942* (Washington, DC: Office of the Chief of Military History, 1953), 285–86. The Roosevelt quotation is from Robert E. Sherwood, *Roosevelt and Hopkins: An Intimate History* (New York: Enigma Books, 1948, 2008), 489. See also Clark, *Calculated Risk*, 62; DDE to Harry Butcher, September 2, 1942, and DDE to Thomas T. Handy, September 7, 1942, both in PDDE, 1:546–47, and 2:525.
6. On the Dieppe raid, see Bernard Fergusson, *The Watery Maze: The Story of Combined Operations* (New York: Holt, Rinehart and Winston, 1961), 175–81; Brian Loring Villa, *Unauthorized Action: Mountbatten and the Dieppe Raid* (New York: Oxford University Press, 1989), which is very hard on Mountbatten; and Robin Neillands, *The Dieppe Raid: The Story of the Disastrous 1942 Expedition* (Bloomington: Indiana University Press), 2005). Eisenhower's quotation is from DDE to Harry Butcher, September 2, 1942, PDDE, 1:526.
7. Clark, *Calculated Risk*, 54–55.
8. After the war, Churchill read Butcher's published diary and learned that Ike considered these meetings a burden. Churchill expressed skepticism about that, but even if it were true, he wrote, they were "necessary for the conduct of the war." Winston Churchill, *The Hinge of Fate* (Boston: Houghton Mifflin, 1950), 526–27.
9. Clark, *Calculated Risk*, 45–46. See the Task Organization tables in Samuel Eliot Morison, *Operations in North African Waters, October 1942–June 1943* (Boston: Little, Brown, 1947; reprinted Annapolis, MD: Naval Institute Press, 2010), 36–40. Also DDE to GCM, August 17, 1942, PDDE, 1:477; Fergusson, *The Watery Maze*, 197.
10. George E. Mowry, *Landing Craft and the War Production Board, April 1942 to May 1944* (Historical Reports on War Administration, Special Study No. 11, July 15, 1944), 1–4.

11. Jerry E. Strahan, *Andrew Jackson Higgins and the Boats That Won World War II* (Baton Rouge: Louisiana State University Press, 1994), 76; Maury Klein, *A Call to Arms: Mobilizing America for World War II* (New York: Bloomsbury, 2013), 188–91.

12. Officially, the Navy had thirteen different types of landing ships or landing craft in early 1942, plus a half dozen tracked amphibious vessels and other specialized landing craft. By the end of the war, the Allies would have forty-six different types of landing ships or landing craft. See Mowry, *Landing Craft and the War Production Board*, 5 (also Appendix C, 72–73); Strahan, *Andrew Jackson Higgins*, 57–58, 64; Morison, *Operations in North African Waters*, 29.

13. Strahan, *Andrew Jackson Higgins*, 89.

14. Morison, *Operations in North African Waters*, 137.

15. DDE to GCM, August 24, and September 21, 1942, PDDE, 1:492, 570; L. S. O. Playfair and C. J. C. Molony, *The Mediterranean and Middle East*, vol. 4 of *History of the Second World War* (London: Her Majesty's Stationery Office, 1966), 127. See the Task Organization Table on 139.

16. DDE to Thomas T. Handy, September 7, 1942, PDDE, 1:546.

17. Dwight D. Eisenhower, *Crusade in Europe* (Baltimore: Johns Hopkins University Press, 1997), 106; DDE Notes, November 8, 1942, PDDE, 2:675.

18. Patton to Beatrice Patton, August 11, 1943, in Martin Blumenson, ed., *The Patton Papers* (Boston: Houghton Mifflin, 1974), 2:320. See also William B. Breuer, *Operation Torch: The Allied Gamble to Invade North Africa* (New York: St. Martin's Press, 1985), 32–33.

19. Hewitt to C in C, Atlantic, November 28, 1942, BAOR (Mss 416), box 3, USNA; Playfair and Molony, *The Mediterranean and Middle East*, 130; H. Kent Hewitt, *The Memoirs of H. Kent Hewitt*, ed. Evelyn M. Cherpak (Newport, RI: Naval War College Press, 2004), 149–50; Morison, *Operations in North African Waters*, 43–45.

20. Morison, *Operations in North African Waters*, 48.

21. Breuer, *Operation Torch*, 82–84; Leslie W. Bailey, *Through Hell and High Water: The Wartime Memories of a Junior Combat Infantry Officer* (New York: Vantage Press, 1994), 11–12.

22. Hewitt, *Memoirs*, 159; Clark, *Calculated Risk*, 67–89.

23. Morison, *Operations in North African Waters*, 74.

24. H. Kent Hewitt, "TORCH Operation Comments and Recommendations," December 22, 1942, BAOR (Mss 416), box 4, USNA.

25. Playfair and Molony, *The Mediterranean and Middle East*, 130; Orr Kelly, *Meeting the Fox: The Allied Invasion of Africa from Operation Torch to Kasserine Pass to Victory in Tunisia* (New York: John Wiley & Sons, 2002), 55.

26. Kelly, *Meeting the Fox*, 69–70; Bailey, *Through Hell and High Water*, 45–50.

27. Kelly, *Meeting the Fox*, 75.

28. Hewitt to C in C Atlantic, November 28, 1942, BAOR (Mss 416), box 3 (hereafter Hewitt Report).

29. Morison, *Operations in North African Waters*, 84.

30. Hewitt Report.

31. Morison, *Operations in North African Waters*, 63, 65, 79; Hewitt Report.

32. Hewitt Report, 12; Morison, *Operations in North African Waters*, 123.
33. DesRon 19 to C in C, Atlantic, November 20, 1944, BAOR (Mss 416), box 3, USNA.
34. Morison, *Operations in North African Waters*, 144–48.
35. DDE to Walter Bedell Smith, November 10, 1942, and to WSC, December 5, 1942, both in PDDE, 2:686, 801; DDE Memorandum, November 22, 1942, PDDE, 2:761. The historian is George F. Howe, *Northwest Africa: Seizing the Initiative in the West* (Washington, DC: Office of the Chief of Military History, 1957), 3.
36. DDE to GCM, November 17, 1942, and DDE to Thomas T. Handy, December 7, 1942, both in PDDE, 2:729–32, 812.
37. DDE to GCM, November 9, 1942, PDDE, 2:680.
38. For a vivid narrative account of American soldiers in the North African campaign, see Rick Atkinson, *An Army at Dawn: The War in North Africa, 1942–1943* (New York: Henry Holt, 2002). The casualty figures are from Atkinson, 536–37.
39. Quoted in Atkinson, *An Army at Dawn*, 535.

Chapter 5: Casablanca to COSSAC

1. Cabinet Meeting Minutes, January 7, 1943, and January 14, 1943, both in FRUS (Special Conferences Series), 1:509; Gordon A. Harrison, *European Theater of Operations: Cross Channel Attack* (Washington, DC: Office of the Chief of Military History, 1951), 39–40.
2. WSC to FDR, November 25, 1942, FDR to WSC, December 2, 1942, and WSC to FDR December 3, 1942, all in FRUS (Special Conferences Series), 1:488–90, 494–95, 496.
3. Robert E. Sherwood, *Roosevelt and Hopkins: An Intimate History* (New York: Harper, 1948; reprinted, Enigma Books, 2008), 522–25; David Roll, *The Hopkins Touch* (New York: Oxford University Press, 2012), 244–47.
4. "Proceedings of the Conference," January 14, 1943, FRUS (Special Conferences Series), 1:538–41; Brooke Diary (entry of January 14, 1943), 358–59.
5. Patton to Handy, January 31, 1943, and GCM to Andrew Bruce, January 30, 1943, both in PGCM, 3:520–21, 521n; Alexander to Brooke, April 3, 1944, *Memoirs of Field Marshal Viscount Montgomery*, 185.
6. Eisenhower's estimate regarding landing craft is from CCS Minutes, January 16, 1942; the GCM quotation is from FDR conference with JCS, January 7, 1942, both in FRUS (Special Conferences Series), 1:582, 510.
7. Brooke Diary (January 15 and 16, 1943), 359, 360.
8. CCS Minutes, January 16, 1943, FRUS (Special Conferences Series), 1: 581–91.
9. See, for example, WSC to War Cabinet, January 20, 1943, in Winston Churchill, *The Hinge of Fate* (Boston: Houghton Mifflin, 1950), 683.
10. Brooke Diary (January 17 and 18, 1943, plus subsequent commentary), 361–62; GCM to FDR, February 20, 1943, PGCM, 3:557. The final agreement is in Minutes of CCS Meeting including FDR and WSC, January 18, 1943, in FRUS (Special Conferences Series), 1:598, 628.
11. Albert C. Wedemeyer, *Wedemeyer Reports!* (New York: Henry Holt, 1958), 211.

12. Minutes of CCS meetings, January 18, 21, and 22, 1943, FRUS (Special Conferences Series), 1:634, 678, 689.

13. Quoted in William H. McNeill, *America, Britain and Russia: Their Cooperation and Conflict, 1941–1946* (New York: Johnson Reprint, 1970), 275.

14. Sherwood, *Roosevelt and Hopkins*, 543; FDR and JCS minutes, January 7, 1943, FRUS (Special Conferences Series), 1:506. Churchill later claimed that he had been surprised by Roosevelt's comment, but the record shows that they had discussed it days earlier, and Churchill himself used the term in a report to the War Cabinet four days before. The only surprise was that Churchill did not know that Roosevelt would announce it at that particular press conference. See Churchill, *The Hinge of Fate*, 684.

15. Morgan's orders, dated April 26, 1943, are in FRUS (Special Conferences Series), 3:287. Operation FORTITUDE included sending as many as 6,000 bogus Army messages and 4,000 bogus Navy messages per day. COMNAVEU (Stark) to CNO (King), April 3, 1944, ComUSNavEu, Subject File, RG 313, box 16, NA.

16. See Frederick C. Morgan, *Overture to Overlord* (Garden City, NY: Doubleday, 1950); Harrison, *European Theater of Operations*, 48.

17. Roger Heskith, *Fortitude: The D-Day Deception Campaign* (Woodstock, NY: Overlook Press, 2000), 1–3; Joshua Levine, *Operation Fortitude: The Story of the Spy Operation That Saved D-Day* (London: Collins, 2011), 193–95. Rieve's war diary is in National Archives Microfilm Publication T-1022, *Records of the German Navy, 1850–1945*, received from the Naval Historical Division, roll 4302, record item PG 38467. I am indebted to Tim Mulligan of the National Archives for bringing this source to my attention.

18. Morgan, *Overture to Overlord*, 57.

19. Ibid., 86–87.

20. Ibid., 132–42.

21. Ibid., 128.

22. CCS Minutes, May 12, 1943, FRUS (Special Conferences Series), 3:25.

23. William D. Leahy, *I Was There: The Personal Story of the Chief of Staff to Presidents Roosevelt and Truman Based on His Notes and Diaries Made at the Time* (New York: Whittlesey House, 1950), 157; Wedemeyer, *Wedemeyer Reports!*, 215–16.

24. Churchill, *The Hinge of Fate*, 785; CCS Minutes, May 12, 1943, FRUS (Special Conferences Series), 3:30, 32.

25. Churchill, *The Hinge of Fate*, 794, 795–96.

26. The American briefing paper is in FRUS (Special Conferences Series), 3:222–24; the CSS Minutes of May 13 and 14, in which the brief is discussed, are on 41–44, 53–54. The numbers are from Maurice Matloff, *Strategic Planning for Coalition Warfare, 1943–1944* (Washington, DC: Office of the Chief of Military History, 1959), 45–46.

27. DDE to GCM, March 12 and May 25, 1943, both in PDDE, 2:1033, 1156; Samuel E. Morison, *The Two-Ocean War* (Boston: Little, Brown, 1963), 245; Frederick C. Lane, *Ships for Victory: A History of Shipbuilding Under the U.S. Maritime Commission in World War II* (Baltimore: Johns Hopkins University Press, 1951), 144. The Bulgarian request is from notes Hopkins took at a CCS meeting on March 27, 1943, quoted in Sherwood, *Roosevelt and Hopkins*, 560.

28. CCS Minutes, May 21, 1943, FRUS (Special Conference Series), 3:348.

29. Ibid.

30. "Draft of Agreed Decisions," May 21, 1943, FRUS (Special Conferences Series), 3:348; Churchill, *The Hinge of Fate*, 810–11; Dwight D. Eisenhower, *Crusade in Europe* (Garden City, NY: Doubleday, 1949), 167; Harry C. Butcher, *My Three Years with Eisenhower: The Personal Diary of Captain Harry C. Butcher, USNA* (New York: Simon & Schuster, 1946), entries of May 29 and 30, 1943, 315–18 (hereafter Butcher Diary); GCM to DDE, April 19, 1943, and DDE to GCM, April 27, 1943, both in PGCM, 3:664–65.

31. Butcher Diary (July 11, 1943), 355.

32. Minutes, CCS Meeting, May 25, 1943, FRUS (Special Conference Series), 3:287; FDR-WSC Press Conference, May 25, 1943, ibid., 3:216.

33. Morgan, *Overture to Overlord*, 137, 97. The quip is quoted in Michael Harrison, *Mulberry: The Return in Triumph* (London: W. H. Allen, 1965), 89.

34. Morgan, *Overture to Overlord*, 137–42.

35. Morgan's preliminary report is in Morgan, *Overture to Overlord*, 148–50. The final report, dated July 15, 1943, is in FRUS (Special Conferences Series), 3:488–96. Quotations are from 493, 496.

36. Morgan, *Overture to Overlord*, 71, 161 ff.

37. Ibid., 161–62.

38. Arthur Bryant, *The Turn of the Tide: A History of the War Years Based on the Diaries of Field-Marshal Lord Alanbrooke, Chief of the Imperial General Staff* (Garden City, NY: Doubleday, 1957), 577–80; William D. Leahy, *I Was There: The Personal Story of the Chief of Staff to Presidents Roosevelt and Truman Based on His Notes and Diaries* (New York: Whittlesey House, 1950), 17 (entry of August 14, 1943).

39. Brooke Diary (August 15, 1943, and subsequent commentary), 441–42.

40. Ibid. (August 19, 1943), 444.

41. Ibid. (August 19, 1943, and subsequent commentary), 444–46. This story is told with particular vividness by Michael Harrington in *Mulberry: The Return in Triumph* (London: W. H. Allen, 1965), 143–45.

42. Winston S. Churchill, *Closing the Ring* (Boston: Houghton Mifflin, 1951), 84; Morgan, *Overture to Overlord*, 165.

Chapter 6: Brits and Yanks

1. Norman Longmate, *The G.I.'s: The Americans in Britain, 1942–1945* (London: Hutchinson, 1975), xiii.

2. David Reynolds, *Rich Relations: The American Occupation of Britain, 1942–1945* (New York: Random House, 1995), 242–43; Longmate, *The G.I.'s*, 42–52; Donald O. Good Oral History, NMPW, 3.

3. John L. Horton, "Getting the Troops 'Over There,'" in Paul Stillwell, ed., *Assault on Normandy: First Person Accounts from the Sea Services* (Annapolis, MD: Naval Institute Press, 1994), 131–32; Gene Jaeger, *Flat-Bottom Odyssey: From North Africa to D-Day* (Henry, IL: Prairie Ocean Press, 2010), 64.

4. Longmate, *The G.I.'s*, 48.

5. Carleton F. Bryant, "Battleship Commander," in Stillwell, ed., *Assault on Normandy*, 182; Kenneth Newberg Oral History, NWWIIM-EC, 3.

6. Reynolds, *Rich Relations*, 174–75; Norman Longmate, *The Home Front: An Anthology of Personal Experience, 1938–1945* (London: Chatto & Windus, 1981), 171.

7. Longmate, *The G.I.'s*, 1–2.

8. Reynolds, *Rich Relations*, 49.

9. Longmate, *The G.I.'s*, 57; Reynolds, *Rich Relations*, 49; Walter Martini Oral History, NWWIIM-EC, 4–5.

10. Longmate, *The G.I.'s*, 70, 242–46.

11. A particularly devastating portrait of Lee is in Duncan Anderson, "'Remember This Is an Invasion': Planning and Buildup," in Jane Penrose, ed., *The D-Day Companion* (New Orleans: D-Day Museum, 2003), 40–42. Eisenhower's letter of caution is DDE to J. C. H. Lee, March 22, 1944, PDDE, 3:1788. See also Reynolds, *Rich Relations*, 105.

12. Anderson, "Remember This Is an Invasion," in Penrose, *D-Day Companion*, 45; Frederick Morgan, *Overture to Overlord* (Garden City, NY, 1950), 75.

13. Longmate, *The G.I.'s*, 39, 60.

14. Reynolds, *Rich Relations*, 278–79.

15. Ibid., 197; Longmate, *The G.I.'s*, 38–39. The story of billeting "Jones and Smith" is from Sidney Salomon, in D. M. Giangreco with Kathryn Moore, *Eyewitness D-Day* (New York: Barnes & Noble Books, 2004), 39. "A great treat" is from Robert H. Miller Oral History, NWWIIM-EC, 2.

16. Angus Calder, *The People's War: Britain, 1939–45* (London: Jonathan Cape, 1969), 308.

17. Stark to U.S. Naval Forces Europe, September 16, 1943, ComUSNavEu, Subject File, RG 313, box 18, NA; Reynolds, *Rich Relations*, 148–49; Roy Carter Oral History, USNA, 21.

18. Longmate, *The G.I.'s*, 218–24.

19. The quotation is from A. V. Dicey, British constitutional scholar, quoted in Reynolds, *Rich Relations*, 145–46.

20. DDE to R. L. Hartle, August 15, 1942, PDDE, 1:497; Calder, *The People's War*, 309–10; Longmate, *The G.I.'s*, 62; Frederick Morgan, *Overture to Overlord* (Garden City, NY: Doubleday, 1950), 125.

21. Calder, *The People's War*, 321–22; Brenda Devereux is quoted in Longmate, *The Home Front*, 172; Cornelius A. Burke, "Liberty Ship Signalman," in Stillwell, ed., *Assault on Normandy*, 143.

22. Eden and Adams are both quoted in Reynolds, *Rich Relations*, 187, 167. American authorities, including Generals Jacob Devers and Ira Eaker, protested that none of this was true. They made every effort, they insisted, to encourage fraternization. Nevertheless, in the wake of Eden's letter, they established a Special Committee on "Anglo-American Relations."

23. DDE to J. C. H. Lee, September 5, 1942, PDDE, 1:544. Later in the war, when Ike returned as SHAEF, he issued another even more pointed notice: "Equal opportunities of service and of recreation are the right of every American soldier regardless of branch, race, color, or creed." Eisenhower ordered this to be read aloud to all enlisted men. DDE to J. C. H. Lee, February 26, 1944, PDDE, 3:1750.

24. Quoted in Reynolds, *Rich Relations*, 303, 322. This story appears in a number of sources, but significantly, a Devon resident told it to me when I was a visiting professor at the British Naval Academy at Dartmouth in 1994.

25. Graham Smith, *When Jim Crow Met John Bull: Black American Soldiers in World War II Britain* (New York: St. Martin's Press, 1987).

26. First quotation: COMNAVEU (Stark) to COMINCH (King), June 18, 1943; second quotation: "Naval Assault Forces for Operation OVERLORD," June 15, 1943, both in ComUSNavEu, Subject File, RG 313, box 16 and box 20, NA.

27. Longmate, *The G.I.'s*, 290; Reynolds, *Rich Relations*, 125, 135.

28. Paul S. Fauks, "My Only Job Was to Stay Alive," in Stillwell, ed, *Assault on Normandy*, 79; LT Howard Vander Beek, in Edward F. Prados, ed., *Neptunus Rex: Naval Stories of the Normandy Invasion, June 6, 1944* (Novato, CA: Presidio Press, 1998), 130.

29. Longmate, *The G.I.'s*, 292.

30. Nigel Lewis, *Exercise Tiger: The Dramatic True Story of a Hidden Tragedy of World War II* (New York: Prentice Hall, 1990), 14–15; Longmate, *The G.I.'s*, 295.

31. Longmate, *The G.I.'s*, 290; Reynolds, *Rich Relations*, 112.

32. Morgan and Churchill are quoted in Gordon A. Harrison, *The European Theater of Operations: Cross-Channel Attack* (Washington, DC: Office of the Chief of Military History, 1951), 111, 109.

33. The "very senior" British officer was Admiral Sir Bertram Ramsay, who will be introduced in Chapter 8. See W. S. Chalmers, *Full Cycle: The Biography of Admiral Sir Bertram Home Ramsay* (London: Hodder & Stoughton, 1959), 137.

34. Morgan, *Overture to Overlord*, 75.

35. James E. Arnold, "NOIC Utah," in Stillwell, ed., *Assault on Normandy*, 86.

36. Stimson to FDR, August 10, 1943, FRUS (Special Conferences Series), 3:496–97; Note by the British Chiefs of Staff, November 25, 1943, FRUS (Special Conferences Series), 2:409.

Chapter 7: "Some God-Dammed Things Called LSTs"

1. Brooke's statement is in Cabinet Meeting Minutes, January 7, 1943, FRUS (Special Conferences Series), 1:509. See also Frederic C. Lane, *Ships for Victory: A History of Shipbuilding Under the U.S. Maritime Commission in World War II* (Baltimore: Johns Hopkins University Press, 1951), 12–13.

2. Knox to Stimson, February 8, 1943, PGCM, 3:535n; Minutes of White House Conference, June 23, 1943, FRUS (Special Conferences Series), 1:441.

3. Lewis W. Douglas in Minutes, White House Conference, June 23, 1942, FRUS (Special Conferences Series), 3:441; Knox to Stark, August 29, 1942, ComUSNavEu, Subject File, RG 313, box 24, NA.

4. CCS Minutes, September 18, 1942, ComUSNavEu, Subject File, RG 313, box 9, NA.

5. Lane, *Ships for Victory*, 650.

6. The various landing craft types and their acronyms are listed in *ONI 226—Allied Landing Craft and Ships* (Washington, DC: Office of Naval Intelligence, 1944).

7. U.S. Navy, *"Skill in the Surf": A Landing Boat Manual* (February 1945), 9–10. Available at www.history.navy.mil/library/online/surfskill.htm.

8. Ibid., 13.

9. William T. O'Neill Oral History, NWWIIM-EC, 10–11.

10. The authority is Gordon L. Rottman in *Landing Ship Tank (LST), 1942–2002* (Westminster, MD: Osprey, 2005), 18.

11. Ralph A. Crenshaw Oral History, NWWIIM-EC, 3; Walter Trombold, "Civilians in Uniform," in Paul Stilwell, ed., *Assault on Normandy: First-Person Accounts from the Sea Services* (Annapolis, MD: Naval Institute Press, 1994), 154–57; Vernon L. Paul Oral History, NWWIIM-EC, 6.

12. Clendell Williams, *Echoes of Freedom: Builders of LST's, 1942–1945* (Kearney, NE: Morris, 2011), 19; Edward F. Prados, *Neptunus Rex: Naval Stories of the Normandy Invasion, June 6, 1944* (Novato, CA: Presidio Press, 1998), 79; Roy Carter Oral History, USNA, 6–8.

13. VCNO to Com 8th Naval District, September 29, 1943, ComUSNavEu, Subject File, RG 313, box 18, NA; George T. Foy Oral History, NMPW, 13–15; Roy Carter Oral History, USNA, 6–8.

14. Gene Jaeger, *Flat-Bottom Odyssey: From North Africa to D-Day* (Henry, IL: Prairie Ocean Press, 2010), 16; Reed Dunn, "War Stories," in LCI(L) 335 file, LCI Association Collection, NMPW, series A, box 2, 21–22.

15. Phil Goulding, "Address to LCI Association," April 13, 1996, LCI(L) 506 file, LCI Association Collection, NMPW, series B, box 11, 25.

16. Don Wolfe, *USS LST 655: A Ship's History, 1944–1946* (Sonora, CA: Don Wolfe, 2002), 41; Jaeger, *Flat-Bottom Odyssey*, 54.

17. Wolfe, *USS LST 655: A Ship's History, 1944–1946*; Trombold, "Civilians in Uniform," in Stillwell, ed., *Assault on Normandy*, 161.

18. Gordon Rottman, *Landing Ship Tank (LST), 1942–2002* (Oxford: Osprey, 2005), 10.

19. Jaeger, *Flat-Bottom Odyssey*, 73. For details about the operation of LSTs, I am grateful to Otis Bingemer, former crewmember of LST-235 and a veteran of Operation Neptune, who gave me a tour of his ship at Evansville, Indiana, where it was built.

20. Stimson to FDR, March 27, 1942, in Henry L. Stimson with McGeorge Bundy, *On Active Service in Peace and War* (New York: Harper & Brothers, 1947), 417–18; CCS Minutes, April 28, 1942, and June 2, 1942, both in ComUSNavEu, Subject File, RG 313, box 9, NA.

21. Lane, *Ships for Victory*, 610; George Elsey, "Strategy and Security," in Stillwell, ed., *Assault on Normandy*, 14; CCS Minutes, September 18, October 2, and November 6, 1942, ComUSNavEu, Subject File, RG 313, folder 9, NA; George E. Mowry, *Landing Craft and the War Production Board, April 1942 to May 1944* (Washington, DC: War Production Board, 1946), 11–13, 21–22, 34. See also the list of "Shipyards Participating in LST and Destroyer Escort Production," in Mowry, *Landing Craft*, 75.

22. CCS Minutes, June 16, 1942, ComUSNavEu, Subject File, RG 313, box 9, NA; Knox to FDR, October 19, 1942, ibid., box 24; Mowry, *Landing Craft and the War Production Board*, 34.

23. Mowry, *Landing Craft and the War Production Board*, 27–29, 34, 40, 58; Frederick C. Morgan, *Overture to Overlord* (Garden City, NY: Doubleday, 1950), 170. Morgan does not name the person with whom he had this conversation, only that it

was one who "should know," but internal and circumstantial evidence suggests it was Nelson.

24. Lane, *Ships for Victory*, 183–84, 311.

25. Ibid., 144, 149; Mowry, *Landing Craft and the War Production Board*, 14–15, 17.

26. Williams, *Echoes of Freedom*, 24.

27. Ibid., 37.

28. Lane, *Ships for Victory*, 183–94.

29. Prados, ed., *Neptunus Rex*, 79; Mowry, *Landing Craft and the War Production Board*, 30.

30. DDE to CCS, October 31 and November 4, 1943, PDDE, 3:1545, 1549. See also DDE to GCM, December 25, 1943, PDDE, 3:1614.

31. McCarthy to Thackery, October 29, 1943, ANCXF Papers, Subject File, box 6, folder 4, NA; WSC to COS, December 25, 1943, in Winston S. Churchill, *Closing the Ring* (Boston: Houghton Mifflin, 1951), 431–32.

32. King to Stark, May 9, 1944, and Sextant to Agwar, December 1, 1943, both in ComUSNavEu, Subject File, RG 313, box 16, NA; Churchill to Brooke, December 19, 1943, in Churchill, *Closing the Ring*, 429.

33. Brynes to FDR, November 24 and November 27, 1943, FRUS (Special Conferences Series), 2:395–97, 444; Knox to Stark, April 14, 1944, ComUSNavEu, Subject File, RG 313, box 24, NA. Italics added.

34. Moses D. Manning Jr. Oral History (p. 2), and Ralph A. Crenshaw Oral History (p. 3), both in NWWIIM-EC.

35. Gordon A. Harrison, *The United States Army in World War II: The European Theater of Operations, Cross-Channel Attack* (Washington, DC: Department of the Army, 1951), 64.

36. FDR to Pershing, September 20, 1943, PGCM, 4:129n; Frederick Morgan, *Overture to Overlord* (Garden City, NY: Doubleday, 1950), 169.

37. Stimson to FDR, August 10, 1943, FRUS (Special Conferences Series) 3:497.

38. Arnold to Handy, September 29, 1943, PGCM, 4:178; Robert E. Sherwood, *Roosevelt and Hopkins: An Intimate History* (New York: Enigma Books, 1948, 2008), 593–94.

39. GCM, Memorandum for JCS, November 5, 1943, PGCM, 4:180–81; Memorandum by the U.S. Chiefs of Staff, November 25, 1943, FRUS (Special Conferences Series), 2:405.

40. Marshall to Sherwood, February 25, 1947, PGCM, 4:195.

41. Minutes, November 28, FRUS (Special Conferences Series), 2:487, 490, 500.

42. Minutes kept by Chip Bohlen, November 29, 1943, FRUS (Special Conferences Series), 2:534.

43. Ibid., 534–35.

44. The attribution of these views to FDR is derived from Elliott Roosevelt's summary in a conversation with Eisenhower in November. See DDE, Memorandum for Diary, December 6, 1943, PDDE, 3:1586.

45. Dwight D. Eisenhower, *Crusade in Europe* (Garden City, NY: Doubleday, 1949), 207. Roosevelt sent a telegram to Stalin the next day (the second anniversary of Pearl Harbor) to notify him of Eisenhower's appointment. See PDDE, 3:1606n.

Chapter 8: SHAEF and ANCXF

1. DDE, Memorandum for Diary, February 7, 1944, PDDE, 3:1712.

2. DDE to GCM, December 28, 1943, and DDE to Morgan, December 26, 1943, both in PDDE, 3:1627, 1616. Morgan's comment is in Elliott B. Strauss, "Disaster at Dieppe, Success at Normandy," in Paul Stillwell, ed., *Assault on Normandy: First Person Accounts from the Sea Services* (Annapolis, MD: Naval Institute Press, 1994), 12.

3. Martin Blumenson, ed., *The Patton Papers* (Boston: Houghton Mifflin, 1974), 2:237 (diary entry of April 29, 1943); Brooke Diary (entry of December 11, 1943), 496; Bernard Montgomery, *The Memoirs of Field-Marshal the Viscount Montgomery of Alamein* (London: Collins, 1958), 198–99.

4. DDE to GCM, December 31, 1943, March 3 and March 21, 1944, all in PDDE, 3:1648–49, 1758–59, 1781–82.

5. W. S. Chalmers, *Full Cycle: The Biography of Admiral Sir Bertram Home Ramsay* (London: Hodder & Stoughton, 1959), 21, 29.

6. Ibid., 50, 134–36.

7. Ramsay Diary (February 22, 1944), 30.

8. Montgomery, *Memoirs*, 213; Ramsay to his wife, January 1944, in Chambers, *Full Cycle*, 187; Ramsay Diary (January 14, 1944), 7–8.

9. Montgomery subsequently asserted in his memoirs that the expansion of the assault force from three divisions to five was his idea, and that he had to persuade Eisenhower to do it. Some historians have taken this seriously, but as Ike wrote in a letter to Marshall: "About the end of December... I had General Montgomery come to see me and General [Beetle] Smith and told him to go to England... to seek for an intensification of effort to increase the troop lift in OVERLORD." Thus when Monty insisted on an enlargement of the landing front at a meeting at St. Paul's School on January 3, 1944, it was in fulfillment of Ike's orders. See DDE to GCM, February 8, 1944, PDDE, 3:1713–14; Montgomery, *Memoirs*, 210.

10. Gordon A. Harrison, *The European Theater of Operations: Cross-Channel Attack* (Washington, DC: Office of the Chief of Military History, 1951), 123–25.

11. Ramsay Diary (January 18 and 20), 10–11.

12. Chambers, *Full Cycle*, 191; DDE to CCS, January 23, 1944, PDDE, 3:1673–75.

13. JCS to DDE, January 25, 1944, PDDE, 3:1691–92n. King's concerns are in Harrison, *The European Theater of Operations*, 127; Ramsay's annoyance is in Ramsay Diary (January 26, 1944), 15.

14. The "Loading Tables, South West Coast," for October 12, 1943, are in ANCXF Papers, Subject File, box 6, folder 3, NA; DDE to JCS, January 27, 1944, PDDE, 3:1688–91; DDE to JCS, March 9, 1944, PDDE, 3:1763.

15. Harrison, *The European Theater of Operations*, 170; DDE to GCM, February 6, 1944, PDDE, 3:1707; Ramsay Diary (February 2, 1944), 19.

16. Ramsay Diary (February 5, 1944), 20.

17. DDE, Memorandum for Diary, February 7, 1944, PDDE, 3:1711–12.

18. Brooke Diary (March 29, 1944), 535. The proposal to swap LSTs from the Med is in DDE to British COS, February 18, 1944, PDDE, 3:1732, and GCM to DDE, March 25, 1944, PGCM, 4:374–75. Ike's note to Marshall is in DDE to GCM, February 14, 1944, PDDE, 3:1725.

19. Brooke Diary (March 17, 1944), 532.
20. Ramsay Diary (February 29 and March 6), 35, 39; Brooke Diary (April 1 and January 24, 1944), 537, 516.
21. DDE to JCS, March 9, 1944, PDDE, 1763–64; DDE to GCM, March 20 and March 21, 1944, and DDE, Memorandum for Diary, March 22, 1944, all in PDDE, 3:1775, 1777, 1783. Marshall's letter to DDE, dated March 25, is in PGCM, 4:374–75.
22. Brooke Diary (April 19, 1944), 541; Ramsay Diary (March 25, 1944), 48.
23. Montgomery discusses his travels in his *Memoirs*, 223–24, 227, 231. The story of the beret is in Anthony Beevor, *D-Day: The Battle for Normandy* (New York: Penguin, 2009), 6.
24. Montgomery, *Memoirs*, 225–26; Ramsay Diary (February 17, 1944), 28. Italics in original.
25. Ramsay Diary (January 1, 1944), 1.
26. Philip Vian, *Action This Day: A War Memoir* (London: Frederick Muller, 1960), 124–25.
27. Ibid., 126–27.
28. Ramsay Diary (March 3, 1944), 37.
29. Kirk's orders to command the Western Task Force are in COMINCH to COMNAVEU, October 13, 1943, ComUSNavEu, RG 313, box 16, NA; Alan G. Kirk Oral History, Columbia University, 233–34, 251.
30. Alan G. Kirk Oral History, Columbia University, 252–53.
31. Ibid., 261, 296. Italics in original.
32. The undated letter of Ramsay to Kirk is in W. S. Chambers, *Full Cycle*, 197.
33. Alan G. Kirk Oral History, Columbia University, 248.
34. Ramsay Diary (January 21, 1944), 12.
35. Admiralty to COMINCH, April 27, 1944, ComUSNavEu, Subject file, RG 313, box 16, NA; Ramsay Diary (March 7, 1944), 39.
36. Ramsay Diary (January, 21, 1944), 12; DDE to GCM, March 20, 1944, PDDE, 3:1773–74; John Lesslie Hall Jr. Oral History, Columbia University, 177–78.
37. Bernhard Bieri Oral History, USNI, 143–45.
38. COMNAVEU (Stark) to CNO (King), April 17, 1944, ComUSNavEu, Message File, RG 313, box 13, NA.

Chapter 9: Duck, Fox, Beaver, Tiger

1. Gene Jaeger, *Flat-Bottomed Odyssey: From North Africa to D-Day* (Henry, IL: Prairie Ocean Press, 2010), 104–5.
2. Edwin Gale Oral History, NWWIIM-EC, 2–3.
3. Ibid.; George Goodspeed Oral History, NWWIIM-EC, n.p.
4. Kenneth Edwards, *Operation Neptune: The Normandy Landings, 1944* (Fonthill Media, 2013), 84.
5. William E. Heavy, *Down Ramp! The Story of the Army Amphibious Engineers* (Washington, DC: Infantry Journal Press, 1947), 22.
6. Nigel Lewis, *Exercise Tiger: The Dramatic True Story of a Hidden Tragedy of World War II* (New York: Prentice Hall, 1990), 20–22.

7. William T. O'Neill Oral History, NWWIIM-EC, 12; Training Schedule of "U.S. Naval Advanced Amphibious Training Base, Appledore," General File 2002.570, NWWIIM-EC; Dean Rockwell Oral History, and Ralph A. Crenshaw Oral History (p. 5), both in NWWIIM-EC.

8. William Steel Oral History, NWWIIM-EC, 8.

9. "Procedure for Marrying LCT(5) and LCT(6) to LST," George Keleher File, NWWIIM-EC.

10. Don Irwin, "The U.S. LCT 614 Following D-Day at Omaha Beach, Normandy," in Don Irwin File, NWWIIM-EC, 7–8.

11. Ibid.

12. Wallace Bishop Oral History, NWWIIM-EC, 3.

13. Kenneth C. Newberg Oral History (p. 8), and Donald W. Nutley Oral History (p. 2), both in NWWIIM-EC.

14. U.S. Naval Academy *Lucky Bag* (1913), 92; John Lesslie Hall Jr. Oral History, Columbia University, 10, 177.

15. Ramsay Diary (March 10, 1944), 41; John Lesslie Hall Jr. Oral History, Columbia University, 164. See also Susan Godson, *Viking of Assault: Admiral John Lesslie Hall, Jr., and Amphibious Warfare* (Washington, DC: University Press of America, 1982), 121.

16. Kirk to King, February 5, 1944, ComUSNavEu, Subject File, RG 313, box 16, NA; Ramsay Diary (March 8, 1944), 40; U.S. Naval Academy *Lucky Bag* (1916), 113. Moon's daughter remembered that it was a family mantra "to always do one's best." Meredith Moon to the author, May 15, 2013, author's collection. Long after Moon's death, a trunk containing his old check stubs was discovered in an Annapolis home that was being demolished. It may or may not illustrate Moon's meticulous attention to detail that every cancelled check had been carefully reattached to the stub.

17. John R. Lewis Jr. Oral History, NWWIIM-EC, 3; John A. Moreno, "The Death of Admiral Moon," in Paul Stillwell, ed., *Assault on Normandy: First-Person Accounts from the Sea Services* (Annapolis, MD: Naval Institute Press, 1994), 225; John Lesslie Hall Jr. Oral History, Columbia University, 162. Moreno recalled that Moon and his chief of staff, Captain Rutledge Tomkins, "were not compatible."

18. J. Lawton Collins, *Lightning Joe: An Autobiography* (Baton Rouge: Louisiana State University Press, 1979), 193; John R. Lewis Jr. Oral History, NWWIIM-EC, 3. At the baseball game between British and American sailors, Moon was watching from a distance when an errant ball bounced near him. He ran to it, picked it up, and threw it back into the field of play. The British sailors were stunned that an admiral would condescend so much. No British admiral, they asserted, would do such a thing.

19. See a summary of all the Allied practice landings in www.history.army.mil/documents/WWII/beaches/bchs-7.htm.

20. Ramsay Diary (March 1 and March 10–11, 1944), 36, 40–42.

21. www.history.army.mil/documents/WWII/beaches/bchs-7.htm; Heavy, *Down Ramp!*, 75.

22. Frederick C. Morgan, *Overture to Overlord* (Garden City, NY: Doubleday, 1950), 261.

23. Guy Hartcup, *Code Name Mulberry: The Planning, Building and Operation of the Normandy Harbors* (London: David & Charles, 1977), 18–19; Michael Harrison, *Mulberry: The Return in Triumph* (London: W. H. Allen, 1965), 170.

24. Eisenhower's concerns are in COMNAVEU (Stark) to CNO (King), February 1, 1944, ComUSNavEu, Subject File, RG 313, box 16, NA.

25. Ibid.; Hartcup, *Code Name Mulberry*, 13–27, 95.

26. Alfred Stanford, *Force Mulberry: The Planning and Installation of the Artificial Harbor off U.S. Normandy Beaches in World War II* (New York: William Morrow, 1951), 74; COMINCH to C in C, Atlantic Fleet, October 9, 1943, ComUSNavEu, Subject File, RG 313, box 18; and COMNAVEU to COMINCH, April 12, 1944, ComUS-NavEu, Message File, RG 313, box 13, NA.

27. Ramsay Diary (February 3, 1944), 19; Harrison, *Mulberry*, 14, 82.

28. Harrison, *Mulberry*, 94.

29. For a discussion of Hobart's Funnies, see Richard C. Anderson Jr., *Cracking Hitler's Atlantic Wall: The 1st Assault Brigade Royal Engineers on D-Day* (Mechanicsburg, PA: Stackpole Books, 2010). Dwight D. Eisenhower, *Crusade in Europe* (Garden City, NY: Doubleday, 1949), 236–37; John J. Guilmartin Oral History, NWWIIM-EC, 10.

30. Dean Rockwell, "DD Spelled Disaster," in Stillwell, ed., *Assault on Normandy*, 68–71; Karl D. Everitt Oral History, NWWIIM-EC, 20.

31. Joseph H. Esclavon Oral History, NWWIIM-EC, 2; Ramsay Diary (February 7 and 12, 1944), 22, 25. The story of salvaging the DD tank and the creation of a memorial is in Ken Small, *The Forgotten Dead* (London: Bloomsbury, 1988).

32. Norman Friedman, *U.S. Amphibious Ships and Craft: An Illustrated History* (Annapolis, MD: Naval Institute Press, 2010), 218.

33. Lewis, *Exercise Tiger*, 4.

34. Elliott B. Strauss, "Disaster at Dieppe, Success at Normandy," in Stillwell, ed., *Assault on Normandy*, 12. There is circumstantial evidence that Moon pressed Kirk to do something about the threat from Cherbourg. After the war, both Robert Lewis and Mark Dalton, who served on Moon's staff, remembered Moon's efforts to neutralize the E-boat threat from Cherbourg. It is not clear if Kirk acted in response to this prodding from Moon or on his own. In addition, Strauss identifies the British officer Struble talked to as Vian, but Vian had no authority to draw new command boundaries, and it was very likely Ramsay that Struble talked with. Interview with Meredith Moon, May 3, 2013. See also Alan Kirk Oral History, Columbia University, 290.

35. Lewis, *Exercise Tiger*, 73–74. The "no luck" message is CTF122 to NCWTF, April 24, 1944, ComUSNavEu, Message File, RG 133, box 16, NA.

36. Lewis, *Exercise Tiger*, 74; Edwin Hoyt, *The Invasion Before Normandy* (New York: Stein and Day, 1985), 93.

37. Lewis, *Exercise Tiger*, 66.

38. M. J. Whitley, *German Coastal Forces of World War Two* (London: Arms and Armour, 1992), 23.

39. Lewis, *Exercise Tiger*, 79.

40. Eugene V. Eckstam, "Exercise Tiger," in Stillwell, ed., *Assault on Normandy*, 43.

41. Ibid., 43–44; Lewis, *Exercise Tiger*, 92, 101.

42. Eckstam, "Exercise Tiger," 44; Lewis, *Exercise Tiger*, 90–93.

43. Lewis, *Exercise Tiger*, 101.

44. Ibid., 67.
45. Ibid., 104–5.
46. Robert L. Evans Oral History, NWWIIM-EC, 3–4.
47. The exact number of killed in Exercise Tiger is uncertain. The number given here (639) is from the official Navy report. Once the event became a matter of public discussion, some argued that the actual number was higher. The number engraved on the monument at Slapton Sands is 739. There is a lengthy and thoughtful discussion of this question in Nigel Lewis, *Exercise Tiger*, 219–34.
48. DDE to GCM, April 29, 1944, PDDE, 3:1838–39; Com 12th Fleet (Stark) to COMINCH (King), May 2, 1944, COMINCH to Com 12th Fleet, May 3 and May 4, 1944, and CINCMED (Cunningham) to Admiralty, May 4, 1944, all in ComUS-NavEu, Message File, RG 313, box 13, NA.
49. COMINCH to COMNAVNAW, May 13, 1944, ComUSNavEu, Message File, RG 313, box 13, NA; Alan G. Kirk, "Admiral Ramsay and I," in Stillwell, *Assault on Normandy*, 25; Ramsay Diary (May 7 and 15, 1944), 65, 70.
50. Alan G. Kirk Oral History, Columbia University, 281; Ramsay Diary (May 8, 1944), 65–66.
51. COM 12th Fleet (Stark) to CTF 122 (Kirk), May 1, 1944, ComUSNavEu, Message File, RG 313, box 16, NA.
52. The witness to this confrontation was Moon's Assistant Plans Officer, CDR John Moreno, who recalled it several times, including his essay "The Death of Admiral Moon," in Stillwell, *Assault on Normandy*, 225–30, and in a conversation with Nigel Lewis that is included in *Exercise Tiger*, 127. He offers additional insights in a letter dated October 6, 1984, now in the Meredith Moon Collection, Maui, Hawaii.
53. Ramsay Diary (May 4–5 and 15, 1944), 62–63, 70.
54. Donald Irwin, "The U.S. LCT 614 Following D-Day," in the Donald Irwin File, NWWIIM-EC, 6; William T. O'Neill Oral History (p. 18), and Edwin Gale Oral History (p. 14), both in NWWIIM-EC.
55. Winston Churchill, *Closing the Ring* (Boston: Houghton Mifflin, 1951), 614–15; Eisenhower, *Crusade in Europe*, 245.

Chapter 10: "A Hum Throughout the Country"
1. The diarist is J. L. Hobson, and the Dorset resident was the British pacifist Vera Brittain. Both are quoted in Angus Calder, *The People's War: Britain, 1939–45* (London: Jonathan Cape, 1969), 557, 558. The villagers' reaction is in William G. Bacon in Edward F. Prados, ed., *Neptunus Rex: Naval Stories of the Normandy Invasion, June 6, 1944* (Novato, CA: Presidio Press, 1998), 187.
2. George R. Hackett Oral History, NWWIIM-EC, 5.
3. Western Naval Task Force, Neptune Operation Order No. BB-44, May 20, 1944, John Lesslie Hall Jr. Papers, box 14, folder 1, Swem Library, W&M; Edwin Gale Oral History, NWWIIM-EC, 6.
4. William F. Heavey, *Down Ramp! The Story of the Army Amphibian Engineers* (Washington, DC: Infantry Journal Press, 1947), 74–78; Nelson Dubroc Oral History (p. 2), Orval Wakefield Oral History (p. 4), and Joe G. Smith Oral History (p. 1), all in NWWIIM-EC.

5. Michael Harrison, *Mulberry: The Return in Triumph* (London: W. H. Allen, 1965), 101.

6. Robert H. Miller Oral History (n.p.), Orval Wakefield Oral History (p. 4), and Curtis Hansen Oral History (p. 6), all in NWWIIM-EC.

7. George Goodspeed Oral History, NWWIIM-EC, 4–5; Joel E. Garner and William G. Bacon, in Prados, ed., *Neptunus Rex*, 20, 187; Western Naval Task Force, Neptune Operation Order No. BB-44, May 20, 1944, John Lesslie Hall Jr. Papers, box 14, folder 1, Swem Library, W&M.

8. Harrison, *Mulberry*, 98–100.

9. Calhoun Bond Oral History, NWWIIM-EC, 3.

10. Roy Carter Oral History, USNA, 11; Armond Barth Oral History, NWWIIM-EC, 3.

11. "Suggested Operating Procedures for LCT," Flotilla Nine, in George Keleher File, NWWIIM-EC.

12. Armond J. Barth Oral History, MWWIIM-EC, 1.

13. George Hackett Oral History, NWWIIM-EC, 5.

14. Wallace Bishop Oral History (pp. 2–4) and Donald E. Irwin Oral History (p. 5), both in NWWIIM-EC; Quentin R. Walsh, "The Capture of Cherbourg," in Paul Stilwell, ed., *Assault on Normandy: First-Person Accounts from the Sea Services* (Annapolis, MD: Naval Institute Press, 1994), 195.

15. Logistics Plan for Overlord, May 15, 1944, in John Lesslie Hall Jr. Papers, box 12, Swem Library, W&M.

16. Action Report, USS *Barnett* (APA-5), June 24, 1944, USNA.

17. Vincent del Giudice Oral History, NWWIIM-EC, 3.

18. William T. O'Neill Oral History (p. 14), John O'Rourke Oral History (p. 6), James Watts Oral History (p. 3), James Goodspeed Oral History (pp. 4–5), Calhoun Bond Oral History (pp. 4, 15), and Curtis Hansen Oral History (p. 11), all in NWWIIM-EC.

19. Ted Billnitzer Oral History (p. 3), and Robert H. Miller Oral History (n.p.), both in NWWIIM-EC.

20. Robert L. Evans Oral History, NWWIIM-EC, 6; John D. Bulkeley, "Ike Remembered Me," in Stillwell, *Assault on Normandy*, 51.

21. George VI to Churchill, June 2, 1944, in Winston S. Churchill, *Closing the Ring* (Boston: Houghton Mifflin, 1951), 618–22; Dwight D. Eisenhower, *Crusade in Europe* (Garden City, NY: Doubleday, 1949), 251.

22. Edwin Gale to his father, June 6, 1944, in Edwin Gale File, NWWIIM-EC; Moon to Mrs. (Sybil) Moon, June 2, 1944, Meredith Moon Collection, Maui, Hawaii.

23. Edwin Gale Oral History, NWWIIM-EC, 5.

24. Sunset was recorded in the logs of several ships including USS *Carmick* (DD493), Action Report, June 23, 1944, USNA. The senior officer was Lt. Gen. Lewis Brereton, who is quoted in Joseph Balkoski, *Utah Beach: The Amphibious Landing and Airborne Operations on D-Day, June 6, 1944* (Mechanicsburg, PA: Stackpole Press, 2005), 73.

25. Howard Vander Beek on LCC-60, in Prados, ed., *Neptunus Rex*, 131; Wallace Bishop Oral History, NWWIIM-EC.

26. Carleton F. Bryant, "Battleship Commander," in Stillwell, ed., *Assault on Normandy*, 183; K. L. Dyer, *50 North: An Atlantic Battleground* (London: Eyre & Spottiswoode, 1963), 249.

27. Antony Beevor, *D-Day: The Battle for Normandy* (New York: Penguin, 2009), 11; Carlo D'Este, *Eisenhower: A Soldier's Life* (New York: Henry Holt, 2002), 519–20; Ramsay Diary (June 3, 1944), 81.
28. Stagg offers the best firsthand account of this meeting in *Forecast for Overlord, June 6, 1944* (New York: W. W. Norton, 1971), 100–102. See also Ramsay Diary (June 4, 1944), 82; Bernard Montgomery, *The Memoirs of Field-Marshal the Viscount Montgomery of Alamein* (London: Collins, 1958), diary entries of June 4 and 5, 1944, 248–49; and D'Este, *Eisenhower*, 520–21.
29. Alan G. Kirk Oral History, Columbia University, 311.
30. Ibid.; Morton Deyo, "Naval Guns at Normandy," Personal Papers Collection of Admiral Samuel Eliot Morison, box 87 (p. 26), NHHC.
31. John Lesslie Hall Jr. Oral History, Columbia University, 179.
32. William T. O'Neill Oral History, NWWIIM-EC, 17.
33. James E. Arnold, "NOIC Utah," in Stillwell, ed., *Assault on Normandy*, 86.
34. Edwin Gale Oral History (p. 6), and Dean Rockwell Oral History (p. 8), both in NWWIIM-EC.
35. Howard Vander Beek, in Prados, ed., *Neptunus Rex*, 131; Richard G. Laine Jr. Oral History (p. 4), and August Leo Thomas Oral History (p. 3), both in NWWIIM-EC; William G. Bacon, in Prados, ed., *Neptunus Rex*, 187.
36. Robert L. Evans Oral History, NWWIIM-EC.
37. Harry C. Butcher, *My Three Years with Eisenhower: The Personal Diary of Captain Harry C. Butcher* (New York: Simon & Schuster, 1946), 562.
38. D'Este, *Eisenhower*, 522–24.
39. The "concern" is from Ramsay's Diary (June 5 and 6, 1944), 82, 83. See also Gordon A. Harrison, *Cross-Channel Attack* (Washington, DC: Department of the Army, 1951), 273–74. D'Este discusses the various iterations of this subsequently famous phrase in footnote 38, p. 782, of his biography of Eisenhower.
40. Butcher, *My Three Years with Eisenhower*, 561.

Chapter 11: D-Day: The Invasion
1. COMNAVEU to COMNAVNAW, May 19, 1944, ComUSNavEu, Message File, RG 313, box 13, NA; Ramsay Diary (March 24, 1944), 47–48.
2. Tamara M. Melia, *"Damn the Torpedoes": A Short History of U.S. Naval Mine Countermeasures* (Washington, DC: Naval Historical Center, 1991), 55–58; "Intelligence Bulletin Number 2," Naval Commander, Western Task Force (Kirk), May 29, 1944, NWWIIM-EC.
3. John D. Bulkeley, "Ike Remembered Me," and John R. Blackstone, "The Best Seat for a Really Big Show," both in Paul Stillwell, ed., *Assault on Normandy: First Person Accounts from the Sea Services* (Annapolis, MD: Naval Institute Press, 1994), 52, 100; COMNAVEU (Stark) to ANCXF (Ramsay), May 13, 1944, COMNAVEU, Message File, RG 313, box 13, NA.
4. Ship's log of Minelayer 137, printed in Brendan A. Maher, *A Passage to Sword Beach: Minesweeping in the Royal Navy* (Annapolis, MD: Naval Institute Press, 1996), 114–15. Captain Rhea's testimonial is from the *Nevada*'s Action Report, June 23, 1944, USNA. See also Kenneth Edwards, *Operation Neptune: The Normandy Landings, 1944* (Fonthill Media, 2013), 110–13.

5. Philip Vian, *Action This Day: A War Memoir* (London: Frederick Muller, 1960), 135; R. G. Watts, personal memoir, available at www.bbc.uk/history/ww2peopleswar/stories.

6. George Hackett Oral History (p. 5), and Edwin Gale Oral History (p. 7), both in NWWIIM-EC.

7. Martin Waarvick Oral History (p. 4), Wallace Bishop Oral History (p. 3–4), and William T. O'Neill Oral History (p. 18), all in NWWIIM-EC; Arthur Struble Oral History, USNI, 166; Alan G. Kirk Oral History, Columbia University, 315.

8. The text of Eisenhower's broadcast is in PDDE, 3:1913. The story of men singing on Moon's flagship is in John R. Lewis Oral History, NWWIIM-EC, 4.

9. Dean Rockwell Oral History, NWWIIM-EC, 10.

10. The quotation is from Curtis Hansen Oral History, NWWIIM-EC, 6. The numbers are from various sources including Max Hastings, *Overlord: D-Day and the Battle for Normandy* (New York: Simon & Schuster, 1984), 348.

11. Jacob Brouwer, in Prados, ed., *Neptunus Rex*, 100; Action Report, USS *Laffey* (DD-724), June 27, 1944, USNA.

12. George Hackett Oral History, NWWIIM-EC, 6, 8; Action Report, USS *Ancon* (Hall's flagship), June 21, 1944, USNA.

13. Curtis Hansen Oral History, NWWIIM-EC, 6; Bush, *Bless Our Ship*, 256; James E. Arnold, "NOIC Utah," in Stillwell, ed., *Assault on Normandy*, 87; Vian, *Action This Day*, 137.

14. James E. Arnold, "NOIC Utah," in Stillwell, ed., *Assault on Normandy*, 87; James Jones to his father, June 27, 1944, in Prados, ed., *Neptunus Rex*, 63; John Kepchar, *Keppy's War: A Memoir of World War II* (Bloomington, IN: Xlibris, 2005), 69.

15. Quoted in Paul Carell, *Invasion! They're Coming* (New York: E. P. Dutton, 1963), 78.

16. George Elsey, "Strategy and Secrecy," in Paul Stillwell, ed., *Assault on Normandy: First-Person Accounts from the Sea Services* (Annapolis, MD: Naval Institute Press, 1994), 17; Morrison, *The Invasion of France and Germany*, 33.

17. Kepchar, *Keppy's War*, 69; George W. Goodspeed Oral History, NWWIIM-EC, 7–8; William B. Kirkland Jr., *Destroyers at Normandy: Naval Gunfire Support at Omaha Beach* (Washington, DC: Naval Historical Foundation, 1994), 22; Thomas B. Allen, "Gallant Destroyers on D-Day," *Naval History* (June 2004), 18–23.

18. The phrase is borrowed from the title of Cornelius Ryan's classic book, *The Longest Day, June 6, 1944* (New York: Simon and Schuster, 1959).

19. Morison, *The Invasion of France and Germany*, 33; Joseph Balkoski, *Omaha Beach, June 6, 1944* (Mechanicsburg, PA: Stackpole Books, 2004), 124.

20. Neptune Operation Order No. BB-44, May 20, 1944, Papers of John Lesslie Hall Jr., box 14, folder 1, Swem Library, W&M; Balkoski, *Omaha Beach*, 98, 102.

21. Handwritten report of Ensign Albert Pelligrini to Rockwell, n.d., in Rockwell file, NWWIIM-EC.

22. Neptune Operation Order BB-44, May 20, 1944, John Lesslie Hall Jr. Papers, box 14, folder 1, Swem Library, W&M; Dean Rockwell Oral History, NWWIIM-EC, 12.

23. Pellegrini to Rockwell, n.d., in Rockwell File, NWWIIM-EC; Rockwell Oral History, NWWIIM-EC, 13.

24. Hall to King, July 27, 1944, John Lesslie Hall Jr. Papers, box 1, folder 5, Swem Library, W&M; Sullivan to Rockwell, June 15, 1944, in Rockwell file, NWWIIM-EC; Richard H. Crook Jr., "Traffic Cop," in Paul Stillwell, *Assault on Normandy*, 66.

25. Action Report, LCT Group 35, July 14, 1944, USNA; Staff Sergeant Paul Ragan, quoted in Balkoski, *Omaha Beach*, 103; Joseph Esclavon Oral History, NWWIIM-EC, 11; McKee to Rockwell, July 20, 1944, and Rockwell to Steven Ambrose, November 23, 1944, in Rockwell file, NWWIIM-EC.

26. Morison, *The Invasion of France and Germany*, 100.

27. Philip Vian, *Action This Day*, 141; Rockwell Oral History, NWWIIM-EC, 13. Rockwell later claimed that his was the first landing craft to touch Omaha Beach, which is possible, but several others claimed the same distinction and in the confusion of the morning, it is impossible to know for certain.

28. Wallace Bishop Oral History, NWWIIM-EC, 13–16.

29. DDE to WSC, May 2, 1944, PDDE, 3:1842; Balkoski, *Omaha Beach*, 78.

30. Balkoski, *Omaha Beach*, 85–89; and Joseph Balkoski, *Utah Beach, June 6, 1944* (Mechanicsburg, PA: Stackpole Books, 2005), 87–89.

31. Morton Deyo, "Naval Guns at Normandy," in Personal Papers of Samuel Eliot Morison, box 87 (p. 18), NHHC. See also Adrian Lewis in *Omaha Beach: Flawed Victory* (Chapel Hill: University of North Carolina Press, 2001).

32. NCWTF (Kirk) to COM O (Hall) and COM U (Moon), April 21, 1944, ComUS-NavEu, Message File, RG 313, box 13, NA; Boatswain's Mate Joel Garner, in Edward F. Prados, ed., *Neptunus Rex: Naval Stories of the Normandy Invasion, June 6, 1944* (Novato, CA: Presidio Press, 1998), 20–21, 24.

33. Deyo, "Naval Guns at Normandy," 37.

34. Ibid., 36.

35. Executive Officer's Report, U.S. *Nevada*, June 23, 1944, Action Reports, USNA; Millard Cloutman, in Prados, ed., *Neptunus Rex*, 32; August Leo Thomas Oral History, NWWIIM-EC, 3; Kepchar, *Keppy's War*, 70.

36. Donald Irwin Oral History, NWWIIM-EC, 5; Balkoski quoting Ensign Victor Hicken and Associated Press reporter Don Whitehead in *Omaha Beach*, 83.

37. Rick Atkinson, *Guns at Last Light: The War in Western Europe, 1944–1945* (New York: Henry Holt, 2013), 57.

38. Vian, *Action This Day*, 138; Yves Buffetout, *D-Day Ships: The Allied Invasion Fleet, June, 1944* (London: Conway, 1994), 114–16; John McClelland Oral History, NMWWI-EC, 5.

39. Winston S. Churchill, *Closing the Ring* (Boston: Houghton Mifflin, 1951), 618–22.

40. Deyo, "Naval Guns at Normandy," NHHC, 24; Dorr Hampton Oral History, NWWIIM-EC; Buffetaut, *D-Day Ships*, 82–84.

41. Supplement to Action Report, USS *Tuscaloosa*, July 18, 1944, USNA.

42. Executive Officer's Report, USS *Nevada*, June 23, 1944, Action Reports, USNA; Action Report, USS *Doyle*, June 8, 1944, USNA.

43. Kirkland, *Destroyers at Normandy*, 34.

44. Balkoski, *Omaha Beach*, 86; Action Report, USS *Carmick*, June 23, 1944, USNA.

45. Balkoski, *Utah Beach*, 89–91.

46. Action Reports of USS *Carmick* (DD-493), June 23, 1944; USS *Emmons* (DD-457), June 22, 1944; and USS *Doyle* (DD494), June 8, 1944, all USNA.

47. W. N. Solkin Oral History, NWWIIM-EC, 3.

Chapter 12: D-Day: The Beaches

1. Neptune Operation Order No. BB-44, May 20, 1944, John Lesslie Hall Jr. Papers, box 14, folder 1, Swem Library, W&M; Samuel Eliot Morison, *The Invasion of France and Germany* (Boston: Little, Brown, 1957), 131.

2. George W. Goodspeed Oral History (pp. 7–8); and Joseph H. Esclavon Oral History (p. 22), both in NWWIIM-EC.

3. Joseph H. Esclavon Oral History (p. 14), and Edwin Gale Oral History (p. 11), both in NWWIIM-EC.

4. Brendan A. Maher, *A Passage to Sword Beach: Minesweeping in the Royal Navy* (Annapolis, MD: Naval Institute, 1996), 113; Edwin Gale Oral History, NWWIIM-EC, 11.

5. James E. Arnold, "NOIC Utah," in Paul Stillwell, ed., *Assault on Normandy: First Person Accounts from the Sea Services* (Annapolis, MD: Naval Institute Press, 1994), 90. See also Joseph Balkoski, *Utah Beach, June 6, 1944* (Mechanicsburg, PA: Stackpole Books, 2005), 194.

6. Ken Ford and Steven J. Zaloga, *Overlord: The D-Day Landings* (Oxford: Osprey, 2009), 54–59, 334.

7. The reluctant volunteer was Richard Coombs, quoted in D. M. Giangreco with Kathryn Moore, *Eyewitness D-Day* (New York: Barnes & Noble Books, 2004), 22.

8. Ibid., 67; Nelson Dubroc Oral History, NWWIIM-EC, 2.

9. Robert H. Miller Oral History (n.p.), Nelson Dubroc Oral History (pp. 2–3), and Orval Wakefield Oral History (p. 4), all in NMWWII-EC.

10. Nelson Dubroc Oral History (pp. 2–3), and Orval Wakefield Oral History (p. 5), both in NWWIIM-EC; Ford and Zaloga, *Overlord: The D-Day Landings*, 79–18; Hall to King, July 27, 1944 (p. 8), John Lesslie Hall Jr. Papers, box 1, folder 5, Swem Library, W&M.

11. Action Report, USS *Thurston* (AP-77), June 19, 1944, USNA. Two of the five boats abandoned after the first wave were later recovered and returned to service.

12. Karl D. Everitt Oral History (pp. 11–12) and George T. Poe Oral History (p. 3), both in NWWIIM-EC.

13. Hall to King, July 27, 1944, John Lesslie Hall Jr. Papers, box 1, folder 5, Swem Library, W&M; Phil Goulding, "Address to LCT Association," April 13, 1996, LCI Association Collection, LCI(L) 506 file, both in Series B, box 11, NMPW.

14. William T. O'Neill Oral History, NWWIIM-EC, 23–24.

15. Ibid., 25, 27, 31.

16. Joel G. Smith Oral History, NWWIIM-EC.

17. Donald Irwin, "The U.S. LCT 614 Following D-Day at Omaha Beach," in the Donald Irwin file, NWWIIM-EC, 7–8.

18. Horace G. "Skip" Shaw Oral History (p. 5) and George Goodspeed Oral History (p. 10–11), both in NWWIIM-EC.

19. Seth Shepherd, "The Story of the LCI(L) 92 in the Invasion of Normandy," LCI Association Collection, LCI(L) 92 folder, Series B, box 10, NMPW.

20. Report of LT(jg) Vyn to SECNAV, June 19, 1944, LCI Association Collection, LCI(L) 91 file, Series B, box 10, NMPW.

21. Annex to Operation Order No. 2-44, in Action Report, USS *Thurston*, June 19, 1944, USNA; Report of LT(jg) Vyn, June 19, 1944, LCI Association Collection, LCI(L) 91 file, Series B, box 10, NMPW.

22. Seth Shepherd, "The Story of the LCI(L) 92 in the Invasion of Normandy," LCI Association Collection, LCI(L) 92 file, Series B, box 10, NMPW; William C. Bacon, "Omaha's Wrath," in Prados, ed., *Neptunus Rex*, 189.

23. Action Report of LCI(L) 489, June 20, 1944, LCI Association Collection, Series B, boxes 10 and 11; Hall to King, July 27, 1944, John Lesslie Hall Jr. Papers, box 1, Folder 5, Swem Library, W&M; Chief Yeoman William G. Bacon, "Omaha's Wrath," in Prados, ed., *Neptunus Rex*, 190; Lorenzo S. Sabin, "Close In Support on Omaha Beach," in Stillwell, ed., *Assault on Normandy*, 59–60.

24. Ken Ford and Steven J. Zaloga, *Overlord: The D-Day Landings* (Oxford: Osprey, 2009), 232–53.

25. Ibid., 244–45.

26. Ibid., 247–57; Paul Carrell, *Invasion! They're Coming* (New York: E. P. Dutton, 1963), 85, 101.

27. Harry C. Butcher, *The Personal Diary of Captain Harry C. Butcher, USNR* (New York: Simon & Schuster, 1946), 566–67; DDE to GCM, June 6, 1944, PDDE, 3: 1914–15.

28. Max Hastings, *Winston's War: Churchill, 1940–1945* (New York: Knopf, 2010), 393–94; Winston Churchill, *Triumph and Tragedy* (Boston: Houghton Mifflin, 1953), 5.

29. Doris Kearns Goodwin, *No Ordinary Time: Franklin and Eleanor Roosevelt: The Home Front in World War II* (New York: Simon & Schuster, 1994), 505–6.

30. "Joint Agreement Between Commanding General First U.S. Army and Commander Task Force 122 for Amphibious Operations," John Lesslie Hall Jr. Papers, box 12, folder 10, Swem Library, W&M.

31. Jacob Brouwer, in Prados, *Neptunus Rex*, 102; Alan G. Kirk Oral History, Columbia University, 292, 329; Omar Bradley, *A General's Life* (New York: Simon & Schuster, 1983), 251.

32. James E. Arnold, "NOIC Utah," in Paul Stillwell, *Assault on Normandy*, 91.

33. Talley is quoted by Max Hastings in *Overlord: D-Day and the Battle for Normandy* (New York: Simon & Schuster, 1984), 92.

34. John Lesslie Hall Jr. Oral History, Columbia University, 199–200.

35. Lorenzo Sabin, "Close-In Support on Omaha Beach," in Stillwell, ed., *Assault on Normandy*, 61.

36. John Lesslie Hall Jr. Oral History, Columbia University, 200.

37. Paul Longrigg Oral History, NWWIIM-EC, 18.

38. Alan G. Kirk, "Admiral Ramsay and I," in Stillwell, ed., *Assault on Normandy*, 25–26; Kirk Oral History, Columbia University, 329–30; Ramsay Diary (June 6, 1944), 84.

39. Bradley, *A General's Life*, 251.

Chapter 13: D-Day: The Crisis

1. Alan G. Kirk, "Admiral Ramsay and I," in Paul Stillwell, ed., *Assault on Normandy: First Person Accounts from the Sea Services* (Annapolis, MD: Naval Institute Press, 1994), 25. Bryant's statement was overheard by Cecil Carnes, a reporter from the *Saturday Evening Post* who was on the bridge and subsequently quoted it in a postwar story. It is quoted as well by Samuel Eliot Morison in *The Invasion of France and Germany, 1944–1945* (Boston: Little, Brown, 1957), 143.

2. Robert Miller Oral History, NWWIM-EC.

3. Richard H. Crook Jr., "Traffic Cop," in Stillwell, ed., *Assault on Normandy*, 67; Gordon Gaskill, "Bloody Beach," *American Magazine*, September 1944, 101. See also William B. Kirkland Jr., *Destroyers at Normandy: Naval Gunfire Support at Omaha Beach* (Washington, DC: Naval History Division, 1994); Morison, *The Invasion of France and German*, 142–49; and Theodore Roscoe, *United States Destroyer Operations in World War II* (Annapolis, MD: Naval Institute, 1953), 347–51. Water depth is estimated by Alfred Stanford in *Force Mulberry: The Planning and Installation of the Artificial Harbor off U.S. Normandy Beaches in World War II* (New York: William Morrow, 1951), 66.

4. William Steel Oral History, NWWIIM-EC, 7–8.

5. Leonard G. Lornell, quoted in D. M. Giangreco with Kathryn Moore, *Eyewitness D-Day* (New York: Barnes & Noble, 2004), 100–104.

6. COMDESDIV 36 Action Report, in Kirkland, *Destroyers at Normandy*, 28; Ken Ford and Steven J. Zaloga, *Overlord: The D-Day Landings* (Oxford: Osprey, 2009), 95–104; Action Reports, USS *Thompson*, June 21, 1944, and USS *Ellyson* June 26, 1944, both USNA.

7. Joseph H. Esclavon Oral History, NWWIIM-EC, 19; Action Reports of the USS *Frankford*, June 24, 1944, USS *Carmick*, June 23, 1944, and USS *Doyle*, June 8, 1944, all in USNA.

8. U.S. Naval Academy *Lucky Bag* (1932), USNA; Action Report, USS *Carmick*, June 23, 1944, USNA.

9. U.S. Naval Academy *Lucky Bag* (1935), USNA; Action Report, USS *McCook*, June 27, 1944, USNA.

10. Action Reports, USS *Doyle*, June 8, 1944, and USS *Thompson*, June 21, 1944, both USNA; U.S. Naval Academy *Lucky Bag* (1934), USNA.

11. Kirkland, *Destroyers at Normandy*, 54; Joseph H. Esclavon Oral History, NWWIIM-EC, 22.

12. George Bauernschmidt Oral History (p. 152), and Joel G. Smith Oral History (p. B), both in NWWIIM-EC; Paul Carell, *Invasion! They're Coming* (New York: E. P. Dutton, 1963), 86.

13. Action Report, LCI(L) 408, June 16, 1944, LCI(L) 408 file, LCI Association Collection, Series B, box 11, NMPW; Action Reports of USS *Emmons*, June 22, 1944, *McCook*, June 27, 1944, and *Carmick*, June 23, 1944, all USNA; NCWTF (Kirk) to CTF 124, 125, etc., June 9, 1944, ANCFX Files, box 6, folder 4, NA; Felix C. Podolak Oral History, NWWIIM-EC, 8. See also Morison, *Invasion of France and Germany*, 142–49.

14. Morton Deyo, "Naval Guns at Normandy," Personal Papers Collection of Admiral Samuel Eliot Morison, box 87 (p. 42), NHHC; Howard Anderson in Prados, ed., *Neptunus Rex*, 53; Action Report, USS *Baldwin*, June 22, 1944, USNA.

15. Action Reports, USS *Ellyson*, June 26, 1944, and USS *Laffey*, June 27, 1944, both USNA.
16. Action Report, USS *Frankford*, June 24, 1944, USNA; Curtis Hansen Oral History, NWWIIM-EC, 11; Bryant, "Battleship Commander," in Stillwell, ed., *Assault on Normandy*, 184; James Jones to his father, June 27, 1944, in Pardos, ed., *Neptunus Rex*, 65.
17. Action Report, USS *Frankford*, June 24, 1944, USNA; Morison, *Invasion of France and Germany*, 150; Bradley, *A Soldier's Life*, 251.
18. Rick Atkinson, *Guns at Last Light* (New York: Henry Holt, 2013), 73. Taylor's statement is often attributed to Cota, as it is in the film *The Longest Day*.
19. Karl Everitt Oral History, NWWIIM-EC, 13; Adrian Lewis, *Omaha Beach: Flawed Victory* (Chapel Hill: University of North Carolina Press, 2001), 25.
20. Action Report, USS *Carmick*, June 23, 1944, USNA. Bingham later attributed the supporting fire to tanks of the 743rd Battalion, which, he said, "saved the day."
21. Robert Giguere Oral History, NWWIM-EC, 5. Giguere received both the Silver Star and the Croix de Guerre for his actions on Omaha Beach.
22. Karl Everitt Oral History, NWWIIM-EC, 13–14.
23. Ford and Zaloga, *Overlord*, 108–11; Morison, *The Invasion of France and Germany*, 150.
24. Hall to King, July 27, 1944, John Lesslie Hall Jr. Papers, box 1, folder 5 (pp. 9–10), Swem Library, W&M; Atkinson, *Guns at Last Light*, 128; Curtis Hansen Oral History, NWWIIM-EC, 11–12.
25. Hall to King, July 27, 1944, John Lesslie Hall Jr. Papers, box 1, folder 5 (p. 10), Swem Library, W&M.
26. Robert L. Evans Oral History (p. 10) and Clifford H. Sinnett Oral History (p. 14), both in NWWIM-EC.
27. Ibid.; Jackson Hoffler, in Prados, ed., *Neptunus Rex*, 168.
28. Lewis, *Omaha Beach*, 4; Morison, *The Invasion of France and Germany*, 152; U.S. War Dept., *Omaha Beachhead* (Washington, DC: War Department Historical Division, 1945), 109.
29. Philip Vian, *Action This Day: A War Memoir* (London: Frederick Muller, 1960), 139–40. The E-boat threat was all but eliminated by an Allied air assault on Le Havre on June 14 that virtually wiped out the German *Schnellboote* squadrons.

Chapter 14: "The Shoreline Was Just a Shambles"
1. Neptune Operation Order No. BB-44, May 20, 1944, copy in John Lesslie Hall Jr. Papers, box 1, Swem Library, W&M; Frederick Morgan, *Overture to Overlord* (Garden City, NY: Doubleday, 1950), 154–55.
2. DDE to GCM, February 8, 1944, PDDE, 3:1715.
3. Gordon A. Harrison, *The European Theater of Operations: Cross Channel Attack* (Washington, DC: Office of the Chief of Military History, 1951), 336; Alfred Stanford, *Force Mulberry: The Planning and Installation of the Artificial Harbor off U.S. Normandy Beaches in World War II* (New York: William Morrow, 1951), 66; Hall to King (Action Report), July 27, 1944, John Lesslie Hall Jr. Papers, box 1, Swem Library, W&M (hereafter Hall Action Report).
4. Hall Action Report, 12–13; Bauernschmidt Oral History, USNI, 148; Calhoun Bond Oral History, NWWIIM-EC, 7. Ramsay is quoted in Samuel E. Morison, *The Invasion of France and Germany, 1944–1945* (Boston: Little, Brown, 1957), 165.

5. DDE to CCS, June 8, 1944, PDDE, 3:1916; Hall Action Report, 12; Donald W. Nutley Oral History, NWWIIM-EC, 4.

6. Hall Action Report, 12; Wallace Bishop Oral History, NWWIIM-EC, 9–10.

7. William J. Milne Oral History (p. 4), and Wallace Bishop Oral History (p. 11–13), both NWWIIM-EC.

8. Wallace Bishop Oral History, NWWIIM-EC, 29–31. Bishop was on Rhino 7, which was one of only nine to offload a cargo on D-Day.

9. Russell Weigley, *The American Way of War: A History of United States Military Strategy and Policy* (Bloomington: Indiana University Press, 1973); COMINCH (King) to COMNAVEU (Stark), June 2, 1944, ComUSNavEu, RG 313, box 13, NA.

10. Alan Kirk, "Admiral Ramsay and I," in Paul Stillwell, ed., *Assault on Normandy: First-Person Accounts from the Sea Services* (Annapolis, MD: Naval Institute Press, 1994), 26; Edmond J. Moran Oral History, USNI, 63–66.

11. Paul Longrigg Oral History, NWWIIM-EC, 8–10, 20; Harold J. O'Leary, "A Destroyer Destroyed," Edward F. Prados, ed., *Neptunus Rex: Naval Stories of the Normandy Invasion, June 6, 1944* (Novato, CA: Presidio Press, 1998), 59–60; Theodore Roscoe, *United States Destroyer Operations in World War II* (Annapolis, MD: Naval Institute Press, 1953), 352–54.

12. Action Report, USS *Ancon*, June 21, 1944, USNA: William F. Heavy, *Down Ramp! The Story of the Army Amphibious Engineers* (Washington, DC: Infantry Journal Press, 1947), 83; Carleton Bryant, "Battleship Commander," in Stillwell, ed., *Assault on Normandy*, 184; Ferris Burke Oral History (p. 2), and Calhoun Bond Oral History (p. 6), both in NWWIIM-EC.

13. John R. Lewis Jr. Oral History, NWWIIM-EC, 6; Louis Putnoky to Meredith Moon, June 17, 2013, Meredith Moon Collection.

14. Hall Action Report, 12–13; Action Report, USS *Jeffers* (DD-621), Exec's Report, June 22, 1944, USNA.

15. Tonnage figures are from Stanford, *Force Mulberry*, Appendix Five, p. 229. LCTs seeking dry loads is from George Hackett Oral History, NWWIIM-EC, 12.

16. Richard G. "Jack" Laine Jr. Oral History, NWWIIM-EC, 5–6.

17. Donald Irwin, "The LCT 614," in Donald Irwin file, NWWIIM-EC, 17.

18. Ibid., 18–19.

19. Karl Everitt Oral History, NWWIIM-EC, 15.

20. George Goodspeed Oral History, NWWIIM-EC, 13.

21. Ibid., 14, and George Hackett Oral History (pp. 8–9), both NWWIIM-EC.

22. Roy Carter Oral History, USNA, 13; Robert T. Robertson Oral History, NWWIIM-EC, 9. The story of the wayward LCI is in Morison, *The Invasion of France and Germany*, 188.

23. Hall to Kirk, July 9, 1944, "Record of Unloading," in John Lesslie Hall Jr. Papers, box 1, Swem Library, W&M.

24. David R. Minard, "The Death of the 'Susie Bee,'" in Prados, ed., *Neptunus Rex*, 241; William T. O'Neill Oral History, NWWIIM-EC, 33; Orwin C. Talboll, "Shipwrecked in the Channel," in Stillwell, ed., *Assault on Normandy*, 119–22.

25. Howard Vander Beek, "Guiding Light," in Prados, *Neptunus Rex*, 145.

26. Stanford, *Force Mulberry*, 114.

27. John Lesslie Hall Jr. Oral History, Columbia University, 154; Stanford, *Force Mulberry*, 90-91, 97; SHAEF (Eisenhower) to COMNAVEU (Stark), May 3, 1944, ComUSNavEu, Message file, RG 313, box 13, NA.

28. Guy Hartcup, *Code Name Mulberry: The Planning, Building and Operation of the Normandy Harbors* (New York: Hippocrene Books, 1977), 99-100.

29. Ellsberg, "Mulberries and Gooseberries," in Stillwell, ed., *Assault on Normandy*, 172.

30. Hartcup, *Code Name Mulberry*, 111; George Goodspeed Oral History, NWWIIM-EC, 12.

31. Stanford, *Force Mulberry*, 160-61.

32. Ibid., 89, 110.

33. Ibid., 172-74. The daily tonnage numbers are from Hall to Kirk, July 9, 1944, "Record of Unloading," in John Lesslie Hall Jr. Papers, box 1, Swem Library, W&M. The total numbers vary slightly from source to source, but all agree that the number of American and British or Canadian soldiers was almost exactly even: 314,514 Americans and 314,547 British and Canadians. The Americans landed more tons of supplies (116,000 to 102,000), while the British landed more vehicles (54,000 to 41,000). These numbers are from Gordon A. Harrison, *Cross Channel Attack* (Washington, DC: Office of the Chief of Military History, 1951), 423, who took them from the SHAEF report of June 20. See also Hartcup, *Code Name Mulberry*, 122, who offers slightly different totals, but the same general ratios.

34. George Goodspeed Oral History, NWWIIM-EC, 16-17.

35. Stanford, *Force Mulberry*, 181; Edward Ellsberg, "Mulberries and Gooseberries," in Stillwell, ed., *Assault on Normandy*, 173.

36. Edward Ellsberg, "Mulberries and Gooseberries," in Stillwell, *Assault on Normandy*, 173-74, 177; Ferris Burke Oral History, NWWIIM-EC, 3.

37. Clifford H. Sinnett Oral History, NWWIIM-EC, 19-20. Italics added.

38. Stanford, *Force Mulberry*, 181, 188, 193-94.

39. Alan G. Kirk Oral History, Columbia University, 346; Arthur Struble Oral History, USNI, 146; Hall Action Report, 17.

40. Stanford, *Force Mulberry*, 197.

41. Alan G. Kirk Oral History, Columbia University, 346; Hall Action Report; NCWTF (Kirk) to ANCXF (Ramsay), June 22, 1944, ANCXF Papers, Subject File, box 6, folder 4, NA. No less an authority than Samuel Eliot Morison has written that "the 'Mulberries'…were absolutely essential for the success of Operation Overlord" (from Morison's introduction to Stanford's *Force Mulberry*), a view followed by many historians since. In asserting that, Morison may have sought to validate the enormous sacrifices the Allies made to sustain the project, for in the end, the artificial harbors added relatively little to the Allied logistical effort.

42. Ramsay's suggestion is in a handwritten note in staff meeting minutes, January 11, 1944, in Office of ANCXF, ComUSNavEu, Subject File, RG 313, box 6, folder 1, NA.

43. Leo H. Scheer, "Salve and Salvoes," in Prados, ed., *Neptunus Rex*, 210-14.

44. William J. Milne Oral History (p. 5), and Wallace Bishop Oral History (p. 13), both NWWIIM-EC.

45. William Bacon, "Omaha's Wrath," in Prados, ed., *Neptunus Rex*, 196; Calhoun Bond Oral History (p. 13), and Ferris Burke Oral History (p. 3), both in NWWIIM-EC.

46. Roy Carter Oral History, USNA, 11; Walter Trombold, "Civilians in Uniform," in Stillwell, ed., *Assault on Normandy*, 162; Vincent del Guidice Oral History, NWWIIM-EC, 10–11.
47. William DeFrates, "Let's Get On with It," in Prados, ed., *Neptunus Rex*, 202–3.
48. Vernon L. Paul Oral History, NWWIIM-EC, 18; Leo Scheer, "Salve and Salvoes," in Prados, ed., *Neptunus Rex*, 214.
49. Ralph A. Crenshaw Oral History, NWWIIM-EC, 9.
50. John J. Guilmartin Oral History (p. 10), and Paul Longrigg Oral History (p. 33), both in NWWIIM-EC.
51. The diary entries are from Kenneth C. Newberg Oral History, NWWIIM-EC, 21.

Chapter 15: "A Field of Ruins"

1. Frederick Morgan, *Overture to Overlord* (Garden City, NY: Doubleday, 1950), 144.
2. DDE to CCS, June 8, 1944, PDDE, 3:1915–1917; Ken Ford and Steven J. Zaloga, *Overlord: The D-Day Landings* (Oxford: Osprey, 2009), 171–72.
3. Samuel Eliot Morison, *The Invasion of France and Germany, 1944–1945* (Boston: Little, Brown, 1957), 156–59; Hall to King, Action Report, July 27, 1944, John Lesslie Hall Jr. Papers, box 1, Swem Library, W&M, 14.
4. Russell Weigley, *Eisenhower and His Lieutenants: The Campaign of France and Germany, 1944–1945* (Bloomington: Indiana University Press, 1981), 98–100; Gordon A. Harrison, *The European Theater of Operations: Cross Channel Attack* (Washington, DC: Office of the Chief of Military History, 1951), 416–22; Quentin Walsh, "The Capture of Cherbourg," in Paul Stillwell, ed., *Assault on Normandy: First Person Accounts from the Sea Services* (Annapolis, MD: Naval Institute Press, 1994), 197.
5. Harrison, *Cross Channel Attack*, 408–22. The quotation is on 411.
6. Weigley, *Eisenhower and His Lieutenants*, 103–5; J. Lawton Collins, *Lightning Joe: An Autobiography* (Baton Rouge: Louisiana State University Press, 1979), 218–19; Ford and Zaloga, *Overlord*, 189. Von Schlieben is quoted in Paul Carell, *Invasion! They're Coming* (New York: E. P. Dutton, 1963), 91.
7. Hitler is quoted in Harrison, *Cross Channel Attack*, 430.
8. Alan G. Kirk, "Admiral Ramsay and I," in Stillwell, ed., *Assault on Normandy*, 26.
9. Morison, *The Invasion of France and Germany*, 197–98.
10. Action Reports, USS *Nevada*, June 30, 1944, and USS *Laffey*, June 30, 1944, both USNA; Jack Jacobson Oral History, NWWIIM-EC, 2; Theodore Roscoe, *United States Destroyers in World War II* (Annapolis, MD: Naval Institute Press, 1953), 361.
11. Collins, *Lightning Joe*, 199–200.
12. Roscoe, *United States Destroyers*, 361; Irvin Airey, "A Strange Place for a Marine," in Stillwell, ed., *Assault on Normandy*, 191.
13. Jack Jacobson Oral History, NWWIIM-EC, 2; Acton Report, USS *O'Brien*, June 29, 1944, USNA.
14. See the discussion of this in Morison, *The Invasion of France and Germany*, 212.
15. Action Reports, USS *Walke* June 29, 1944, and USS *Nevada*, June 30, 1944, both USNA.
16. Action Report, USS *Nevada*, June 30, 1944, USNA; Charles Sehe, letter to his family, June 6, 1994, in Sehe file, NMPW; O. Alfred Graham, "Straddling a Battle

Wagon," in Edward F. Prados, ed., *Neptunus Rex: Naval Stories of the Normandy Invasion, June 6, 1944* (Novato, CA: Presidio Press, 1998), 30.

17. Action Report, USS *Hobson*, June 25, 1944, USNA; Carleton F. Bryant, "Battleship Commander," in Stillwell, ed., *Assault on Normandy*, 185.

18. Action Reports, USS *Hobson*, June 25, 1944, and USS *Laffey*, June 30, 1944, both USNA; Carleton F. Bryant, "Battleship Commander," in Stillwell, ed., *Assault on Normandy*, 185. See also Morison, *The Invasion of France and Germany*, 206–7.

19. Bryant, "Battleship Commander," in Stillwell, ed., *Assault on Normandy*, 185; Action Report, USS *O'Brien*, June 29, 1944, USNA. The *O'Brien* had only been in commission for four months and 70 percent of her crew had never before been to sea.

20. Carleton Bryant, "Battleship Commander," in Stillwell, *Assault on Normandy*, 184–85; Action Report, USS *Ellyson*, June 29, 1944, USNA.

21. Action Reports, USS *Hobson*, June 25, 1944, and USS *Chickadee*, June 26, 1944, both USNA.

22. Action Report, USS Ellyson, June 29, 1944, USNA.

23. Action Report, USS *Tuscaloosa*, July 26, 1944, USNA; Morison, *The Invasion of France and Germany*, 203.

24. Action Reports, USS *Tuscaloosa*, July 26, 1944, USS *Ellyson*, June 29, 1944, and USS *Hobson*, June 25, 1944, all USNA. See also Morison, *The Invasion of France and Germany*, 201–9.

25. Weigley, *Eisenhower and His Lieutenants*, 105–6; Action Reports, USS *Tuscaloosa*, July 26, 1944, and USS *Nevada*, June 30, 1944, both USNA.

26. Bryant, "Battleship Commander," in Stillwell, ed., *Assault on Normandy*, 186; Ramsay is quoted in Morison, *The Invasion of France and Germany*, 211.

27. Von Schlieben and Rommel are both quoted in Harrison, *Cross Channel Attack*, 434.

28. Harrison, *Cross Channel Attack*, 436.

29. Ibid., 438.

30. Collins, *Lightning Joe*, 223.

31. Morison, *The Invasion of France and Germany*, 214–15; Collins, *Lightning Joe*, 225.

32. Quentin Walsh, "The Capture of Cherbourg," in Stillwell, *Assault on Normandy*, 197–98.

33. Alfred Stanford, *Force Mulberry: The Planning and Installation of the Artificial Harbor off U.S. Normandy Beaches in World War II* (New York: William Morrow, 1951), 199. See also Appendices 5 and 6, 229–33.

Epilogue

1. Max Hastings, *Overlord: D-Day and the Battle for Normandy* (New York: Simon & Schuster, 1984), 175.

2. George Patton, *The Patton Papers*, ed. Martin Blumenson (Boston: Houghton Mifflin, 1974), 2:477.

3. Hastings, *Overlord*, 196.

4. Philip Vian, *Action This Day: A War Memoir* (London: Frederick Muller, 1960), 151–57; ComUSNavEu, to COMBATDIV5, June 30, 1944, ComUSNavEu, Subject file, box 16, NA; ComUSNavEu, to COMINCH, July 6, 1944, Message file, box 13.

5. Author interview of Don Moon, Washington, DC, February 2013.

6. Testimony of Commander F. R. Lowe at a Board of Enquiry held on board USS *Bayfield*, printed in Jonathan P. Alter, *"My Dear Moon": Rear Admiral Don Pardee Moon* (privately printed, 2003), no page numbers.

7. Testimony of Captain Rutledge Tompkins at a Board of Enquiry held on board USS *Bayfield*, ibid.

8. John R. Lewis Jr. Oral History, NWWIIM-EC, 7. Moon's note is from Meredith Moon Collection. See also Alter, *"My Dear Moon."* Officially, the cause of Moon's death was "a gunshot wound to the head that was self-inflicted during a period of insanity which was the direct result of overwork and mental fatigue incident to planning and executing combat operations against the enemy." Since then, some have speculated that in addition to the overwork, Moon could also have suffered from a physical malady. The near miss of the German bomb off Utah Beach (see Chapter 13) could have caused an undiagnosed internal brain hemorrhage. If so, the slow seepage of blood into his brain would have caused Moon periodic intense pain and confusion—or, as the Navy report put it, "a period of insanity." Moon's daughter, who was ten at the time of her father's death and who later became a clinical psychologist, believes that this may well have contributed to her father's desperate action on August 5, 1944.

9. Karl Bischoff Oral History, LCI Collection, series B, box 11, NMPW.

BIBLIOGRAPHY

Bibliographical Note

Though a complete bibliography follows, several particularly useful sources deserve special mention. On strategic issues, an indispensable source is a fifty-eight-volume history of the United States Army in World War II that is often referred to by historians as "The Green Book" series because of the binding. These detailed studies on particular campaigns of the Second World War were sanctioned and funded soon after the war by the Office of the Chief of Military History (formerly the Historical Division, Department of the Army). Though they were authored by different scholars, they constitute a kind of quasi-official military history of the United States Army during the Second World War. Many of them include invaluable maps—large, detailed, full-color fold-out maps placed in sleeves at the back of the original volumes. The most useful volumes for this study were Mark Skinner Watson's *Chief of Staff: Pre-War Plans and Preparations* (1950); Maurice Matloff and Edwin M. Snell's *Strategic Planning for Coalition Warfare, 1941–1942* (1953); George F. Howe's *Northwest Africa: Seizing the Initiative in the West* (1957); Maurice Matloff's *Strategic Planning for Coalition Warfare, 1943–1944* (1959); and Gordon A. Harrison's *Cross-Channel Attack* (1951). They are listed individually in the notes and bibliography.

A parallel version of this source from the British perspective is a six-volume set entitled *Grand Strategy*, which was authorized and published by Her Majesty's Stationery Office between 1956 and 1976. Like the American Green Book series, the volumes have different authors and were published at different times. Volumes 3 and 5 proved most useful for this project. Volume 3, covering the period June 1941 to August 1942, is divided into two parts because J. M. A. Gwyer, who wrote Part I, found himself unable to complete the assignment, which was taken up by the general editor, J. R. M. Butler, who completed Part II. Both volumes (collectively listed as Volume 3) were published in 1964. Volume 5, which covers the period from August 1943 to September 1944 and includes the cross-Channel attack, is by John Ehrman and was published in 1956.

On the naval side, the semiofficial history of the U.S. Navy during the war was supervised and written by Samuel Eliot Morison and consists of fifteen volumes. The most useful volumes for this book were *Operations in North African Waters, October 1942–June 1943* (1946) and *The Invasion of France and Germany, 1944–1945* (1955). All fifteen volumes are available in a new paperback edition from the Naval Institute Press.

In the belief that history is essentially the product of the decisions made and actions taken by individuals, I have relied heavily on memoirs, letters, and especially oral histories in the compilation of this narrative. There are several particularly rich sources of these, including those recorded and transcribed as part of the U.S. Naval Institute's Oral History Program; the large collection assembled by Stephen Ambrose at the Eisenhower Center, located in the National World War II Museum in New Orleans, Louisiana; and the LSI Association Collection at the National Museum of the Pacific War in Fredericksburg, Texas. In addition to these archival holdings, several published works include important firsthand accounts. Among these are *Assault on Normandy*, edited by Paul Stillwell; *Neptunus Rex*, edited by John Prados; and *Eyewitness D-Day*, edited by D. M. Giangreco with Kathryn Moore. Also, Joseph Balkoski's excellent books on Omaha Beach and Utah Beach include a large number of firsthand accounts. All of these are listed separately below.

In the notes for this work, I have cited the most readily available source. For example, whenever the minutes of a Combined Chiefs of Staff meeting are included in the published *Foreign Relations of the United States* (FRUS), I cited the printed source, citing the originals in the National Archives only for those meetings where the minutes were not published. Similarly, whenever possible, I have cited the published versions of the diaries of Alan

Brooke, Harry Butcher, Harry Hopkins, Bertram Ramsay, Henry Stimson, and others. I have also cited the published versions of the papers of Eisenhower and Marshall, and documents that are printed in Winston Churchill's six-volume *History of the Second World War*. Only when documents do not appear in a published collection did I cite the archival source.

Manuscript Sources
Franklin D. Roosevelt Library, Hyde Park, New York
 Map Room Files
 President's Secretary's Files
Meredith Moon Collection, Maui, Hawaii
 Don P. Moon Letters and Papers
National Archives of the United States, College Park, Maryland (Archives II)
 Action Reports
 Record Group 38: CNO Files
 Record Group 218: Joint Chiefs of Staff
 Record Group 313: Naval Operational Forces
  Commander, U.S. Naval Forces, Europe (ComUSNavEu)
  Allied Naval Commander, Expeditionary Forces (ANCXF)
  Records of Amphibious Forces (Flag Files)
  Amphibious Forces, Atlantic Fleet (Red 619)
  Historical Section, Overlord and Neptune
 Record Group 337: Records of Army Group Headquarters
 Record Group 407: Records of the 21st Army Group
 Records of the German Navy, 1850–1945
National Museum of the Pacific War, Fredericksburg, Texas
 LCI Association Collection
 Oral histories (see list below)
National World War II Museum (Eisenhower Center), New Orleans, Louisiana
 Oral histories (see list below)
Naval History and Heritage Command, Washington Navy Yard, Washington, DC
 Morton L. Deyo, "Naval Guns at Normandy."
  (Personal Papers Collection of Samuel Eliot Morison)
 Ernest J. King Papers
 Oral histories (see list below)
Swem Library, College of William & Mary, Williamsburg, Virginia
 John Lesslie Hall Jr. Papers
U.S. Naval Academy, Annapolis, Maryland
 Action Reports, Ships Involved in Operation Neptune
  USS *Ancon* (AP-66)
  USS *Arkansas* (BB-33)
  USS *Barnett* (APA-5)
  USS *Barton* (DD-722)

USS *Carmick* (DD493)
USS *Chickadee* (AM-59)
USS *Chimo* (ACM-1)
USS *Davis* (DD-395)
USS *Doyle* (DD-494)
USS *Ellyson* (DD-454)
USS *Emmons* (DD-457)
USS *Forrest* (DD-461/DMS-24)
USS *Frankford* (DD-497)
USS *Gerhardi* (DD-637)
USS *Hambleton* (DD-455)
USS *Hobson* (DD-464)
USS *Jeffers* (DD-621)
USS *Jouett* (DD-396)
USS *Kiowa* (ATF-72)
USS *Laffey* (DD-724)
LCI and LST reports
USS *Nevada* (BB-36)
USS *O'Brien* (DD-725)
USS *Thompson* (DD-627)
USS *Threat* (ACA-124)
USS *Thurston* (AP-77)
USS *Tuscaloosa* (CA-37)
USS *Walke* (DD-723)
World War II Battle Action and Operational Reports (Mss 416)
U.S. Naval Institute, Annapolis, Maryland
Oral histories (see list below)
U.S. Naval War College, Newport, Rhode Island
H. Kent Hewitt Papers

Oral Histories
(a) *At the National World War II Museum (Eisenhower Center), New Orleans, Louisiana*
Wallace Bishop
Calhoun Bond
Ferris Burke
Ralph A. Crenshaw
Vincent Del Guidice
William H. Derbins
Nelson Dubroc
Joseph H. Esclavon
Robert L. Evans
Karl D. Everitt
Edwin Gale
Robert Giguire
George Goodspeed

John J. Guilmartin
George Hackett
Dorr Hampton
Curtis Hansen
Donald Irwin
Jack Jacobson
George Keleher
Richard G. "Jack" Laine
John R. Lewis Jr.
Paul Longrigg
Moses D. Manning
John McClelland
Robert H. Miller
William J. Milne
Kenneth C. Newberg
Donald W. Nutley
William T. O'Neill
Vernon L. Paul
Robert T. Robertson
Dean Rockwell
Horace G. "Skip" Shaw
Clifford H. Sinnett
Joel G. Smith
W. N. Solkin
William Steel
August Leo Thomas
Martin Waarvick
Orval Wakefield

(b) *At the National Museum of the Pacific War (Nimitz Educational and Research Center), Fredericksburg, Texas*
Karl Bischoff
George T. Foy
Donald O. Good
Claude F. Olds
Charles Waters

(c) *At the United States Naval Institute, Annapolis, Maryland*
George W. Bauernschmidt
Bernhard Bieri
Phil Bucklew
Roy Carter
Edmond J. Moran
Alfred A. Richmond
Elliott B. Strauss
Arthur D. Struble

(d) *At Columbia University*
    John Lesslie Hall Jr.
    Alan Goodrich Kirk

Printed Primary Sources

Alanbrooke, Field Marshal Lord [General Alan Brooke]. *War Diaries, 1939–1945*. Edited by Alex Danchev and Daniel Todman. London: Weidenfeld & Nicholson, 2001.

Alter, Jonathan P. *"My Dear Moon," Rear Admiral Don Pardee Moon: A Literary Collection—Life, Death and the Untold Story*. Privately printed, 2005.

Bailey, Leslie W. *Through Hell and High Water: The Wartime Memories of a Junior Combat Infantry Officer*. New York: Vantage Press, 1994.

Bradley, Omar, with Clay Blair. *A General's Life: The Autobiography by General of the Army Omar N. Bradley*. New York: Simon & Schuster, 1983.

Bradley, Omar, with Clay Blair. *A Soldier's Story*. Chicago: Rand McNally, 1978.

Bryant, Arthur. *The Turn of the Tide: A History of the War Years Based on the Diaries of Field-Marshal Lord Alanbrooke, Chief of the Imperial General Staff*. Garden City, NY: Doubleday, 1957.

Bush, Eric. *Bless Our Ship*. London: Allen & Unwin, 1958.

Butcher, Harry C. *My Three Years with Eisenhower: The Personal Diary of Captain Harry C. Butcher, USNR*. New York: Simon & Schuster, 1946.

Churchill, Winston S. *The Second World War*. 6 vols. Boston: Houghton Mifflin, 1950.

Clark, Mark W. *Calculated Risk*. New York: Harper and Brothers, 1950.

Collins, J. Lawton. *Lightning Joe: An Autobiography*. Baton Rouge: Louisiana State University Press, 1979.

Easton, Alan. *50 North: An Atlantic Battleground*. London: Eyre & Spottiswoode, 1963.

Edwards, Kenneth. *Operation Neptune: The Normandy Landings, 1944*. Fonthill Media, 2013.

Eisenhower, Dwight D. *Crusade in Europe*. Garden City, NY: Doubleday, 1949, 1997.

Eisenhower, Dwight D. *The Papers of Dwight David Eisenhower*. Edited by Alfred D. Chandler Jr. Baltimore: Johns Hopkins University Press, 1970.

Eisenhower, John S. D. *General Ike: A Personal Reminiscence*. New York: Free Press, 2003.

Giangreco, D. M., with Kathryn Moore. *Eyewitness D-Day: Firsthand Accounts from the Landing at Normandy to the Liberation of Paris*. New York: Barnes & Noble Books, 2004.

Guingand, Francis. *Operation Victory*. New York: Charles Scribner's Sons, 1947.

Hewitt, Henry Kent. *The Memoirs of Admiral H. Kent Hewitt*. Edited by Evelyn M. Cherpak. Newport, RI: Naval War College Press, 2004.

Ickes, Harold. *The Secret Diary of Harold L. Ickes*. 3 vols. New York: Simon and Schuster, 1954.

Ismay, Hastings Lionel. *The Memoirs of General Lord Ismay*. New York: Viking, 1960.

Jaeger, Gene. *Flat-Bottom Odyssey: From North Africa to D-Day: A Memoir*. Henry, IL: Prairie Ocean Press, 2010.

James, W. M. *The Portsmouth Letters*. London: Macmillan, 1946.

Kepchar, John. *Keppy's War: A Memoir of World War II*. Bloomington, IN: Xlibris, 2004.

Kimball, Warren F., ed. *Roosevelt and Churchill: The Complete Correspondence*. Princeton, NJ: Princeton University Press, 1984.

Loewenheim, Francis L., Harold D. Langley, and Manfred Jones, eds. *Roosevelt and Churchill: Their Secret Wartime Correspondence.* New York: Saturday Review Press/E. P. Dutton, 1975.

Longmate, Norman, ed. *The Home Front: An Anthology of Personal Experience, 1938–1945.* London: Chatto & Windus, 1981.

Maher, Brendan A. *A Passage to Sword Beach: Minesweeping in the Royal Navy.* Annapolis, MD: Naval Institute Press, 1996.

Marshall, George C. *George C. Marshall: Interviews and Reminiscences for Forrest C. Pogue.* Edited by Larry I. Bland. Lexington, VA: George C. Marshall Foundation, 1996.

Marshall, George C. *The Papers of George Catlett Marshall.* Edited by Larry I. Bland. Baltimore: Johns Hopkins University Press, 1991.

Montgomery, Bernard. *The Memoirs of Field-Marshal the Viscount Montgomery of Alamein.* London: Collins, 1958.

Morgan, Frederick. *Overture to Overlord.* Garden City, NY: Doubleday, 1950.

Morgenthau, Henry. *The Presidential Diaries of Henry Morgenthau, Jr.* New York: Clearwater, 1984.

Mowry, George E. *Landing Craft and the War Production Board, April 1942 to May 1944.* Historical Reports on War Administration: War Production Board (Special Study No. 11), 1944.

Operation Report Neptune, Omaha Beach, 26 February–26 June 1944. Provisional Engineer Special Brigade Group. History Section, European Theater of Operations, U.S. Army, 1944.

Patton, George. *The Patton Papers.* Edited by Martin Blumenson. Boston: Houghton Mifflin, 1974.

Prados, Edward F., ed. *Neptunus Rex: Naval Stories of the Normandy Invasion, June 6, 1944.* Novato, CA: Presidio Press, 1998.

Ramsay, Bertram. *The Year of D-Day: The 1944 Diary of Admiral Sir Bertram Ramsay.* Edited by Robert W. Love Jr. and John Major. Hull, England: The University of Hull Press, 1994.

Roosevelt, Franklin D. *Complete Presidential Press Conferences of Franklin D. Roosevelt.* 12 vols. New York: Da Capo Press, 1972.

Schofield, B. B. *Operation Neptune: The Inside Story of Naval Operations for the Normandy Landings, 1944.* Barnsley, England: Pen & Sword, 1974.

Sherwood, Robert E. *Roosevelt and Hopkins: An Intimate History.* New York: Enigma Books, 1948, 2008.

Stagg, J. M. *Forecast for Overlord: June 6, 1944.* New York: W. W. Norton, 1971.

Stanford, Alfred. *Force Mulberry: The Planning and Installation of the Artificial Harbor off U.S. Normandy Beaches in World War II.* New York: William Morrow, 1951.

Stillwell, Paul, ed. *Assault on Normandy: First-Person Accounts from the Sea Services.* Annapolis, MD: Naval Institute Press, 1994.

Stimson, Henry L. with McGeorge Bundy. *On Active Service in Peace and War.* New York: Harper & Brothers, 1947.

Tully, Grace. *F.D.R.: My Boss.* New York: Charles Scribner's Sons, 1949.

U.S. Congress. *Pearl Harbor Attack, Hearings Before the Joint Committee on the Investigation of the Pearl Harbor Attack.* Washington, DC: Government Printing Office, 1946.

U.S. Navy Department. *Detail and Special Specifications for Building Landing Craft Infantry (Large)*. Washington, DC: Government Printing Office, 1943.

U.S. Navy Department. *ONI 226—Allied Landing Craft and Ships*. Washington, DC: Division of Naval Intelligence, 1944.

U.S. Navy Department. "Skill in the Surf: A Landing Boat Manual." (February, 1945). Available at www.history.navy.mil/librry/online/surfskill.htm.

U.S. State Department. *Foreign Relations of the United States, 1942, 1943, 1944*, plus supplementary volumes *The Conference at Cairo and Tehran, 1943* and *The Conferences at Washington and Quebec, 1943*. Washington, DC: Government Printing Office, 1961, 1970.

U.S. War Department, Historical Division. *Omaha Beachhead (6 June–13 June 1944)*. Washington DC: Center of Military History, 1945, reprint 1984.

Vian, Philip. *Action This Day: A War Memoir*. London: Frederick Muller, 1960.

Wedemeyer, Albert C. *Wedemeyer Reports!* New York: Henry Holt, 1958.

Wolfe, Don. *USS LST 655: A Ship's History, 1944–1946*. Sonora, CA: Don Wolfe, 2002.

Books

Ambrose, Stephen E. *D-Day, June 6, 1944: The Climactic Battle of World War II*. New York: Simon & Schuster, 1994.

Ambrose, Stephen E. *Eisenhower: Soldier and President*. New York: Simon and Schuster, 1990.

Anderson, Richard C. Jr. *Cracking Hitler's Atlantic Wall: The 1st Assault Brigade Royal Engineers on D-Day*. Mechanicsburg, PA: Stackpole Books, 2010.

Astor, Gerald. *June 6, 1944: The Voices of D-Day*. New York: St. Martin's Press, 1994.

Atkinson, Rick. *An Army at Dawn: The War in North Africa, 1942–1943*. New York: Henry Holt, 2002.

Atkinson, Rick. *The Guns at Last Light*. New York: Henry Holt, 2013.

Bailey, Thomas A., and Paul B. Ryan. *Hitler vs. Roosevelt: The Undeclared Naval War*. New York: Free Press, 1979.

Balkoski, Joseph. *Omaha Beach: D-Day, June 6, 1944*. Mechanicsburg, PA: Stackpole Books, 2004.

Balkoski, Joseph. *Utah Beach: D-Day, June 6, 1944*. Mechanicsburg, PA: Stackpole Books, 2005.

Barbier, Mary Kathryn. *D-Day Deception: Operation Fortitude and the Normandy Invasion*. Westport, CT: Praeger Security International, 2007.

Beevor, Antony. *D-Day: The Battle for Normandy*. New York: Penguin, 2009.

Breur, William B. *Hitler's Fortress Cherbourg: The Conquest of a Bastion*. New York: Stein & Day, 1984.

Breur, William B. *Operation Torch: The Allied Gamble to Invade North Africa*. New York: St. Martin's Press, 1985.

Buell, Thomas B. *Master of Sea Power: A Biography of Fleet Admiral Ernest J. King*. Boston: Little, Brown, 1995.

Buffetaut, Yves. *D-Day Ships: The Allied Invasion Fleet, June, 1944*. London: Conway Maritime Press, 1994.

Burns, James MacGregor. *Roosevelt: The Soldier of Freedom*. New York: Harcourt Brace Jovanovich, 1970.

Calder, Angus. *The People's War: Britain, 1939–45*. London: Jonathan Cape, 1969.

Carrell, Paul. *Invasion! They're Coming*. New York: E. P. Dutton, 1963.

Chalmers, W. S. *Full Cycle: The Biography of Admiral Sir Bertram Home Ramsay*. London: Hodder & Stoughton, 1959.

Cross, Robert F. *Sailor in the White House: The Seafaring Life of FDR*. Annapolis, MD: Naval Institute Press, 2003.

D'Este, Carlo. *Decision in Normandy*. New York: Dutton, 1983.

D'Este, Carlo. *Eisenhower, A Soldier's Life*. New York: Henry Holt, 2002.

Divine, Robert A. *Roosevelt and World War II*. Baltimore: Johns Hopkins University Press, 1969.

Eisenhower Foundation. *D-Day: The Normandy Invasion in Retrospect*. Lawrence: University Press of Kansas, 1971.

Fergusson, Bernard. *The Watery Maze: The Story of Combined Operations*. New York: Holt, Rinehart and Winston, 1961.

Ford, Ken, and Steven J. Zaloga. *Overlord: The D-Day Landings*. Oxford: Osprey, 2009.

Godson, Susan. *Viking of Assault: Admiral John Lesslie Hall, Jr., and Amphibious Warfare*. Washington. DC: University Press of America, 1982.

Goodwin, Doris Kearns. *No Ordinary Time: Franklin and Eleanor Roosevelt: The Home Front in World War II*. New York: Simon & Schuster, 1994.

Harrison, Gordon A. *The European Theater of Operations: Cross Channel Attack*. Washington, DC: Office of the Chief of Military History, 1951.

Harrison, Mark. *The Economics of World War II: Six Great Powers in International Comparison*. Cambridge: Cambridge University Press, 1998.

Harrison, Michael. *Mulberry: The Return in Triumph*. London: W. H. Allen, 1965.

Hartcup, Guy. *Code Name Mulberry: The Planning, Building and Operation of the Normandy Harbors*. New York: David & Charles, 1977.

Hastings, Max. *Overlord: D-Day and the Battle for Normandy*. New York: Simon & Schuster, 1984.

Heavey, William F. *Down Ramp! The Story of the Army Amphibious Engineers*. Washington, DC: Infantry Journal Press, 1947.

Hesketh, Roger. *Fortitude: The D-Day Deception Campaign*. Woodstock and New York: The Overview Press, 2000.

Howe, George F. *Northwest Africa: Seizing the Initiative in the West*. Washington, DC: Office of the Chief of Military History, 1957.

Kelly, Orr. *Meeting the Fox: The Allied Invasion of Africa from Operation Torch to Kasserine Pass to Victory in Tunisia*. New York: John Wiley & Sons, 2002.

Kersaudy, Francois. *Churchill and De Gaulle*. London: Collins, 1981.

Kirkland, William B., Jr. *Destroyers at Normandy: Naval Gunfire Support at Omaha Beach*. Washington, DC: Naval Historical Foundation, 1994.

Klein, Maury. *Call to Arms: Mobilizing America for World War II*. New York: Bloomsbury Press, 2013.

Lacey, Jim. *Keep from All Thoughtful Men: How U.S. Economists Won World War II*. Annapolis, MD: Naval Institute Press, 2011.

Lane, Frederic C. *Ships for Victory: A History of Shipbuilding Under the U.S. Maritime Commission in World War II*. Baltimore: Johns Hopkins University Press, 1951.

Levine, Joshua. *Operation Fortitude: The Story of the Spy That Saved D-Day*. New York: Collins, 2011.

Lewis, Adrian. *Omaha Beach: A Flawed Victory*. Chapel Hill: University of North Carolina Press, 2001.

Lewis, Nigel. *Exercise Tiger: The Dramatic True Story of a Hidden Tragedy of World War II*. New York: Prentice Hall, 1990.

Longmate, Norman. *The G.I.'s: The Americans in Britain, 1942–1945*. London: Hutchinson, 1975.

Love, Robert William, Jr. *History of the U.S. Navy*, vol. 2, *1942–1991*. Harrisburg, PA: Stackpole Books, 1992.

Matloff, Maurice. *Strategic Planning for Coalition Warfare, 1943–1944*. Washington, DC: Office of the Chief of Military History, 1959.

Matloff, Maurice, and Edwin M. Snell. *Strategic Planning for Coalition Warfare, 1941–1942*. Washington, DC: Office of the Chief of Military History, 1953.

McNeill, William H. *America, Britain, and Russia: Their Co-operation and Conflict, 1941–1946*. New York: Johnson Reprint Corporation, 1970.

McNeill, William Hardy. *American, Britain, and Russia: The Co-Operation and Conflict, 1941–1946*. New York: Oxford University Press, 1953. Reprinted New York: Johnson Reprint Corporation, 1970.

Melia, Tamara Moser. *"Damn the Torpedoes": A Short History of U.S. Naval Mine Countermeasures*. Washington, DC: Naval Historical Center, 1991.

Miller, Edward. *War Plan Orange: The U.S. Strategy to Defeat Japan, 1897–1945*. Annapolis, MD: Naval Institute Press, 1991.

Morison, Samuel E. *The Invasion of France and Germany, 1944–1945*. Boston: Little, Brown, 1957.

Niellands, Robin. *The Dieppe Raid: The Story of the Disastrous 1942 Expedition*. Bloomington: Indiana University Press, 2005.

Parrish, Thomas. *Roosevelt and Marshall: Partners in Politics and War*. New York: William Morrow, 1989.

Penrose, Jane, ed. *The D-Day Companion: Leading Historians Explore History's Greatest Amphibious Assault*. New Orleans: National D-Day Museum, 2003.

Playfair, I. S. O., and C. J. C. Molony, with F. C. Flynn and T. P. Glave. *The Mediterranean and Middle East: The Destruction of the Axis Forces in Africa*. London: Her Majesty's Stationery Office, 1966.

Pogue, Forrest C. *George C. Marshall: Organizer of Victory, 1943–1945*. New York: Viking Press, 1973.

Prados, John. *Normandy Crucible: The Decisive Battle That Shaped World War II in Europe*. New York: New American Library, 2011.

Reynolds, David. *Rich Relations: The American Occupation of Britain, 1942–1945*. New York: Random House, 1995.

Roll, David. *The Hopkins Touch: Harry Hopkins and the Forging of the Alliance to Defeat Hitler*. New York: Oxford University Press, 2012.

Roscoe, Theodore. *United States Destroyer Operations in World War II*. Annapolis, MD: Naval Institute Press, 1953.

Rottman, Gordon. *Landing Ship Tank (LST), 1942–2002*. Oxford: Osprey, 2005.

Ryan, Cornelius. *The Longest Day: June 6, 1944*. New York: Simon & Schuster, 1959.

Schofield, Brian B. *Operation Neptune*. Annapolis, MD: Naval Institute Press, 1974.

Small, Ken. *The Forgotten Dead: Why 946 American Servicemen Died off the Coast of Devon in 1944*. London: Bloomsbury, 1988.

Smith, Graham. *When Jim Crow Met John Bull: Black American Soldiers in World War II Britain*. New York: St. Martin's Press, 1987.

Stafford, David. *Ten Days to D-Day: Citizens and Soldiers on the Eve of the Invasion*. New York: Little, Brown, 2003.

Stoler, Mark A. *Allies and Adversaries: The Joint Chiefs of Staff, the Grand Alliance, and U.S. Strategy in World War II*. Chapel Hill: University of North Carolina Press, 2000.

Strahan, Jerry E. *Andrew Jackson Higgins and the Boats That Won World War II*. Baton Rouge: Louisiana State University Press, 1994.

Tent, James Foster. *E-Boat Alert: Defending the Normandy Invasion Fleet*. Annapolis, MD: Naval Institute Press, 1996.

Villa, Brian Loring. *Unauthorized Action: Mountbatten and the Dieppe Raid*. New York: Oxford University Press, 1989.

Watson, Mark Skinner. *Chief of Staff: Prewar Plans and Preparations*. Washington, DC: Historical Division, Department of the Army, 1950.

Weigley, Russell F. *The American Way of War: A History of United States Military Strategy and Policy*. Bloomington: Indiana University Press, 1973.

Weigley, Russell F. *Eisenhower and His Lieutenants: The Campaign of France and Germany, 1944–1945*. Bloomington: Indiana University Press, 1981.

Whitley, M. J. *German Coastal Forces of World War Two*. London: Arms and Armour, 1992.

Wilson, Theodore A., ed. *D-Day 1944*. Lawrence: University Press of Kansas, 1971, 1994.

Yung, Christopher D. *Gators of Neptune: Naval Amphibious Planning for the Normandy Invasion*. Annapolis, MD: Naval Institute Press, 2006.

Ziegler, Philip. *Mountbatten*. New York: Alfred A. Knopf, 1985.

Unpublished Sources

Shoulders, Troy A. "The U.S. Navy in Operation Overlord Under the Command of Rear Admiral Alan G. Kirk." Trident Scholar Project, U.S. Naval Academy, 1994.

Strange, Joseph L. "Cross-Channel Attack, 1942: The British Rejection of Operation Sledgehammer and the Cherbourg Alternative," Ph.D. dissertation, University of Maryland, 1984.

INDEX

in North Africa, 94
special weapons of, 312–13
See also Hitler, Adolf
Gerow, Leonard, 197, 202, 205, 220
at Normandy, 284, 286–87, 302
Ghormley, Robert L., 11, 16
Giguere, Robert, 301–2
Giraud, Henri, 93–94, 104
Glasgow (RN cruiser), 264, 343
Gleaves-class destroyers
ammunition of, 297–98
described, 290–91, 291n
at Omaha Beach, 291–300
Glennon (USN destroyer), 313
Gold Beach, 188, 202, 227, 315
DD tanks at, 257
landings on, 281
Goodspeed, George, 225
gooseberries, 207, 233, 320, 327
Graves, Frederick, 356
Gray, T. L., 318
Greer (USN destroyer), 5, 19
Guingand, Francis "Freddy", 203
Gymnast, 41, 45, 53, 64
vs. Sledgehammer, 67–70, 71–72
See also North Africa; Torch

H-hour (on Normandy beaches), 252
Hackett, George, 223, 249
Hall, John Lesslie Jr., 193, 220, 220,
319, 355
characterized, 202–3
off Omaha Beach, 286–88, 304–4,
308, 317
in Operation Neptune, 226–27,
244, 284
Hambleton (USN destroyer), 92
Handy, Thomas T., 168
Hansen, Curtis, 225, 230–31, 303
Harding (USN destroyer), 291, 299
hards (loading platforms), 226–27
Harley, Arthur, 208
Harriman, Averell, 25, 25n
Harriman, Pamela, 25n
Harris, Arthur, 173

Harris, Joel Chandler, 95
Hartland (RN corvette), 88
Hawkins (RN cruiser), 212
Hennecke, Walther, 349
Herndon (USN destroyer), 298
Heubner, Clarence, 227, 303
Hewitt, H. Kent, 115
in Anvil campaign, 355
in Torch campaign, 83–84, 91, 202
Hicken, Victor, 263–64
Higgins, Andrew Jackson, 78–79, 149, 163
Higgins boats (LCP, LCVP), 154, 163
construction program, 159–60
described, 78–79, 149–50
landings in Normandy, 252–53, 270–76
problems with, 91–92
repair of, 316
in Torch landings, 88–91
utility of, 200
Hitler, Adolf, 4, 7–8, 27
declares war on U.S., 28–29
forbids retreat, 338–39, 348–49,
353–54, 357
Hobart, Percy, 208–9, 210
Hobson (USN destroyer), 346
Hoffler, Jackson, 304
Hopkins, Harry, xvii, 33, 60
at Arcadia conference, 37–42
diplomatic efforts of, 53–54, 57–59,
67–70, 98
and Lend Lease, 27–28
and Pearl Harbor, 3–4, 25
Hopkins, Robert, 99
Hornet (USN carrier), 77
Hughes-Hallet, John, 206, 208
Hull, Cordell, 23
Husky (invasion of Sicily), 102
map, 116

Iceland, American troops in, 35–36
Ickes, Harold, 6
India, 56
Ingersoll, Royal E., 8
Ireland, American troops in, 35–36, 128
Irwin, Donald, 263, 278, 315–16